mazda
Rotary-engined cars
From Cosmo 110S to RX-8
Marc Cranswick

Some other great books from Veloce:

1½-litre GP Racing 1961-1965 (Whitelock)
AC Two-litre Saloons & Buckland Sportscars (Archibald)
Alfa Romeo 155/156/147 Competition Touring Cars (Collins)
Alfa Romeo Giulia Coupé GT & GTA (Tipler)
Alfa Romeo Montreal – The dream car that came true (Taylor)
Alfa Romeo Montreal – The Essential Companion (Classic Reprint of 500 copies) (Taylor)
Alfa Tipo 33 (McDonough & Collins)
Alpine & Renault – The Development of the Revolutionary Turbo F1 Car 1968 to 1979 (Smith)
Alpine & Renault – The Sports Prototypes 1963 to 1969 (Smith)
Alpine & Renault – The Sports Prototypes 1973 to 1978 (Smith)
An Austin Anthology (Stringer)
An Austin Anthology II (Stringer)
An English Car Designer Abroad (Birtwhistle)
An Incredible Journey (Falls & Reisch)
Anatomy of the Classic Mini (Huthert & Ely)
Anatomy of the Works Minis (Moylan)
Armstrong-Siddeley (Smith)
Art Deco and British Car Design (Down)
Autodrome (Collins & Ireland)
Automotive A-Z, Lane's Dictionary of Automotive Terms (Lane)
Automotive Mascots (Kay & Springate)
Bahamas Speed Weeks, The (O'Neil)
Bentley Continental, Corniche and Azure (Bennett)
Bentley MkVI, Rolls-Royce Silver Wraith, Dawn & Cloud/ Bentley R & S-Series (Nutland)
Bluebird CN7 (Stevens)
BMC Competitions Department Secrets (Turner, Chambers & Browning)
BMW 5-Series (Cranswick)
BMW Classic 5 Series 1972 to 2003 (Cranswick)
BRM – A Mechanic's Tale (Salmon)
BRM V16 (Ludvigsen)
Bugatti – The 8-cylinder Touring Cars 1920-34 (Price & Arbey)
Bugatti Type 40 (Price)
Bugatti 46/50 Updated Edition (Price & Arbey)
Bugatti T44 & T49 (Price & Arbey)
Bugatti 57 2nd Edition (Price)
Bugatti Type 57 Grand Prix – A Celebration (Tomlinson)
Carrera Panamericana, La (Tipler)
Car-tastrophes – 80 automotive atrocities from the past 20 years (Honest John, Fowler)
Chevrolet Corvette (Starkey)
Chrysler 300 – America's Most Powerful Car 2nd Edition (Ackerson)
Chrysler PT Cruiser (Ackerson)
Citroën DS (Bobbitt)
Classic British Car Electrical Systems (Astley)
Classic Engines, Modern Fuel: The Problems, the Solutions (Ireland)
Cobra – The Real Thing! (Legate)
Cobra, The last Shelby – My times with Carroll Shelby (Theodore)
Competition Car Aerodynamics 3rd Edition (McBeath)
Competition Car Composites A Practical Handbook (Revised 2nd Edition) (McBeath)
Concept Cars, How to illustrate and design – New 2nd Edition (Dewey)
Cortina – Ford's Bestseller (Robson)
Cosworth – The Search for Power (6th edition) (Robson)
Coventry Climax Racing Engines (Hammill)
Cranswick on Porsche (Cranswick)
Daily Mirror 1970 World Cup Rally 40, The (Robson)
Daimler SP250 New Edition (Long)
Datsun Fairlady Roadster to 280ZX – The Z-Car Story (Long)
Dino – The V6 Ferrari (Long)
Dodge Challenger & Plymouth Barracuda (Grist)
Dodge Charger – Enduring Thunder (Ackerson)
Dodge Dynamite! (Grist)
Dodge Viper (Zatz)
Draw & Paint Cars – How to (Gardiner)
Drive on the Wild Side, A – 20 Extreme Driving Adventures From Around the World (Weaver)
Driven – An Elegy to Cars, Roads & Motorsport (Aston)
Dune Buggy, Building A – The Essential Manual (Shakespeare)
Dune Buggy Files (Hale)
Dune Buggy Handbook (Hale)
East German Motor Vehicles in Pictures (Suhr/Weinreich)
Essential Guide to Driving in Europe, The (Parish)
Fast Ladies – Female Racing Drivers 1888 to 1970 (Bouzanquet)
Fate of the Sleeping Beauties, The (op de Weegh/Hottendorff/ op de Weegh)
Ferrari 288 GTO, The Book of the (Sackey)
Ferrari 333 SP (O'Neil)
Fiat & Abarth 124 Spider & Coupé (Tipler)
Fiat & Abarth 500 & 600 – 2nd Edition (Bobbitt)
Fiat in Motorsport
Fiats, Great Small (Ward)
Ford Cleveland 335-Series V8 engine 1970 to 1982 – The Essential Source Book (Hammill)
Ford F100/F150 Pick-up 1948-1996 (Ackerson)
Ford F150 Pick-up 1997-2005 (Ackerson)
Ford Focus WRC (Robson)
Ford GT – Then, and Now (Streather)
Ford GT40 (Legate)
Ford Midsize Muscle – Fairlane, Torino & Ranchero (Cranswick)
Ford Model Y (Roberts)
Ford Mustang II & Pinto 1970 to 80 (Cranswick)
Ford Small Block V8 Racing Engines 1962-1970 – The Essential Source Book (Hammill)
Ford Thunderbird From 1954, The Book of the (Long)
Ford versus Ferrari – The battle for supremacy at Le Mans 1966 (Starkey)
Formula 1 - The Knowledge 2nd Edition (Hayhoe)
Formula 1 All The Races - The First 1000 (Smith)
Formula One – The Real Score? (Harvey)
Formula 5000 Motor Racing, Back then ... and back now (Lawson)
The Good, the Mad and the Ugly ... not to mention Jeremy Clarkson (Dron)
Grand Prix Ferrari – The Years of Enzo Ferrari's Power, 1948-1980 (Pritchard)
Grand Prix Ford – DFV-powered Formula 1 Cars (Robson)
Great British Rally, The (Robson)
GT – The World's Best GT Cars 1953-73 (Dawson)
Hillclimbing & Sprinting – The Essential Manual (Short & Wilkinson)
Honda NSX (Long)
Honda S2000, The Book of The (Long)
Immortal Austin Seven (Morgan)
India - The Shimmering Dream (Reisch/Falls (translator))
Inside the Rolls-Royce & Bentley Styling Department – 1971 to 2001 (Hull)
Intermeccanica – The Story of the Prancing Bull (McCredie & Reisner)
Jaguar - All the Cars (4th Edition) (Thorley)
Jaguar from the shop floor (Martin)
Jaguar E-type Factory and Private Competition Cars (Griffiths)
Jaguar, The Rise of (Price)
Jaguar XJ 220 – The Inside Story (Moreton)
Jaguar XJ-S, The Book of the (Long)
Jeep CJ (Ackerson)
Jeep Wrangler (Ackerson)
The Jowett Jupiter – The car that leaped to fame (Nankivell)
Karmann-Ghia Coupé & Convertible (Bobbitt)
KTM X-Bow (Pathmanathan)
Lamborghini Miura Bible, The (Sackey)
Lamborghini Murciélago, The book of the (Pathmanathan)
Lamborghini Urraco, The Book of the (Landsem)
Lambretta Bible, The (Davies)
Lancia 037 (Collins)
Lancia Delta HF Integrale (Blaettel & Wagner)
Lancia Delta Integrale (Collins)
Land Rover Design - 70 years of success (Hull)
Land Rover Emergency Vehicles (Taylor)
Land Rover Series III Reborn (Porter)
Land Rover, The Half-ton Military (Cook)
Land Rovers in British Military Service – coil sprung models 1970 to 2007 (Taylor)
Le Mans Panoramic (Ireland)
Lexus Story, The (Long)
Lola – The Illustrated History (1957-1977) (Starkey)
Lola – All the Sports Racing & Single-seater Racing Cars 1978-1997 (Starkey)
Lola T70 – The Racing History & Individual Chassis Record – 4th Edition (Starkey)
Lotus 18 Colin Chapman's U-turn (Whitelock)
Lotus 49 (Oliver)
Lotus Elan and +2 Source Book (Vale)
Making a Morgan (Hensing)
Maserati 250F In Focus (Pritchard)
Mazda MX-5/Miata 1.6 Enthusiast's Workshop Manual (Grainger & Shoemark)
Mazda MX-5/Miata 1.8 Enthusiast's Workshop Manual (Grainger & Shoemark)
Mazda MX-5 Miata, The book of the – The 'Mk1' NA-series 1988 to 1997 (Long)
Mazda MX-5 Miata, The book of the – The 'Mk2' NB-series 1997 to 2004 (Long)
Mazda MX-5 Miata Roadster (Long)
Mazda Rotary-engined Cars (Cranswick)
Maximum Mini (Booij)
Mercedes-Benz SL – R230 series 2001 to 2011 (Long)
Mercedes-Benz SL – W113-series 1963-1971 (Long)
Mercedes-Benz SL & SLC – 107-series 1971-1989 (Long)
Mercedes-Benz SLK – R170 series 1996-2004 (Long)
Mercedes-Benz SLK – R171 series 2004-2011 (Long)
Mercedes-Benz W123-series – All models 1976 to 1986 (Long)
Mercedes G-Wagen (Long)
MG, Made in Abingdon (Frampton)
MGA (Price Williams)
MGB & MGB GT– Expert Guide (Auto-doc Series) (Williams)
MGB Electrical Systems Updated & Revised Edition (Astley)
MGB – The Illustrated History, Updated Fourth Edition (Wood & Burrell)
The MGC GTS Lightweights (Morys)
Mini Cooper – The Real Thing! (Tipler)
Mini Minor to Asia Minor (West)
Mitsubishi Lancer Evo, The Road Car & WRC Story (Long)
Montlhéry, The Story of the Paris Autodrome (Boddy)
MOPAR Muscle – Barracuda, Dart & Valiant 1960-1980 (Cranswick)
Morgan Maverick (Lawrence)
Morgan 3 Wheeler – back to the future!, The (Dron)
Morris Minor, 70 Years on the Road (Newell)
Motor Movies – The Posters! (Veysey)
Motor Racing – Reflections of a Lost Era (Carter)
Motor Racing – The Pursuit of Victory 1930-1962 (Carter)
Motor Racing – The Pursuit of Victory 1963-1972 (Wyatt/ Sears)
Motor Racing Heroes – The Stories of 100 Greats (Newman)
Motorsport In colour, 1950s (Wainwright)
N.A.R.T. – A concise history of the North American Racing Team 1957 to 1983 (O'Neil)
Nissan 300ZX & 350Z – The Z-Car Story (Long)
Nissan GT-R Supercar: Born to race (Gorodji)]
Nissan – The GTP & Group C Racecars 1984-1993 (Starkey)
Northeast American Sports Car Races 1950-1959 (O'Neil)
Patina Volkswagen, How to Build a (Walker)
Patina Volkswagens (Walker)
Pontiac Firebird – New 3rd Edition (Cranswick)
Porsche 356 (2nd Edition) (Long)
Porsche 356, The Ultimate Book of the (Long)
Porsche 908 (Födisch, Neßhöver, Roßbach, Schwarz & Roßbach)
Porsche 911 Carrera – The Last of the Evolution (Corlett)
Porsche 911R, RS & RSR, 4th Edition (Starkey)
Porsche 911 SC, Clusker
Porsche 911, The Book of the (Long)
Porsche 911 – The Definitive History 1963-1971 (Long)
Porsche 911 – The Definitive History 1971-1977 (Long)
Porsche 911 – The Definitive History 1977-1987 (Long)
Porsche 911 – The Definitive History 1987-1997 (Long)
Porsche 911 – The Definitive History 1997-2004 (Long)
Porsche 911 – The Definitive History 2004-2012 (Long)
Porsche 911, The Ultimate Book of the Air-cooled (Long)
Porsche – The Racing 914s (Smith)
Porsche 911SC 'Super Carrera' – The Essential Companion (Streather)
Porsche 914 & 914-6: The Definitive History of the Road & Competition Cars (Long)
Porsche 924 (Long)
The Porsche 924 Carreras – evolution to excellence (Smith)
Porsche 928 (Long)
Porsche 930 to 935: The Turbo Porsches (Starkey)
Porsche 944 (Long)
Porsche 964, 993 & 996 Data Plate Code Breaker (Streather)
Porsche 993 'King Of Porsche' – The Essential Companion (Streather)
Porsche 996 'Supreme Porsche' – The Essential Companion (Streather)
Porsche 997 2004-2012 'Porsche Excellence' – The Essential Companion (Streather)
Porsche Boxster – The 986 series 1996-2004 (Long)
Porsche Boxster & Cayman – The 987 series (2004-2013) (Long)
Porsche Racing Cars – 1953 to 1975 (Long)
Porsche Racing Cars – 1976 to 2005 (Long)
Porsche - Silver Steeds (Smith)
Porsche – The Rally Story (Meredith)
Porsche: Three Generations of Genius (Meredith)
Powered by Porsche (Smith)
Preston Tucker & Others (Linde)
RAC Rally Action! (Gardiner)
Racing Camaros (Holmes)
Racing Colours – Motor Racing Compositions 1908-2009 (Newman)
Racing Mustangs – An International Photographic History 1964-1986 (Holmes)
Rallye Sport Fords: The Inside Story (Moreton)
Rolls-Royce Silver Shadow/Bentley T Series Corniche & Camargue – Revised & Enlarged Edition (Bobbitt)
Rolls-Royce Silver Spirit, Silver Spur & Bentley Mulsanne 2nd Edition (Bobbitt)
Rover P4 (Bobbitt)
Runways & Racers (O'Neil)
Russian Motor Vehicles – Soviet Limousines 1930-2003 (Kelly)
Russian Motor Vehicles – The Czarist Period 1784 to 1917 (Kelly)
RX-7 – Mazda's Rotary Engine Sportscar (Updated & Revised New Edition) (Long)
Sauber-Mercedes – The Group C Racecars 1985-1991 (Starkey)
Schlumpf – The intrigue behind the most beautiful car collection in the world (Op de Weegh & Op de Weegh)
Singer Story: Cars, Commercial Vehicles, Bicycles & Motorcycle (Atkinson)
Sleeping Beauties USA – abandoned classic cars & trucks (Marek)
SM – Citroën's Maserati-engined Supercar (Long & Claverol)
Speedway – Auto racing's ghost tracks (Collins & Ireland)
Standard Motor Company, The Book of the (Robson)
Steve Hole's Kit Car Cornucopia – Cars, Companies, Stories, Facts & Figures: the UK's kit car scene since 1949 (Hole)
Subaru Impreza: The Road Car And WRC Story (Long)
Supercar, How to Build your own (Thompson)
Suzuki Motorcycles - The Classic Two-stroke Era (Long)
Tales from the Toolbox (Oliver)
Tatra – The Legacy of Hans Ledwinka, Updated & Enlarged Collector's Edition of 1500 copies (Margolius & Henry)
Taxi! The Story of the 'London' Taxicab (Bobbitt)
This Day in Automotive History (Corey)
To Boldly Go – twenty six vehicle designs that dared to be different (Hull)
Toleman Story, The (Hilton)
Toyota Celica & Supra, The Book of Toyota's Sports Coupés (Long)
Toyota MR2 Coupés & Spyders (Long)
Triumph & Standard Cars 1945 to 1984 (Warrington)
Triumph Cars – The Complete Story (new 3rd edition) (Robson)
Triumph TR6 (Kimberley)
Two Summers – The Mercedes-Benz W196R Racing Car (Ackerson)
TWR Story, The – Group A (Hughes & Scott)
TWR's Le Mans Winning Jaguars (Starkey)
Unraced (Collins)
Volkswagen Bus Book, The (Bobbitt)
Volkswagen Bus or Van to Camper, How to Convert (Porter)
Volkswagen Type 4, 411 and 412 (Cranswick)
Volkswagens of the World (Glen)
VW Beetle Cabriolet – The full story of the convertible Beetle (Bobbitt)
VW Beetle – The Car of the 20th Century (Copping)
VW Bus – 40 Years of Splitties, Bays & Wedges (Copping)
VW Bus Book, The (Bobbitt)
VW Golf: Five Generations of Fun (Copping & Cservenka)
VW – The Air-cooled Era (Copping)
VW T5 Camper Conversion Manual (Porter)
VW Campers (Copping)
Volkswagen Type 3, The book of the – Concept, Design, International Production Models & Development (Glen)
Volvo Estate, The (Hollebone)
You & Your Jaguar XK8/XKR – Buying, Enjoying, Maintaining, Modifying – New Edition (Thorley)
Which Oil? – Choosing the right oils & greases for your antique, vintage, veteran, classic or collector car (Michell)
Works MGs, The (Allison & Browning)
Works Minis, The Last (Purves & Brenchley)
Works Rally Mechanic (Moylan)

For current books, more information about our other imprints, special offers, newsletters, ebooks and apps please visit our website.

www.veloce.co.uk

First published in September 2016 by Veloce Publishing Limited, Veloce House, Parkway Farm Business Park, Middle Farm Way, Poundbury, Dorchester DT1 3AR, England. Fax 01305 250479 / e-mail info@veloce.co.uk / web www.veloce.co.uk or www.velocebooks.c
ISBN: 978-1-787117-71-6; UPC: 6-36847-01771-2. Reprinted August 2021.

Readers with ideas for automotive books, or books on other transport or related hobby subjects, are invited to write to the editorial director of Veloce Publishing at the above address. British Library Cataloguing in Publication Data – A catalogue record for th book is available from the British Library. Typesetting, design and page make-up all by Veloce Publishing Ltd on Apple Mac. Printed and bound by CPI Group (UK) Ltd, Croydon, CR0 4YY.

MAZDA

Rotary-engined cars

From Cosmo 110S to RX-8

Marc Cranswick

Contents

Introduction

How often does something new come along in the car world? According to leading automakers: all the time – there isn't a year goes by without 'new' and/or 'improved' being tacked onto what companies hope to sell. Something genuinely new happened in 1959, when West German company NSU unveiled the rotary engine powerplant to the world: it had so few moving parts and could spin so fast. Dr Felix Wankel is rightly credited with inventing the rotary engine that will forever be linked to his name, but history shows that it was Mazda that made rotary reliable as a production and racing powerplant on an international basis.

This is the account of the vehicles that Mazda fitted with its rotary engines. From 1967 to 2012 model year, Mazda produced some kind of rotary car, bus or truck on a successful and continuous basis. There were reliability problems, World Fuel Crises and business reorganizations along the way, but Mazda overcame such trials and tribulations. Rotary Mazdas typified the successful rise of Japan's car industry in the '60s and '70s, from conventional, well-made cars with generous standard equipment to cutting edge, high tech performance cars by the early '90s. Rotary could cut it on the street and track, with Mazda's racers quickly becoming known as V8 giant killers. To date, a rotary-powered Mazda has been the only Japanese car to win the 24 Hours of Le Mans outright.

Finally, I would like to acknowledge the assistance of Mazda Japan, Knight Sports and VeilSide in the making of this book. Although currently out of production, Mazda rotaries will always have a place in Mazda's corporate image; and remain a part of the Japanese tuner aftermarket.

Marc Cranswick

この本は、日本の素敵な友人である英美さんと礼子さんからインスピレーションを受け生まれました。

This international project is inspired by my two wonderful Japanese friends, Hidemi san and Reiko san

The world needed a rotary

Current motoring demands may question the need for rotary power, but, back in the '50s, the rotary engine concept seemed perfect for the era's needs. Fifties' driving, on both sides of the Atlantic, usually involved an OHV four-stroke piston gasoline engine, that wasn't interested in visiting 5000rpm, let alone staying there. Two of the most popular cars of the day, the VW Beetle and Fiat 500, were rear-engined, air-cooled, four-cylinder small European family cars. While quick in tuned editions, Oettinger and Abarth respectively, the standard cars were small-engined and underpowered.

To make more power, just spin faster, but the pushrod or 'broomstick' valve actuation and oil lubrication of the time conspired against reaching and maintaining high rpm. It was often necessary to change oil seasonally in the '50s and '60s, four times a year, as it lacked the longevity of modern synthetic equivalents. In North America, power wasn't lacking – the OHV V8 was extremely forceful by the late '50s/early '60s – yet there were performance woes here too. Whether in America or Europe, production OHV engines, even V8 ones, exhibited engine wear and overheating problems during continuous high speed travel (70mph plus cruising) on the increasingly common super highways or Continental autoroutes. Indeed, racing rear-engined Fiats and NSUs had their engine compartment lids propped open as a cool aid.

Furthermore, contemporary engines inhibited handling. A more powerful engine meant a larger, bulkier and heavier unit. By the mid-'60s, GM, with its blown BOP 215ci aluminum V8 and Corvair flat-six, was the only company mass-producing turbo cars, but normally more power involved more displacement and more cylinders. A larger engine made the archetypal front engine, rear-drive live axle chassis running on bias belted tires even more unwieldy.

A big block V8 in one's Impala, or straight six in an MGC, spelt understeer, and no one has ever liked understeer. Ideally, it would have been nice to have a small, powerful, compact and lightweight engine, capable of high rpm, and impervious to the low octane gas and mediocre oil available to the average driver. Such a powerplant panacea started in the Black Forest.

Dr Felix Wankel – the ideas man

Dr Felix Wankel, father of the rotary engine, wasn't a doctor in the traditional sense. His doctorate was an honorary degree bestowed upon him by Technische Universitat Munchen in 1969. Felix Wankel's family's lack of money stopped him from going to university. In addition, he never learnt to drive, but such details didn't prevent him from taking out his first rotary patent in 1929.(1)

Felix Wankel was born on August 13 1902, in Lahr, located in Germany's Black Forest. Reputed to have been a difficult pupil, who argued with teachers, he also didn't get along with Hitler's Nazi regime. However, his rotary concept work with BMW, in 1934, impressed Hermann Goering, enabling Wankel to start a research institute in Lindau on Lake Constance. Rotary was useful in the aviation field.(2)

Felix Wankel worked on the rotary engine in the '50s with research partner, Ernest Hoppner, and it was during this decade that he hooked up with the West German firm, NSU, regarding rotary's application to motorcycles. In 1951, Wankel and NSU signed their first contract concerning rotary valve work, adapted for NSU's racing motorcycle program. Indeed, a NSU bike with rotary piston supercharger proved a great competition success and set a number of world records in 1956.(3)

Herr Wankel was behind the 1954 discovery that the familiar four-stroke engine cycle could be done by a three-lobed rotor. NSU management was not too enthusiastic, and rather concerned, about trying to reinvent the wheel. However, the persuasive Wankel pushed NSU to share development costs and future patents on a rotary engine. Acknowledgment of that joint patent would be seen on Mazda adverts in the future.

What makes a Wankel tick?

In essence, a Wankel is a couple of triangular rotors spinning on an eccentric shaft within a beer keg-sized housing, as typified by the 1967 Mazda Cosmo Sport 110S and 1967 NSU Ro80. Wankel's triangular piston exhibited rotational and orbital movements in a figure eight. The rotor followed an epitrochoidal path, with three points of contact between itself and the inner surface of an ovoid casing, using ferrous alloy apex seals as a medium. Space between the rotor's sides and casing increase and decrease twice with every rotor revolution.(4)

Fuel and air enter the casing through an inlet port; the mixture is compressed between rotor side and casing, whereupon it is ignited, courtesy of a sparkplug fitted to the combustion chamber. This explosion forces the rotor around, with the spent mixture exiting the rotary casing via an exhaust port.[5] The rotor casing has a cooling jacket, although, like an air-cooled motor, the rotary partly relies on engine oil for cooling.

The combustion chambers are partly sunk into the rotors. It was also discovered that the use of two rotors, mounted opposite one another, yielded superior efficiency and balance for smoothness. Although the same four-stroke cycle of intake, compression, expansion and exhaust are present, the rotary has only around one-third the parts of a conventional reciprocating engine. In addition, the Wankel design produces three power strokes for each turn of the rotor: that equals seriously high output for displacement.

Part of the rotary's smoothness, and ability to spin very fast, comes from the fact the engine's rotor turns in only one direction. It doesn't have to contend with the out-of-balance motions of pairs of conventional pistons moving up and down. Nor does the rotary concept require extraneous cams, valves, tappets and such. Plus, given that all the action takes place in a single combustion chamber, rotary allows the four-stroke cycle to happen simultaneously.

The above describes a perfectly functioning brand new 1967 NSU Ro80 with nominal capacity of 995cc, an equivalent of 1990cc of conventional displacement.[6] However, Herr Wankel and NSU took the scenic engineering route getting there. The motor Felix Wankel and Ernest Hoppner brought to NSU was the rotary piston engine or Drekohlbenmotor (DKM). The DKM had a few practical problems, like poor, low-end performance and high rotational inertia. There was also the inconvenience of having to dismantle the whole motor to change sparkplugs.

Changing sparkplugs was quite a frequent event before the '80s, so poor Felix was forced to compromise with the Kreiskohlbenmotor (KKM), or circuit piston engine. This NSU-influenced change involved a stationary rotor housing and cycloidal gears. The rotating rotor's energy was transmitted to the output shaft using the subsequently famous Wankel-type eccentric, or 'wobble,' shaft. The output shaft rotated three times for each rotation of the rotor.

Felix Wankel wasn't wild about the move from DKM to KKM suggested by NSU research chief Dr Walter Froede, feeling this to be an inferior concept. However, neither time nor funds were available to explore alternative designs and needs must when the devil and the banker drives. NSU had only recently returned to car production, and immediate results were necessary for a cash-strapped concern struggling to get a new motor concept to market.

NSU took its name from the town of Neckarsulm, where its factory was located. By 1955, NSU was the world's largest motorcycle maker, producing 343,000 bikes that year. However, the firm had given up car production in the interwar years, selling its car division to Fiat. Almost 30 years later, in 1957, NSU got back into four-wheelers, with the rear-engined NSU Prinz (a car in the Fiat 500, Austin Mini, Hillman Imp class), but had its sights set far higher.[7]

Its rotary was going to be in a very upscale kind of car. That was the long-term plan, but, first, a few protos: in 1957, NSU built versions of the rotary concept as an automobile engine, and as a pump. The first unit made 22 horses at 17,000rpm. In theory, a rotary can spin to an infinite number of revs, but, physically, the engine would blow up before that happened. In any case, NSU publicly unveiled its rotary engine to stunned, worldwide acclaim, in 1959.[8]

Mazda hears about rotary

Rotary's fewer engine parts promised cheaper manufacture and fewer wear-related problems. Recall the dreaded top end overhaul, or one's 'big end' going? The Wankel didn't have valvegear or a big end. There were as many interested parties as there were possible rotary applications. The first production single rotor Wankel NSU made weighed just 275lb, with ancillaries included.[9] However, this was only the beginning; NSU wanted – needed – licensees to part-fund their own rotary R&D.

NSU didn't have to look hard, rotary was tempting tech bait and, within a few years, it had received over 100 license requests. This included one from American aviation company, Curtiss-Wright, paying $2.1 million, in October 1958, and a 5% cut on every engine eventuating and sold to NSU. This gave Curtiss-Wright the North American entitlement to sublicense rotary, and it set about doing so. Desiring an in-house rotary for its upcoming Pacer, American Motors paid Curtiss-Wright $1.5 million, on February 7 1973, for the right to build rotary motors in the 80-200bhp range.

Rotary dreams weren't limited to gasoline/ diesel cars, or the aeroplane engine CW was cooking up. Applications considered included lawnmowers, outboard marine boat motors and even motorcycles. Licensees included GM, Ford, Citroën, Daimler-Benz – and a little Japanese company called Mazda.(10)

Mazda – from cork to cars

Mazda and NSU had some historical common ground. Both companies made motorcycles and both were associated with a single geographic location, Hiroshima and Neckarsulm respectively. The firms also released iconic dual rotor production rotary automobiles in 1967. However, Mazda's parent company, Toyo Kogyo Co Ltd, had a background in cork products. The company had started life, in Hiroshima, in January 1920, as Toyo Cork Kogyo Co Ltd. The synthetic cork product industry soon fell on hard times, and, in 1921, creditors appointed 45-year-old Jujiro Matsuda as company president.

Jujiro Matsuda had a background in firearms manufacture, and took the corporation in a new direction: machinery. In 1923, the Kanto earthquake leveled Tokyo, and president Matsuda was impressed by the efficiency of the Ford Model T trucks brought to Japan to facilitate earthquake relief work. This prompted him to take Toyo Cork Kogyo into motorcycles. At the time, most Japanese transportation involved cattle, carts and wagons.

With the corporation producing machine tools and motorcycles, the company needed a name change. What's in a name? In the case of Mazda, the company president, and an ancient religion. Mazda was a variation on the president's myouji or surname, and was also derived from the Avestan language of the Zoroastrian religion – Ahura Mazda was 'Lord of Wisdom.' This Persian religion was based on the recognition of good and evil, and Mazda represented good.

Given the importance of commercial vehicles in the early days of Japan's auto industry, Mazda's first non-bike vehicle, in 1930, was understandably a three-wheel truck that drew on overseas designs. The GO DA truck, a cargo-capable three-wheel motorcycle with 500cc engine, reached full production by October 1931, and was rather successful. At this stage, Mazda vehicles were Mitsubishi-distributed, but Toyo Kogyo's input was immense, even early on.

From the get go, Mazda established a reputation for in-house engineering and design. Whilst other Japanese companies used bought-in components, Mazda made its own. The GO DA microtruck was produced at a new, custom-built factory, next to the birthplace of president Matsuda, Niho Village. By June 1937, Mazda was making over 300 three-wheelers per month, and Matsuda san was eyeing up production of regular passenger cars.

Machinery to make a production car, including a body press, was imported, and a completed running prototype was created, by 1940. However, it was not until 1960 that Mazda could offer a normal car to the private Japanese motorist. Progress did continue with commercial vehicles. 1950 saw Mazda introduce its first four-wheel truck. In September that same year, the company made Japan's first one-ton cargo-capacity three-wheel commercial vehicle, called the CT.

By 1954, commercial vehicle production was 32,094, and there were even some concessions to cabin comfort, in the form of a dual ventilator system. Mazda kept pace with the increasing sophistication of the commercial sector. Anticipating the widespread transition to four-wheelers, it brought out the 35-horse, two-ton, four-wheel Romper pickup in April 1958. This was followed by the 42bhp Romper II of July 1959. Once again, Mazda was up to speed, with Romper II featuring OHC tech. October 1959 saw the firm launch its final new three-wheel model.

In the '50s, Mazda was working on the move from OHV to OHC power. At first, it made air-cooled engine parts, like cylinder heads, blocks and cranks, using the shell mold technique. Mazda progressed to producing water-cooled motor parts from ductile cast iron. In the '60s, Mazda got into passenger car production with the 'Kei' class air-cooled R360 and water-cooled P360 Carol microcars. The company even sniffed out diesel power.

Mazda needed a rotary

Although Japan and Japanese auto companies aren't closely associated with diesel, in 1965 Mazda signed an agreement with Perkins Engines (UK). This resulted in the development of Mazda's first diesel, which was the 2.5-liter unit used in the E2500 pickup, launched in January 1967. However, in spite of this, and steadily improving its series of inline four-cylinders, the most important motor for Mazda, in the '60s and beyond, was the rotary. It was to become a question of survival.

As an independent car maker, it was essential that Mazda offer something in products or technology that other Japanese companies did not. In 1951, Jujiro Matsuda had been succeeded by his son, Tsuneji, who believed that Mazda needed a special element to give it an edge over the competition and to survive and prosper. There was an urgency to his credo in the late '50s, as Japan's Ministry of International Trade and Industry had a plan to consolidate Japan's car makers into a few large entities. There was a fear, a justifiable one, that Japan might get inundated by small European and British cars if steps weren't taken soon. The average Japanese consumer was rising in affluence, and private car ownership was increasing. Japanese companies, concentrating as they had on commercial vehicles, didn't have products to match overseas competition. Thus, the Japanese government felt a smaller number of large Japanese automakers would provide a stronger vanguard against a flood of Fiat 500s, Austin A35s and Citroën 2CVs. To this end, Mazda and other smaller companies would be forced to join one of the big boys, Toyota or Nissan.

Tsuneji Matsuda thought rotary might provide Mazda's salvation. He had heard about it in late 1959, and contacted NSU, early in 1960, to see if the Wankel wonder might make a new home in Hiroshima. In October 1960, Tsuneji san and six Mazda representatives went to Neckarsulm, to inspect NSU rotary test stands and negotiate a licensing agreement.

Under the agreement, Toyo Kogyo was able to use and sell rotary engines in Japan and Asia. The licensing agreement cost ¥280 million or $780,000, and was approved by the Japanese government in mid 1961. The deal included a few freebies: sample units, the first of which arrived at Mazda's R&D center in November 1961. This single rotor Wankel wasn't too good. There was a great deal of vibration at idle, copious amounts of white smoke, and too much oil consumption. Adding insult to injury, the Wankel only lasted 200 hours before its power output dropped off appreciably, and the combustion chamber's electroplating fell off.

NSU had sold an idea to Mazda and others, but it was up to the licensees to make it work. At Mazda, that task fell to Kenichi Yamamoto and his team. Yamamoto had graduated in mechanical engineering from Tokyo's Imperial University. Brought into the company by Matsuda senior, he had been instrumental in the design of Mazda's first OHV motor. But he was also, initially, one of Mazda's harshest critics of the Wankel rotary. The company president's enthusiasm for the concept, along with a speech he made, in June 1963, to Mazda's component suppliers, about the Ministry of International Trade and Industry's plan to force automaker consolidation, convinced Yamamoto that Mazda's future depended on rotary's success.

Given his initial skepticism, Yamamoto san was surprised that president Matsuda appointed him boss of the new Rotary Engine Research Department, but now, in April 1963, he had to find a way to overcome its faults … and fast. However, there was a major stumbling block: the Wankel had a major rotor tip seal wear problem. Felix Wankel had informed NSU about it early on, pre-Prinz prototype. It's very likely NSU didn't mention this at all during license fee negotiations.

This problem was the result of the modification that NSU's Dr Froede had made to the Wankel to productionize it fast: introducing planetary motion for the rotor inside the combustion chamber. It was now possible for fuel and air to enter via an intake manifold and ports placed in the rotor housing. It also meant sparkplugs could be moved from the rotor face to the housing. Sounds great, but in the transition from DKM to KKM, tinkerer Herr Wankel told the good doktor that fluctuations in apex seal loads would occur.[11]

This apex seal conundrum …

If the seals on the edges of the triangular rotor wore, compression was lost, power went down and pollution/economy worsened. The rotary dream went up in a puff of smoke – white smoke, as Mazda found out from NSU's single rotor samples. Okay, just make the seals harder, so they don't wear out, but Mazda discovered this introduced major scratch marks on the rotor housing.

Often is the story recounted of how one enlightened Mazda R&D engineer observed his pencil, and was inspired to try carbon rotor apex seals. However mythical this story is, there is no doubt Mazda engaged in an intense, systematic and continuous program to get the rotary engine working, and then improve upon it. For his research department, Kenichi Yamamoto selected a group of skilled engineers, known as the 47 Samurai, and in 1964, a cutting edge rotary engine laboratory with 30 test cells commenced R&D action. Yamamoto was given lots of resources by president Matsuda to make the Wankel work. Computers were utilized to process test data, and the department's staff quadrupled between 1964 and 1967. All those Mazda R360s, Carols and first gen Familias sold, helped to pay for Tsuneji Matsuda's rotary dream.

Research came up with two key fixes to get rotary on the road. Firstly, to combat rotor housing scratching, early Mazda rotaries used 6mm aluminum-impregnated carbon apex seals. Lightly spring-loaded, these seals satisfactorily maintained the compression ratio, without rotor housing scratching. Such seals had a Mazda R&D proven minimum 60,000 mile life – more, if one didn't continually cane one's 10As. Mazda also plated the rotor housings with chrome, and scrapped hundreds of test motors to overcome the seal wear/scratching woes – that's real R&D commitment.

The other major problem with rotary concerned oil. With its rotor apex, corner seals, and o-rings between the rotor housings and sideplates, the Wankel has a complex oil sealing situation. Plus, the rotary engine tends to run cool, and the poor thermal efficiency calls for a relatively large radiator system, and often an oil cooler. Early Mazda rotaries even injected some oil into the carb, to aid rotor lubrication and cope with general heat disappation. NSU's Ro80's dual rotor motor leaked or burnt up so much oil, that one never really needed to do an oil change, as top ups were standard operating procedure for owners.[12] Mazda felt this would rub consumer activists the wrong way, so tried to curb the oil issue. Working with Nippon Oil Seal Co and Nippon Piston Ring Co, Mazda was able to get oil consumption to a tolerable level by the '67 release of its dual rotor engine.

The 1964 Cosmo Sport 110S prototype, shown at that year's Tokyo Auto Salon with a 10A motor. Note the contemporary 'clap hands' windshield wipers. (Courtesy Mazda)

Yamamoto and the 47 Samurai also went their own way on rotary driveability versus the Neckarsulm Ninjas. The vibration displayed by NSU's single rotor freebies made Mazda go dual rotor for its production engine. Counterweights, mounted at either end of the eccentric shaft, also reduced the rotary eccentric motion wobble. The rotary wasn't always vibration-free –Toyo Kogyo helped get it there!

Opening prototype L8A rotary engines had a two-stage intake system, but this was to change. Early on, the Mazda L8A combined peripheral exhaust ports, with combination side and peripheral intake ports in conjunction with a 4bbl carb. Cruising around on primaries, the rotary would be using the side port, full throttle would bring in the secondaries and peripheral intake port. While peripheral porting remains a speed racer trick for top end performance, with the L8A the overall effect was an engine with insufficient torque and poor idle smoothness.

Team Yamamoto decided it was better to just use the side intake ports and increase displacement. This move took the L8A from 798cc to the L10A's familiar 982cc of total swept volume. Four barrel carburetion was retained with one Zenith-Hitachi unit. To further compensate for rotary's characteristic weak torque, Mazda used two spark plugs per chamber and two complete ignition systems. The dual distributor (one per rotor) set up would be normal Mazda practice until 1974.

It was also usual for Mazda's rotary to have the trailing sparkplug firing five to 15 degrees after the leading plug. This was to achieve more complete combustion, and reduce the risk of detonation. The pinch-waisted oval combustion chamber size and shape was well suited to dealing with lower octane gas, and Mazda's sparkplug firing lag made a good thing even better. In the '60s, high-performance engines were notorious for misfiring. Higher compression ratios, sportier profile camshafts and advanced ignition timing made premium gas or high test mandatory for certain high-performance cars, imported and domestic. The rotary freed the owner from having to hunt for high test.

Valve float was a well known high rpm hang up of hi po reciprocating engines; the rotary avoided that problem by not having valves. Mazda refinements over NSU's Prinz involved moving the intake ports from the edge of the combustion chamber, to the front and rear faces of the chamber. Mazda's leading and trailing sparkplug firing order, adapted ignition timing to the moving position of the rotary combustion chamber as revs rose.(13)

Having two sets of sparkplugs firing simultaneously, and two ignition systems, balanced out the leading/trailing plug practice and contributed to Mazda's smoothness. The latent promise of NSU's rough idling single rotor motor had been realised by Toyo Kogyo. Mazda was happy to show its wares at the October 1963 Tokyo Auto Salon; the firm brought two: a 399cc single rotor version of the 798cc L8A was on hand, and Mazda could have shown even more if it wasn't for NSU.

Hiroshima challenges Stuttgart, Maranello et al ...

In September 1963, at the Frankfurt Auto Show, NSU unveiled the first production rotary-engined car in the world, the 1964 model year single rotor NSU Spider. At the October 1963 Tokyo Auto Salon, Mazda's dual rotor L8A made a claimed 75PS. However, more important than either, was a mystery proto car that Mazda president Tsuneji Matsuda drove to the 1963 Tokyo Auto Salon, powered by Mazda's L8A. Toyo Kogyo was going to showcase its new dual rotor rotary in a brand new sports car, to be called the Mazda Cosmo Sport 110S.

As if introducing a new engine format wasn't audacious enough, small Japanese microcar-making Mazda was dreaming up a sports car. At the time, Britain dominated this area. America had the live-axled, drum-braked C1 Vette, and Italy did its exotic handmade creations for tycoons, dictators and movie stars.

The profile and roofline of this Cosmo Sport Series I hint at a modernized '50s two-seater Ford Thunderbird. Next to the Cosmo Sport, cars like the MGB and Volvo 1800S coupe seemed so yesterday! (Courtesy Mazda)

Now, along came Mazda. The Hiroshima crew began design work on the Cosmo Sport 110S, arranged from the start to accept the Wankel wonder, in 1962.

Feverishly and simultaneously doing the rotary engine and the new Cosmo Sport 110S, Mazda had a prototype of the latter powered by its own version of the former (L8A), ready to roll by August 1963. Mazda had to be content with showing just its two rotary engines at the 1963 Tokyo Auto Salon. Whether it was out of respect to NSU, or legal embargo from Neckarsulm, Mazda didn't reveal its new sports car to the public until the 1964 Tokyo Auto

Pictured in May 1967, this Cosmo Sport 110S Series I shares photo space with a DC4 for aviation flavor! Sadly, the Cosmo Sport didn't reach as many international destinations as the DC4. (Courtesy Mazda)

Mazda's first production rotary engine, pictured in May 1967, and backed by the Cosmo Sport's four-speed manual. The dual rotor L10A represented the work of Kenichi Yamamoto and his 47 Samurai. (Courtesy Mazda)

The Mazda Cosmo Sport 110S was initially public-released on May 30 1967, as the world's first dual rotor rotary engine production car. It used Mazda's 110PS (DIN) L10A rotary. (Courtesy Mazda)

Salon. At this show Mazda even displayed a four rotor engine prototype.

There is no doubt a dual rotor sports car of an unusual and striking nature, such as the Cosmo Sport 110S, would have stolen the thunder of the single rotor NSU Spider. The diminutive Spider wasn't nearly as exciting as NSU's upcoming Ro80, and no doubt NSU wanted as few to know about the Cosmo Sport 110S, for fear it might upstage the Ro80 in the interim. Although the Ro80 was attractive and modern, Mazda's new sportster had a touch of Flash Gordon about it, and in time would be driven by a Japanese super hero.

The Cosmo Sport 110S styling had a range of influences, and yet looked like no MGB known to man nor aardvark. From the late '50s to the mid '60s, Japanese passenger cars were influenced by the Italian autoworld. In March 1962, Mazda had signed a design license agreement with Italian styling house, Bertone. The delicate Italianesque flavor, dare one even say Fiat-like, was apparent in the 1964 proto show car, and yet there were also American overtones. The latter was a trend to affect Mazdas, and Japanese cars in general, from the late '60s.

If Ford had persevered with the spirit of the original '50s two-seater Thunderbird, it might not have been a million miles away from the Cosmo Sport 110S by the mid '60s. Add in inspiration from Chrysler's '63 gas turbine show stopper, as well as some unique Japanese style, and the end result wasn't going to slip between the cracks of your local sidewalk. At this time, Mazdas weren't sold outside Japan very much, and the Cosmo Sport 110S would be an international ambassador for Toyo Kogyo. It may not have been at a dealer near you, but word of mouth was aided by international car shows, posters, playing cards, toys and magazines.

Car collecting comedian, Jay Leno, recalled seeing the Cosmo Sport 110S on the US car show circuit in the late '60s. In *Popular Mechanics*, Leno mentioned the Mazda was overshadowed by the Toyota 2000 GT two-seater sports car. The Toyota was of more conventional appearance, with pop-up headlamps, and, as the car featured in the 1967 James Bond film *You Only Live Twice*, it had a TV screen in the dashboard. Being the '60s, having a TV made the Toyota more of a showcar magnet than a strange-looking sports car with a new kind of engine, from an automaker most Americans hadn't heard of.

A TV is more visible than a hood-hidden motor, and the Mazda cost a substantial ¥1.48 million. Expensive as it was, the Cosmo Sport 110S still undercut the Toyota 2000 GT, and with under 1550 produced, exclusivity was assured. However, image wasn't everything to Mazda's engineers, the car had substance to back up the style. Japan was just beginning its major car export push at this time. (Mazda only started selling cars in the UK in 1968.) If one encountered a Japanese car, it was most likely a small Datsun or shovel nose Toyota Corona, not a sports car and yet, Britain's LJK Setright was impressed by the Cosmo Sport 110S, "I remember how impressive the Cosmo 110 seemed at Silverstone, before we came to know and love the RX-7."(14)

Apart from its styling, rotary motor and rear suspension twist, the Cosmo Sport 110S was quite conventional. The body was a steel monocoque measuring 163in long with 45.9in height. Front suspension was by double wishbones, coils and swaybar. The rear suspension had a live axle, de Dion tube, with location aid from trailing arms and semi-elliptic leaf springs. Braking was via non power 10in front disks (254mm) and rear 7.9in (201mm) drums. The Cosmo Sport 110S weighed only 2024lb and the front brakes of a car do most of the work, so the disk/drum format was fine. The two-seater sat on an 86.6in wheelbase.

As per '60s sports car practice, the Cosmo Sport 110S was front-engined and rear-drive. However, the compact 10A powerplant allowed Mazda to place the motor far back and down, allowing the company to coin the term 'front midship' layout. The 982cc 0810 L10A rotary engine produced 110PS (DIN) at 7000rpm and 100lb/ft at 4000rpm, with the Cosmo Sport's 110S moniker taken from its gross power rating. Mazda claimed a top speed of 115mph and standing 400 meter time of 16.4 seconds. This was achieved via a four-speed all synchro transmission. The Cosmo Sport 110S was only available with manual transmission.

For comparison, the Volvo 1800S, a popular two-seater coupe of the time, had an OHV 1.8-liter inline four-cylinder producing 115bhp at 6000rpm and 112lb/ft at 4000rpm on twin SU carbs using premium gas. The Swedish coupe could do around 110mph with a 19 second ¼ mile. The Cosmo Sport 110S used a single four-barrel carb, and its engine weighed 225lb complete. The Mazda 10A motor used aluminum for rotor housing and side plates, in its Cosmo Sport 110S application. The Volvo B18 four-cylinder unit weighed 90lb more. Handling benefits of less nose weight were obvious.

In short, overseas motoring scribes took a shine to the Cosmo Sport 110S, and thought

The Cosmo Sport kicked-off styling heritage at Mazda. The general look of the rear valence panel and back-up lights would be seen on the 1978 RX-7! (Courtesy Mazda)

the 10A was noisily charming when pressing on. However, some criticisms were directed at the feel of the non-boosted brakes, and the Mazda's susceptibility to crosswinds. From the cockpit, the Mazda seemed light years ahead of the Volvo 1800S, MGB and Triumph TR6. Often an over-used comparison in the autoworld, but the Mazda's interior really did have aviation flavor.

Full analogue, circular gauge instrumentation was at hand, with gauges for ampheres, oil and water temperatures. Toyo Kogyo wanted to get into export markets early on. In 1981, Mazda would publish a Japanese-language brochure, using Switzerland as the photo setting for its range.(15) The Cosmo Sport 110S had dashboard controls written in longhand English, no international symbols were used. The steering

The 1967 Cosmo Sport 110S dashboard with aircraft flavor, which was added to by the Series II option of a/c with rear parcel shelf mounted evaporator/ blower box. Useful amp, oil and water temp gauges were standard. (Courtesy Mazda)

wheel was most certainly a major control. It was connected to a rack and pinion system, no less. However, it seems some of the rack and pinion set up's expected accuracy was lost in translation. Some testers noted an on center vagueness.

Manufacture chronology saw Mazda assemble two L8A-powered Cosmo Sport prototypes in 1963. One L10A-engined car was made in 1964, for that year's Tokyo Auto Salon. During 1965-66, 80 more pre-production Cosmo Sports were constructed for testing purposes. This period coincided with the completion of Mazda's Miyoshi Proving Grounds, another venue for Cosmo Sport evaluation. Of the 80 1965-66 Cosmo Sports made, 20 went to Mazda's test department, the other 60 went to Mazda dealers. The objective was to thoroughly try out this all-new sports car, before any member of the general public or press got hold of one.

It seems unlikely NSU had the budget, opportunity or plan to carry out a similar testing program for the NSU Ro80. So it was that Mazda became the first company to release a production two-rotor rotary-engined car, when its Cosmo Sport 110S went on sale, on May 30 1967. The sports car's release was over four months before the NSU Ro80 came out. Curtiss-Wright had fitted its own designed two-rotor RC2-60 U5 engine to a Ford Mustang test mule prior to the release of either the Mazda or NSU, but this vehicle wasn't available for public sale.

The interior of the Cosmo Sport 110S Series II, with the sporty refinement of a remote shift linkage and full analogue instrumentation. However, the separate lap and shoulder belts of the era were less welcome. (Courtesy Mazda)

Designed under internal code Project L402A, the Cosmo Sport 110S was now market available for around $4100 US. However, that wasn't to say one could buy the new car in America or the usual export markets. Mazda did revise its NSU license agreement, so its Wankel engine and Cosmo Sport 110S could be sold outside Japan and even beyond Asia. That said, the Cosmo Sport 110S would mainly stay at home. Given the Cosmo Sport 110S was mostly hand-assembled at a rate of around one per day, that wasn't a problem.

Cosmo Sport 110S Series I & II

The Cosmo Sport 110S wasn't the Datsun 240Z, and Mazda would subsequently have volume-produced rotary models. Firstly, Mazda made 343 0810 L10A-engined Series I Cosmo Sport 110S cars, between May 1967 and July 1968. As a sports car, the Cosmo Sport 110S's competition history was brief and simple: it did just one official race. Mazda entered a factory-backed team of two cars, for the 1968 Marathon de la Route at West Germany's Nürburgring.

There they were, at the Nordshleife, on August 21 1968, with an untried proposition. One Cosmo Sport 110S was driven by an all-Japanese crew, the other was driven by Belgians. Adding to the Continental flavor, the Cosmo Sport 110S in racing decals and livery, bore more than a passing resemblance to the Alpine A110 sports car. Under the hood, the racing Cosmo Sport 110S sported a peripheral port 130-horse version of the 10A Wankel, for the 84-hour enduro. The motor used the idea embodied by the early L8A that Yamamoto san and the 47 samurai had worked on.

The aluminum-housed 130PS 10A used a combination side and peripheral port set up, with a port-switching butterfly shutter valve in the intake manifold. As per early Mazda R&D work, the side port was used for low to medium revs to maximize torque, with the engine switching to the peripheral port for better breathing and high end performance. Given the endurance nature of the race, the 10A with single Weber 4bbl carburetion was held to the road car's 7000rpm limit.

Unfortunately, in the 81st hour the Japanese crew's Cosmo Sport 110S suffered a broken rear axle and was forced to retire. The remaining Belgian-crewed car finished fourth overall, behind a Lancia in third, with Porsche 911s coming first and second. It was the first time any rotary car had been entered in a race. It was a nice publicity boost for the Cosmo Sport 110S Series II, introduced in the fall of 1968. Although retaining the '110S' tag, porting, carb and intake revisions saw power climb to 130PS at seven grand. Series I and II cars can be told apart by a quick check under the hood.

Cosmo Sport 110S Series I cars with the L10A motor had a yellow single-snorkel air cleaner. Series II cars featured a twin-snorkel blue air cleaner for the revised L10B motor. Mazda increased rotor diameter to get from L8A to L10A displacement. However, there was no displacement increase from L10A to L10B. Determining an equivalent reciprocating motor displacement has long been a contentious Wankel matter. Displacement determines vehicle registration fees and taxation in countries like Japan and France, so what did the 10A equal?

According to the Japanese Ministry of Transportation, the 10A was considered to be 1473cc, or 1.5 times its nominal size. For racing, that figure was two times, making the 10A 1964cc, which neatly slotted any 10A-powered Mazda into the under 2-liter class. Given the Wankel's high output, that made Alfa Giulia and BMW 2002 racers rather unhappy. Most of the rotary motors Mazda would make in the years ahead would have the same rotor thickness.

The bore and stroke of a rotary accords with rotor diameter and eccentricity respectively of said rotor's movement. Displacement can also be affected by the number of rotors and, with production cars, Toyo Kogyo has issued two- and three-rotor Wankel units between 1967 and 1995. Such statistical differences are hard to discern underhood, although Mazda's triple-rotor 20B would have an intake manifold callout testifying to the power of three.

The Series II's wheelbase increase to 92.5in was also hard to pick up. The front wheels had moved 5.9in forward, even though the Cosmo Sport's overall length was down a pinch. Easier to see was the larger under-bumper air aperture, with two additional vents to each side of such grillework. The Mazda Wankel 2-liter had always possessed a torque advantage over the NSU Ro80's 2-liter Wankel, but the revised 10A increased torque from 100 to 103lb/ft at the same four grand torque reading. One could exploit such bounty with the Series II's newly available overdrive five-speed manual transmission.

A Cosmo Sport 110S Series II pictured in July 1968. The Cosmo Sport sports car was driven by Ultraman's human alter ego Hideki Goh, and the Hiroshima Prefecture Police in the '70s! (Courtesy Mazda)

Thus, the Series II cars could cruise quieter, ride better and have more interior space to enjoy the Cosmo Sport's newly optional air-conditioning. The a/c evaporator/blower box was placed on the rear parcel shelf, aft of the seating. Although the Series II cars weighed 110lb more, they used their more powerful 10A to spin larger 15inch wheels onto a manufacturer-claimed 200kph. Formerly, the Cosmo Sport 110S rode on 14-inchers. The Cosmo Sport 110S Series II retailed for ¥1.58 million, and continued in low volume production until September 1972.

1176 Series II cars were made, and, right to the end, the Cosmo Sport remained right-hand drive only. The limited exports of the Cosmo Sport 110S were mostly L10A/four-speed editions, although the model was always a rarity. At the annual *Classic & Sports Car* Action Day held at the Castle Combe racing venue, on September 9 2000, around 1000 classics were present, but only one Cosmo Sport 110S made an appearance. This particular example was known to be the only Cosmo Sport 110S in the UK in working order.[16]

It is thought six Cosmo Sport 110S Series IIs were brought to America, as gray market

Although never sold in North America, interest in the original Cosmo Sport is always rising. Jay Leno and Mazda North America own some of the few Cosmo Sports that made it Stateside, during the model's currency. (Courtesy Mike Glore)

specials. Considering the handbuilt nature of the Japanese sports car, it represented good value for money. ¥1.58 million was about $4390, whereas the fuel-injected 1970 MY Volvo 1800E listed for $4655 on the West Coast. The Volvo also had 130 gross horses, but its 17.5 second ¼ mile time couldn't touch the Series II Mazda's 15.8 second equivalent. The Mazda was also almost 10mph quicker on top speed than the popular 115mph Volvo.

The US dollar may have been weakening in the late '60s, but Mazda's performance was strong. Of the two surviving Stateside Cosmo Sport 110S cars, one belongs to Mazda America. Its car was bought from Phoenix car collector, Glenn Roberts. It was featured in the article 'A Tale of Two Rotaries,' from the September 2007 issue of *Car and Driver*. The other US Cosmo Sport 110S Series II belongs to US comedian, Jay Leno. Leno's 1970 car was shown on the Speed Channel series *My Classic Car*, in March 2006.

Jay Leno also discussed his Cosmo Sport in *Popular Mechanics* magazine. The car was originally owned by an American U2 pilot stationed in Japan, who brought the sports car to Florida upon his US return. The car came with two factory-fitted rear parcel shelf black box audio speakers. As per other private import US Cosmo Sports, it was a right-hand drive Japanese spec edition. In common with other surviving Cosmo Sports around the world, the Leno car has some modern upgrades. In place of the original L10B motor is a later 12A edition, with custom intake manifold and Weber sidedraft carb supplied by rotary specialist Mazdatrix of Signal Hill, California. Off-the-shelf braking components and suspension shocks from later Mazdas complete the classic.

Always an icon in its native Japan, the Cosmo Sport 110S Series II was featured in the 1971 Japanese TV series, *Return of Ultraman*. In the show, the Mazda served as transport for super hero Ultraman's human alter ego, Hideki Goh. It was also only natural that the police of Hiroshima Prefecture use the sports car. Hiroshima's police had at least one Cosmo Sport 110S in its fleet until the mid 1970s.

The success of Japanese industry and its products were often accompanied by statements by Western commentators during the 1960s to 1980s, that such success was achieved via reverse engineering. Creating new products from existing ideas was mentioned by American auto journalist, Ron Wakefield, "The Japanese have a fascinating way of starting with existing technology and taking it that extra step to make it more competitive. In fact, this is an important reason why their position around the world is now so strong. Toyo Kogyo's development of the rotary engine is one example: the use of robots in production is another."[17]

The facts show that the Wankel motor as a reliable production reality was barely an existing technology. The NSU/Wankel license granted by Neckarsulm to many companies was more

This 1970 Cosmo Sport was privately imported to Mississippi from Japan, in April 2015. The importation was facilitated by the Passion USA (1.310.985.5525) collector company, and Japanese contact Ayumi Nakao san. (Courtesy Mike Glore)

like an invitation to dream than an assured path to glory. Mazda succeeded where others didn't dare try. Mighty Mercedes came closest to producing a rotary car outside Hiroshima or Neckarsulm. Stuttgart's rotary was going to power its planned '70s gullwing sports car, called C111. The 1970 model year sports car was going to debut with a 350bhp four-rotor engine, that would accelerate the car from 0-60mph in 4.7 seconds and achieve a top speed of 186mph, but no dice.

The C111 came within one vote of being produced at a rate of 1000 copies per annum, but Stuttgart lost its nerve. The mid-engined C111 wasn't put into series production, because of worries over the Wankel's durability. Between 1969 and 1979, the C111s Mercedes built served an internal role as a 'continuing research car.'[18] In contrast, Mazda was happy to mention in its ads that, by June 15 1971, over 150,000 rotary-powered Mazdas had been sold worldwide. Actions speak louder than words, and all those whirring 10As made quite a statement.

Two-seater Ford Thunderbird styling overtones are clearly discernible in this shot. Ironic, given the number of times Ford would cross paths with Mazda, concerning rotary and other matters. (Courtesy Mike Glore)

An iconic part of Mazda history. However, in 2015, when discussing its new baby CX3 SUV, and economical high compression gasoline engines, Mazda answered questions about a future rotary-powered sports car in the negative. (Courtesy Mike Glore)

2 R100, the Family Rotary

The 1960s saw a sustained rise in the output of Japan's auto industry. The continual setting of new records coincided with increasing popularity of new car ownership at home, and an immense export drive that saw Japanese cars find new homes and make new friends overseas. Between 1966 and 1970, Mazda and Mitsubishi sales more than doubled.[19] In 1967, the Japanese car industry reached an annual total of one million units for the first time in history. In 1968 the total was over two million, and by 1971 it was a nifty ten million.[20] There was also an air of sophistication and confidence to developments.

The 1966 six-cylinder Mitsubishi Debonair offered reclining seats and air-conditioning as options. In 1967, the *Japan Auto Trade Federation's Handbook* spoke with great pride about the international outlook of Japan's auto industry. However, before this industry could reach across oceans, it started with microcars at home. Europe had these small-engined devices in the '50s, Germany was famous for them. A step up from a motorcycle sidecar combination and far more comfortable, but inexpensive. Japan offered much the same through its 'Kei' class.

The Kei class fitted in well with Japan's congested urban areas, and desire for low cost private motoring. Kei class required a microcar to have an engine smaller than 360cc, be shorter than three meters and have a width equal to or less than 1.5 meters. As a result, many Japanese micromodels had the figure '360' in their names, Mazda was no exception. On May 23 1960, the Mazda R360 became Toyo Kogyo's first production passenger car. Stylistically and technically, it had much in common with the Iso/BMW 'Bubble Cars' of the day.

Measuring 2980mm in length, with height and width equal to 1290mm, the R360 was powered by a rear-mounted, air-cooled V-twin all-alloy 16-horsepower motor. There was also much use of aluminum in the unibody, helping the 837 lb micromobile scoot to a 90kph top end. The R360 was available in standard three-speed manual all synchro KRBB spec for ¥300,000. There was also the optional torque converter automatic KRBC edition retailing at ¥320,000. With either, civility was aided by standard four-wheel all-independent rubber torsion bar sprung suspension.

Mazda's R360 also featured the refinements of rack and pinion steering and hydraulic brakes. Thus, auto historian, Michael Sedgwick, rightly stated, that the R360 was as sophisticated as any European microcar.[21] Style even dictated a rear fender chrome script and the merest hint of a tailfin. Although bubble

The 1960 Mazda R360 Kei class coupe was the first passenger car Toyo Kogyo put into series production. The little microcar had four-wheel independent torsion bar suspension, and continued into 1966. (Courtesy Mazda)

Mazda's Carol was a more refined, upscale Kei class microcar that Mazda introduced in February 1962. The 1962 P360 Carol complemented the smaller R360, and featured a rear-mounted 358cc OHV I4. (Courtesy Mazda)

The successful Carol had a four-door variant from September 1963, and this '67 MY edition came with a standard four-speed all-synchro manual. The Carol nameplate ended in 1970, but was revived in 1989. (Courtesy Mazda)

cars mostly resemble mobile saunas or eggs on wheels, Mazda's car came closer than most to living up to its 'R360 coupe' appellation. Inside the two-seater had separate front buckets, a floorshift and radio on the passenger side in deluxe spec. In the late '50s, early '60s cars like the R360 coupe, NSU Sport Prinz and BMW 700 coupe served as 'poor man' sports cars.

Subaru even had a tuned version of its R360, and in the US recessionary times of the late '50s to early '60s, a fair few German microcars made it to America. However, it would be another ten years before Mazda was introduced to North America. In the meantime, Mazda moved onto the larger, and more refined, Carol. Whether Mazda chose this nameplate because of the popular Neil Sedaka tune of the time, no one will ever know. However, Mazda were bounding along so merrily, it is known it skipped the planned and displayed two-seater Mazda 700, in favor of its first four-seater.

The two-door P360 Carol, of February 1962, not only had four seats, it also had four cylinders. However, at 358cc the OHV I4 'DA' 18PS (DIN) water-cooled motor still allowed the Carol to fly in the Kei class, and with a five-bearing crankshaft. The Carol followed the R360's rear engine-mounted, all-independent torsion bar suspension layout, but had a longer wheelbase and was more refined. The Carol had a four-speed manual, with synchromesh on the top three gears. The heftier monocoque structure and torsion bar suspension made for refined ride comfort.

Quickly known for its solid construction and relative Kei class luxury, the Carol was a hit. In 1962, it captured 67% of the important Kei class market, answering the Japanese motorist's call for more sophistication. In the drive for more upscale transport, the R360 was discontinued in 1966. In the interim, the Carol improved: September 1963 saw the introduction of a four-door Carol. This intro roughly coincided with the inline four-cylinder being upgraded to 20PS via a revised combustion chamber.

Enter Mazda's Familia

For 1967 model year, the Carol got an all synchro four-speed box, with the nameplate chugging onto August 1970. By the time production ended, 265,226 Carols had been made, but it wouldn't be until 1972 that its Kei class replacement, the Chantez, would surface.

This Familia 800 commercial two-door mauve wagon marked the October 1963 debut of the long-running Mazda Familia small family car range. Private car ownership was still in its infancy in Japan. Thus, Mazda launched the commercial edition of the Giugiaro styled Familia first. (Courtesy Mazda)

Mazda was moving further upscale than even the plushest four-door Carol, and beyond the Kei class. As the '60s unfolded, a new, larger small family car was increasingly supplanting the Carol. The newcomer was fittingly called the Familia. Although known by various names in overseas markets, the Mazda Familia would come to serve as Mazda's family transport staple until 2003; but, in the beginning, there was a panel van.

Cautious over the newness of Japanese consumers buying cars for private transport, the Familia was launched, in October 1963, as a commercial two-door delivery paneled wagon. It wasn't until November 1964 that the regular passenger car version made its debut as the Familia 800 two-door sedan. Too big for the Kei class, but a small car by world standards, the initial two-door was 145.7in long, on an 86.2in wheelbase and tipped the scales at 1587lb.

Larger engined than the Carol, but still modestly powered, the Familia was motorvated by a water cooled, front-mounted, OHV four-stroke inline four-cylinder of 782cc. Making 42PS (DIN) at 6000rpm and 43lb/ft at 3200rpm, the Familia 800 could touch an honest 65mph. Stylewise, the Familia had Italian and US overtones. Courtesy of the design licensing agreement Mazda signed, in March 1962, with Bertone, it got Giorgetto Giugiaro to do its Familia.

Italian style was prevalent in the '60s, with the work of Pininfarina and Michelotti being much admired. Triumph had great links with the latter. The need to be fashionable even saw the adoption of Italian terminology. The '60s family Daihatsu was called the Compagno Berlina, which simply means family sedan. However, in the midst of this fashion homage, US auto impact was coming to the fore. Young Giugiaro channeled the contemporary Chevy Corvair into the Familia.

The 'Flat Deck' Familia sedan certainly took styling cues from the Corvair, as did many European cars of the time. The Familia looked pleasant, and was underpinned by conventional early '60s small car engineering. Thus, there was A arm/coil independent front suspension, with a live axle supported by semi-elliptic leafs out back. The small rear-driver came with four-wheel drums and four-speed manual transmission, with two-speed autobox optional. Not the most exciting of spec sheets, but Mazda's Japanese rivals offered no better, and, unlike the separate chassis Daihatsu Compagno Berlina, the Familia did boast a modern unibody.

Everyone has to start somewhere, but the Familia soon cooked up spicier menu offerings. The November 1965 Familia 1000 coupe featured a single overhead cam (SOHC) 1-liter I4, that whisked the little two-door onto 90mph. Sales of the successful first gen Familia moved quickly, and there was even a little foray into racing. In 1966, the Familia 800 entered the Singapore Grand Prix with Mazda factory racing team backing, and won its class. However, the Familia's reach was hardly international. Around 400,000 original Familias were made, but only approximately 10,000 were exported, mostly to Australia and the Asian region.

Japan did experience an economic slump in 1964-65, but the '60s were generally a growth time for the Japanese domestic scene. Japanese consumers were happily able to take up the increasing supply of cars and other goods made in the home market, but there always comes a saturation point. Eventually, Japanese companies knocked on overseas doors to take their increasing output. Such was the plan for the second gen FA2 Familia. The first gen Familia continued in production to February 1968, but the new second gen FA2 was introduced in November 1967.

Released in the fastback pony car era, the new Familia had a trendier Coke bottle look, with tapered tail in two- and four-door sedan forms. Sedans they most certainly were, both possessing pillars as they did. However, given the plentiful style quotient in the groovy psychedelic era, the charitable could call the two-door variant a coupe. As before, the Familia was available in wagon, and commercial-directed panel van and pickup variants. Mazda was experiencing a very good era up to the FA2's launch, so there were plenty of funds for its development and the rotary program.

It took Toyo Kogyo 29 years and four months to make a ½ million vehicles, but only a further two years and two months to make another ½ million. So in March 1963, Mazda made its one millionth vehicle. The firm reached the two millionth milestone in 1966, coinciding with the completion of the company's new Ujina factory. It was time the Familia traveled to France. Thus, the FA2 made its European debut, in the fall of 1968, at the Paris Auto Salon. The Familia shown was the 1200cc version.

When the FA2 came out in Japan, it did so in 1-liter form. The engine utilized was the carryover OHV 987cc I4 from the Familia's first generation. The 1200 boasted a bigger 58 horsepower 1.2-liter motor. With a 1200 engine the FA2 won the 1970 Monte Carlo Rally, with the driver pairing of M & H Castaing. A prestigious event, and perfect timing to celebrate both Toyo Kogyo's 50th birthday, and the launch of the new Familia 1300. The 1300cc variant used a 1.3-liter version of the 1-liter OHC four-cylinder seen in the first gen Familia coupe.

The up-engined Familia 1300 took over from the 1200cc edition, as the 'Export Familia' in many overseas markets. Outside Japan, the Familia cars were simply known by their displacements, ie Mazda 1000, 1200 etc. Technically, the FA2 was similar to the first gen cars: front engine, rear-drive, a live axle with leaf springs and unitary steel body construction. However, MacPherson struts and high mount

A 1970 Familia Presto 1200 four-door sedan. The second generation Familia made its European debut at the 1968 Paris Motor Show as the 58bhp 1200. (Courtesy Mazda)

The RX-85 accompanied the big RX-87 as concept coupes at the 1967 October Tokyo Auto Salon. This RX-85 shows how very close the concept model was to the 1968 Familia Rotary coupe. The 2nd gen Familia itself made a November 1967 debut. (Courtesy Mazda)

front coils featured at the front, as part of Mazda's revised suspension geometry. The Familia 1300 was a sporty little number, and Mazda publicity interior photos showed that Toyo Kogyo wanted the public to adopt the 'youth mindset.'

The 1300 had a three-spoke sports steering wheel, four on the floor, buckets, a 180kph speedo extreme right and a center circular tach. Extreme left lived a combination fuel/temp/amphere gauge, so that full instrumentation complemented the wood veneer trimmed dash. Black and yellow racing gloves were casually placed in the console's cubby hole, and a map resided in the open under-passenger-side glovebox.

As adventuresome as the 1970 Familia 1300 seemed, 14% of Mazda's output that year was glamorously accounted for by a more powerful Familia that made its debut at the 1967 Tokyo Auto Salon. Appearing in RX-85 guise, alongside the regular Familia, the Familia Rotary coupe, or Familia Presto Rotary coupe to state its full Japanese title, was the little terror everyone was really waiting for. As an export model, this rotary pocket rocket was internationally known and recognized as the R100 coupe. Whatever the name, the diminutive car re-wrote the rulebook on small car performance.

R100, Chiisai Kyojin – Small Giant!

The R100, an easier name to say, was the first non-European small high-performance sedan. It was also the first popular rotary-powered car in the world. The Cosmo Sport 110S was very small scale, and NSU's Ro80 was foundering from day one, so call the R100 the planet's first true mass production rotary vehicle. And one didn't even have to prop the hood open when racing. Choices in this small size hot shoe sector had been limited to rear-engined, rear-drive cars like the Fiat-Abarth 500s or NSU TTS. Then there was the front-drive, front-engined Mini Coopers.

Performance never stands still, the aforementioned sports sedans took one up to 100mph at best, but to go beyond this and get from 0-60mph in under 12 seconds, turn to The Land of the Rising Sun. The R100 could blow the doors off all the Euro crowd, because it came with a dry shipping weight of 1775lb and a de-tuned version of the 0820 10A Wankel seen in the Cosmo Sport Series II. It was like putting a tuned version of the MGB's 1800cc motor in the Mini, but the old B series I4 could never touch the smoothness of rotary.

A conventional four-cylinder also wouldn't have the racing build-up potential of rotary, which would stand the R100 in good stead concerning international competition. However, the stock standard R100 was no shrinking violet on its July 1968 release. Mazda's Japanese TV commercial for the Familia Presto Rotary coupe flashed in large numbers on screen the factory 16.4 second 400m sprint time, Japan's ¼-mile equivalent, as the coupe sped along. Then suddenly the little car materialized on a cliff top; Mazda wanted the public to think it flew there. With a manufacturer-promised 175kph top end, perhaps it did.

The R100's debut price was ¥660,000. Costing around 40% of the retail price of the like-engined Cosmo Sport 110S, the R100's 10A Wankel had to sport some cost-cutting measures. There was less aluminum, with cast iron center and end plates, even though the rotor chamber featured aluminum. At

The RX-87 prototype shown at the 1967 Tokyo Auto Salon. It would soon go into production as the Luce Rotary coupe or R130. Underhood was the new, and unique, high torque 13A Wankel. (Courtesy Mazda)

The RX-87 would provide Mazda with its first front-driver, and styling reflected the transition from Italian to Detroit influence. The long hood, short deck and screened headlamps were all in vogue. The last feature didn't find its way into R130 production during 1967-72. (Courtesy Mazda)

the equivalent of $1840, the R100's cast iron side housings were accompanied by a chrome steel version of the Cosmo Sport's chrome-molybdenum eccentric shaft. The R100 also had a smaller Hitachi four-barrel carb, altered porting and more modest outputs.

Rated at 100PS DIN gross at 7000rpm and 92lb/ft at 4000rpm, the R100's 982cc 10A rotary put it handily ahead of the 59PS Familia 1200 in terms of home market specs. In spite of the great strides in rotary durability, Mazda's engineers built in some 10A safeguards. Fuel feed to the secondaries shut down at 7000rpm courtesy of a cut out on the aforementioned secondaries. There was also something Mazda rotary owners would soon become familiar with, a warning buzzer. With seven grand on the tach, the buzzer would sound and it was prudent to change up.

At the time, reciprocating engines normally informed the driver it was time to change gear through vibration, noise racket or running out of breath. The 10A didn't exhibit any of these symptoms, so smooth was the rotary. In an era before ECU managed electronic redlines, Mazda was concerned about careless owners and rotor tip seal wear, hence the precautions. In a 1971 ad, Mazda was happy to quote *US Road Test* magazine on the topic: "The lack of vibration and noise makes it difficult to be aware of the engine." Mazda added that was partly why it specified a tachometer as standard R100 equipment.

Tachs weren't always standard on sporty cars of the time. Often an option, they were considered desirable, especially on stick shift cars and the R100 was stick shift only. Being so much cheaper than the Cosmo Sport, the R100's four-speed came courtesy of the Familia 1200, as did much of its spec. It should be noted that whilst the Familia was the first mainstream Mazda to get the 10A, it wasn't designed from the outset to accept the rotary. Thus, the R100 was a Familia with apt mods. The usual recirculating ball manual steering, MacPherson strut/coil front, leaf suspended rear live axle was in evidence.

Early on, the R100 utilized an altered version of the 1200's rear suspension. Amongst geometry alterations, there was an additional rear suspension leaf and front/rear springing was firmer at 103lb/in, compared to the 1200's 71lb/in. The R100 also wisely sported standard front 9.6in Girlock solid disk brakes, complementing the rear 7.9in drums. In very early times the Familia Presto Rotary coupe even retained the 1200's 40-liter gas tank. Something the 10A was adept at emptying speedily.

Manufacturer dimensions for the R100 involved 3830mm length, 1480mm width and 1345mm height. The most obvious external difference between the R100 and its piston brethren, was the use of paired round taillights. These were in the trendy style of the new C3 Corvette, Opel GT et al. However, followers would have less time to admire such R100 items, compared to those on the slower accelerating Opel GT. Piston-engined Familias just had square taillights. At the front, the R100 sported a slightly different shaped black out front grille. Blacked out trim was code for sport edition in the '60s and '70s.

Mazda's 'M' logo of the day was displayed within a front rotor-shaped mid-front grille badge, once again not for piston Familias.

Introduced in 1970, the up-engined Familia Presto 1300 took over as the export Familia, and shared its rear suspension spec with the rotary R100. (Courtesy Mazda)

R100-specific decorative raised hood louvers were a popular, non-functional 'tack on' of the era. Suggestive of air intake trumpets feeding a 'Vee' motor underhood, their presence on a rotary car was better explained by a psychologist than an engineer. Of more value to the enthusiast was the standard baseball bat-sized front swaybar. The R100's narrow track, 47.3in front and 46.9in rear, relatively soft suspension, and 160mm manufacturer-stated ground clearance, made that swaybar a lifesaver.

The R100 was a tall, narrow car and, to aid cornering control, the Japanese spec 6.15in footprint bias belted rubber was replaced by wider 145/70 SR14 radials in most export markets. Japanese market Familias, piston and rotary, possessed 13in wheels at best. However, to utilize the wider rubber, the R100 moved up to a 14in rim. This provided an odd technical distinction, since all Mazda's subsequent rotary heroes (RX-2 to RX-4) rode around on 13-inchers. The 14in rims made the diminutive R100 seem even taller and more toylike: the rims were only 4in wide after all. That said, such concerns matter little in racing.

Racing that R100

Trackside applications usually see flared fenders to accommodate spacers, wide rims and wider rubber. Thus amended, the R100 looked just about right and headed towards competition with factory support. A peripheral ported 10A was good for 200 horses plus, but Team Mazda chose something milder for the R100's debut outing. That first footstep was the April 1969 Singapore Grand Prix, where the R100 won its class using a 195bhp 10A. From there, it was on to Belgium and the Spa-Francorchamps 24-hour race. Mazda fielded three 187bhp R100s at the August 1969 event, with the little coupe coming fifth and sixth overall. The first four places were claimed by Porsche 911s, which were racing in a different category.

Retracing the Cosmo Sport's 1968 path, Mazda sent three R100s to the Nürburgring for 1969's Marathon de la Route. However, only one R100 completed the event, achieving fifth overall. After its European foray, the R100 appeared in its first Japanese race, the November 1969 All Japan Suzuka Automobile Grand Cup Race. The R100 handily won this domestic event on 214bhp. Returning overseas, the R100 entered the June 1970 British RAC Tourist Trophy Rally, coming eighth overall. In July 1970, it was the turn of the West German Touring Car Grand Prix, which saw the rotary coupe finish a creditable fourth overall. The R100 was certainly challenging the European establishment.

The challenge was no more apparent than in the 1970 Spa-Francorchamps 24-hour enduro. In a field of 58 entrants, the R100 would be up against the BMW 2800CS and Alfa GTA. In the 1969 event, the R100 had been in competition with factory-backed Porsche 911s. The CS coupe wasn't factory backed at this time, BMW preferring to leave its big two-door in the hands of German tuners. Thus, for 1970, the little Mazda would be racing against the Alpina 2800CS, and the aforementioned special Alfa. The GTA was a homologation light alloy-paneled, tuned 1300cc Alfa GT Junior. It was good for 120mph as a road car, and very exotic.

Unperturbed by big name opponents, Mazda's 'Small Giant,' as the R100 soon became known, battled fiercely. By the 12th hour, the R100, piloted by driver pairing Yoshimi Katayama and Toshinori Takechi, wrestled the lead from the Alpina 2800CS for the first time. At this hour, the other three R100s entered were lying in third, fourth and eighth places. The leading R100 and 2800CS continued to fight hard until the 18th hour, when the R100 was forced to pull out from proceedings. Unfortunately, only one R100 finished the 24-hour race, coming fifth overall.

Honor had been upheld: the R100 had made a big splash in the competition pond. Racing R100s utilized the aluminum-intensive racing Cosmo Sport 10A motor. The fiery furnace of European racing competition accelerated Mazda's development of rotary hop-up parts. These improved items were soon available over selected Mazda dealer counters as 'Sport Kits,' for public and racing privateers alike. The effectiveness of the R100 as a racecraft weapon was immense, and the cars it competed against were of higher price and speed as roadcars.

The Porsche 911, BMW 2800CS and Alfa GTA were much more expensive than the R100, and had top speeds of between 120 and 140mph, with 0-60mph acceleration in well under 10 seconds. The standard R100 was quick, but not *that* quick. The race results showed the power-making potential of the Wankel concept, and the effectiveness of porting in race preparation. Once race-tuned,

The Cosmo Sport 110S Series II and R100 following in July 1968 on Mazda's test track. Both made their debut that month, and used versions of the 10A rotary engine. (Courtesy Mazda)

A home market 1970 Familia Presto Rotary coupe (R100) with stock 6.15in footprint bias belted rubber. 10A cost cutting helped the diminutive two-door retail, for around 40% the price of the like-engined Cosmo Sport. (Courtesy Mazda)

The R100's debut Japanese TV ad, flashed its 16.4 second 400m (¼ mile) time large on the small screen. At under 1800lb and 100 horses strong, the R100 was a late '60s pocket rocket. (Courtesy Mazda)

the Mazda 10A rotary motor allowed the R100 to move up the performance class ladder, something that would put racing officials on alert for decades to come.

Even at home the Small Giant was challenging convention, by giving the already legendary Nissan Skyline GT-R plenty to worry about. The diminutive Mazda placed fourth in the country's national tin top championship, which was a bonus for sales promotion. The rotary Familia was a slow starter in the sales race to win hearts, minds and yen. In 1968 the total sold was just 6925. However, Mazda added to the rotary appeal, with a cheaper ¥638,000 Familia Rotary SS four-door variant in July 1969. Another step in normalising the rotary concept, and 1969 sales of the rotary Familias stepped up to a much more impressive 28,000 unit approximate figure.

In 1970, that number improved again to 31,328. The rotary Familias were gaining ground inside and outside Japan, but hadn't really reached North America yet. The R100 export model sold in Western export markets was coupe only. Even when the R100 arrived on Australian shores in June 1969 at $2790 AUD, the four-door SS wasn't to be seen. At this hour, the R100 coupe was a rather expensive novelty in Europe; a novelty because of the 10A motor, expensive because of all that fuel the 10A liked to drink. In 1970 and the years that followed, the high price Europeans pay at the gas station to fill up due to steep government excise duties, would always make the rotary a hard sell on that continent.

The R100 travels to North America

America held more promise for the R100, and the 1970 *Kodansha Children's Color Encyclopedia* suggested why. Describing the world motor car status quo, American cars were stated as being generally large and possessing powerful engines. Cars from Europe and Asia were characterised as being smaller and thriftier on gasoline.[22] This presented an opportunity for Mazda, but when official exports started reaching America, the model lineup was all piston. In 1970, Mazda started out selling the Familia as the 1200 sedan, coupe and wagon. Its big car, in the US compact class, the 1800, was present in sedan and wagon forms. Mazda also sold its small four-cylinder B1600 pickup, taking advantage of rising demand in America for that segment of vehicle.

The US Mazda sales operation started modestly, with regional center sales offices. The first opened on May 27 1970, as Mazda Motors of America (North West) Inc. This entity handled Washington and Oregon. The first exports of US-bound Mazdas occurred in April 1970, with the first allotment of 60 R100s shipped six weeks later. Further regional centers that opened during 1970 were Mazda Motors of Florida Inc, located in Jacksonville, and Mazda Motors of Texas Inc, in Houston.

The R100 was introduced in Canada in late 1969, at a price of $2929 Canadian dollars.[23] Canada was the R100's first North American port of call, while Mazda's engineers got the 10A smog-ready for America. When the R100 did reach America, the distribution network implied the rotary coupe's availability was initially limited to some Northwestern states. Washington, Oregon as well as Idaho, Montana, Wyoming and Alaska were the first places to greet the R100 in America.

The vehicle they got was shod with the export 14in 145 SR radials, and round headlamps, to comply with American vehicle lighting laws. Normally, the Familia Rotary coupe came with round-edged square lamps. The US round lamps made the R100 look even cuter, as did the 1971 US MY price of $2495, but success wasn't quite instant. 1970 US sales for the whole Mazda lineup was only around 2300 units.

Mazda was just another Japanese import, in a competitive area where Toyota and Datsun (Nissan) were already established. Japanese cars of the day were known for being relatively small, well made and fuel efficient. The R100 was certainly small, it was in the subcompact Corolla ballpark, but it was also fast, much more expensive than its piston 1200 cousin, and quite gas hungry. In 1970, Americans were still used to gaining extra horses cheaply. Air-conditioning and upgraded interior appointments were pricey, but gas and larger engine options were inexpensive.

GM president, Ed Cole, gave his blessing to a retail surcharge of $1 per extra cubic inch, and $50 to go from a two-barrel to four-barrel carburetion. So, moving from a 2bbl 350 V8 to a 4bbl 400 V8 cost $100. It cost a lot more than that to shift from the 58bhp 1200 to the 100bhp R100. Such a jump was more in keeping with the European import crowd. Obviously a different strategy was needed to promote Mazda in North America than 'performance by the pound.' The solution was to hire Dick Brown as the first General Manager of Mazda Motors of America, in December 1970. Dick Brown was a young sales executive from AMC Canada, and had strong ideas on how to get Mazda humming in America.

A 1971 Familia Presto Rotary coupe is shown. The mid 1970 Series II edition had a 50-liter gas tank, and Familia 1300 rear suspension as upgrades. (Courtesy Mazda)

The strategy was: upscale and value added. Mazda Motors of America Inc's national office was a small building in Compton, California, that started in February 1971. In this place Mr Brown asked for freedom from Mazda Japan concerning arranging the US sale of Mazdas, and he got its blessing. Whereas in Japan most Mazda dealers were small, single-brand mom and pop outfits, Brown wanted large shared-brand dealers in America. No shade tree operations, but large, well-funded dealerships.

Some large concerns combined brands like Datsun and Mercedes. Thus, when a client achieved sufficient means, it was easy to go upscale under one roof. It also brought in a range of buyers to see a marque of car they may not have previously considered or encountered, helping to spread the word. The combination of Audi with Porsche certainly helped the former brand get some glamor, and a foothold in the US market, during the '70s.

Brown set the Mazda dealer franchise price high to attract the big fish, with the bait of a high mark-up per car. Normally no one wanted to make, or even sell, small cars in America, because the profit margin was low. However, with Brown's plan, dealers could have a difference between wholesale and retail on a compact or subcompact equal to that usually found on an American full-size car. The Mazda R100's east coast list price of $2495 was $550 higher than the 1200 coupe. The big fish dealers swallowed the bait and got in line to sign up and promote Mazda as something rather special. Something worth spending that little bit extra on.

When it came to convincing North American buyers Mazdas were special, the rotary engine would prove an indispensible asset. NSU was not Stateside at the time, so Mazda alone had the open track to sell the rotary sizzle. The first 1970 R100 brochure for this continent had the Mazda marketing plan's two cornerstones, the special nature of rotary and an upscale flavor. Given the newness and alien nature of the powerplant, the brochure devoted much time and space to explaining and showing how the 10A motor worked. Trying to give consumers a handle, terms like 'Dual-Rotor' motor and 'Rotary Piston Engine' were used.

Fitting in with the psychedelic era, the R100 brochure invited prospects to "Get with the rotary experience – Mazda R100 coupe." The cover showed a young lady sailing overhead via tethered parachute. An appropriate contemporary soundtrack would have been The 5th Dimension's tune *Up, Up and Away* (in my beautiful balloon). There was some uncertainty about how to present the R100. Small cars of this size were usually very slow, and the Mazda 1200 coupe shape was pretty cute. This suggested the car would be favored by ladies, which explained the great presence of female models and the 'girl power' nature of the brochure.

The R100's Japanese 16.4 second 0-400m manufacturer sprint time was mentioned. This was enough to put the R100 in the same acceleration class as a pony car with a base V8, or Triumph TR6. However, the brochure's nature didn't accord with the equivalent literature for those kinds of sporty cars. To spice up proceedings, the R100's Canadian description involved the Cosmo Sport Series I's power and torque figures, described as being SAE gross. The Cosmo Sport figures were 110PS

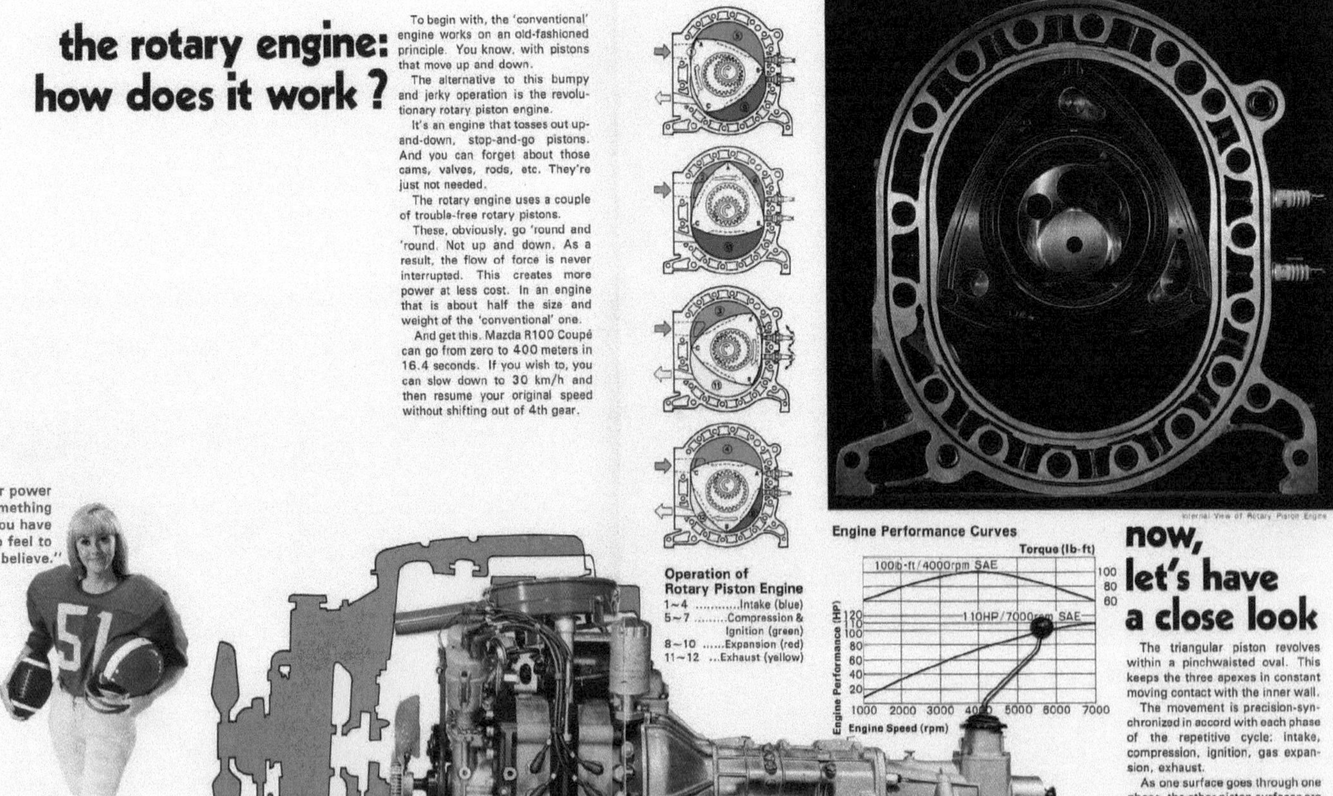

The first (1970) North American R100 brochure showed the Wankel's compact layout, and explained the technical workings of the new engine to the public. (Courtesy Mazda)

and 100lb/ft in DIN gross, a more overstated measure than SAE gross. In addition, the R100's 10A was always a de-tuned version, and made 100PS and 92lb/ft. However, the first casualty of advertising copy is always the truth.

By claiming 110bhp, the R100's brochure could set up a cute colored overlay diagram, comparing a domestic I6, high-output imported I4 and the 10A Wankel. The former two were said to make 100 horses, the Mazda rotary trumped that by 10% and took up ½ the space underhood versus the HO four-cylinder. The latter space claim was absolutely true, and there was a proven handy weight saving. A star of the day was the quick Datsun 1600, with an I4 that made 96 horses and weighed 421lb. The Mazda's 10A made similar power, but weighed just 269lb with ancillaries and had that aforementioned space saving.[24]

One couldn't believe so much power came from such a small package. This quality no doubt motivated the ad men to put a young blonde dressed in gridiron football attire in the R100's brochure with the line: "Her power is something you have to feel to believe." The R100 four-speed was right in the 0-60mph race with the six-cylinder 135bhp AMC Gremlin 232 and 113bhp BMW 2002. In addition, the R100's accelerative enthusiasm was something to behold. In an age when smog tuning was already taking the edge off performance heroes, the Mazda rotary kept on rushing for the redline.

Popular Mechanics timed a R100 tested in Vancouver at 15.1 seconds for 70-90mph, but 80-90mph only took 5.8 seconds.[25] The 10A could deliver a pre-emissions power surge, which endeared the little Mazda to many. The BMW 2002 was a good comparison for the R100, especially given the 10A was considered a 2-liter piston engine equivalent. The R100 was lineball on performance with the less tightly controlled 1968 BMW 2002, and weighed around 200lb less. There was also a reduction in price, the 1968 BMW was already $2988 or $500 more than the R100 two-door was two years later.

The BMW was also a worthy R100 comparo car, since the Mazda was no stripped out Plymouth Road Runner special. The R100 was brochure-pictured in the environs of a posh house, and a scuba gear-wearing gal provided affluent leisure time connotations. The R100 cockpit lived up to the upscale talk. Apart from the universal aircraft cabin comparison, the Mazda coupe had all the high end refinements one associated with expensive sports cars. The dashboard looked a lot like the contemporary C3 Corvette's equivalent. There were huge circular 8000rpm rev counter on the left, and speedometer on the right. Supplemental analogue gauges and radio were in the dash center pad, and the sports steering wheel had real wood. The shifter surround integrated into the dash and console surround neatly. With Italian flair, the shifter lever projected from the dashboard at an angle, just like an Alfa Spider. Unlike the Alfa, the R100 was well made and finished, in the manner all Japanese cars seemed to be at the time. Elvis famously shot his Jag XKE; there was no call for that with the R100. The early North American R100 brochure stated that radio, heater and seatbelts were optional. However, it is unlikely any US R100 appeared at a dealer without all three present.

Further in keeping with imported sporty car nature, front reclining buckets were standard and a handbrake lever resided between said buckets. The front seats had plenty of track travel to accommodate even the tallest driver, but this did dent the already cramped rear quarters. At least the rear compartment was well padded, unlike the pony car torture chambers of the day. A small child or pet would have been happy in the R100's rear, but not a large example of either. Still, do consider the fact that the R100 was 10in shorter than a VW Beetle, and almost 25in shorter than the original Ford Mustang. There was a comfort price to pay for the Familia's physical brevity.

The R100 introduced overseas buyers to Mazda's excellent flow through ventilation system. The round swivel vents, placed at the dashboard ends, would become a familiar and effective sight on the Familia rotaries and their successors. This was just as well, because the new rotary Mazdas and their piston cousins lacked vent wings. Michael Lamm described the experience, "... vents really blow you out of car at high speed."[26] There were also stale air extraction slots on the C pillars, and the rear windows opened out.

The abundance of fresh airflow through was pretty key at a time when ventilation on domestic cars without a/c was very poor. If one didn't specify a/c, the stock dash vents found on a Mustang or Camaro were largely

A Cosmo Sport 110S, R100 and RX-2 at the 2011 Japanese Nationals in Australia. Note the height of the 14in R100 export rim/tire, compared to the RX-2 coupe's 13-inchers! (Courtesy www.ausrotary.com)

for display purposes only. Plus, the swing-out rear panes were a boon, given the Detroit bean counter propensity to stop glass rolling all the way down, or even worse, keep 'em fixed. However, the R100 seemed to be the gift that kept on giving. The R100 brochure said, "And remember, you get two rotary pistons in every Mazda R100 coupe."

The ad copy line about two rotary pistons was purposely made at an hour when popular piano duo Ferrante & Teicher always promised two pianos with their recordings. However novel and wonderful the R100 was, Mazda had to mention where the rotary story started. That place was Neckarsulm, and the acknowledgment was "Mazda Rotary Engine: License NSU-Wankel." However, it was a mention made in absentia. It was 1972 before NSU could ship an emissions-compliant NSU Ro80 to America.

In the meantime, the R100 provided the only opportunity for Americans to sample the rotary, and it was love at first whir. In spite of a possible dealer mark-up of $600, Dick Brown's strategy saw US Mazda sales increase to around 21,000 units in 1971. In 1972, over 53,000 Mazdas were sold in America. The R100 North American consumers were getting, was largely the R100 Series II introduced in mid 1970. This model encompassed a larger 50-liter gas tank, to store a few more extinct dinosaurs before the 10A gobbled them up. The R100 had used the 1200's 40-liter tank.

The R100 Series II also adopted the 1970-introduced Familia 1300's rear suspension. On the smaller items, there has been found to be some interchange between Series I and II cars. Not all the believed Series II items are on Series II cars. Mazda achieved greater spec consistency with the R100's successor, the RX-2. One ceremonial change was the re-rating of the R100's 10A from gross to net SAE horsepower and torque figures, between 1970 and 1971 calendar years. Thus, 1971 North American R100s carried the more truthful description of 77bhp and 80lb/ft. No real drop in performance, and still emissions complying with the aid of a thermal reactor. The industry as a whole was changing to net ratings for all vehicles in 1971/72.

Coincidentally, also produced between 1968 and 1973 was the Opel GT mini Corvette clone, although the US R100 was available over a shorter timeframe. The two cars had four rear circular taillights and seemed to cater to niche needs. A further similarity was in production totals, the Opel GT 1900 totaling 103,373 and the 2-liter Familia Rotary reaching 95,706 by the time all was said and done. The Opel was left-hand drive only, but could draw on US distributive help, courtesy of parent GM. The R100 was sold in left and right-hand drive, but had to rely more on Asian region sales.

Overall, it was a wash, but the contest highlighted Mazda's commercial success. The Opel's fanciest feature was its looks; under that was pretty humdrum Kadett hardware and a motor that wasn't particularly willing. With swoopy good looks and absolutely vanilla flavor, down the middle engineering, the GT was the perfect recipe to please Joe Q Public. The Mazda seemed too spicy, kara sugimasu. However, Mazda's thorough engineering allowed North America to sample an unknown brand and new kind of engine, with confidence. A further historical coincidence was that Japanese cuisine was successfully introduced on the east coast around this time, as the 'California Roll.'

Next to the Opel, the R100 looked more sedan than coupe, but proved to be a reasonable A-to-B road machine. The export 145 section 14in radial tires and front swaybar allowed one to corner quickly, and with less lean than the tall body suggested. Unlike with the '90s Mercedes A class, there was no 'moose swerve test' to trip the R100 up, but its chassis seemed capable of containing the 10A rotary. Braking from the non power disk/drum combo also seemed up to snuff. Durability and maintenance seemed greater possible pitfalls. Letting loose a new product on North America can create a product liability minefield, as consumers creatively find new ways to use said product that the manufacturer never envisaged.

The R100's 12-volt electrics were a boon concerning starting in colder climes. The 14.7-quart cooling system also seemed able to prevent a sweat being raised. The rotary chamber water passages lay between the round holes of the case securing studs. Chief concern with the Wankel was oil usage. US motorists had experienced the joys of adding oil with gas to two-stroke Saabs, and the need to use the gas pedal whilst braking to maintain lubrication. Mazda were looking to make R100 motoring less esoteric, but there were foibles.

The exported R100 cost $2495 in America for 1971 MY. For that, the coupe came with the larger export 145 section 14in tires. Not as large as the set on this car show-located R100! Rising collector values mean R100s get preserved, more than modified, now. (Courtesy Alex Tong)

Mazda's rotor tip sealing R&D had reduced oil consumption levels from the NSU Prinz era, but one was still going through a pint every 1200 miles. Oil was an important heat transference medium for the thermally inefficient rotary, but the R100's sump capacity was only 5.5 quarts. An oil change was recommended every 2000 miles. Around the late '60s, an oil/filter change on an import like a BMW 2002 would be done every 4000 miles. On a sporty domestic, the interval was 6000 miles.

To cope with the Wankel's thermal load, the R100 was in keeping with the Mazda common practice of having a separate oil cooler just below the radiator. American cars mostly had longer service intervals, and less work required at a service, than imported cars. How would the R100 cope with potentially unsympathetic owners? Where the tires hit the road, the Familia Rotary coupe was reliable enough to stay off Consumer Reports' and Ralph Nader's hit list. Mazda's oversize radiator and additional oil cooler seemed to ward off overheating.

Conventional piston-engined sporty European imports were notorious for overheating. Often 'Old Faithful' would pay an underhood visit when crawling through rush hour traffic or lining up at a tollway booth. What was their thermal excuse? The little 10A-powered Mazda sidestepped this, plus

British Lucas electrics, and got a good word from *Popular Science* concerning the R100's drama-free motoring longevity. The title of the January 1972 *Popular Science* story was "PS Puts 10,000 Miles on the New Mazda: Wankel-Powered Car Proves Silent, Powerful, and Trouble-free," a solid start for the 10A motor.[27]

The R100 winds down

As nice as the R100 was, it was but a 10A appetizer, and 1972 would be the little pocket rocket's last model year in the US. Sales of the Familia Rotary coupe and SS sedan were slowing in all markets, as Mazda introduced larger, more refined rotary follow-up models. The R100 coupe was sold in Australia from June 1969 to the fall of 1971, during which its price rose from $2790 to $2890 Australian dollars. Coupe and sedan lived on in Japan through 1973.

The fall 1973 lineup at Mazda for the 1974 MY included the revised FA3 Familia. The FA3 featured wider bodywork, altered front and rear fascias, but no 10A, or any Wankel for that matter. The FA3 non commercial range continued in production until January 1977, with the final Japanese version the 1978 two-door pickup truck edition. The normal Familia range ended on the 'Anti-Pollution' note of the 72PS 'TC'-engined Familia Presto 1300 AP. However, the rotary motor had already achieved its goal: the independent survival of Toyo Kogyo.

In 1960, Toyo Kogyo's first year of passenger car production, around 23,000 Mazdas emanated from Hiroshima. In 1970, that figure was approximately 200,000. The four millionth Mazda rolled off the assembly line on March 30 1971. The three millionth arrived just 14 months earlier. The rotary engine certainly contributed to Mazda's growth as an automaker, and its rising international profile. This would continue for some years after the R100, too. This was the whole point of Mazda president Tsuneji Matsuda's decision to pursue the rotary dream.

Mazda was able to avoid the '60s fate of Prince Motors, gobbled up by Nissan. The 10A was the one ace up Mazda's sleeve, to prevent it from befalling the destiny of other minnows. Tsuneji Matsuda passed away in November 1970, whereupon the Mazda presidency was taken up by his 48 year old son, Kouhei Matsuda. Kenichi Yamamoto, leader of the 47 samurai that got the 10A working, became Mazda's rotary advocate through the '70s and beyond. The R100 itself has also progressed to icon status as a collector classic.

The R100 is one of a wave of nostalgia mobiles, reflecting the rising value of '60s and '70s Japanese cars. At a mid 2012 auction, held by auctioneer company Shannons in New South Wales, Australia, an immaculate, unmodified 1971 Mazda R100 coupe sold for a little over $40,000 US dollars. A big part of the appeal, as when the car was new, was the rotary engine. This has resulted in the creation of R100 clones, as enterprising souls swap in 10As to what were originally piston-powered 1200s and 1300s. Genuine R100s have a chassis number starting with M10A, whereas the number for 1200s and 1300s start with STA and STB/C respectively. It's proof one has a bona fide Small Giant at hand.

1970 – The future has arrived

Originally published in 1970, the *Kodansha Children's Colour Encyclopedia* had a volume on transport, with an auto section written by Kiyoshi Takagishi of JAMA (Japan Automobile Manufacturers Association). Takagishi san described the Wankel rotary to junior readers thus, "The rotary engine has the same four-stroke cycle as an ordinary petrol engine – that is, induction, compression, ignition and exhaust. The energy released by the burning of the petrol and air mixture turns the triangular rotor."[28]

The Wankel was introduced as the third type of motor vehicle engine, after gasoline and diesel four stroke piston motors. The two spark plugs in the rotor housing and illustration suggested Mazda's 10A rotary. 1970 was the starting point for Mazda taking its engine of the future mainstream, and Kiyoshi Takagishi made some predictions about what vehicles of the future might be like.

Most of the technical predictions have come to pass. It was thought cars of the future would have TV screens showing what was going on rearwards. Takagishi san also foretold of vehicles with smart cruise control, using radar, that would automatically maintain safe vehicle distance gaps and apply the brakes, if an obstacle lay ahead. Electrically actuated aerodynamic aids, that automatically came into play at speed to improve vehicle stability, also got a mention.[29]

In 1970, the world was still wedded to the pony car ideal of long hood, short deck, even outside America, but what did the car of the future look like? The encyclopedia depicted sleek, glass bubble-topped manta rays silently moving at high speed about eerie blue-gray cityscapes. The scene was worthy of contemporary sci-fi TV series like *Star Trek* or *Space 1999*. Earth was shown to be a manmade, sterile-looking and atmosphereless concoction, at least in terms of major metropolitan centers. This was the common view of 'Tomorrowland' in the '50s and '60s.

Thus, not all predictions came to pass. Urban planners do insist on the inclusion of foliage, and capitalism dictates that not all vehicles of a given type look identical in shape and color. Kodansha's illustrations of the 21st century left out product differentiation, and 6500lb SUV behemoths. Always be wary of predicting the future. An absolute auto darling of the '50s and '60s was the gas turbine engine. Takagishi san did mention this powerplant as a future method of high, smooth power production with low pollution.

Think green, think rotary

The utopia-residing gas turbine powerplant has yet to be adopted as the mainstream motor of choice. Many companies in the '50s and '60s were working on gas turbine, including General Motors. GM's supremo Ed Cole saw the rotary engine as a cheaper way to get the benefits of gas turbine, and the need to obtain such benefits was rather pressing. The issue was auto pollution, and the engine controls necessary to tame it. For the first US smog years of 1968-70, ad hoc methods to turn engines green had been adopted, like transmission controlled spark, air pumps and thermal reactors, but it looked like more would be needed.

Recognising the growing problem of urban pollution, and the contribution cars and trucks make, December 1970 saw passage of the US *Federal Clean Air Act*. This act, informally known as the 'Muskie Smog Bill,' set strict emissions standards for the future 1975 autofleet. In 1970, it was ok for a car to emit 4.1g of hydrocarbons, and 34g of carbon monoxide per mile. Come 1975, a new car would be limited to 0.41g and 3.4g per mile concerning the aforementioned respective pollutants. Plus, an additional limit of 3.1g of nitrogen oxide. There had been no previous standard for this last pollutant, and it was worrying automakers, because existing pollution controls seemed powerless over nitrogen oxide.

The thermally cool running rotary was good on NOx, not so hot on the other two pollutants. However, hydrocarbons and carbon monoxide could be dealt with using existing emissions hardware. This put Mazda the closest to meeting the Muskie smog bill, and raised Detroit's interest in rotary and Mazda to fever pitch. A 1972 model year Mazda print ad was titled: "Detroit is spending $50 million to study the rotary car engine. Experience a new Mazda and you'll know why."

GM paid Curtiss-Wright $50 million in November 1970, as a NSU sub licensee with a right to develop and produce a Wankel in North America. Similarly spooked by the specter of emissions, Ford got into negotiations with Mazda to buy in rotary engines from Hiroshima,

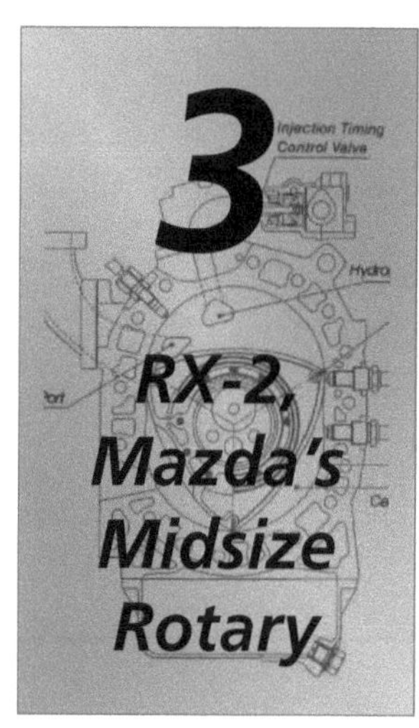

for Ford cars. One could indeed imagine a 10A-powered Maverick GT. The irony was that being impressed by Ford Model T trucks is what helped persuade Mazda president Jujiro Matsuda to push Toyo Kogyo into vehicle manufacture in the first place.

A little over a decade later, Ford did buy in diesel engines from BMW for its Lincoln brand. These historical developments reflect a trend since the mid '60s where US industry has done less innovation. Mazda was happy to show the way to the future. At the major 1970 World Expo held in Osaka, Mazda revealed ten electric prototype vehicles. However, closer to powering one's future ride was the 10A rotary, and 1970 saw Toyo Kogyo unveil its first rotary-powered concept vehicle. That vehicle was the RX-500.

Mazda's RX-500 mid-engined sports car was first shown at the 1970 Tokyo Auto Salon. It celebrated Toyo Kogyo's 50th birthday, and used a 250PS 10A! Styling drew influence from the Ferrari 250 GTO 'Breadvan.' (Courtesy Mazda)

RX-500, Mazda's breadvan

The RX-500 concept car coincided with a time when many automakers were trying their hand at mid-engined sports cars, often of the gullwing variety. 1970 was also a period when concerns about auto safety laws saw manufacturers experiment with how much active/passive safety could be built into a normal car, without creating a tank. Often, all the above came together in a single showcar, and, in Mazda's case, it threw in the 10A Wankel as well. Coincidentally, Rolls-Royce did do a military rotary diesel engine application for tanks, but most people preferred the RX-500's lines. So much more discreet when going shopping!

The RX-500 was so named, because Mazda was celebrating its 50th birthday. As Enzo Ferrari would later say, concerning the 1987 Ferrari F40, the best gifts are the ones we give ourselves. Mazda showed its birthday present at the 1970 Tokyo Auto Salon, and it drew inspiration from Maranello. The RX-500's styling was greatly influenced by the Ferrari 250 GTO 'Breadvan.' The RX-500 two-seater had 'butterfly wing doors,' which rotated upward to permit easier ingress and egress. In keeping with many show and safety cars of the day, the RX-500 had timed tricolor taillights. As an effective safety measure, the taillights illuminated green when accelerating, yellow during coasting and turned red when the brakes were depressed. However, the driver wouldn't get depressed, because a 250PS 10A Mazda rotary was placed just aft of the RX-500's two seats. No turbo, just creative porting and no race-organising authority breathing down the engineers' necks, allowed Mazda to redefine 'hi output.' The mid-engined showcar weighed 1873lb, and has been said to have reached almost 150mph on Mazda's test track.

The RX-500 attracted widespread attention when new, and was considered innovative. However, it wasn't put into production and was quietly forgotten about. In the 2000s, the RX-500 was restored, in partnership with the Hiroshima City Transportation Museum. The former showcar was then displayed in this museum, until reappearing at the Tokyo Auto Salon in 2009, looking just as fresh and future focused as ever.

Capella Rotary – star of the highways

In actual 1970 production, Mazda was doing something bigger than the Familia and 10A – on a practical level it had to. Consult Michael Lamm's opinion on the R100's rear seating commodiousness: "Back seat too small for anything but penguins."[30] There was also the front geometry observation that, whilst there was no front disk fade, the brake pad was too near the suspension arm. Plus, there was a need to get beyond the Familia's front and rear track to improve handling.

Mazda also had a psychological need to move upscale with confidence. In 1965, Toyo Kogyo introduced its first executive car, the Mazda Luce 1500. Late in 1968, this was joined by the up-engined 1800. These models were only a moderate success, so, for many reasons, Mazda needed its next 'large' car to do well. That new car was the Capella, Japanese market introduced on May 13 1970. The range consisted of a Japanese standard midsize four-door sedan, in the Nissan Bluebird, Toyota Corona class, and accompanying pillared coupe. Mindful of possible US roof strength tests, Mazda kept the pillar.

The Capella name was taken from the heavenly constellations, which explained the new car's advertising slogan "Star of the Highways." Capella is also an African antelope, with this wildlife species represented in vehicle badging. However, the Capella was certainly down to earth in engineering. It was an utterly conventional, unitary construction front engine, rear-driver, which Toyo Kogyo constructed in Hiroshima using the medium of steel. As per normal Mazda '70s practice, there was MacPherson strut front independent suspension, recirculating ball manual steering and live axle rear suspension.

The Capella did have one chassis aberration: rear coils. Whereas most '70s Mazdas circulated with rear leaf springs, the Capella employed the refinement of coils. The midsizer also improved upon the Familia's front and rear track. This was now at 51/50in front and rear respectively. Early Japanese and Asian region market Capella piston-engined variants sported four-wheel drums, adequate for the power on tap but not inspiring. However, export versions sent to western countries had front power disk and rear drum brakes.

Apart from rear coils, the Capella range also topped the Familia's sophistication by having a four-link Salisbury arrangement to manage the live axle. All these conservative mechanicals were housed in styled bodies, where even the four-door had a tapered profile with short rear deck that somewhat compromised luggage capacity. Its dimensions were 163.4in length, 62.2in width and 56in height on a tight 97.2in wheelbase. On the same wheelbase, the Capella coupe had equivalent dimensions of 163.2in length, 62.2in width and 54.9in height. The trunk was 8cu ft, and the Capella range was without a wagon variant.

The Capella coupe's swoopy styling carried the price of 3in less rear headroom compared to the sedan. However, coupes were king in the fastback era, and certainly Mazda's most popular variant across its '70s rotary ranges. Price for the most basic Capella in Japan was ¥696,000, ¥36,000 higher than the plushest Familia. For the outlay, one received a four-door Capella with the 1490cc four-cylinder SOHC motor taken from the starter Luce sedan. Upwards of this was a 1586cc inline four, but most eyes were looking at the newly introduced 12A rotary powerplant option. Yes, the 1.6-liter was a new I4 Mazda addition, but real excitement started with spinning rotors.

The 12A followed established 10A Noah's Ark practice of having two rotors, two sparkplugs per combustion chamber and two complete ignition systems, but engine capacity and power were up. Rotor diameter rose from 60 to 70mm, taking displacement to 1146cc, or a reciprocating piston engine equivalent of 2292cc. The new 2.3 motor, as it was commonly described in magazine data panels and tests, put out 130PS and 117lb/ft in Japanese market gross ratings. Compared to the '2-liter' 10A, which still continued, albeit not in the Capella, the new 12A utilized three smaller peripheral exhaust ports to cut noise. The rorty 10A used one large exhaust port.

No doubt thoughts of strict drive-by noise standards in California, soon to render the mighty Pontiac Trans Am's hoodscoop non functional, weighed on the minds of Mazda's engineers. The Capella wasn't in California, or even America yet, but it soon would be with gusto. The 12A still retained Mazda's Wankel road car side intake and peripheral exhaust porting, but the intake porting was larger for better breathing. The 12A also exhaled in superior fashion, thanks to an extractor-type cast iron exhaust manifold. When this smog free 12A motor reached Australia with the Capella in October 1970, the 950 kilo four-speed manual coupe recorded a 16.3 second ¼ mile in local testing.

The Capella sedan tipped the scales 20lb heavier than the coupe, but, either way, this was a speedy mover. 12A powered Capella Series Is, were initially four-speed manual console stick shift cars exclusively. As for naming practice, in Japan the 12A was marketed as a Capella engine option, not a distinct model. So, in the home market, they were simply Capella Rotary coupe and sedan. For export, rotary Capellas were marketed as distinct models. Toyo Kogyo initially chose the R612 moniker. This was an amalgam of the piston Capella's 616 export name, alluding to the 1.6-liter I4 motor, and the 12A Wankel powerplant.

The R612 also fitted in with the rotary export model names used thus far, R100, R130 and even the Cosmo Sport used a triple digit 110S tag to reflect power rating. However, after two weeks, Mazda strangely changed the export name from R612 to the well known RX-2 nomenclature, and started a legendary overseas marketing practice that would last for decades. Visual differences between piston and rotary Capellas started with the Mazda front grille 'M' logo being surrounded by a circle on the former and a triangular rotor shape on the latter. Rotary Engine 'RE' front and rear fascia badges are easy telltales, and the first port of call for RX-2 clone creators.

The greater thirst of the rotary motor saw Mazda specify a larger gas tank for the rotary Capellas, 65 liters versus the piston car's 50-liter tank. This meant that the rotary version's spare tire had to reside on the trunk floor. Piston Capellas could have the spare mounted under the trunk floor, since the gas tank was smaller. The 12A-powered car's larger gas tank also caused the exhaust muffler exit point to be nearly 6in towards the midpoint of the rear lower valence panel, compared to the piston editions.

RX-2 visits America

The success of the R100 and 10A motor in North America, invited the successful follow-up that was the RX-2. The RX-2 made its US debut early in 1971 calendar year, with Mazda ads stating that rotary choices lay with the R100 coupe and sleek new RX-2. In a country where Detroit pushed long, low, sleek and wide, Mazda dealers were happy to see the RX-2. If the R100 carried on solo for too much longer, Mazda might have become known as the VW of performance cars. However, whether it was in four-door or coupe editions, the RX-2 had the look and power America was used to.

The RX-2 coupe could out swoop a Vega, and the RX-2 sedan made Valiants look like mobile lunchboxes, and asthmatic ones at that. Forget about those wheezing 200 cube domestic sixes, the RX-2's 70ci Wankel knocked out a smog legal 120bhp SAE gross. More than that, it performed better than the label said it would. It wasn't so much the power figure, but the way the punch was delivered. To meet emissions standards, ever tightening since 1968, automakers used methods that curbed a piston engine's enthusiasm.

Family favorites in the GM car line were Transmission Controlled Spark (TCS), and the lower compression ratios the auto giant sort of forced on every other car maker. TCS killed vacuum advance on first and second in one's typical GTO three-speed auto V8 chariot. The drop in compression ratios also reduced off-the-line sparkle. Ford had been relying on its 'Thermactor' air injector pump since the pollution party started, and like any smog hardware all the above were party poopers.

Emissions even got engineers to grind specific auto and manual camshaft profiles. This wasn't a problem for Mazda's rotary, it didn't have a camshaft. The other big issues of the day were VSR and pinking. The move to get rid of leaded gas saw forced increased availability of low lead and no lead. Ads promised great performance on these gasolines, but once again claims were seldom realised. Apart from missing the octane-boosting properties of lead, and bringing misfiring or pinking, there was the associated run on woe of VSR or valve seat recession.

Lead used to deposit on the valve seats as the engine ran, adding a protective layer. Take away the lead and wear would set in, if severe enough, noticeable motor malfunction would arise. To ward off pinking, and even worse, manufacturers suggested alternate tankfuls of leaded and unleaded, in mild cases every third fill up. VSR didn't phase Mazda's 10A or 12A, a Wankel didn't have valves. In addition, all independent magazine testing, without exception, showed there was no performance benefit to using more expensive High Test gas on a rotary Mazda. A necessary action on other performance cars to achieve manufacturer speed claims, but a waste on a Wankel.

Beware performance stats, they didn't reveal why so many Americans were signing on the dotted line for an RX-2. *Motor Trend*'s

A 1972 model year US Mazda rotary ad with the R100 and RX2 coupes. Mazda had sold over 150,000 rotary cars by this stage. With stricter 1975 US emissions laws on the horizon, Detroit wanted to know what made rotary tick. (Courtesy Mazda)

Detroit is spending $50 million to study the rotary engine.

Experience a new Mazda and you'll know why.

Subversive Activity

After ten hard years of applied engineering, research and testing, Toyo Kogyo has perfected an extraordinary new power unit that is shaking the automotive establishment.

It's the Mazda rotary engine. And it's far simpler and more efficient than the engine in your car.

Revolutionary

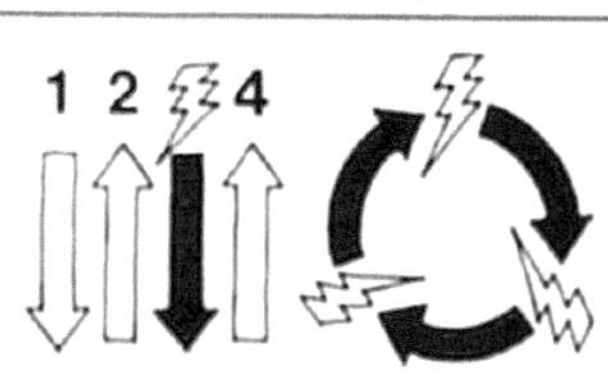

Piston engine

As gasoline burns in cylinders, pistons are forced up and down. This vertical motion must be changed into rotary motion to turn car wheels.

Rotary engine

This logically-designed engine has no wrong-way motion. No need to change directions. It spins out smooth, constant rotary motion from the beginning.

MAZDA ROTARY ENGINE LICENSED BY NSU/WANKEL

*As of June 15, 1971

Firepower

The Mazda rotary is a totally different automotive design. Our regular two-rotor engine equals any of the establishment's six-cylinder engines in 'firepower'. It runs turbine-smooth with much less of the vibration that wears a car out. As Road Test Magazine of the U.S. said, "The lack of vibration and noise makes it difficult to be aware of the engine." (That's partly why we decided to fit tachometers.) Mazda's performance has attracted widespread attention, too. In the major 1970 European endurance races, our rotary cars consistently humbled others two and three times bigger.

Absent Friends

Even so, the Mazda rotary engine lacks a terrible lot.

Things like pistons, rods, valves, cams, and chains. But don't worry about it. Because our rotary engine doesn't need them. It functions at full output with only a few moving parts.

Democracy

We know – the Mazda rotary may be new to you. But it's not new to the rest of the world. Over 150,000* have proved their rugged reliability in more than fifty countries. Now it's here. And for those of you who feel ready to switch, we've built two beautiful cars around the rotary engine. There's the world-famed R100 coupé and the sleek new RX-2.

They're a totally new driving experience. At your nearest Mazda dealer.

Toyo Kogyo Co., Ltd., Hiroshima, Japan

November 1972 report on an RX-2 four-door four-speed sedan produced a 17.7 second ¼ mile at 75mph. An identical time to a 1966 Ford Ranchero, with 225bhp four-barrel 289 V8 and the first Thermactor smog pump. However, the RX-2, on a mere 120 SAE gross horses felt much better. In the words of *Motor Trend*'s Steve Smith "... when you need the fire of Zeus, you just put your foot in it all the way ..." That 12A motor was the gift that kept on giving.

The Thermactored Ford may have delivered the same figures, but the reduced sparkle off the line, and breathlessness towards the redline, had one wishing it was still 1965. 1967 didn't even have the stricter smog dictates of 1972. That explained why US automakers were so keen to set sail on the good ship rotary. One didn't have to floor the RX-2's gas pedal to get the feeling of yesteryear, and it didn't develop rough lethargy when approaching the redline.

Due to rotary's good showing on emissions, the Wankel could still sport a high compression ratio of 9.4 to one. Normal piston engines for 1971/72 had to go much lower than that, which helped explain the RX-2's spry nature. However, it wasn't all utopia, and Mazda's thermal reactor method of dealing with hydrocarbon and carbon monoxide produced what sounded like auto indigestion. This exhaust manifold mounted furnace burnt up pollutants that the cool natured Wankel let through to the exhaust.

Automakers in 1971/72 were usually meeting emissions with leaner carb settings and retarded ignition, which made nice engines sound and feel unwell. The thermal reactor helped the 10A and 12A avoid those tuning compromises, but, whenever you obstruct exhaust airflow, you create back pressure and audio unpleasantness. The unpleasantness was backfiring, experienced during warm up and on deceleration. You didn't want to lower a window when the Wankel backfired. It was as frightening as a Dick Cheney pheasant hunt.

The Mazda RX-2 utilized the larger 12A rotary engine. As the rotary-motorvated Capella, the RX-2 was the first volume Mazda designed to take a rotary powerplant. (Courtesy Mazda)

A pity, because in the spirited, redline-shifting fever the RX-2 encouraged, lifting off the gas unleashed that exhaust cannon. The problem was somewhat exacerbated by the RX-2's excellent ventilation system. As per the R100, no vent wings, but a modern dash with adjustable round swivel outlets at the dash ends. There was also an additional outlet directly in front of the driver with the RX-2. Mazda's fresh air system let in a goodly amount of air even with the car's natural forward motion, no need to turn on the fan. However, the vent system also let in a lot of engine noise.

Magazines suspected a good part of Mazda's Wankel refinement and quietness was down to excellent R100 and RX-2 noise insulation. That said, *Road & Track*'s May 1972 comparison test, between Alfa 1750 Berlina, BMW 2002tii and RX-2 coupe, threw up a maximum decibel first gear wind out recording that put Alfa on 84 dBA, BMW on 82 dBA and Mazda on just 74 dBA. This stat, where a Mazda rotary recorded the lowest noise level in first, by an appreciable margin, would be repeated in comparison tests for years to come.

Buyers and critics alike really dug the rotary engine, especially the 12A's added torque. *Road & Track* said the 12A was "absolutely exciting." In many ways the Mazda rotary seemed well suited to American life, for one it used a four-barrel carb and for another gas was still cheap. The European course involved dual two-barrel carbs, mechanical fuel-injection, and with smog gear times electronic fuel-injection. Intended to create precise fuel metering to some, rather than all, cylinders – think of the Valiant's base one-barrel carb – such exotic methods were hardware expensive and often troublesome.

The Mazda's four-barrel conformed to the US V8 norm of cruising on primaries, with secondaries for full acceleration. The RX-2's single Hitachi/Stromberg 4bbl conformed to this economy/performance compromise, but did little to modify the rotary's intrinsic thirst. The rotary's appetite for gas even concerned Americans, in spite of gas being relatively cheap at the RX-2's intro time. The facts show the

RX-2 12A recorded 18mpg overall, the same as that aforementioned Ranchero 289 4 barrel V8 pickup. If both vehicles delivered the same performance, why begrudge the RX-2 its meal?

In spite of Ford's Ranchero V8 needing premium gas to match the RX-2 on regular, begrudge the consumers did. A *Popular Mechanics* owners' report involving RX-2 carried the title "Enthralled by performance, appalled by mileage."[(31)] The Mazda's physical size had something to do with this view. North Americans had been buying smaller cars for some years to achieve lower overall transport costs, with a vehicle that was easier to maneuver and park. Since 1965, that role was increasingly played by Japanese vehicles. They offered the small size of a VW, but with more modern accoutrements and much lighter controls, which the fairer sex appreciated.

Rotary Mazdas confused North American buyers. They took up around the same amount of space as a Datsun 610 or Toyota Corona, and had those light and easy gas, clutch and brake controls, but what about the gas mileage? In addition, Japanese cars were known for being very quiet, so the rorty RX-2 sedan came across as Clark Kent with a drinking problem. Mazda were continuing to R&D the 10A and 12A's oil consumption down, but an RX-2 was still using a quart of oil every 800-900 miles. Fortune tellers were delighting Arab sheiks with events that were yet to unfold.

In the meantime, buyers weren't able to conflate the idea of small sedan and US V8 midsize performance. With reference to the new hit TV show *M*A*S*H*, *Motor Trend*'s Steve Smith likened the RX-2 in full song moan, to sounding like Hawkeye's impersonation of Hot Lips Hoolihan. A fitting comparison, because Mazda would become the last of the Mohicans when it came to Wankel perseverence. Smith did note that the 12A was silent the rest of the time, and very smooth, but too late – the Mazda's war cry had already been heard by Joe Q Public.

Of the over-53,000 Mazdas sold in 1972 model year America, over 80% were rotary-powered. It seemed buyers were satisfied with the overall performance/economy trade off. *Motor Trend* felt the RX-2 had a lot more moxie than the carb-fed BMW 2002, the previous acceleration champ in this sector. RX-2 garnered *Road Test*'s Import Car of the Year title for 1972. Critically acclaimed, and with demand outstripping supply, US dealers exploited the situation by charging well above msrp.

However, it seemed the consumer was willing to accept the free market set price for an RX-2. Alongside the 12A cars, the piston-engined Capella, called 616 in North America and many export destinations, existed. As usual the 616 took its name from the 1.6-liter inline four stashed underhood. In 1971 smog trim, the 1586cc SOHC I4 was rated at 88bhp SAE gross, and retailed for around $500 under the RX-2's suggested retail price. A decent car, and a fair cost saving, but most chose the rotary-powered editions.

Mazda US persevered and offered the up-engined 618 for 1972 MY. This version replaced the 616 Stateside, and featured the 1.8-liter four-cylinder from the now defunct North American 1800. It carried a 74 horse net rating, but still no interest. Buyers must have reasoned that if they wanted this size of Japanese sedan with a piston engine, then why not get a Datsun 610 or Toyota Corona? Those brands had larger dealer networks, majored in good gas mileage and one doesn't go to Fifth Avenue to buy a Timex.

This was Tsuneji Matsuda san's reasoning for Mazda concentrating on rotary. Who was going to go to Mazda for a Japanese economy car, when the big boys undercut on price and gave better dealer coverage? It suited Mazda, and its US dealers, to follow the value added route. In 1972 a four-door RX-2 retailed for $3050, the stylish RX-2 coupe costing $45 more. That rotary two-door was Mazda's most expensive US chariot. No problem, said the consumer, and, come 1973 MY, the RX-2 was the only Capella variant sold in North America.

Mazda also took steps to uncork the bottleneck and increase supply. During 1972, Mazda distribution was still limited to the North West, West Coast and South. However, come December 1, East Coast and Midwest dealers were due to open their doors. It didn't bother folks that the 618 was absent, 1973 North American Mazda sales surged towards over 119,000. Happy to play a niche market, Mazda was the only non-European provider of a sports sedan in North America.

Based on the prerequisites of full instrumentation, radials, firm suspension and high output low displacement motor in a subcompact unibody, the segment didn't have many players, but was growing. Smog,

A Capella Rotary coupe Series I pictured in 1970. Whether piston or 12A powered, the Capella midsize was the only mainstream, non sports car Mazda range not available in wagon form. (Courtesy Mazda)

higher noise and desire for comfort saw many increasingly give up their Sunbeam Alpines and Triumph TR4s, for cars like the Alfa Giulia, Lancia Flavia and BMW 2000/2002. Now Mazda put forth its RX-2.

Apart from coming from Japan, the major difference was price. The Mazda cost around three grand, whereas the Europeans lived north of $4000. *Road & Track* compared the BMW 2002 with the RX-2 and Alfa 1750 Berlina Giulia revision, and remarked on Japan's low labor cost. In the '70s, Japan was also known for the high productivity of its workers, making more cars per person than factory workers in any other car-making nation.

Japan has always offered a cost conundrum, how could a country where goods and services are relatively expensive have such low wages? The company worker, or kaishain, may have been paid less than their UAW counterpart, but could draw on benefits provided by their benevolent corporate employer. At one time guaranteed long-term employment with company subsidized accommodation, children's music lessons and even an inhouse computerized matchmaking service were the Japanese norm.[32]

At $2750, in 1971, for a US RX-2, buyers must have thought that Christmas or Kurisumasu had come. The three kings from the east had indeed come bearing much standard equipment, and unlike a Fix-It-Again-Tony sedan (Fiat), all the stuff usually worked. One received power front disks, locking gas cap, oil cooler, electrically heated rear window defogger, electric dashboard clock and tachometer. The RX-2 sedan also came with a full width underdash parcel tray, locking glovebox and center console. Many of these items were options on domestic and imported cars, but standard on Japanese cars. Like many Japanese cars the RX-2 came with infinitely adjustable seatbacked front buckets, and that wasn't available on GM's F body until 1982.

Export spec trim names often ran to 'Deluxe' and 'Super Deluxe' for the sedan, and just Super Deluxe for the coupe. Series I cars, up to the fall of 1971, had rectangular headlamps in Japan and many export markets. However, due to US lighting laws, the Stateside RX-2s, and 616/618s had pairs of equal-sized circular lights. This visage was adopted by Japan and all markets for the RX-2 Series II, introduced in Japan in the fall of 1971. At this hour the RX-2 also became available with automatic transmission, a three-speed torque converter JATCO unit.

The JATCO (Japanese Automatic Transmission Company) unit represented a late 1969 joint venture between Mazda, Ford and Nissan. Indeed, the automatic had been seen on shiftless Datsun 240Zs, but the RX-2 application was tailored to suit the rotary's power and torque curves. Being short on low end torque, the RX-2 JATCO had a special high stall torque converter and different shift points to the 240Z. After a slower take off compared to the manual edition, the remaining acceleration spectrum was little affected, due to the Wankel's excellent top end go.

Automatic rotary Mazdas are like automatic turbo cars, they rely on the torque amplifying effect of the torque converter for low end acceleration. Once the torque converter assistance wears off, the engine's strong middle and high rpm performance take over. A seamless slingshot effect, and handy in North America, where most buyers prefer automatic transmission. The automatic option was introduced in Australia in February 1972, and on December 1 of the same year in America, and most of the 1.2 second ¼-mile penalty came at the sprint start.

The RX-2's four-speed box was judged very nice, almost as light and direct feeling as the class leading BMW 2002 four-speed manual.

The only problem was a curiously large ratio gap between second and third, which *Motor Trend* noted was in keeping with British practice of having max torque at 3000rpm, so one could remain in a three-speed box's top gear. However, the RX-2 couldn't be driven like a big six Brit sports car. Much shifting was needed around town to overcome rotary's torque shortfall, so the JATCO auto may have been a wise choice.

Options also ran to the usual audio choices of AM radio for $52 (1972 prices), or AM/FM unit for $93. Japanese radios were offering conspicuously good reception for the money, at a time when expensive Becker or Blaupunkts fitted to a BMW 2002 didn't do as good a job at over twice the price. These RX-2 radios could be combined with a power antenna for just ten bucks. Some good words about Japanese air-conditioning too. An integrated factory a/c unit for the RX-2 was available for $345.

Japanese a/c was building up a good reputation for powerful cold, good airflow distribution and flexible usage. The rival BMW 2002 eventually offered a dealer-fitted Behr unit, which slowly took over from the Frigiking units dealers had been fitting. Both were add-on units that lived in the center console, cooled adequately rather than brilliantly, and were a bit pricey. The RX-2 unit wasn't as integrated in its controls or usage as an American car's a/c, but it was a much better deal than the aftermarket dealer-installed units fitted to European imports.

In the 1960s and 1970s, a/c was an expensive option on all cars. With imports, a dealer-installed aftermarket unit was cheaper than the factory system, and many took up the offer. On the RX-2, the a/c option was only $279. The pitfall with a dealer a/c option was that it wasn't specifically designed for the car. This could cause idling woes with the engine under a/c load. It could also cause handling problems by adding additional nose weight that the front stock springs weren't tuned for; a/c hardware was quite heavy during these years.

Dealer-installed a/c often didn't cool as effectively, or look as 'console tidy' as the

An Australian RX-2 coupe. Series I and II RX-2s came with four circular Familia Rotary (R100) sourced taillights. The RX-2 coupe made an October 1970 Australian debut in Super Deluxe trim for $3298. (Courtesy Dimitri Papastergou)

factory a/c, due to its more add-on nature.

So those were the features with which the RX-2 could match its Euro competition, but could it deliver where the rubber met the road? As *Road & Track* asked in May 1972, "Is the Japanese rotary an alternative to the more expensive European sports sedans?" Handling wasn't quite up to snuff. The RX-2 came equipped with just a front antisway bar, whereas the opposition usually sported two. With export spec 165-13in Bridgestone radials it was lineball on paper, but in practice the RX-2 didn't encourage like a Euro sedan.

In spite of the RX-2's trailing links and Panhard rod, the sedan and coupe would be bumped off line, if a corner was less than smooth. *Road & Track*'s test Alfa had a sophisticatedly located live axle, the BMW 2002 independent rear semi trailing arms, and both could better maintain course on imperfect pavement. Logic would dictate that possessing a suspension unable to process bumps and undulations, would make the RX-2 a demon handler on glass smooth surfaces, but not so.

As per many imported cars, the RX-2 rode rather soft. It seemed Jaguar, Audi, Mazda et al tuned their North American chariots for the comfort they thought Americans wanted. There was a handling package available for the RX-2 in Japan, but not America. There was also a five-speed manual gearbox option for the sporty Japanese market Capella Rotary coupe GSII, but not for America. As importers chose the spec they felt would best suit North American tastes, the hardware heroes got left at home. It was the start of a trend that affected all import brands.

The RX-2's relatively narrow track also didn't do any handling favors in tight cornering situations. In the American sporty car idiom, the RX-2 was a safe understeerer, with lower cornering limits than Euro opponents. So it was that the *Road & Track* RX-2 coupe recorded 0.679g on the skidpad. The Alfa got to 0.692g and the BMW 2002tii 0.726g. If the RX-2's suspension was made firmer, that would just have exacerbated the car's poorer rough road roadholding. That's probably why *Road & Track* had the RX-2's handling down as merely passable. The magazine did say the RX-2 could be driven quickly, it just wasn't up to the easy confidence of a Euro chassis.

However, value was displayed in other areas. Before the 1973/74 fuel crisis made everyone try to pare down the pounds, Japanese cars came with a good amount of metal. The RX-2 coupe was 3.3in shorter than the BMW 2002tii, but weighed the same 2645lb, and the 2002 lost sedan races to Alfas because it was too heavy. It must also have brought joy to owners' hearts upon realising their RX-2 didn't need periodic valve clearance adjustments. High output engines sans hydraulic tappets did, but the 12A didn't have valves.

A testimony to Mazda R&D was apparent in the RX-2 matching the BMW's 4000-mile oil change interval, the Alfa twin-cam I4 needed one at 3000 miles. It was important to prospects that they could treat a rotary like a normal car. The only oddity was the RX-2 needing a chassis lube every 32,000 miles. The other two cars didn't, and a chassis lube on a unibody car was a strange thing in the modern era. However, the RX-2 was modern in its controls and ergonomics. The sentiment was that one didn't need to buy a rotary to get a well-thought out car, even a piston Capella would suffice.

Motor Trend titled its November 1972 report 'With or Without Rotary Power, This Car is Ergonomic Perfection.' Apart from well-sized footwell pedals, a single upper left steering wheel stalk did turn signals, headlight flasher, headlight dimmer, two-speed windshield wiper action and windshield washers. There was also mention of Mercedes-like chair high seats with good driving position, and handy return spring action for the adjustable seatback. Whilst all the above doesn't make a sports car, the world was moving beyond the Mrs Robinson Alfa Spider era, to something more practical.

Soon the RX-2's successor would have the Volvo 244 as a sports sedan rival, and no one would find the Triumph GT6's bent spine seatback amusing anymore. Problems directed at the RX-2 concerned its plethora of body add ons, like excess badging and sculptured body panels suggestive of horsepower. In copying the stylistic ways of V8 pony cars, contemporary Japanese cars were considered over-ornamented. Rotary Mazdas were targets of such criticism. However, more affluent Japanese consumers didn't want the plain rides of just a few seasons earlier, that used to play well with US economy car fanciers. The value added look also had charm for American small sporty car buyers that might have gone for a Comet GT V8. Critical nitpicking saw testers remark on how the RX-2's general hush made the sounds of electric microswitches, eg brake lights and turn signals, very noticeable. However, there were no complaints about the 12A derived performance. *Road & Track*'s Alfa, BMW, RX-2 comparo saw Mazda as top speed champ on 120mph. The Alfa and BMW managed only 108mph and 110mph respectively. 120mph was a very impressive top speed for a subcompact sports sedan of the early '70s, and testified to the 12A's power characteristics.

The North American smogger 12A had been re-rated from 120bhp SAE and 110lb/ft gross to net figures of 102 horses and 98lb/ft during 1972. Much less than its Euro rivals, but that rotary power curve that wouldn't quit, and, to a lesser degree, the coupe's slippery shape, helped the RX-2 win out. In 0-60mph acceleration, the RX-2 neatly split the BMW 2002tii's 9.8-second time and Alfa's 11-second clocking, with 10.4 seconds. *Road & Track*'s stats showed the gas mileage penalty for the RX-2's enthusiasm. The Mazda got 15.3mpg, whilst the other two managed 20mpg.

To compensate for its thirst, the RX-2 came with a 17.3-gallon tank: the Alfa's and BMW's gas tanks were over five gallons smaller. More important to US buyers was the Mazda's diet of 85 octane gas, whereas the Alfa and BMW needed 96 and 91 octane respectively. With a 3.70 final drive ratio, the RX-2 was also cruising quietly at 70mph with 3600rpm on the tach, perfect for dealing with miles of interstate. The rotary engine seemed better able to cope with smog restrictions than European rivals, on paper and in practice.

When tested by UK's *Autocar*, the carb BMW 2002 had a top speed of 107mph and did 0-60mph in 10.1 seconds. The RX-2 registered 111mph and 10.3 seconds when featured in the same journal.[33] Normally the fuel injected BMW 2002tii could do 0-60mph in well under 9 seconds, but in US smog trim it was little quicker than its Euro carb counterpart. However, *Autocar*'s 130PS RX-2, with or without thermal reactor, turned in almost the same 0-60mph time as the *Road & Track* RX-2 with thermal reactor. Thus, apart from the occasional backfire, it seemed consumers had little to fear concerning the RX-2's smog gear.

Gas mileage relativities also seemed maintained across the Atlantic pond. The

An Australian spec RX-2 sedan. The RX-2 Super Deluxe sedan made its Australian debut at $2998. The RX-2 Series I & II R100 taillights were deep-sixed at the end of 1973 MY, due to changes in Japanese safety lighting laws. (Courtesy www.ausrotary.com)

Autocar BMW 2002 and RX-2 managing 25.5 and 17.8 UK mpg respectively. The 17.8mpg figure according nicely with *Road & Track*'s 15.3 US mpg. Once again *Autocar*'s 2002 needed four-star 98 octane UK gas, whereas the RX-2 merely required two-star, and one also saved on purchase price, the BMW and RX-2 costing £2265 and £1500 respectively. The BMW was in keeping with the German expression 'sinfully expensive.' An appropriate Japanese translation for the RX-2 would be 'kono kuruma ga taka sugi masu.'

In the US and UK, importers were adding a comfy margin with both cars, but the RX-2 seemed to maintain its two-thirds price advantage and relative bargain nature. The Mazda's mere 70ci on paper displacement could even fool an insurance company or two. On the question of whether the RX-2 was a viable alternative to the European crusaders, *Road & Track* answered "yes." It won five test categories and tied with the Alfa, leaving the BMW the winner – at a price. That price was a base $4360 for the 2002tii, making US importer, Max Hoffman, jubilant.

Logic dictated one should choose the RX-2, pocket the nearly $1300 saving, and endure the Mazda's slightly lower roadburner standards. Value aside, could the RX-2 be trusted? Such was the newness of Mazda, the 10A/12A and absence of owner surveys, in 1972 *R&T* said "Mazda? Don't know yet."[34] So it was with some uncertainty that *Car and Driver* editor Patrick Bedard suggested the magazine should race an RX-2 in the 1973 BF Goodrich Radial Trophy Series.

RX-2, track time

The BF Goodrich-sponsored races were in the IMSA Racing Stocks or IMSA class for lightly modified showroom stock small sedans, the 'grocery getter' class, if you will. In this mix, one would find Ford Pintos, Datsuns and even a Saab 96. There were subclasses for less powerful and more powerful cars. The latter involved 2-liter overhead cam powered rides, and those with OHV engines greater than two liters. The AMC Gremlin 232 and BMW 2002 were leaders in the powerful group.

Car and Driver got the best in the business to handle its RX-2. The Mazda was prepared by Roy Woods Racing (RWR). RWR ran the American Racing Associates (ARA) outfit that grabbed the 1972 SCCA Trans Am Driver's and Manufacturer's Championships. George Follmer drove the #1 ARA AMC Javelin to glory in what was fast becoming a cash-starved, deflated series. There was more interest in small cars in showrooms and on the racetrack. Buyers in America were selecting more compacts and subcompacts to combat inflation, insurance and, soon, steeply rising gasoline prices. So why not race what people were actually buying?

The C&D RX-2 certainly had the right stuff underhood, thanks to a 12A tuned up by Jim Mederer of Anaheim, Californian Mazda specialist Racing Beat. Mederer stuck with the stock 70mm dual Wankel rotors, but did much carb and porting mods. The latter involved opening up the 12A's housing aperture, so that the motor could ingest more air and fuel to make more power. In this case, very large auxiliary intake ports to each side of the sideplate housing, or a 'Bridge Port.'

Created by racing royalty, and ready for an IMSA baptism of fire, but the RX-2 wasn't a complete unknown. In Japan, the RX-2 made its race debut at the Fuji 1000 in July 1971, winning its class and finishing third overall. In Mazda's own assessment, whilst the RX-2 didn't win the 1971 Japanese Touring Car Championship, it did show promise. The trouble was that, when the R100's spiritual successor arrived, the RX-3 coupe, Mazda put its racing efforts behind that car, leaving the larger RX-2 overshadowed.

The RX-2, like the R100, had a narrow track, but other properties augured well. The light 12A gave the RX-2 a 54/46% weight distribution, the best on test against the Alfa and BMW in *R&T*'s May 1972 comparo. That 12A motor was also making some serious horsepower. In 1973 federalized spec, the 12A made 97 net horses at 6500rpm and 98lb/ft at four grand. Even though Mr Mederer stuck to the RS rulebook of stock rotors, the *Car & Driver* RX-2 got to 198 net horses, 30bhp over *C&D*'s original goal. Then, just to be safe, a Mazda factory racing exhaust system was added, which gave a grand total of 218bhp at 8400rpm.

By this time, the RX-3 (Savanna) had already been racing in Japan with 12A power, so the factory had homologated a super exhaust system that *C&D*'s RX-2 could utilize. The RX-2's output was more than AMC's I6 or BMW's 2-liter four could manage, and helped qualify Patrick Bedard a little too well for the RX-2's first race outing in June 1973. The IMSA officials immediately added 300lb of ballast for the remainder of the 1973 racing season. However, the Mazda RX-2 won its third race with Bedard driving at Lime Rock. John Morton came second in his BMW 2002, with title contender, Amos Johnson, third in the AMC Gremlin.

On September 30, Bedard pulled off a second triumph at Road Atlanta, beating George Alderman's Gremlin into second place. The IMSA officials demanded a tear down of the RX-2's 12A motor, and then conceded it was 100% legal. The officials then banned porting for the 1974 racing season. No porting

The 1972 MY Capella Rotary coupe in Japan. As the RX-2, Mazda's bigger, more refined 12A-powered R100 follow-up, was *Road Test* 1972 Import Car of the Year. The coil sprung, live axle rear and narrow track limited handling compared favorably to pricier Euro Sports sedans. However, in SCCA Racing Stock, the 12A's power more than compensated. (Courtesy Mazda)

was like getting a piston car to race with a stock cam and intake manifold, ie it would have rendered the RX-2 uncompetitive in RS, so *C&D* pulled the plug on the program.

The *C&D* RX-2 was then sold to Mazda salesman and racer, Walt Bohren. Things looked up when IMSA loosened the rules and allowed some porting. Bohren brought the RX-2 back to IMSA RS, and lap records along with victories were achieved in 1976 and 1977, by which time the RX-2 was no longer sold new in America. Better than that, Bohren's RX-2 won the driver's championship in 1978 and Mazda got the manufacturer's cup. There was some irony in the fact that RX-2 departed North America's new car market at the end of '74 MY. In addition, rotary was on the decline in America and elsewhere by the late '70s.

The ex *C&D* RX-2 proved that yesterday's hero could be today's winner. The very same car continued with different owners in the IMSA and SCCA mediums, achieving SCCA divisional championships in 1982 and 1983. The car was then sold to Mazda racer and constructor, Jim Downing. Success for the RX-2, in general, also transpired during the model's currency downunder in Australia. A number of good performances were displayed at the famous Mount Panorama circuit, during the Australian Bathurst endurance race.

Rotary Mazdas would reveal their performance prowess at Bathurst for decades to come. In October 1971, at the Bathurst-held Hardie-Ferodo 500, Gary Cooke's RX-2 won class C (2- to 3-liter class) and came 26th overall. For 1972, the RX-2 made the switch to Class B (1.3- to 2-liter class) and finished second and third in class, improving to 13th and 14th overall. The European rear-drive Ford Escort GT came first in class. Not bad, considering, as elsewhere, racing officialdom took an unenlightened view of porting.

However, needs must when the devil drives, the RX-2 did its best amidst the slings and arrows of outrageous officialdom. 1973 was to be the RX-2's final Bathurst appearance, whereupon it returned to Class C, coming first and second in said class. The cars were classified 10th and 12th overall, the RX-2's best showing at Mount Panorama. As Mazda said, the Capella Rotary did show promise. The RX-2's talents were more appreciated in Australia and New Zealand than in Europe, where high government fuel excise made the RX-2's thirst worrisome.

Southern hemisphere RX-2 exploits

In the cheaper gas environment of the Antipodes, the RX-2's straight-line performance outweighed gas mileage concerns. V8 and big six-cylinder cars were popular locally produced fare, and the Mazda rotaries offered grunt at a relatively affordable price the European imported cars couldn't match. Zoom zoom in the traffic light grand prix, rather than the doom, doom experienced in the Peugeot 504 versus Holden Kingswood V8 match up. On release, Mazda Australia wanted $2998 (AUD) for the RX-2 Super Deluxe sedan and $3298 for a like-trimmed coupe.

Not cheap, but priceless if one was to avoid the 'wait for the paint to dry' acceleration of a four-cylinder Mercedes Compact or Citroën DS. Certainly the RX-2 coupe assumed the performance leader position in Australia, until the smaller, cheaper RX-3 coupe gained momentum. At that point Australian Mazda marketing put the Grand Familia-based rotary two-door in the sport sector driver's seat, leaving RX-2 to do the premium price medium size family class.

No RX-2 coupes came to Australia after 1973. Newer Mazda releases cannibalised RX-2 sales, leaving just the 1974 RX-2 manual transmission sedan at $3668 and $3958 automatic equivalent. In New Zealand, they actually made RX-2s. To beat import duty and meet government policy of encouraging local manufacturing, piston Capellas (616) and RX-2s were assembled from CKD kits. These vehicles were assembled under contract, from 1972, for Mazda New Zealand, by Motor Industries International (MII) in Otahuhu, South Auckland.

The RX-2 was the only rotary Mazda made in New Zealand. Manual and automatic RX-2 sedans were assembled, as were manual only coupes. MII also built the much less popular 616. New Zealand buyers followed American and Australian logic: buy a rotary Mazda, the Wankel was the special feature. Anyone wanting a vanilla flavor Japanese sedan would have taken the Datsun 180B (610) route. Globally, 225,004 buyers took the rotary route and chose an RX-2, although, for various reasons, most of those sales were generated before 1975.

The fuel crisis and new release rotaries drew attention from the Capella rotary cars, but Mazda continued to update the range nevertheless. Major changes occurred with

The revised Series III 1974 MY pollution compliant, Japanese spec Capella 1800 AP. The piston engined Capella was called 616 in overseas markets. The 1.8-liter I4 started life in the 1960s Luce. (Courtesy Mazda)

the fall 1973 launch of the 1974 model year Mazdas. In the Capella's case, this heralded the Series III and a restyle that continued with the Series II's front quad circular headlamps, but introduced hexagon taillights rearwards. The Series I and II Capellas had utilized the R100's quad Italianesque round taillights, but the Familia Rotary was gone by the end of 1973 MY, and Japan had new 1974 lighting safety laws.

The RX-2 sported a revised front fascia, whilst the updated interior had a highly styled new dashboard and larger RX-4 derived steering wheel. Revised suspension settings and wider international market availability of the optional overdrive five-speed manual, and 165SR 13in tires, improved the breed. It was also possible to get the previously automatic spec 3.9:1 differential ratio, on manual RX-2s. However, the biggest change concerned underhood, and wasn't RX-2 exclusive. The 12A motor became the 12B, with a single dizzy.

In the interests of greater reliability, Mazda dumped the dual ignition system; the 12B had a single distributor to handle both rotor chambers. The dual sparkplugs per chamber continued. The '12B' nomenclature was tried for some time, before the realization dawned that existing marketing had promoted the better known 12A name. Thus, it wasn't long before the new single distributor motor was again called 12A. No displacement change occurred in the dual to single distributor change, the 12A still registered 70 cubes.

There was also no change in the Japanese market 130PS rating and associated 117lb/ft of torque. This was surprising, because the 12B had Mazda's new REAPS pollution control system. REAPS stood for Rotary Engine Anti-Pollution System. A fancy title, but, in substance, it represented the adoption of the thermal reactor emissions set-up seen on American spec R100s and RX-2s. This was the familiar exhaust side oven that burnt up combustion leftovers before they exited the tailpipe.

Auto armageddon!

REAPS had an exhaust system overheat thermosensor. If one's REAPS muffler heated up beyond a set limit, the thermosensor would short circuit and the malfunction would illuminate as a dashboard warning light to inform the driver of pending doom. With fears about coming tighter US federal laws, some car makers were trying emissions and safety strategies for world markets. Volvo and Porsche tried 5mph bumpers everywhere in 1974. Salesmen outside the US would allay fears by telling prospects, "Don't worry, sir, soon, all cars will look like this."[35]

Similarly, Mazda went global on the thermal reactor approach, even though many markets outside Japan and America didn't require such environmental civic mindedness. To Mazda's credit, its 12A's adoption of said reactor was less noticeable, and irritating, than Volvo's American market-motivated seatbelt warning buzzer. If there was a performance pollution price, new 1974 RX-2 owners were okay with it.

The North American market got most of the RX-2's 1974 changes, including the highly styled new dash, but kept the 1973 front visage, whilst incorporating 5mph bumpers at both ends. The beefier bumper bars were directed at protecting the car more than its occupants, spare the looks and spoil the insurance premium. US insurance companies, loathe to pay out for 'park by ear' damage to the previously pretty chrome bumpers, were at the bottom of the bumper conspiracy.

Allstate et al had relatively little to do with RX-2's 1974 American demise. Blame the newer

RX-3 and RX-4 for taking up the sports and luxury sides of the ledger. The former undercut and the latter over-luxoed the poor RX-2 into obscurity. In the North American market, the fine Japanese size distinction between RX-2 and RX-4 was lost. They both seemed alike except one was newer, so RX-4 got the vote. Mazda was somewhat of a niche US brand in the early '70s, a Japanese BMW equivalent, if you will. That made RX-3 wagon more kookily appealing than a like-sized RX-2, if one wants to get into the psychology of it all.

As a practical matter, depreciation of the US dollar was making RX-2 less attractive too. The demise of the Bretton Woods 1949-1970 system of tied international currencies to the US dollar was bad news for RX-2 in particular. Under Bretton Woods, each dollar was worth ¥360. With this fixed relationship over and the yen free to appreciate and correct trade imbalances, Mazdas became more expensive. The RX-2 had crept up from 1971's $2750 to 1974's $3695.

The RX-2 lingers on ...

A very niche RX-3 wagon with zero rivals could better weather a price rise, than the relatively plain RX-2 sedan, worthy though it was and still improving. The Series IV Capellas, still with optional 12A, were released in Japan in mid 1974. The revised Capella Rotary had a new front fascia with smooth pointed hood, RX-4 style grille, RX-3 influenced headlights/surrounds and improved engine cooling. However, there seemed few takers for the rotary-powered Capellas, even in Japan, and elsewhere the RX-2 was noticeable by its absence.

The RX-2 was listed for sale throughout 1974 model year in the UK, and the RX-2 coupe carried a £1500 price by the end of said year. However, it is believed there were no RX-2 imports to the country after 1973 calendar year, due to poor sales sparked by the fuel crisis. A similar cool off happened in Australia, although at least the RX-2 Series IV did reach Downunder. Since the Series III, Australia had only been receiving the RX-2 sedan. The Series IV was supposed to reach Australia at the end of 1974 calendar year, but a glut of unsold Series IIIs and a seven- to eight-week ordering delay, meant it was mid-1975 before Series IV stock reached showrooms.

The presence of the RX-3 and RX-4, together with the oil crisis, did the Australian RX-2 Series IV no favors either. However, Australian dealers still managed to sell around 300 RX-2 Series IVs, and continued to take orders until April 1976. In theory, the RX-2 lived on in some markets into 1978, even though the non-rotary third generation Capella made its Japanese debut in the fall of 1977. The final 1978 RX-2s represented lingering stock made before the summer break of 1977.

The fuel crisis had boosted the popularity of piston Capellas. In the rotary-available Capella era, the piston and 12A cars weren't far apart on sales. Indeed, minus the fuel crisis, the 12A cars may well have wound up ahead. For piston and 12A, the production numbers were 254,919 and 225,004 respectively during 1970-77. However, the next Capella managed a huge 723,709 during 1978-82; around a ¼ million more in a shorter timeframe. The world was getting over the gas crunches in this period, and Mazda was on the corporate recovery path, but this 'new' Capella was piston only. Engine options now ran to the 1970 Capella-introduced 1.6-liter, first gen Luce-featured 1.8-liter, and 2nd gen Luce 1970cc motor. All worthy and reliable single overhead cam inline four-cylinder fare, but sadly no 12A excitement. That dipsomaniac motor found a svelte new Mazda companion for 1978, but the Capella was now very midsize family vin ordinaire.

The 1978-82 Capella was basically the 1970-77 rear-drive chassis, dressed in new crisper, if more anodyne, clothing. In auto industry parlance, Mazda had reskinned the earlier 616, and so fresh were the new duds that the latest Capella was rechristened 626. In most places that is, except the UK. In Great Britain, the 626 was called Montrose, in honor of the area where a notable Mazda dealership was located.

By now competing in the UK against the Toyota Carina, and also upscale and rear-drive Colt Sigma (Mitsubishi Galant), there was little to excite beyond the expected Japanese high build quality and generous equipment levels. However, technically, substituting in a 12A engine, wide alloy wheels and firm suspension, would create a new RX-2. The Montrose was available as a four-door sedan and coupe, as per previous Capellas, but with a Japanese bank and Ford USA looking over Toyo Kogyo's financial shoulder, Mazda couldn't afford to be so enlightened.

Swapping 10As and 12As into what were rotary chassis, and older piston Familias and Capellas, was up to enthusiast tinkerers. To avoid finding rotary Capella clones, the vehicle VIN is a place to start. Capella Series Is have the number stamped flush on the firewall, and raised on the Series II cars. Legit RX-2s carry the chassis number prefix S122A, whereas the piston Capella starts with SNA. Rotary engine 'RE' front grille and rear deck badges can be bought by nefarious parties, but the chassis number should never lie.

Series III and IV RX-2s also differ from piston Capellas and RX-2 Series Is and IIs, due to the REAPS emissions hardware. A larger rear valence panel cutout was necessary for the REAPS rear muffler. Similarly, the intrusive underhood nature of the REAPS thermal reactor furnace necessitated a redesigned and repositioned steering box, unique to RX-2 Series III and IV cars.

As a new model, the RX-2 excited many, but newer models come by. Buyers are always seeking new pastures; the grass is always greener on the other side. At Mazda, that grass had a name, and the name was Savanna.

The 1978 MY Capella, known internationally as the 626, was a reskin of the 1970-77 Capellas. Conventional rear-drive, with blander, universal neat styling and no rotary option, the 1978-82 Capella was also available in coupe form. (Courtesy Mazda)

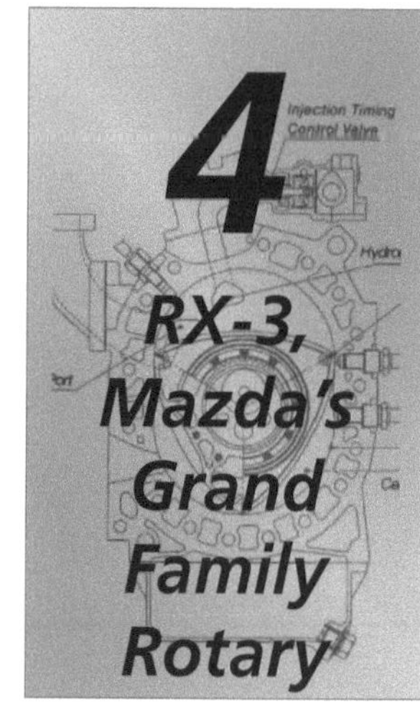

Bigger is better

Sometimes one gets an exception that honors the rule that most advertising is complete baloney. That exception occurred with the Mazda RX-3. For its 1972 debut in America, Mazda's advertising stated that it simply wasn't enough just to build a better engine: "We had to sit down and build a better car around it." The R100 wasn't actually mentioned, but spectacles weren't required to read between the lines.

The statement was made that the new RX-3 was longer and wider than earlier 982cc Mazda rotaries. Given the R100 was the only officially imported Mazda in North America to use the 982cc 10A Wankel, and the North American RX-3 was only ever 12A-powered, the conclusion was inescapable. As cute as the R100 was, a larger car with wider track would provide better accommodation and superior handling. Introduced in Japan as the Savanna, the new RX-3 addressed these concerns, although the R100 and RX-3 continued to be sold together in Japan, until the end of 1973 MY.

Just as the Familia Rotary coupe and sedan were derived from the piston Familias, the fourth-launched Mazda rotary was related to the new Grand Familia range. Those living outside Japan would better know the Grand Familia and Savanna as the 808/818 and RX-3 models respectively. Living up to its name, the Grand Familia was indeed a big Familia: a larger, more refined range of coupes, four-door sedans and wagons, in the European Ford Escort, VW Golf class. The Familia and Grand Familia would continue to sell alongside each other, right to the end of the FA3's final pickup truck vestige, in 1978.

The engineering between Familia and Grand Familia was similar. The front engine/rear-drive format continued with front MacPherson strut independent coil suspension, with a leaf sprung live axle at the rear. Disk front and drum rear brakes, along with recirculating ball manual steering were expected Mazda 1970s fare. However, at 160in long, 62.8in wide and having a 91in wheelbase it lived up to its 'Grand' title. Such dimensions made the Grand Familia 9.2in longer, and 4.5in wider than the plain Familia.

In terms of weight, the four-door rotary RX-3 tipped the scales at 865kg, the coupe was heavier at 885kg for Japanese spec 10A-powered cars. This gave the portlier two-door a kerb weight under 2000lb, not bad, but still nearly 200lb more than the 10A-powered R100. The Japanese spec Savannas made their debut with uprated 105PS 10A motors solely, five units up on the R100. However, the extra 'Grand' weight coupe versus coupe meant a lower top speed of 109mph, compared to 112mph for the R100. Australian testing of the 10A RX-3 coupe produced a 17.6 second ¼ mile at 76mph, not bad, but slower than the R100.

Mirroring an international early '70s trend, new, heavier and more luxurious sporty cars were flashier and slower than '60s predecessors. Customers favored the more stylish appearance, and stopwatch starts were of less importance. Symbolic of a need for flash was the Mazda RX-510 coupe showcar, which made its debut at the 1971 Tokyo Auto Salon. This light green bolide was Savanna coupe-based, and intended to promote the new Grand Familia range and associated rotaries. Thus the RX-510 married special front and rear fascias to a Grand Familia center section. The effect from the front was that of a heavy-duty, butch-looking, Zagato-bodied 1971 Lancia Fulvia 1.6 Sport.

With pending US federal 5mph bumper law, many car makers were experimenting with concealed impact bumpers. The RX-510 stepped up to this '70s reality, and incorporated what Mazda thought would be another '70s mainstay, the rotary. Apart from the 1971

Note the funky Japanese market fender-mounted side mirrors. The Savanna coupe was Japan's pony car for a whole generation of young drivers. Early Japanese market Savanna Series Is were powered by the 105PS 10A Wankel alone. (Courtesy Mazda)

Savanna 10A/4 speed manual power team, the RX-510's custom aluminum rims had rotor-shaped cutouts. Such alloy rims in the '70s and '80s were usually concave and covered, not showing much brake rotor/caliper, with such hardware being quite small at the time. Thus, the rotor cutouts were a visual highlight.

The RX-510's interior was stock standard Savanna, except for special front buckets. For production, the RX-2 experience had convinced Mazda bean counters that trim and insignia differences between piston and rotary variants should be kept in check. On debut, the Grand Familia prices were not far removed from Familia, with the basic Grand Familia 1300 standard commencing at ¥600,000. For that, one received a very bare spec 1272cc 'TC' I4-powered four-door sedan, with two-barrel carb and 87PS DIN at 6000rpm. Most would want to spec up to the ¥700,000 GR trim sedan, with the 1500 GLII as the top piston luxo designation.

The 'UB' 1.5-liter four-cylinder was of first gen Luce origin, and was rated at 92PS at 5800rpm. This 1490cc motor was the top choice for the sportiest of piston engine Grand Familia coupes, the GSII variant. A trim equivalent to the GR sedan was the GS coupe. For 1974 model year, the new top Grand Familia Japanese market piston engine became the 100PS 1586cc I4 motor. This 'NA' inline four was introduced in November 1973, and was first seen in the 1970 Capella.

A 1972 model year Savanna Coupe GSII may show a striking resemblance to the also 1972-introduced Ford Gran Torino Coupe. However, Ford had no connection with Mazda at the time. Visual similarity was purely coincidental. (Courtesy Mazda)

The rotary equivalent Savanna cars followed the Grand Familia trim levels, but were marketed as distinct entities in Japan. Whereas the 12A had merely been a Capella engine option, the rotary Savanna was a model in its own right. After all, it came with its own nameplate. This latest home for the 10A Wankel was initially four-speed manual only, like the Grand Familia. However, the Savanna had shorter first to third gear ratios to keep that 10A on the boil. That 100lb/ft never felt like the same torque belonging to a piston engine.

Marketing distinction in Japan and elsewhere pushed the Savanna as the youth sport, affordable rotary, whereas the Capella Rotary was more midsize executive. In early 1972, the Savanna range embraced the JATCO auto option, and became the first rotary wagon in the world. This utilitarian sports holdall was available in Japan and US markets, but not everywhere. The five-door RX-3 wagon, to use its export title, was available in the UK, powered by the 10A Wankel alone. However, the wagon wasn't available in Australia or New Zealand.

Built on the same 91in wheelbase as the sedan and coupe, the wagon was 1in longer and 80lb heavier. It was also 1in taller at 55in than the 54in tall sedan, the RX-3 coupe was 53in tall. Another 1972 calendar year arrival in the Japanese market was the Savanna GT coupe. This was an even sportier variant with lowered suspension, 12A motor, and a five-speed gearbox, mostly limited to the Japanese domestic market. All Savanna/RX-3 Series I cars sold outside the US were 10A-powered, except the GT. For America, the RX-3 used the federal RX-2 smog motor, which implied a thermal reactor and 120 net SAE horses.

RX-3 redefines the pony car

Road & Track tested an RX-3, upon the rotary reaching the US market, in 1972. Its August 1972 report revealed a four-speed, four-door that could do 0-60mph in 10.9 seconds, stop from 80mph in 281 feet, generate 0.692g on the skidpad and consume an average of 18mpg. That said, don't compare this RX-3 with a Datsun or Toyota; compare it with a small block V8-powered domestic compact or subcompact. Such comparison would reveal the RX-3's superiority. US 1972 advertising said, "Some people will call it the Silent Express." That was an accurate assertion, since the

RX-3 was so quick, quiet and smooth, one would think there was a six- or eight-cylinder underhood. Precedent would say that was impossible. The RX-3 was a small car, and how could a domestic cast iron 6 or V8 fit in there without really upsetting weight distribution? Shoehorning in a small block V8 would also have necessitated removing the fenders when the sparkplugs were changed! Domestic subcompacts with V8s – witness Mustang II and Gremlin V8 – certainly had underhood access and weight distribution woes, but there was also the catalytic converter issue. Apart from AMC, the domestics quickly wedded their emissions plans to the cat converter – and people were afraid of cats.

There was public concern that hot cats, being a sub chassis exhaust muffler device, could start forest fires. It was also feared that the streets would be full of the smell of sulphur from the aforementioned cats. Coming out of the counter culture, conspiracy late '60s era, the public's imagination was quite fertile. Contemporary movies like *The Omega Man*, *Soylent Green* and *Damnation Alley* also fueled fears of pending doomsday scenarios. Apart from the idea of sulphur-induced zombie cats and dogs running amok with mutant cockroaches, catalytic converters tied owners to unleaded gas.[36]

Lead would coat the inner workings of a catalytic converter, making them less effective as a pollution filter and eventually fail. The RX-3 allowed one to use cheaper, leaded, gas. If one lifted the hood on an RX-3 running at night, a glowing red hot thermal reactor would give a visual greeting. However, this device was far enough from the ground not to worry forest ground cover or Smokey the Bear. After all, the RX-3's home name was Savanna.

Apart from better weight distribution, the RX-3 also featured staggered rear shocks. This was an old pony car trick to keep wheel hop and axle tramp at bay under hard acceleration and braking. One shock absorber was placed behind the live axle, with the other ahead. Unlike the increasingly emissionized V8 small cars, the Mazda still made decent power, so controlling that live axle was very key. Taking a leaf from the 'Wide Track Pontiac' era, the RX-3's wider stance was also a handling boon. A shorter, but wider car than the RX-2, the RX-3's 51in front and rear track contributed to more surefooted handling.

Using 155 section metric footprint 13in radial tires, with optional perforated sports steel rims, the RX-3's handling was praised, and judged an improvement over RX-2. However, the RX-3 wagon was felt by many to have a harsh ride. The firmed-up rear suspension, necessary to keep the extra rear unibody weight under control, worsened ride comfort compared to the RX-3 coupe and sedan and all other small wagons on the market. However, as a niche vehicle, the RX-3 wagon hit the bullseye and was a big hit in America. In that competitive car mecca called California, the RX-3 wagon was the newest flavor no one had yet tried.

Small wagons were in vogue at this time, and having a pollution-friendly rotary in smog Nazi California was an ace up the sleeve. Mazda zoomed to fourth amongst import brands in California within six months of market entry. By late 1972, its bestseller was the RX-3 wagon. In spite of its strict smog dictates, California was a popular place for ponycars and sports cars. The RX-3 wagon seemed to cover all bases in offering sprightly V8-type performance, and a fifth door for a lifestyle-orientated environment.

The RX-3 wagon might have been all the cars one ever wanted rolled into one. *Road Test* magazine certainly thought so. This esteemed journal anointed the RX-2 coupe as 1972 Import Car of the Year. Under three months later, *Road Test* declared the RX-3 wagon was 1973 Import Car of the Year in its 1973 March

The interior of the new Savanna Coupe, pictured on its September 1971 debut, in top GSII spec. Fashionable early '70s fare included 8-track and AM auto radio tuner, vinyl buckets and four on the floor! Note the 100kph speedo marking, representing Japan's national speed limit. (Courtesy Mazda)

Shown on debut in January 1972, the Savanna Sports Wagon was the world's first rotary-powered series production wagon! With the entire market to itself the Savanna/RX-3 wagon was a smash hit! (Courtesy Mazda)

issue. It was easy to chart the relative success of the RX-3 Stateside, because of its unique Series I chassis prefix id. 10A-powered Series I RX-3s started with S102A for sedan and coupe, and S102W for wagons.

Early exclusive US use of the 12A motor in the RX-3 produced chassis prefixes of S124A for coupe/sedan and S124W for the wagon California knew and loved so well. Indeed, the popularity of the RX-3 Stateside was illustrated by the large percentage of 12A cars in the approximate 186,000 Savanna/RX-3 Series I total. Of this figure, around 60,000 and 55,000 were North American coupe/sedan and wagon respectively. Inside and out Mazda, the RX-3 choice was easy. The RX-3 could save a buyer up to $270 compared to an RX-2 in America, where the external size difference between the two was felt insignificant. They were both considered small cars.

Outside Mazda dealers, a 1.6-liter Mazda 808 priced out around $200 higher than the smaller Honda Civic, and 808-size-comparable Toyota Corolla. The pricier 808 befitted Mazda's US niche brand status, but most decided to pay even more for the rotary RX-3. The 808/Grand Familia range arrived in America in 1972, kicking out the piston Mazda 1200 in the process. The larger Grand Familia was more 'small car' for the US buyer than the tiny 1200, and coincidentally came in the same model year as the revised Ford Torino, with the like-styled and named '72 Gran Torino.

Ford's close connection with Mazda began at the end of the '70s. Therefore, chalk up the 808/RX-3 coupe's scaled-down Ford Gran Torino Sportsroof look to early '70s fastback fashion and great minds thinking alike. Highlighting Mazda's niche player forte, the RX-3 sedan was the least popular variant. The four-door RX-3 was quietly shown the door at the end of the '74 MY, while the popular wagon and coupe versions continued in North America.

Whatever the RX-3 was doing in America, it was doing on 12A smogged Wankel motorvation. The numbers weren't anything special at 90 net SAE horses and 96lb/ft, but the figures were honest, and the RX-3 seemed to do more than other cars of the day. The Mercedes 450SE and 450SL V8 automatics accelerated from 0-60mph in around the same 10-11 second range, but required 13-16mpg more overall compared to the RX-3's relatively frugal 18mpg. The *Road & Track*-tested figures received less attention than the EPA's gas mileage ratings that put the RX-2 and RX-3 last amongst small cars, but the Mazda wasn't really that kind of car.

In October 1973, *Road & Track* did a 12-small-wagon-comparo test, wherein the automatic RX-3 12A wagon was the fastest, but thirstiest, little wagon scrutinized. It cost the most at $3395, had a buck board jittery ride, and consumed petroleum distillate at around 18mpg. Mercedes V8 and domestic specialty coupe buyers would have really dug the RX-3 wagon; unfortunately, small imports were more in the realm of Datsun buyers and Consumer Union. Such parties were less likely to appreciate the RX-3's avoidance of being a dog-slow, small four-cylinder import. Then again, even Mazda's I4 small car was no slouch.

A 1975 808 coupe came with the ex-616 1.6-liter, making 64 SAE net horses at 5000rpm and 78lb/ft at 3000rpm. Teamed with a four-speed manual and 6.15 13in tires, *Road & Track* found the car capable of 0-60mph in 15.6 seconds, a skidpad figure of 0.683g, 80mph to zero braking in 320 feet and 21mpg overall. Also tested by the same magazine, in January 1975, was the 262 cube V8 automatic Chevy Monza 2+2: it turned in stats of 13.4 seconds, 0.675g, and an identical 320-foot braking performance and 17mpg, or thirstier than the quicker RX-3 automatic wagon.

Thus, if one was willing to work a stick shift, the 808 answered the call of the fuel crisis SOS by delivering more mpg than it lost in acceleration to the Monza. In an efficiency contest, the Mazda SOHC four-cylinder seemed to have a winning hand over the Monza's 4.4-liter OHV V8. The Chevy 262 motor was an economy fiend derived from the famous 350 small block. However, it seemed like a lot of cast iron to haul around, for such modest performance and economy.

Unbeknownst to most, GM wanted to put a rotary engine of its own in the new 1975 Monza. Known as the GMRCE (General Motors Rotary Combustion Engine), this Wankel was larger than any of Mazda's '70s rotaries, and promised much for high output sports performance. A former employee of the GM Delco Moraine factory said the facility was tooled-up and ready to make the rotors for the GMRCE, but management abruptly pulled the plug on the exercise. The internal word amongst GM people was that the GMRCE got canned because of limited rotor seal life. The engine lasted only 30,000 miles, at best, before the seals gave out.

GM had strict requirements on durability of engines, cooling systems, a/c performance etc, before something new got rolled out nationwide. The two-rotor GMRCE wasn't going to meet the different driving styles and climate variations of North America on time, and GM wasn't going to take NSU's 'work in progress' approach to Wankel development. It had enough product recalls with its conventional stuff. A pity, since GMRCEs running in the Delco Moraine plant engine test cells registered a little over 300 SAE net horses on the dyno. As soon as the GMRCE program ended, all plant tooling was scrapped.

It spoke to the good of Mazda R&D that its Wankel was a production reality, and could be bought nationwide. A couple of tech differences between the aforementioned Mazda 808 and RX-3: the 1975 piston 808 drank through a 2bbl Nikki carb, the RX-3 via a 4bbl carb (as per all rotary Mazda passenger cars since the Cosmo Sport 110S). To make up for rotary's weak low end torque, the RX-3 had shorter gear ratios than the 808's four-speed manual. The ratios for first to fourth were 3.68, 2.26, 1.40 and 1.00 compared to the 808's 3.40, 2.01, 1.37 and 1.00.

If the ratios told of the need to keep the 12A on the boil, its 50-state power/torque rating also showed Wankel's clear environmental conscience. At a time when many cars sold in America had a 49-state version, and Californian edition with less power due to tighter emissions, Mazda's rotaries dodged the slings and arrows of outrageous pollution laws, and treated all places the same. The 49-state Mazda 808 had an 8.6:1 compression ratio, and lower Californian bhp rating, whereas the

Note the faux V6 hood intake trumpets. Mazda, and other Japanese companies, were criticized for over-ornamentation in the '70s. The RX-3 12A wagon's only North American opposition was the AMC Hornet Sportabout V8. (Courtesy Mazda)

The 1972 model year Savanna Coupe GSII. In July 1973, UK's *CAR* magazine acidicly observed that the Savanna/RX-3 had a great engine in search of a proper chassis. Factory-backed racing Savannas used a Watts linkage for the live axle, and the Savanna had notched up 100 Japanese race wins by May 1976. (Courtesy Mazda)

Mazda 12A and 13B Wankels had compression ratios of 9.4- and 9.2-to-one respectively. The higher compression ratios showed the Mazda's imperviousness to smog tuning.

Reading between the spec lines, the 808 had an 11.7-gallon tank, whereas the RX-3 had a 15.6-gallon tank. The 12A's greater thirst meant one had serious reasons to fear gas lines, and envy thy neighbor's Mercedes 240D. However, the RX-3 was much sportier than a diesel Mercedes, Peugeot, Cadillac or any of the stone slow rides many endured to get through the fuel crisis. On the minus side, the RX-3's 6in ground clearance made Kojak's Buick Century look like a Can Am racer. On the plus side, the RX-3's recirculating ball manual steering had 3.5 turns lock to lock. This was decidedly quicker than the Chevy Cosworth Vega's yawn-worthy 4.4 turns.

The RX-3 matched the BMW 2002's 3.5 turns, and both cars showed why GM was so interested in its two-rotor GMRCE. The Cosworth Vega promised 170 horses as a prototype, a model announcement suggested 140bhp, but that ended up as 110bhp when the special Vega arrived. The car's 16-valve DOHC cylinder head came courtesy of English company, Cosworth, and proved that high output and emissions can be enemies. Although the Vega's 2-liter four-cylinder outrated the 90 horse 12A and BMW's 96bhp 2-liter, it didn't feel as strong as these latter two motors.

Mazda's secret was the 12A's good nitrogen oxide properties; the BMW used a tri-hemi combustion chamber to thoroughly tame pollutants. The Cosworth may have had electronic Bendix MPC fuel-injection, compared to the 12A's humble Nikki four-barrel and the 2002's even humbler 2bbl Solex, but it takes a special kind of tech to deal with smog. As with other 1974 model year rotary cars, the RX-3 went on to a single distributor, thermal reactor approach when the RX-3 Series II made its Japanese market debut in the fall of 1973.

Mazda translated the NSU Wankel rotary engine into a reliable success. (Courtesy Marc Cranswick)

As a world market model, the 1974 RX-3 shared the RX-2's 12A smog motor, rated at 130PS DIN in the home market. Thus, the US RX-3 was no longer an exclusive member of the S124A and S124W chassis sequence. Japanese manufacturers were taking the lead in introducing pollution controls the world increasingly needed. Mazda envisaged a rotary thermal reactor universe, and Honda chose its famous CVCC method. This 'stratified charge' avenue with three-valves per cylinder inline SOHC four pot, used a segmented combustion chamber. A small part of the chamber had a rich mixture, with most of the chamber working with a lean fuel mix.

The CVCC method worked with leaded gas, no cat converter or any hang on devices. A 1975 1.5-liter five-speed Civic CVCC achieved 0-60mph in 15 seconds and 36.5mpg on 91 octane gas with an 8.1:1 compression ratio. The CVCC method was tested on a full-size car Chevy 350ci V8, with the same great results. Both 12A and CVCC, especially the CVCC, had an absence of driveability quirks, and emissions tuning freedom that allowed horsepower to be maximized. In spite of the CVCC utopia, Toyota and Nissan were looking closely at rotary, to answer the performance/emissions conundrum.

Apart from the automaker-feared 1975 US federal emissions standards, Japan was cooking up some strict rules of its own. No strangers to dense urban environments and auto pollution, the Japanese government was influenced by the US Muskie Smog bill and California's golden state solution. As parliamentary debate raged on how strict the environmental pollutant standards were going to be, the Japanese government, with Kakuei Tanaka san as Prime Minister, offered tax incentives to motorists that chose new low pollution cars. The thermal reactor, single distributor 12A and 13B rotaries, and Honda CVCC cars, were in the class of civic mindedness.

Apart from the universal smog motor, a restyle was in order. The RX-3 Series IIs had revised front fascias which made the detailing around the headlamps and grille more distinct. The rear fascia, along with Mazda's other cars, adopted new Japanese safety lighting. The twin brake lights designed for greater visibility carry the informal nametag of 'Savanna taillights' amongst aficionados. Newly introduced exterior colors were Bottle Green and Alexandria Gold.

The RX-3s continued with 200kph speedos, whereas Grand Familias and 808s had 180kph units, but the ammeter battery gauge was upgraded from 30 to a 50amp/hour scale. Trim and seatbelt changes also accompanied Series II revisions, along with a new twin post radio antenna to improve in-car wireless reception; it had been a single post mast. As per Mazda's other thermal reactor AP (Anti Pollution) 1974 rotaries, the Savanna AP and RX-3 sported a dash exhaust overheat light. Thus, the owner was informed the moment fluffy bunnies were in danger from a malfunctioning thermal reactor system.

If the AP muffler heated up beyond a set limit, car service attention was necessary. US cars received the Series II changes, and also got federal impact bumpers. In 1973, federal law mandated 5mph front and 2½mph rear bumpers for most passenger cars. This pushed RX-3 wagon length to 163in, and, in 1974, US law required 5mph bumpers at both vehicle ends. Thus, 1974 RX-3 coupes were 168in long, with the wagon now 170in long. Coupe and wagon now weighed 2395lb and 2450lb respectively.

Heading trackside ...

The Series II changes for 1974 saw the end of the 10A's availability. By bidding farewell at the end of 1973, the 10A was only ever available in twin distributor form. The irony was that the 10A allowed the RX-3 to enter more categories of racing, and achieve more class wins. The RX-2 was only around with the 12A. This limited the RX-2's participation, but, in any case, Mazda chose to put the Savanna/RX-3 at the forefront of factory racing efforts upon the Grand Familia car's late 1971 entry. The Savanna's competition debut was successful.

On 10A power, the Savanna coupe won the 500-mile Fuji Tourist Trophy held in December 1971. The Savanna prevented the Nissan Skyline GT-R from notching up 50 consecutive race victories. In 1972, factory-racing Savannas moved on to 12A power and dominated qualifying of the TS-b category touring car race event held at the Japanese Grand Prix. Savannas came first, second and third. This prompted mass interest from privateers wanting to campaign their own racing Savannas.

In the tradition of race homologation, Mazda provided performance kits for sprint and endurance applications, over selected dealer outlet parts counters. Upgrade parts for one's Savanna/RX-3, and, as they say, racing improves the breed: win on Sunday, sell on Monday. Mazda were soon selling 5000 RX-3s in Japan alone each month, so the latter saying proved true. The Savanna was doing a lot of winning and selling. Domestically, the Savanna garnered five Japanese GP championships. It took the touring car title in 1972, 1973, 1975, 1976 and 1977.

Contributing to such aforementioned titles, the Savanna won the Japanese Grand Prix touring car event in 1972, 1973, 1975, 1976 and 1978. A dominant vehicle in Japan's super touring class, the Savanna achieved its 100th domestic victory, at the JAF Grand Prix TS/GTS category race, held in May 1976. To mark the milestone, Mazda released a limited run of commemorative road cars. The car was the 1976 Savanna AP-GT; even road-going racers carried the 'Anti Pollution' tag in the '70s.

It seemed only right that the Savanna should do well on the racetracks of desmogged America too. The RX-3 came to the forefront in sedan road circuit racing, in the US, during the late '70s to early '80s era, after the early to

The RE12 grille badge said it all. The 1972 Savanna GT Coupe homologated the bigger 12A Wankel, for use in factory Savanna racers. As a road car, it also brought sportier suspension and a five-speed manual gearbox. (Courtesy Mazda)

A fast mover on the racetrack and in the sales charts, the RX-3 coupe was the most popular version in the RX-3 family. A 1972 advert is shown. (Courtesy Mazda)

IN MOTION

Mazda RX-3 Rotary Power

Some people will call it the Silent Express.
But we call it Mazda RX-3. The car with Rotary Power.

Why the Silent Express?

Because the new Mazda RX-3 can go very quickly...very quietly. And so smoothly you'd swear there's a six- or eight-cylinder engine up front. But you'd be wrong.

There's a Mazda rotary engine. With two rotors that spin out turbine-smooth power. One way only. Without needing the pistons, rods, valves and things that almost every other car needs.

In fact, only a few parts move. So in addition to saving on space and weight, the simple Mazda rotary engine could also save you a lot on repair bills.

But it's not enough just to build a better engine. We had to sit down and build a better car around it. A car that was safe at sustained high speeds. A car that could outperform most of the others in its size and price bracket. A tough, well-balanced car.

Well, we did just that. Mazda RX-3 is wider and longer than earlier 982 cc Mazda rotaries.

You get more space inside. Reclining bucket seats. Non-reflective instruments (which include a tachometer). And a dual-circuit braking system with power-assisted front disc brakes for consistent stopping safety.

In short, the Silent Express is all car. It's the new rotary-powered Mazda RX-3. Climb aboard at your nearest Mazda dealer.

mid-'70s dominance of the AMC Gremlin and BMW 2002.

By this hour, race authorities were beginning to realise it was only fair to allow some porting, the Wankel equivalent of engine tuning. With rulebook enlightenment came victories, and lots of them. Stuart Fisher won the SCCA B-Sedan National Championship, in 1977. One-time Mazda factory driver and race constructor, Jim Downing was also closely associated with the RX-3 12A coupe.

Whether SCCA or IMSA categoried, it was nice to see racecraft not that far removed from the showroom floor. Many sporting brands gained their reputations from such 1960s and 1970s racing adventures. In the opening race of the 1979 IMSA Champion Sparkplug Challenge (Racing Stocks–RS) series, an RX-3 almost won. This February 3 Champion Sparkplug 100 race, held at Daytona, involved a three-way tussle between Amos Johnson's AMC Spirit, James Reeve's venturi-restricted Buick Skyhawk and Jim Downing's RX-3. All were small rear-drive cars.

It was the AMC 3.8-liter I6 against the 3.8-liter Buick V6, and 2.3-liter equivalent Mazda 12A. The three cars broke racing rules seven miles from the finish, and went off the track entering turn one. The RX-3 was forced to retire, the Skyhawk limped back to pitlane with a damaged tire, leaving Johnson to complete the race and win. Jim Downing went on to drive for Team Highball boss, Amos Johnson, in the class winning team of two AMC Spirit AMXs, that contested the October 1979 FIA Group 1 24-Hour Nürburgring touring car race.

If the RX-3 didn't win at Daytona then, it did dominate the IMSA RS series between 1979 and 1983. Jim Downing was 1981 IMSA RS series champion, driving a 1978 RX-3 SP, providing Mazda with its fourth Manufacturer's Championship in said series. The RX-3 got the Manufacturer's Cup for Mazda in 1979, 1980, 1981 and 1983. Within that IMSA RS success lay a 1982 Driver's Championship as well. The rotary underlined its competitive worth with SCCA trophies too. The RX-3 took out the SS/B-Sedan National title, in 1980 and 1981. The coupe also gleaned the 1982 GT-2 National Championship, and Savannas/RX-3s continued tin top success in smaller Japanese and US events for decades to come.

In America, Tom Ellam's 1972 RX-3 won many championships with SCCA Solo II and Pro Solo events into the 2000s. Amongst other wins, Tom Ellam won the 2006 SCCA Solo E-Modified National Championship. The car then went on loan to Jennifer Lee, helping Lee to win the E-Mod Ladies National Championship. In SCCA Super Production Car, Irish driver John Cummins has performed strongly in modern times driving an RX-3.

As an example of flying high, the US-designed Aero Design DG-1 racing plane utilized two tuned 12A motors taken from RX-3s. Driving propellars, one Wankel was located at the front, with the other at the rear. Each 12A was tuned to 330bhp. Racing, on the track, and Mazda's ongoing Wankel R&D, worked hand-in-hand to improve the reliability and efficiency of the rotaries buyers could get from the showrooms.

Mazda development was also directed at producing reliable Wankels more easily. Early 10As had aluminum rotor housings with an electroplated chrome surface. To facilitate getting the chrome onto the aluminum surface, Mazda introduced TCP. TCP or Transplant Coating Process, involved spraying the rotor housing with a thin layer of steel, prior to chrome plating. In mid-1973, TCP was replaced by SIP, or Sheet-metal Insert Process. SIP put a chrome-plated steel insert within the rotor housing. Early on, carbon/aluminum apex seals were used in the TCP era. SIP permitted thinner cast iron apex seals to be used, along with flexible corner seals, to reduce gasoline blow by. The Wankel design had been known for letting unburnt fuel get past the combustion chamber, and into the exhaust system. Thus, the flexible corner seals would improve gas mileage and reduce chances of backfiring.

The search for more mpg after the fuel crisis prompted Mazda to introduce the

The Grand Familia was the piston-engined version of the Savanna/RX-3, known as the 808 or 818 in export markets. This is a 1974 model year Grand Familia 1300 GL four-door sedan. (Courtesy Mazda)

The RX-3 wagon was more popular than the RX-3 sedan, though the RX-3 wagon had a harsh ride reputation. By 1974, the 5mph-bumpered wagon, pictured, was 170in long and weighed 2450lb. (Courtesy Max Tanner)

MDR (Medium Deep Recess) combustion chamber design. Belt-driven engine accessories and ancillaries were also modified to curb mechanical losses. Not content with this improvement, Mazda replaced MDR with the LDR (Long Deep Recess) combustion chamber design, in 1975. Ignition, porting and carb alterations created an overall gas mileage result, greater than the sum of the Wankel's few parts.

In going global with the thermal reactor approach for 1974, Mazda applied pre-heated injection air, to reduce the need for the very rich fuel mixture found with the thermal reactor emission's route. The rich mix had been an essential ingredient to achieve the thorough pollutant burn in the reactor. This was especially so for BMW in California, where reduced ignition advance, to meet emissions, caused very poor gas mileage and throttle response, compared to its 49-state thermal reactor cars.

Mazda applied pre-heated air injection to US federal and AP cars alike. Other changes one would find on the 1974 single-distributored RX-3 included a starter motor moved from the top of the engine to the left hand rear side. A change from dual- to single-row side seals accompanied Mazda's revised apex seal design. Such underhood alterations, combined with taller gearing, helped the 1976 RX-3 earn an EPA highway rating of 30mpg. An impressive improvement, and timely, given past Mazda America and EPA conflict.

Necessity is the mother of invention, and in Mazda's case necessity was called the fuel crisis. The Savanna/RX-3 family zoom-zoomed to 218,842 sales in its first 2½ years, with an all-out total of 286,685 by 1978. Thus, it's obvious the steeply rising price of a barrel of oil cramped the RX-3's style. By the end of 1975 model year, the Savanna/RX-3 was essentially a special order model made in small batches, and was starting to vanish from export markets. The RX-3 sedan already left America at the end of 1974, and the US RX-3 wagon departed at the end of 1976 model year. Plus, it seemed that the UK RX-3 was no more, in any bodystyle, by the close of 1975 calendar year.

So it was that the Savanna/RX-3 Series III got a selective world release, that included America and Australia as well as the Japanese domestic market. The nosecone now sported a lower spoiler lip, and former exterior 'rotor' badging was simplified to Mazda 'M' badges, as differences between the RX-3 and 808 diminished.

Differences between rotary and non-rotary Grand Familias will help one spot clone cars – Grand Familias/808s pretending to be Savannas/RX-3s. Genuine rotary cars with S102A and S102W chassis prefixes for 10A-powered sedan/coupe and wagon respectively. The prefix changes to S124A and S124W for 12A-powered editions. However, 1.3-liter and 1.6-liter 808s sport chassis number starts of STC and SN3A respectively. The 1.3-liter 808 has a very small rear differential, although the 1.6-liter 808s have normal RX-3-sized differentials. Cosmetically, the RX-3 Series I has a rear licence plate frame, whereas the 808 doesn't.

All RX-3s have rear bumpers with square reflectors, and RX-3 Series IIs have a front bumper with a cutout for oil cooler airflow. The piston 808s lack either front and rear bumper features. Mazda acknowledged the greater thirst of the Savanna by giving it a 60-liter gas tank, stamped with the letter 'L.' 808s came with an 'S'-stamped 45-liter tank. There were also electronic and hardware additions to Savanna/RX-3 Series II cars, due to their thermal reactor 'AP' status.

AP cars possessed emission control relays in their computer fusebox, and the associated wiring harness was generally thicker than the 808 equivalent. The harness on AP cars had choke control and special ignition relay, or an unused plug for the purpose. The 12A REAPS rear muffler had an associated exhaust overheat

A 1975 Mazda 808 four-door sedan. The Grand Familia was called the 808 in Australia. This car has had its original inline four cylinder engine replaced with an RX-4-sourced 13B rotary. (Courtesy Justin Kowal)

thermo sensor located in the right corner of the trunk, near the shock tower. A genuine Savanna/RX-3 AP will have thermo sensor mounting holes, with an associated wiring loom plug.

As with RX-2/RX-4 AP cars, the thermo sensor would shortcircuit if the REAPS muffler got too hot, and this would be relayed to a dash warning light via the wiring loom. The REAPS rear muffler had protective heat shields, and there should be mounting brackets for them. However, there were many more Grand Familias/808s made than Savanna/RX-3s – 625,439 to be precise – so the clone temptation is great.

In the UK market, the 808 was called 818. This happened, in places where Peugeot had the naming rights, to triple-digit figures with a center zero. The UK Mazda 818 was sold only with the Japanese starter 1272cc TC inline four-cylinder. Like this market's RX-3 choice, the usual sedan, coupe and wagon bodystyles were around, as the 818 sold as a mildly premium alternative to the also rear-drive Toyota Corolla and Datsun 120Y (Sunny). America got the 1.3-liter 808 later on. North America started with the 616 1586cc NA I4, before the Japanese Grand Familia.

Ebenezer's 808

The 808 came to America in 1972, displacing the 1200 as the 'butter and egg' economy small car choice. Never a big seller in the US Mazda fleet, it made up under 10% of sales. Why have the 1.6-liter motor when gas was cheap, and the RX-3 was so exciting? However, when gas got pricey after the 1973/74 gas crunch, Mazda America started pushing that piston 808, and came up with the Mizer. In the '70s, it seemed like an import would never strike it big Stateside, until it got a real nameplate instead of a number, and this one spelt economy.

In 1976, the Porsche 912 returned with a VW motor; Chevrolet sold its Chevette minus a back seat as the 'Scooter;' and the Mizer was an 808 with the TC 1.3-liter I4 instead of the usual 1.6-liter. One would certainly be a mizer if the thought of a 1600cc four was avarice. Others also had their fuel crisis specials; in the Mizer's case, the vital stats were a two-barrel

There was a four-door 808-based RX-3, but such cars got only the 10A and 12A Wankels. This originally-piston 808 now uses a J port RX-4 13B, with the tried and tested Weber 48mm IDA carb. (Courtesy Justin Kowal)

carb feeding a 1272cc SOHC I4 that made 69bhp and 67lb/ft. It came with great EPA numbers, and made stock-emissionized US VW Bugs seem stone slow.

The Stepford RX-3

Mazda America probably wished it had kept the 616, because, the world over, Mazda's piston engine wallflowers were quickly finding dance partners. With sales of the Savanna/RX-3 slower than molasses in winter, and 808s selling in just tens of thousands, Mazda seemed to have created an inhouse rotary clone: the Savanna/ RX-3 Series III appears to have used the humble Grand Familia/808 as its production basis. In terms of chassis numbers, in Japan, the so-called small volume V-100 cars were right-hand drive Savannas using a 460000 number range chassis sequence, in keeping with the Grand Familias of the day. It is generally understood that later RX-3s continued with the worldwide S124A prefix until the 85,000th car, to VIN S124A-185000. US RX-3s continued in the VIN S124A prefix pattern, but the nature of the North American Series III cars shows their 808 links.

The interior and dashboard were similar to 808 style, foregoing previous rotary distinctions. Exterior rotary badging was simplified to a 'Rotary Engine' trunklid badge and RX-3 rear fender script. RX-3s had previously come with chrome window dripRails and rocker panel trim, but both were absent from Series III cars and contemporary 808s.

This 1975 808 was found with virtually no rust, and still has an almost all original body and interior. RX-3 taillights and some Autometer gauges have been added. Either 15in or 17in alloys are used, with a lowering job that makes this 808 sit 4in lower at the rear than stock. (Courtesy Justin Kowal)

For 1976, the US RX-3 eschewed its long-standing 4bbl Nikki carb, in favor of a two-barrel edition to save gas. However, Mazda's engineers retuned the 12A to find more power using said two-barrel. The figures were formerly 90bhp and 96lb/ft; they were now 95bhp and 102lb/ft respectively, but one couldn't get this version in California. The 95-horse 12A, with its creative porting, was a 49-state beastie. However, it seemed less was indeed more, and, for Golden State rotary fans, one could look good with a special new nationally available model called RX-3 SP.

This US RX-3 SP was a grand finale for the RX-3 in this locality, available in 1977 and 1978 model years. With the once-loved US RX-3 wagon gone, and rumors of a pending rotary sports car from Hiroshima gaining momentum, something was needed in the interim. The RX-3 SP arrived in the 'paint & tape' depressed disco era of sporty cars. Various domestic and imported models were turning specially liveried 'limited edition' models into an art form. Performance patrons had to have something to match their medallions, but Mazda said from the get go that the RX-3 had the substance to back up the style.

Pictured blazing through a roadbend at breakneck speed, the ad proudly stated "The New Mazda RX-3 SP. (Rest assured, SP does not stand for slowpoke)." So Mazda claimed the SP was closer to Speedy Gonzales than Slow Poke Rodriguez, but what did one get for $3945? 49-state cars had the revised moxified 12A, and all RX-3 SPs came with a five-speed overdrive manual gearbox, semi-monocoque body, and the pedigree of 100-plus international competition race wins.

As soon as the Savanna got to 100 wins in Japan, the 100-win tally was much used for global PR. The semi-monocoque term was more curious: GM had received praise for making the partial unibody on its Camaro/Firebird work, so here was a positive concept that advertising wished to link to the RX-3. The RX-3 SP was also associated with an optional appearance package that consisted of a deep Mr Plough front spoiler, fashionable blackout treatments for grille, headlamp and sidemarker surrounds, plus a rear spoiler.

The SP appearance package also announced its presence with 'RX-3 SP' profile, hood and spoiler decals, but no fire-breathing phoenix or berserk cobras. From the late '60s to the early

Performance mods include a twin exhaust system, which extends as far as the differential, where it joins a single 2½in muffler. The trend with rotary swaps into piston Mazdas is to leave the 808 exterior stock. The desire to create clones has diminished. (Courtesy Justin Kowal)

'80s, a performance car was measured by its decals, and the RX-3 SP was no shrinking violet. With the appearance package – considered essential by general sporty car buyers of the day – the price boosted to a stagflated, Carterfied total of $4290. However, as the final example of the RX-3 already absent from many export markets, it's rare – and priceless – to triangle rotor devotees.

Much vaunted hero models weren't always bestsellers, and, in the recession-hit late '70s, such sporty Saturday Night specials could hang around dealer lots for an eternity. Not many RX-3 SPs were sold. The 1976 calendar year RX-3/Savanna world total was just 9825. 1977 MY RX-3 SPs numbered around 3000 cars, and had build dates late in 1976. 1978 US RX-3 SPs numbered around 800, and were made in the fall of 1977. As for the SP stripe and trim kit, it was Californian-made and port-fitted.

In the 1960s and 1970s, California was the center for car customization and pinstriping. It takes a professional to get those decals and stripes on straight and true. The RX-3 Series IIIs are seen as 808s with rotary, trim changes and driveline upgrades – perhaps a technical inhouse clone, but it looked and sounded just like those SCCA winners.

A 1976 Grand Familia 1600 AP coupe. It's believed that by the end of the Savanna/RX-3's life, Grand Familia/808 base cars were used to create the rotary coupes. (Courtesy Mazda)

The RX-3 SP of 1977/78 was the final RX-3 iteration available in America. The SP appearance kit was port-fitted and Californian-made. (Courtesy Mazda)

The New Mazda RX-3SP.

(Rest assured, SP does not stand for slowpoke.)

Perish the thought. How could it?

The remarkable, improved rotary engine is beneath the hood.

RX-3SP also has things like a slick 5-speed stick shift, semi-monocoque construction, and the breeding of over one hundred racing victories in international competition.

What's more, the world's most remarkable engine is now backed by the world's most remarkable engine warranty.

Mazda warrants that the basic engine block and its internal parts will be free of defects with normal use and prescribed maintenance for five years or 75,000 miles, whichever comes first, or Mazda will fix it free. This transferable, limited warranty is free on all new rotary-engine Mazdas sold and serviced in the United States and Canada.

How much, you might ask, will all this set you back? A very reasonable $4290.* Or, for a mere $3945.* you can have the good stuff minus the special appearance package shown.

Whichever RX-3SP you drive home, it'll make a believer out of you.

Fast.

mazda

Downunder with the RX-3

Appreciative of a rorty ride, and not so concerned about gas mileage, Australian buyers added the RX-3 to their enthusiast list from March 1972. Similarity to the Japanese Savanna was great, the Series I cars were right-hand drive and 10A-powered, but there would be no wagon variant for Australia or New Zealand. Trim levels were like those in other export markets, a Deluxe sedan and Super Deluxe RX-3 coupe – as per the UK, but that market received the wagon. Wagons were not known for being sporty in Australia, so that niche was avoided.

The Australian RX-3 Series I sedan had the 982cc 10A's 100bhp, 100lb/ft and a $3299 (Australian dollar) list price for the four-speed, with the JATCO three-speed auto a $341 option. The RX-3 coupe four-speed rallied in at $3479, but came with all the fruit (minna furutsu-o). This included optional body stripe, clock, rear defogger, center console with high armrest and collapsible steering column. With the extra equipment, the Series I coupe weighed 20kg more than the 865kg sedan. Tested in Australia, the four-speed coupe did the ¼ mile in 17.6 seconds at 76mph – slower than the 12A RX-2, but that didn't stop the RX-3 coupe at Bathurst.

At Bathurst in the RX3

For local touring car racing, eyes always turned to the pinnacle Bathurst endurance race held at Mount Panorama. Called the Hardie Ferodo 1000 during this '70s era, it was here that the RX-3 turned the tables on the RX-2. In fact, worldwide, the RX-3 coupe was to assume the mantle as Mazda's top touring car competitor. In its debut 1973 Bathurst outing, the RX-3 10A came second in Class B for 1.3- to 2-liter cars, and ninth overall; a better overall result than the RX-2 12A that won Class C. During this era, Australia's CAMS body put the kybosh on porting, but the RX-3 coupe battled on to surprise V8 opponents.

In 1974, the RX-2 coupe was shown the door, as marketing concentrated on the RX-3 coupe as the sporty little number; that year it visited Bathurst with 10A and 12A power. Bernie Haehnle's and Geoff Brabham's RX-3 coupe set the Class C (2- to 3-liter) pole position, with a two-minute 51.7-second lap. Second qualifying Class C time was by the RX-3 of Tony Farrell and Brian Reed in two minutes 51.9 seconds.

The very last RX-3 variant available as a new car anywhere was the RX-3 SP. Only around 800 of these US market cars were made. This particular RX-3 SP sports the optional appearance pack. (Courtesy Juan Carlos Lopez)

It was a rain-affected race, and, when all was done and dusted, John Goss and Kevin Bartlett conquered the mountain in their Mad Max Road Warrior-type Ford Falcon V8 coupe. Brian Reed's and Tony Farrell's RX-3 coupe came sixth outright and won Class C.

Normally, all US RX-3s are 12A-powered. However, this 1978 RX-3 SP has been modified with a bridge ported 13B! A Holley 650cfm dual pumper, headers and full 3in exhaust system help festivities. (Courtesy Juan Carlos Lopez)

The similarity between the interior and dashboard of the RX-3 SP and contemporary 808 has contributed to the theory that the Series III RX-3s were 808-based. (Courtesy Juan Carlos Lopez)

The Reed/Farrell RX-3 coupe finished 11 laps behind the winning Falcon V8. If CAMS had allowed porting (and it's an unusual race car that doesn't have the equivalent of a hot cam and boring/stroking), then the gap would have been smaller. A 10A-powered RX-3 managed tenth overall and second in Class B at 1974's Bathurst.[37] A Class C victory was achieved by the RX-3 coupe in 1975 too. Here, Don Holland's RX-3 coupe got the model's best result at Mount Panorama, fifth overall. 1976 saw the RX-3 come second in Class C.

The RX-3 was a dominant performer in US IMSA and SCCA racing during the late 1970s and early 1980s. Jim Downing successfully campaigned a 1978 RX-3 SP. (Courtesy Juan Carlos Lopez)

In 1977, the RX-3 came seventh overall at Bathurst, and there was another Class C win in 1979. 1979 was the year CAMS finally allowed bridge porting, but the RX-3's sporting credentials were well established by then. The RX-3 AP reached Australia in March 1974, and this Series II thermal reactor car came with the bigger 130bhp 12A, 117lb/ft of torque, and a pure 200kph speedo. 1974 also saw Australian market cars switched from mph to metric, with associated road sign changes. However, the kph markers weren't passing as quickly as in the smog-gear-free 10A days.

The 12A-powered RX-3 AP coupe was slower at 17.8 seconds, in the ¼ mile, than previous 10A machines. The Series II Australian cars weighed 44kg more. It was felt that the new REAPS emissions control adversely affected torque delivery. Even so, the new cars did possess a higher top speed. Performance aside, 1972-75 represented peak popularity for the rotary concept in Australia. Specifically, Mazda Motors Pty Ltd (Australia) sold 2866 rotary cars between the fiscal period of May 1973 to April 1974, representing 40% of the company's Australian Mazda sales.

Mazda Motors Pty Ltd (Australia) covered Victoria, Tasmania and southern NSW. The rest of the country was catered for by independent distributors, selling even more Mazda Whir Warriors. The Series II AP cars, emissions clean for 1975 America and Japan, were ahead of their time by meeting Australia's 1986 standard, which normally meant a catalytic converter and unleaded gas. However, such environmental-mindedness soon played second fiddle to the need for good fuel economy.

Even in Australia, buyers wanted more mpg in the wake of the fuel crisis, slowing demand for rotary Mazdas. Thus, the RX-3 was officially out of the Australian Mazda lineup as of March 1976, by which time the coupe cost $4525; a relatively expensive gas guzzler at a time when the future of Australia's own V8s was in doubt. It became hard to sell V8 gruntmobiles. RX-3s lingered on dealer's lots long after March 1976, but people were still buying cars. Mazda was still selling cars too, but they were increasingly piston-powered, and one model in particular soon stole the show: the GLC.

Familia AP/323: such a Great Little Car

In a 1979 episode of the US family TV drama *Eight Is Enough*, family patriarch, Tom Bradford, was convinced by his brood that it was about time they dumped the US full-size family wagon, in favor of something more fuel efficient. The new car chosen was a Mazda 626. Unfortunately, by the time Mr Bradford got home, all the kids had checked out the 626, and it didn't feel brand new any more. Desiring that new car experience, he went back to the dealer and returned with another new car, a GLC wagon.

The GLC was the name for the 1977 Familia AP in America. It stood for Great Little Car – an apt title, and the public the world over agreed. The new small family car was called 323 in most countries outside Japan. Called the fourth generation Familia by Mazda Japan, recall that the 1974-76 FA3 was piston only; the new Familia AP made its Japanese debut in January 1977 and replaced the 1200/1300 and 808 ranges. It was an engineering amalgam of the 1300 and 808, with a fresh, trendy, hatchback body thrown in.

Thus, one had a rear-wheel drive, hatchback VW Golf-size class small family car, with the wide body nature the 808 (Grand Familia) enjoyed over the Familia (1300). The Familia AP had the hatchback advantage over many cars in this class. The Toyota Corolla 30 and Datsun 120Y/B210 were both rear-drive, but lacked hatchback convenience on sedan variants. The Austin Allegro was front-drive, but only had a conventional trunk on the sedan. As with the Corolla and 120Y, the Allegro had to be specified as a wagon to get extra cargo space.

The very popular European Ford Escort of pre-1981 days, also gave the usual sedan choice and was also rear-drive. Many people wanted more space than a conventional trunk, but didn't wish to own a frumpy wagon, and some wagons of the time were especially unlovely looking. The VW Golf was hatch only, no wagon, but some were weary of front-wheel drive. Those in Britain and its export markets had unpleasant recollections of the constant velocity joints of BMC/BL front-drivers.

America was one of the few places outside Japan to receive the Series III RX-3 introduced for 1976 model year. Only RX-3 Coupes were US-available in 1977 and 1978. (Courtesy Juan Carlos Lopez)

This all explained the worldwide popularity of the Mazda GLC/323. Mazda teamed the convenience of hatch, with the security of rear-drive, and even offered a wagon version. US buyers wishing to avoid Ford Pinto's gas tank and VW Rabbit's high price and poor early quality, now had a great little car from Hiroshima. During the 1977 model year, there was some product overlap in America, as the Mizer 808 gave way to the GLC 323. In America, TV adverts had the words 'Great Little Car' set to the tune *Spanish Flea*.

It seems very likely the neat bit of product placement on TV's *Eight Is Enough* had something to do with Ford acquiring a stake in Mazda during 1979. Tom Bradford may no longer have been a country squire, but at least his clan could remain in Henry's family.

The GLC also seemed to owe its popularity to being round, rather than square. The VW Golf favored the cheese wedge school of styling, that made GM's Bill Mitchell quip that the Rabbit looked like a bullfrog that swallowed a square. Eschewing the popular '70s wedge, a red GLC resembled a tomato. The organic, rear-drive Familia/GLC/323 lived on into 1980, registering 904,573 sales. Very successful, and yet the next Familia/GLC/323 would shadow the original Golf very closely.

This 1981 model year car was a front-driver, with aforementioned cheese wedge looks. The new Familia was even more successful than its predecessor, but being a front-driver, with no chassis relation to the RX-3, implied no rotary option once again. However, as per Toyota and

Called the fourth generation Familia AP by Mazda Japan, the GLC (Great Little Car) in America, and 323 just about everywhere else, this new Familia was an engineering amalgam of the 1967-77 Familia (1200/1300) and 1971-78 Grand Familia (808). Rear-drive with a trendy hatchback body, but no rotary. (Courtesy Mazda)

Nissan in the transition to front-drive, Mazda decided to retain the old rear-drive 1977-80 Familia AP for wagon and commercial van variants.

The revised Familia wagons and vans sported new front and rear fascias, to blend in with the new front-drive hatch. However, under that '80s sheetmetal lay the old rear-drive chassis that made these wagons and vans cousins of the by-now long-defunct RX-3. These descendants of the rear-drive Familia/Grand Familia line lived on through the 1981-86 timeframe. Mazda didn't do front-drive wagons/vans in the Familia BD era. This was fortunate for tinkerers, because the last of the rear-drivers have provided project cars to receive 12A and 13B rotary engine swaps. Rear-drive also accommodates big horsepower increases more easily, so such rotary holdalls could contain a 20B!

The Savanna/RX-3 family has proved a long-time favorite with the streetcar crowd. The right size, and width to build up something special. Thus, for many years, a hot peripheral port 13B and shortened Ford 9in differential was, and is, the streetcar combo of choice. A coincidence, given Ford's association with Mazda. The Ford 9in has been the default streetcar choice for handling lots of power. When tuned, the Mazda rotary can certainly make the numbers; hence, a bullet-proof diff is necessary. Whether in sedan, coupe or wagon forms, the Savanna remains Mazda's archetypal street performance car.[38]

Ambitious Mazda was never one to rest on its laurels. In the mid '60s, the average Japanese consumer was just moving from Kei class to normal small Corolla family cars, and yet Mazda and others were already thinking bigger. In August 1966, Mazda launched its 1500 executive sedan, a large live-axled rear-driver featuring the new UB 1490cc single overhead cam inline four, and fancy styling.

Still in that era when Italian style influenced Japanese cars, the 1500 had a tall greenhouse, slim-pillared appearance. There was also the design contract Mazda had with Bertone, which explained the tapered front and rear sections, together with four circular-headlamp nose. Mazda PR described the Italian styling as "superlative in every respect." With hood bulge, the general shape resembled a 1973 BMW 525, and Mazda never tired of dropping the Bertone name into 1500 conversations. When you pay for the bottle, you want folks to read the label.

The range expanded with a wagon variant, and up-engined 1796cc SOHC VB I4 in 1968, boasting 101 gross horses. For the Japanese home market, where the sedan and wagon were called Luce, there was even a sports Luce SS edition, replete with the 1.8-liter VB motor. This version wasn't exported to places like the Australian, UK or US markets. Here, the 1500/1800 machines were regarded as well-equipped and made in the Japanese tradition, but not terribly exciting. No six-cylinder, and by the time production ended in 1972, 121,804 1500s and 39,041 1800s had issued forth from Hiroshima. By Japanese production standards, it was a modest success.

CAR magazine covered the 1966 Tokyo Auto Salon. It mentioned that the Mazda stand featured the rotary Cosmo Sport sports car, and "the beautiful and successful" Luce 1500. It noted Luce wagon and dual carb variants on show, and wondered why no UK company had stepped up to import the exciting Japanese marque? Mazda would reach the British Isles in 1968. A 1969 Luce 1500 is shown. (Courtesy Mazda)

The sporty Luce SS, pictured in January 1968. This was the dual carb 1.8-liter variant of the original 1966-72 Luce. It was a Japanese-only market variant, as most high performance versions of Japanese cars usually are. (Courtesy Mazda)

The other 1st gen Luce – Luce Rotary coupe

A nice looking sedan and wagon, but only average driving dynamics for non SS versions, and no rotary powerplant. Not quite; there was a version of the first gen Luce, that looked like the Luce, but had completely different engineering. It was a pillarless two-door, coupe hardtop, first seen alongside the RX-85 at the 1967 Tokyo Auto Salon. The Luce Rotary coupe was called RX-87, and went on sale in Japan in October 1969. Although the car's formal name was Luce Rotary coupe, it has also been known as the R130. In addition, prototypes and production cars carried 'RX-87' badges on the rear fenders, just behind the doors.

The Luce Rotary Coupe of 1969 made its debut, alongside the RX-85 (R100) at the 1967 Tokyo Auto Salon. It was Mazda's first front-driver. (Courtesy Mazda)

The Luce Rotary Coupe was Toyo Kogyo's automotive flagship between 1969 and 1972. In size, luxury and Super Deluxe ¥1.75 million price, it was the domestic market only Big Daddy of the Mazda range. It would take the arrival of the 1981 MY Familia hatch, before Mazda had another front-driver. (Courtesy Mazda)

The Luce Rotary coupe was the biggest and heaviest car Mazda had put in production. It measured 180.5in long, on a 101.6in wheelbase, with 54.5in height and weighed 1285kg in Super Deluxe trim. A very large car by Japanese standards, but it was only made in RHD form, and not officially exported. However, some gray market imports turned up in the RHD markets of Australia and South Africa. Being much larger than the normal Luce, and thirsty on gas, it was better suited to these countries than Japan. The reason for the thirst was the rotary engine, from which the coupe took its name.

Power was provided by a new and unique 13A Wankel. Larger in displacement than the 10A, but tuned for torque rather than horsepower. Thus, it came with less power than the Cosmo Sport's 130PS, the 13A made 126PS at 6000rpm and 127lb/ft at a Wankel low 3500rpm. Mazda claimed the Luce Rotary coupe could do 190kph, but the two-door's most exceptional quality was its drivetrain layout. The Luce Rotary coupe was Mazda's first front-wheel drive car. The 13A was placed forward of the front axle line, and a four-speed transaxle was employed.

Mid-'60s thinking was that front-drive gave better straight line directional stability, roadholding and better traction by having the engine over the driven wheels. There was also the internal space packaging benefit of driveshaft tunnel elimination. Such theory was employed to the front-drive limit with the 1966 7-liter Oldsmobile Toronado V8 personal car. However, in layout the Luce Rotary coupe had more in common with the NSU Ro80 and Audi 100. Both also placed their engines far forward, in a North-South layout, for handling directional stability. However, the light, small rotary engines promised that the Ro80 and Luce Rotary coupe wouldn't have the Audi's understeer.

The Luce Rotary coupe had double wishbone front suspension, with front disk brakes and standard vacuum servo power assistance. The

Luce Rotary coupe then diverged from the Cosmo Sport of the day, by having a more humble beam axle on coils, located by trailing arms. The aim was a luxury cruiser, and to that end there was a plush interior and much sound insulation. In Deluxe form, the price of admission was ¥1.45 million (pronounced 'en' in Japanese), rising to ¥1.75 million for the Super Deluxe version. All in all a desirable coupe, but size and niche nature equaled just 976 sold by the time production stopped in 1971. Mazda turned to the conventional for rotary in a big car.

The second coming of Luce – 1972

With the non rotary first gen Luce sedan/wagon, and Luce Rotary coupe done and dusted, Mazda launched a new generation Luce in Japan, during October 1972. The second Luce was available in four-door sedan, pillarless coupe and wagon versions. All variants were rear-wheel drive, and both piston and rotary Mazda engines were available in all three bodystyles. Planning for a range with more engine options than 1500/1800, export piston variants adopted the 929 nameplate for the first time. Rotary-engined Luce cars were called RX-4 in overseas markets. The RX-4 was the biggest, and, by 1974 fastest, worldwide exported rotary Mazda.

The first generation Luce Italian style was dumped, in favor of trendy American look fashion done inhouse at Mazda. Indeed, one might have expected Steve McQueen to have exited from a parked RX-4 coupe. Dimensions for the range included a 167in length for the sedan and 170in length for the coupe. Width was 65.6in and the cars were built on a 98.8in wheelbase. Base range weight was 1045kg for the sedan with 5kg more for the coupe, looking at 12A-powered Japanese spec cars.

Compared to the 1500/1800s, the new sedan was 5in shorter, but had a longer wheelbase and wider track. For an RX-4 coupe with wide tires, front and rear track was a useful 54in. In keeping with 808/RX-3 practice, suspension was by front MacPherson struts and independent coils, with a live-axled, leaf-sprung rear. The first generation Hotchkiss

Following a North-South layout, with the engine ahead of the front axle, the Luce Rotary Coupe had much in common with the contemporary NSU Ro80 and Audi 100. However, unlike the German cars, the Mazda was pillarless. (Courtesy Mazda)

The second generation Luce was introduced in October 1972. The 12A rotary version was available as sedan, wagon and the coupe edition shown. Internationally, the rotary Luce was called RX-4. (Courtesy Mazda)

drive rear end was retained. Trim levels for the 1973 model year in Japan involved Mazda's usual Special, GR and GRII steps for sedan and wagon. The two-door hardtop went through SX, GS, GSII and finished with luxurious 'Grande' trim.

The Grande spec was equivalent to the Brougham super lux found on US personal cars. Also along US lines was the Luce Grand Turismo wagon with faux exterior wood paneling, added during the 1973 model year. Powering the second Luce was a range of familiar engines. One started with the trusty 1796cc SOHC inline four, the Luce's former 1.5-liter was now a Grand Familia star. Then there were two versions of the Mazda 12A spinning out 120PS and 130PS. These motors could be teamed with the familiar four-speed, five-speed manual boxes or three-speed JATCO automatic.

Blending with the second Luce US styling was an interrupted character profile line, which kicked up over the rear fender. The suggestion in the pony car era was of horsepower, but other qualities were more important to the Luce. Those priorities concerned luxury and low pollution. The trim levels testified to the luxury, and the Wankel targeted air pollution. Urban pollution was a big issue in Japan; it has always been a country with many people living in a small space. By the early '70s, consider over 100 million people living in an area smaller than California.

Save the cherry blossom trees!

Most Japanese couldn't enjoy the wide open spaces of Hokkaido; they had to face real pollution issues on the main Japanese island of Honshu, where Tokyo is situated. Within Tokyo, it doesn't get more urban or congested than the entertainment district known as the Ginza. At this time, there were electronic billboard signs stating sulphur dioxide and carbon monoxide readings in parts per million. Such signs also gave the urban decibel reading in dba, another form of vehicle pollution. It was understandable that California, with its strict pollution laws and drive by noise requirements, had such common ground.

One didn't need signs to know there was pollution; it was easily felt. The sight of a traffic cop taking breaths of mint-scented oxygen from a portable tank was as amusing as it was disturbing. On the domestic level, most Japanese homes didn't have central heating. 85% relied on kerosene stoves. The upshot of manmade problems in a confined area was that air pollution was affecting the country's much loved cherry trees in Tokyo.

As happened with acid rain in the Black Forest a decade later, there was pressure to reduce pollution in Japanese city areas, and the rotary engine could help. In terms of model distinctions between piston and rotary Luce cars, Mazda's bean counters had been whittling down the cosmetic differences from the RX-2/3. A 'RE12' front grille badge, on the left hand side, told folks a 'Rotary Engine 12A' was afoot; the Luce never had the 10A. However, there were style differences between sedan and coupe. The RX-4 Series I sedan had a flat front fascia, and plainer interior dashboard. Coupes had a pointed snout, and a cockpit style dash in the fashion of the 1971 AMC 'Humpster' Javelin.

Adding to the macho Luce look, Mazda fitted its widest normal car wheels and tires yet. 13in by 5½in steel perforated sports rims with 175/70 or BR70 13in radials, depending on export market. This was as heavy-duty as one would want, given the RX-2/3 and RX-4 were unavailable with power steering. It was an era to fear parking lots and love the open road. Mazdas of this era, the RX-4 in particular, picked up criticism for excessive badgework and over fussy styling detail, but everyone was in agreement that the Wankel afforded excellent performance. Independent testing of export market, non-smogged 1973 RX-4 12A sedans, produced ¼-mile times in the mid 17s for four-speed cars and high 17s for automatics.

Luce Series II with 13B power

Not long after the second gen Luce came out, Mazda was readying Series II improvements for a December 1973 Japanese release. The most important introduction with the Series II cars were the single distributor, thermal reactor 12A and 13B engines. The single distributor approach was to improve Mazda rotary reliability. The thermal reactor emissions method was a move to answer Japan's pollution concerns, and new stricter emissions regulations. New 1974 model year Mazdas, piston and rotary, carried the AP (Anti Pollution) suffix. Indeed, the 1974 RX-4 AP became the first car on the planet to pass the proposed 1975 US emissions regulations.

The thermal reactors may have glowed red,

Utilising the larger 135PS 13B REAPS motor, the Luce GT 13B coupe with 15.8 second quarter mile and 195kph top end, was one of Japan's fastest rides. (Courtesy Mazda)

but AP Wankel Mazdas were green at heart. Their combination of top shelf performance and clean tailpipe, turned Detroit green with envy. In spite of the civic mindedness, Mazda increased performance with the larger displacement 13B rotary. The Mazda 13B rotary would go on to become a long running, two-rotor high-performance icon, but let's allow journalist Mark Hales to describe what a tuned example sounds like. He described the engine in UK's *Motor* magazine as being very loud, like a manic braying donkey on drugs.[39] Perhaps not as enduring as a SCCA Trans Am '60s V8, more like a cross between a jet airplane and an angry bumble bee.

However, the efficiency of the 1308cc engine was undeniable. Fitted to a Hawaiian Tropic-sponsored Ginetta G29 in the Thundersports British sports car series, the racing 13B had a flat torque curve from four to nine grand, no vibration, and a ported output of 280bhp. The 1974 model year Japanese spec thermal reactor 13B didn't make that much; it was rated at 135PS and 132lb/ft. Fitted to a rotary Luce, it allowed Mazda to claim a top speed of 195kph and 0-400m sprint time of 15.8 seconds. This made the RX-4 four-speed sedan a couple of mph slower than the much more expensive BMW 528 four-speed sedan, but one half second or more swifter over the standing 400 meters.

This new motor went well with the new Luce GT sedan or coupe variants, embodying the engineering upgrade of rear torque rods to better laterally locate the rear live axle, making one's 13B Luce RX-4 more stable through corners. Mazda also re-engineered the four-speed manual box to cope with the 13B's additional torque. To create the 13B, Mazda upped rotor and housing width 10mm over the 12A, which was in turn 10mm over the 10A. Thus, from 10A to 12A to 13B, one had 60ci, 70ci and 80ci displacements. Where did all that power come from?

In road car terms the move from 12A to 13B, was effectively like going from a 2.3- to a 2.6-liter motor. For racing and road tax, the formula was usually 1308cc x 2. Where the ponies met the road, the Luce GT employed 195/70 13in radials on 5.5in wide steel rims, super wide when one doesn't have power steering. To lower unsprung mass and improve handling even more, optional four-spoke aluminum rims were available. Staying with style, the Luce sedan Series II shared the coupe's pointy front fascia, and had a more elaborate dashboard than Series Is. The single distributor 12B, now called 12A by Mazda, was rated at 125 horses and 117lb/ft.

In Australia, the RX-4 coupe Series II could now be purchased with the JATCO auto. The RX-4 made its Series I debut in Australia at $3938 and $4168, for the sedan and coupe respectively in Australian dollars. In Japan the Luce GT 13B was one of the fastest cars made in that country. In Australia, the RX-4 Series II arrived in April 1974, with the 13B and four-speed as the standard power team. It gave locally made V8 muscle cars a run for their money. The thermal reactor RX-4 continued the Goliath V8 giant-slaying Mazda Wankel tradition, and coped with tightening Australian Design Rules (ADR) emissions regs better than local cars, and most Japanese, plus European, imports.

Visual changes from RX-4 coupe Series I to II in Australia saw the front passenger side grille badge morph from 'RE12' to 'Rotary Engine.' There was also a larger cutout in the rear valence panel for the oversize REAPS muffler. At this time, Australian-designed large six-cylinder wagons dominated the family car market, so Mazda imported neither the RX-3 wagon nor the RX-4 wagon to Australian shores. The RX-4 had an easier time in Australia than Europe and the UK, where gas mileage was always an issue.

RX-4 in the UK

The piston 929 launched in the UK, in April 1973, was always an easier sell in the British Isles than the rotary RX-4. After the Yom Kippur-timed Arab Israeli 1973 conflict, the energy crisis made V12 Jaguars, V8 Jensens and any thirsty vehicle even more unpopular. Mazda's rotaries quickly gained a gas guzzler reputation, which was hard to overcome. In March 1975, Britain's *CAR* magazine put the RX-4 coupe 12A in the boring section of its infamous 'The Good, The Bad & The Ugly.' Listed in the £2001-3000 price class for 'coupes and sports cars,' the RX-4 2.3 got 108mph and 15mpg overall, when tested by the journal.

Positive points were described as the 12A's smoothness, the RX-4's excellent finish, and the availability of the 2.6-liter 13B. Performance was rated as 'Strong,' but the journal judged the fuel economy trade off as not worth it. Negative points involved poor handling and that 'horrendous thirst' that led *CAR* to say, "Guzzling gets it nowhere." The same magazine, and the British press in general, were more in favor of the Datsun 260Z. Although costing a lot more, £3095, *CAR* thought 125mph and 24mpg were okay. The magazine liked the 260Z's roadholding, character and its reincarnated Austin Healey 3000 style.[40]

Britain's oldest car mag, *Autocar*, tested the RX-4 12A and the home market Rover 3500 V8 sedan. Coincidentally, both models were sold in North America, albeit during different time periods. The Rover was always competitively priced in Britain, and with the ex-Buick all-aluminum V8, a firm favorite with Her Majesty's police force. *Autocar* found the Rover 3500 automatic did 112mph, 0-60mph in 10.8 seconds and recorded 18mpg overall. The equivalent figures for the RX-4 4 speed manual were 106mph, 10.8 seconds and 18mpg.

Given the RX-4's gas mileage was associated with V8 performance, maybe said gas mileage wasn't so horrendous after all? The RX-4 put its gasoline to good use. The also rotary NSU Ro80 tested by *Autocar* had a 107mph top, did 0-60mph in 13.9 seconds with overall economy of 18.2mpg. The Ro80's rotary was sized more like Mazda's smaller 10A, but it could only slightly better the 12A RX-4's economy, whilst being a much slower sprinter.

Being similar sized to the Rover, the RX-4 significantly undercut the British car on price. The RX-4 12A sedan cost £1678, with the automatic transmission version retailing at £1720. Compared to the RX-2 and RX-3, the RX-4 was the only Mazda of the day to offer the larger 13B Wankel. The 13B represented a £300 surcharge. However, even with auto plus 13B, a new RX-4 13B automatic sedan was just £2020. The Rover 3500 automatic cost £2513, and, apart from a de Dion rear suspension, came with much less standard equipment than the Mazda, or any like priced Japanese car.[41]

In the fall of 1974, an RX-4 coupe with 12A cost £1720, at a time when each pound was worth around $2.30 US. It was a sign of the stagflatory times that, by March 1975, the same car cost £2192. With the cost push effect of higher world oil prices, everyone was experiencing reduced economic activity, along with higher prices. To try and get some value for money from the situation, buyers in the UK, and elsewhere, were increasingly selecting Japanese cars. In terms of AM radio, sunroof and, on larger cars, power windows and assorted gadgets, one got more as standard equipment compared to like-priced British cars. Compared to British Leyland, Vauxhall, Chrysler UK (Rootes), and even Ford UK, Japanese cars were better made and more reliable.

A Toyota Corolla or Mazda 808/818 may have been blander machines than a Vauxhall Viva or Ford Escort; however, more and more UK motorists were unwilling to chance it with a Luton Lovely or a Halewood Horror. By the early '70s, a flood of Japanese imports brought about quotas to protect the UK car industry. The changing times prompted *CAR* magazine's May 1975 cover illustration, showing a geisha trying to hitch a ride from a passing RX-4 coupe, with the headline, "DARE you buy Japanese?" The sentiment at the time was that, while Japanese cars were good value for money, well equipped and made, they lacked character and didn't handle as well as comparable European models.

It's arguable how much fact was behind these assertions, since a live-axled Cortina or Vauxhall Victor wasn't exactly the pinnacle of technical achievement. Either way, UK buyers did dare buy Japanese, and such imports quickly gained a reputation as a safe bet. The good reputation this first wave of Japanese imports earned was shown in the letters written to Britain's *Motor* magazine a decade later. The star letter concerned an RX-4 sedan, and was titled 'Thanks A Quarter-Million …' It was written by a Mr EW Collins of Headley Down Hampshire. After owning several cars which had given Mr. Collins problems, the teacher of metalwork and technical subjects, purchased a secondhand 12A-powered 1973 RX-4 four-door sedan with 7000 miles on the odometer, in 1974. Although not mentioned, it's probable the first owner got rid of the RX-4 due to the fuel crisis. Whatever the reason, by late 1985, Mr Collins' RX-4 had accumulated 225,428 miles. His previous best result was 144,000 miles with a Triumph Herald. The British owner was enthusiastic about his RX-4 saying, "I cannot speak for any other make of Japanese car, but for the Mazda I have nothing but praise." He added, "The quality of engineering of the Mazda is better than that of any other car I have owned."

As with his past cars, the RX-4 was serviced by Mr Collins, and this was at a time when not all UK Mazda dealers were registered as being rotary model service providers. Nevertheless, after nearly a quarter of a million miles, this RX-4 was still on its original 12A. The 12A had been rebuilt, but retained one original rotor and the eccentric shaft. The reason for the rebuild wasn't related to rotor apex seal wear. One day, a sparkplug had broken up, fallen into the combustion chamber and scored one of the 12A's rotors, which had to be replaced.[42]

Mr Collins did note that his RX-4 had never broken down, not even during the broken sparkplug/ scored rotor fiasco. He put the RX-4's unstoppability down to the dual ignition system. The irony was that, for 1974, Mazda's 12A and new 13B had a single distributor to improve 12A/13B reliability. Duly impressed by his RX-4, Mr Collins noted that his next car would have to be an RX-7, the FC chassis would arrive in Britain during 1986, or its successor.

It wasn't just Mazda; there were letters from other British owners of Japanese cars, in the magazine, which had given ten years and 70,000 miles of solid service or greater. The '70s models mentioned were the Toyota Celica, Mitsubishi/Colt Celeste coupe, and Datsun Cherry. It was a sudden coming – in the mid '60s, most cars sold in Britain were of British origin and or manufacture; by the mid '70s, Japanese brands and European imports were making large inroads, as British Leyland and the former Rootes Group faltered. General negative comments about Japanese cars, from British owners, centered on poor sporting handling. Japan has long had very good roads, like West Germany, but bumpy British B roads could upset a less than optimally located live axle.

British owners were still overjoyed that, unlike an Austin or Vauxhall, their Japanese cars would start first time and no trim would fall off. The owners were also pleasantly surprised by the minimal and fixable rust their Japanese cars had, after a decade plus of UK winters.

Symbolic of the rising esteem in which Japanese companies were increasingly held was the experience of British TV producer Brian Clemens, the person behind *The Professionals*. Working on the show *The New Avengers* in the mid '70s, he approached Honda for a motorbike for TV show character, Purdey. Honda said no problem, and if given time it would come up with a special edition, pinstriped version for the show at no additional charge. On *The Professionals,* Brian Clemens had originally gone to British Leyland (BL) for the ITV show's cars: a Triumph TR7, Triumph Dolomite and Rover 3500 SD1 V8. BL charged Clemens for the use of the cars, and, when they arrived on set, they proved very unreliable. The vehicle supplier was soon changed to Ford UK.

The high quality of Japanese cars was already well known in America, by the time the RX-4 arrived Stateside as a 1974 model year ride. Given such organizational arrangements occur with a lag, 1974 was a peak in some ways for Mazda's US rotary era. All regional distributors had merged, by this stage, into Mazda Motors

Mazda's rotary engine licensed by NSU-WAN

Tough

Most cars sold in America guarantee their engines for 12,000 miles or 1 year.

But Mazda guarantees its rotary engines for 50,000 miles or 3 years.

How can we do it?

Simple. First, we built a tough engine. An engine with no pistons, no rods, no lifters, no valves and no cams. An engine with fewer moving parts than a piston engine. A rotary engine. Then, we refined that engine for over 10 years.

When you build a good, tough engine, you can back it up longer. So when we say that Mazdas are built to last, we not only promise it. We guarantee it.

Like this:

Mazda's non-transferable warranty is free on all new rotary-engine Mazdas sold and serviced in the continental United States. It guarantees that the basic engine block and internal parts will be free of defects, with normal use and prescribed maintenance, for 50,000 miles or 3 years, whichever occurs first, or Mazda will fix it free.

***Road & Track*'s 1974 RX-4 coupe almost matched the 0-60mph acceleration of the Maserati Merak. Like other new 1974 North American Mazdas, it featured a better, but not transferable, rotary motor warranty. There was also that US Mazda 'humming' ad slogan. (Courtesy Mazda)**

of America Inc. By September 1974, there were 390 US Mazda dealers, selling RX-2, RX-3, RX-4, the piston 808, and rotary B1600 pickup variant called REPU. Somewhat of a high watermark for Mazda that had reached over one third the number of US Toyota dealers … mostly on rotary power.

With the RX-4, the piston 929 cousin wouldn't arrive Stateside until 1988, America received the fastest and most expensive, plus largest, rotary Mazda ever officially imported at that point in time. That time was early 1974, and, although America got the three sedan, coupe and wagon bodystyles, power teams were limited to the federalized 13B with the four-speed manual or three-speed JATCO automatic transmission. Power was 110 horses SAE net with torque at 117lb/ft, and, being a '74 MY vehicle, the RX-4 came with federal-dictated 5mph front and rear bumpers.

As per all 1974 North American domestic and imported passenger cars, the impact bumpers increased weight and length. The federal RX-4 sedan was 179in long, the RX-4 coupe came in at 177in, with the RX-4 wagon the largest at 184in. Large for a Mazda, but in those pre-downsizing Detroit days, the RX-4 was merely a compact class car. However, by the mid '80s, such external dimensions would rate a midsize label, but the RX-4 would be long gone by then from new car price lists. The US debut 1974 base sticker was $4095, a very reasonable charge, given the imported quality and peppy performance of RX-4.

The US spec, complying with federal lighting/ride height laws, and wearing the w-i-d-e BR70 profile 13in radials chosen for North America, *Road & Track* gave the RX-4 coupe's ground clearance as 7in. Front and rear track were an all time Mazda rotary wide 54in front and rear. This combined with a 32.8ft turning circle and 3.4 turns lock to lock. Weight was down as 2745lb, the sedan as 2875lb. The 13B sported a 9.2:1 comp ratio, the 12A was on 9.4-to-one, but either way it was a 50-state coast-to-coast 110 horses for RX-4.

The emissions-friendly nature of the Mazda rotary had worth, at a time when performance was plunging, and Detroit feared implementation of the Muskie smog bill. US automakers were wedded to a two-way catalytic convertor, as a halo device for their piston engines. The EPA authority had a look, in 1973, at how well the 'Recalcitrant 4' were doing on reaching environmental enlightenment. Concerning the proposed 1975 federal clean air tailpipe standards, the EPA's April 1973 estimate showed GM to be 93% ready, Ford was on 55%, and little AMC and International Harvester were 26% towards getting their fleet green.[43]

Sadly, Chrysler Corp was 0% ready. Chrysler was long past its Hemi heyday, with every aspect of its domestic and international operations in a troubled state. To make ends meet, Chrysler sacrificed its R&D budget, spending only a third of the revenue allocated amount on R&D compared to Ford and GM. Whatever the relative position, Detroit didn't want to know. The automakers had their excuses on how the pollution controls would be expensive, make cars unreliable, and worsen fuel economy. Using lobby group pressure, which Detroit had much of at the time, the companies tried to get 1975 deferred to 1990.

Detroit said it needed more time; cynics said if the date got changed, don't expect a compliant car a day before 1990 January 1. The 1973/74 gas crunch proved Detroit's unlikely ally. With America as a major oil importer, a lot for cars and trucks, government was concerned about the effect the crunch was having on the balance of trade. Pollution controls worsen gas mileage; this was especially the case with early '70s tech. With rising vehicle weight, more power accessories and increasingly optional a/c, the 1974 North American autofleet was the thirstiest fleet to that moment.

Mazda's Parkway bus design came out in 1972. This example is pictured in April of that year. In 1974, Mazda produced a version of the Parkway called 'Rotary 26.' This was a 135 DIN PS 13B rotary-motorvated example, that utilized the low emissions properties of the thermal-reactored 13B to deal with Japan's urban pollution. (Courtesy Mazda)

Pollution controls would make things thirstier, increasing oil imports, so the Nixon administration put off stricter emissions targets – for the economic good of the nation, of course. The due date on lower carbon monoxide and hydrocarbons was delayed to 1976. For nitrogen oxides, it was now 1977 or never. All the while, CVCC Hondas and thermal reactor RX Mazdas made Detroit look a little slack.

RX-4 performance: just the facts, ma'am

The performance and economy stats put the RX-4 sedan that *Road & Track* had on its books on a par with the V6 mid-engine Maserati Merak. Perhaps Maserati had benchmarked the RX-4 secretly in the Merak's development?! It all proved Mazda wasn't just another economy import. *Road & Track* tested a four-speed RX-4 sedan, in April 1974, with 0-60mph/80mph-0 braking/skidpad g/mpg stats of 9.7 seconds/228ft/0.720g/17.5mpg. Tested in September 1974 the five-speed Merak managed the same respective categories in 9.5 seconds/310ft/0.791g/17mpg.

The mid-engine, chassis sophistication of the Maserati meant a much higher lateral g in steady state cornering, than the Mazda's sedan worth reading. However, the technical refinement of four-wheel disks provided a result way worse than the RX-4's respected disk/drum combo. The Mazda was the fastest car in the sedan class. At 120mph, its terminal velocity wasn't much lower than the US spec Merak's top speed. The pure stats showed that, in 1974, one could get Maserati performance, with the practicality of four-doors, slightly better gas mileage and a base sticker less than ⅓ the Italian experience.

An ultra rare 1974 RX-4 GTR, awaiting restoration. The GTR edition was a regional dealer appearance package, not unlike the 'Freeway Flyer' packs offered in California during the mid to late '70s. (Courtesy www.rx7club.com)

Although the worth of a car can't be assessed on raw data alone, they were impressive Mazda stats.[44] In addition, it could safely be said that Mazda was better at power tuning with emissions in mind than the Italians and Detroit. It was also quite correct to say that the RX-4 was a high-performance bargain, whether pitted against a Maserati or America's sporty cars. Not that there were many American sporty cars left by the mid '70s. Insurance premiums, pollution controls and the fuel crisis made what was on offer meeker, and harder to sell.

Since the RX-4 was ready for America's 1975 emissions dictates, that would be a good comparison year. The iconic Camaro Z-28 said goodbye at the close of 1974 model year. By 1975, the Corvette had 165bhp's worth of L48 350 V8 as a base motor, but the coveted domestic ride of the time was the Pontiac Firebird Trans Am. The Trans Am had the big inch V8 sizes of yesteryear, wings and fender flares, plus that fiery phoenix hood decal. All this helped one forget that those plain Jane '60s rides could go twice as fast, for half the price.

The Fairlane 390s and El Camino 396s were long gone, so was the 99 octane premium leaded gas. To meet emissions standards that the RX-4 was already okay with, the 1975 Trans Am had to adopt a catalytic converter and, with it, an unleaded-only diet – lest the lead poison poor cat.

In March 1975, *Road Test* magazine published a Trans Am report, titled 'A Bird Without Wings.' Predictably, it concerned a 1975 automatic Trans Am with base L78 400 V8 making 185 horses net. This was the typical Trans Am more and more people were ordering as '70s fashion dictated that the plainer Formula got overlooked. The exceptional thing about this car was its loaded specification. The 'please the dealer' spec boosted weight and price to 4035lb and nearly $6600 respectively. Unfortunately the window sticker from hell didn't include high-performance. Equipped with zombie shift and 'save the mpg' 2.56 final drive ratio, the Trans Am maxed out at just 85mph in top gear. Zero to sixty was a glacial – no, make that continental drift – 11.2 seconds. In spite of this bad news, overall economy was just 12.6mpg. Well, at least the dealer was happy.

The RX-4 had some nifty badges, a well fitting vinyl roof that a UAW member could only dream of, and perforated steel sport rims with trim rings, and those aforementioned BR70 13in wide footprint radials. All this, and the RX-4 coupe's pointy hood, couldn't match the Grand Master Flash Trans Am's showroom appeal, but think of the substance. The practical sedan four-door layout, a real trunk, way better acceleration aided by an easier-to-use four-speed, than that bolted to any GM V8. Most importantly, the RX-4 traveled five extra miles on every gallon of gas. Not all gas guzzlers were created equal.

Pontiac's 1975 ½ follow up to please the faithful was the reborn Trans Am 455 HO four-speed. The addition of a 455 cube V8 improved performance, *Road & Track*'s June 1976 report gave figures of 0-60mph in 8.4 seconds, 110mph top speed and 14.5mpg overall. Not so many options, so this Trans Am weighed 3750lb and cost only, sigh … $5750. Thus, the 7.5-liter Trans Am was around one second quicker in acceleration from 0-60mph, but still slower on top speed, and much, much thirstier than the 13B powered RX-4.

It spoke to the 1308cc RX-4's efficiency that to better its 2.6-liter equivalent rotary, one had to go to a 7.5-liter eight-cylinder coupe, with a trunk just large enough for a spacesaver and overnight toothbrush. With the RX-4, toothpaste and some luggage could be taken as well.

A car of roughly similar size, performance, thermal reactor controls and four-door layout was the BMW 530i. Coincidentally, the RX-4 and 530i were both selected by *Road & Track* for its Top Ten 1975 list, although in different sports sedan price divisions. Outright performance figures were nearly equal, but the RX-4 delivered said performance with greater enthusiasm.

At over nine grand, the BMW charged twice as much to reach 120mph. Its chief advantage over the Mazda was all independent chassis sophistication. However, in terms of quality finish, BMW could offer no advantage, and an inferior engine warranty. The 530i's six-cylinder had a one-year/12,000-mile warranty, the RX-4 covered one for three years/50,000 miles. Fuel economy for both cars was in the high teens. More importantly, come 1975/76, the RX-4 and

Available in various exterior hues, including white, the RX-4 GTR pack had color-keyed rims, bumpers and side marker chrome trim, blacked out lower valences, grille and rear fascia. This particular GTR came with the black vinyl hood and trunk stripes, plus the extremely rare gold/black exterior with optional luggage rack: very dealer-value-added! (Courtesy www.rx7club.com)

Although corrosion necessitates major repair to lower windshield, trunk floor and much of the general floorpan, this example proved very complete. Window trim, glass, interior and bumpers, along with rim trim rings/center caps and lighting were all present. Delon Mazda, now Power Mazda, of Salem, Oregon was one dealer that sold the GTR pack. (Courtesy www.rx7club.com)

This RX-4 GTR has the windshield-embedded radio antenna, although not working anymore, and once had an Auto Power bolt-in rollbar suggesting a competition past. The RX-4 reached North America in 1974 MY, just as interest in rotary was beginning to wane due to the gas crunch. (Courtesy www.rx7club.com)

530i were some of the few non cat cars that could run on cheaper leaded gas. When a gas station ran a low bait price, it was for leaded gas and your RX-4 could use it.

Factor in superior performance, economy, cheaper gas and better reliability, to judge the RX-4 as a much more cost effective, high-performance car, with four on the floor, than the pricier Trans Am 6.6-liter. The three-year warranty Mazda gave on its 12A and 13B really counted for something, in mid-'70s North America. Normal pollution controlled piston engines didn't run well, and emissions controls added a new dimension in unreliability. To offer a better warranty on an alien motor format took guts.

Mazda's new rotary avenue was the flavor of the early '70s. Toyo Kogyo constructed its 600,000th rotary production vehicle in 1973. 1973 Mazda calendar year production was over 450,000 units, or up 50% from 1970. To help give the world the Mazdas it wanted, Toyo Kogyo could draw upon overseas assembly plants set up in Malaysia, Indonesia, New Zealand and South Africa. There was even a new Philippines facility, completed in January 1974. Even bigger Japanese competitors were admiring the rotary success. Nissan and Toyota took out NSU/Wankel rotary licenses in 1971 and 1972 respectively. GM had been a licensee since 1970.

That pesky World fuel crisis!

Unfortunately for the RX-4 and Mazda, negative change was in the air. The RX-4 was chosen in *Road & Track*'s "Ten Best Cars for a Changing World." The RX-4 took out the $3500-$6500 Best Sports Sedan category. *Road & Track* mentioned the RX-4 could be had as a four-door sedan, two-door hardtop and four-door wagon adding, "We got 17.5mpg with the four-speed we tested, and that's for a car that runs like a big American V8." Even though concluding that the gas mileage was commensurate with the performance, *R&T* stated the specter of poor economy in the fuel crisis, and Mazda's well known recent sales woes.[45]

R&T did say the 13B rotary was the RX-4's star feature, but it seemed this one-time asset was dragging Toyo Kogyo into the commercial abyss. With OPEC's 1973 oil embargo, the restriction in supply quadrupled the price of oil, and made perceived gas guzzlers public enemy number one. In America, full-size V8 family cars sat in the Melting Four's showrooms like beached whales, and the trend to thrift occurred globally. Sales of Mazdas in America fell over 40%; in Japan they fell 30%. Comparing 1973 to 1974, Mazda Capella Rotary sales plummeted from 54,962 to just 7656. The star performer, Savanna, fell from rotary grace registering 29,678 compared to 105,819 units the previous year.

In Australia, a former popular rotary market, Mazda Motors Pty Ltd of Australia sold just 999 rotary cars between May 1975 and April 1976. It seemed like the rotary dream had fallen on hard times with the energy crisis. Elsewhere the aim was to conserve energy, enjoying fast cars just wasn't a priority anymore. In some ways, Japan was even more affected by the gas crunch than America. Japan, the second largest economy globally, was the world's No1 oil importer. Apart from coal in Hokkaido, Japan has long been an energy-hungry place with few natural resources.

At the time of the 1973 fall crisis, 85% of Japan's imported oil came from the Middle East, so OPEC's actions really put the economic brake on Japan. To save power, neon lighting in Tokyo's famous Ginza entertainment district was extinguished, TV stations limited their broadcasts, and the Japanese government's cabinet changed both policies and personnel. Apart from slumping sales, Mazda was losing a lot of salesmen from its struggling small, mom and pop type dealer outlets. 20% of sales staff walked away.

In the UK and Europe, rotary became an even harder sell. As the most recently introduced rotary model, it looked like the energy crisis might kill off the worthy RX-4 from all export markets. Energy saving in America, during the winter of 1973/74, saw temporary measures, like changed school busing and classroom hours, to make the most of daylight. Local ordinances against the burning of high sulphur oil and coal were relaxed. For motorists, the new 55mph national speed limit arrived to save gas. However, most wouldn't have known that, amidst the rotary sales problems, Mazda America supremo Dick Brown, the man who engineered Mazda's sales success in North America, resigned in July 1974.

Mazda's North American sales fell from over 119,000 in 1973 to 61,000 in 1974. Although Mr Brown wasn't responsible for the gas crunch, he was replaced by former Chrysler executive, Sidney Fogel. It seems in a crisis you quickly find out who your friends are. In Mazda's case, evidence indicates it wasn't domestic car buyers. The fuel crisis threw up an example of market perversion, that proved who had been buying Mazda imports in the good years. Whereas sales of RX-4s were going through the floor, sales of Pontiac Trans Ams were going through the roof.

Pontiac sold more Trans Ams after the crisis than before. Sales of the winged wonder were under 5000 in 1973, over 10,000 in 1974, around 27,000 in 1975 and over 45,000 in 1976. To add insult to injury, over 7500 Trans Ams sold in 1976 were 7.5-liter cars. Pontiac had outsold Mazda in North America, using the 6.6- and 7.5-liter Trans Ams alone. In 1975 and 1976, Mazda North America sales were 65,000 and 35,000 units respectively. An incredible comparison of fortunes, but true. How could an expensive 3800lb two-door vehicle with gas mileage in the low to mid teens, together with declining yearly smogged performance, outsell Mazda's entire line during such difficult times? The answer was different buyer profiles.

The different success levels showed that Trans Ams were bought by domestic car buyers, desperately holding onto memories of a fading '60s heyday. Plus, many domestic buyers had moved out of intermediate and full-size classes, into smaller rides that were easier to drive and relatively more economical. Finally, the Trans Am scooped up buyers choosing from the dwindling domestic sporty car selection. Mazda's trouble was that domestic buyers didn't normally choose Japanese cars. A domestic buyer looking for V8 performance wouldn't usually consider a rotary Mazda.

The fuel crisis showed rotary Mazdas were bought by import buyers that might have chosen a six-cylinder sporty Japanese car, or a European brand like Alfa or Saab. The Mazda's rotary performance was desirable, and its thirst okay, so long as the price of gas stayed low. The demographic profile at hand wouldn't have tolerated the Trans Am's V8 gas mileage, but they wouldn't have considered a domestic car in the first place anyway, with or without the fuel crisis.

Fixing the rotary – the three-year warranty

The gasoline price exceeded that magic level, where import buyers were no longer comfortable feeding leaded regular to rotaries. With the slump in demand, Mazda's plans for the larger 15A and 21A were shelved. Apart from gas mileage, Mazda had some reliability record problems with earlier sold 10As and 12As. Although not the Ro80 catastrophe that nearly sank NSU, pre-13B units exhibited relatively high oil consumption, the complexity of dual ignition, and a penchant for sparkplugs. More than this, a different kind of rotary seal problem had showed up.

Unlike NSU's equivalents, Mazda's rotary apex and corner seals had proven sufficiently robust. However, the thermally-inefficient Wankel gave the oil seals and gaskets joining

The RX-4 Series II reached Australia in April 1974 with a standard 13B/four-speed power team, that this Tasmanian 1974 coupe had when new. Between its April 1973 debut and 1976 the RX-4 coupe price rose from $4168 to $5195. (Courtesy Chris Stredwick)

The RX-4 coupe pictured trackside with a late model Falcon Ute. When new, the RX-4 13B coupe was an upscale alternative to local Australian V8 coupes from GM Holden and Ford Australia. The 13B coped better with Australian emissions regs than did the local 5-liter V8s. (Courtesy Chris Stredwick)

This 1974 Australian RX-4 Coupe has a JC Cosmo-sourced 20B Wankel, using a single aftermarket Garrett GT42R turbo, custom ceramic-coated exhaust manifold and PWR water to air intercooler for 450 to 500bhp! (Courtesy Chris Stredwick)

rotor housings to side plates a hard time. Ever-vigilant *Consumer Reports* covered the seal failure problem concerning US Mazdas with 10As and 12As. Mazda's continuous R&D produced more durable seals to cope with the waste heat for 1973. To show the public its rotary was up to snuff again, Mazda America brought out an extended warranty. Unfortunately, the new seal design and warranty didn't work retrospectively to aid owners of existing Mazda rotaries.

Disgruntled early R100 and RX-2 Mazda owners started a class action lawsuit against Mazda America, which was settled in 1980. Similarly, and by coincidence, US BMW 530i owners took action against BMW North America, concerning the propensity of their rides to experience cracked cylinder heads. This lawsuit was also settled in 1980. This may not have been a coincidence. The R100, RX-2 and 530i all used thermal reactors to meet emissions standards in America. The heat generated by said thermal reactors may have contributed to the oil seal problems and cracked heads.

Just as Mazda revised its oil seals, BMW introduced a new cylinder head design with wider coolant passages. Mazda reacted to its engineering problem much quicker, and, by March 1974, its revised, extended warranty was used as a selling point. Some companies, like VW and AMC, up to that point, had given two-year warranties, but Mazda went one better with three years. So it was that the 1974 RX-4 coupe ad headlined with "Tough … Mazda Hmmmmm." The non-transferable engine warranty covered the Mazda rotary block and internals for the motor's normal use under prescribed manufacturer servicing, for three years or 50,000 miles, whichever came first.

The warranty applied to the latest RX-4s and REPUs, motivated by the 13B. It also covered new RX-2s and RX-3s using the single distributor 12A. Mazda explained that this was possible because rotary had fewer parts, and Toyo Kogyo had been doing over ten years' worth of R&D. So Mazda could still use its famous US ad slogan, making reference to the rotary power plant, "… and Mazdas go hmmmmm." At this stage, Mazda still wished to be known as the rotary company, and, as with past ads, in the top right-hand corner it said the engine was licensed by NSU-Wankel.

Rotary being as central as it was, Mazda was still keen to show that the 1974 RX-4 was no one-trick ponycar. Qualities included full dash instrumentation with tach, optional automatic console shifter, adjustable velour buckets with front-driver armrest, and radial tires on perforated steel disc rims with chrome trim rings. In America, Mazda's big car was only rotary powered. North America wouldn't get the 929, the RX-4's piston cousin, until 1988. By that hour, the Luce had moved on, to the size up HC platform and could still be 13B motorvated in Japan. However, America said goodbye to the rotary Luce at the end of the 1978 model year.

Arise the real RX-4!

As with the R100, RX-2 and RX-3, some have tried to create RX-4 clones on the sly. Thus, technical differences between RX-4 and 929 are worth noting. Legit RX-4 Series Is have the LA22S chassis prefix. All the pre-929L (Legato) Series I to III 929s started with LA2VS. The RX-4 Series Is were solely 12A-powered, RX-4 Series IIs and IIIs start with LA23S, reflecting the promise of 13B power. Wagon RX-4s carry a 'W' suffix, and have VINs starting with LA22W, or LA23W for 13B cars. The 929 piston wagon has the LA2W id.

As per R100 to RX-3, the RX-4 had a larger gas tank fitted compared to the more economical 929. RX-4s had a 65-liter tank, 929s just 45 liters. A rev counter was standard equipment on all RX-4s, and 929 coupes. A tach wasn't fitted to 929 sedans or wagons. On this sporting topic, the RX-4 rev counter had a higher 6500rpm redline, reflecting the 12A and 13B's high rpm lifestyle. Within the rotary clan, the RX-4 Series II and IIIs have wider diameter axles and larger differentials than the 12A only RX-4 Series I. This reflects the higher torque of the Series II and III available 13B.

American RX-4 revisited

The only better final drive ratio for the RX-4 Series I, due to hardware limitations, is the 4:4 ratio and associated differential from the 1977-1979 Mazda E1600 van. That didn't apply to US RX-4s, which were always 13B-powered. The RX-4 did continue in America, despite the fuel crisis, but its nature had changed, as *Road & Track* discovered in March 1977. The eight-car test was ominously titled 'Separating the pretenders from the contenders.' It had been three years since *R&T* last met RX-4; its price had risen from $4095 to $5034.

A Microtech ECU will maximize this car's 20B. To cope with the power increase from the stock thermal reactored 13B to the 20B, the RX-4 Coupe's front brakes have been upgraded to RX-7 Series V disks and calipers, housed within 16in Simmons alloys. (Courtesy Chris Stredwick)

As with all imports and domestics, American buyers bemoaned the fact that they were paying fast climbing prices for examples of the same models, which were now heavier, slower and didn't run as well. The arrival of smog controls, energy crisis and inflation produced a total enthusiast car crisis. As the pony cars, muscle cars and Brit sports cars quietly exited stage right, there came the rise of the semi affordable Euro sport sedan. They were in the pre-downsized subcompact, compact class, had sophisticated ride/handling and base stickers equal to a high class, luxury US intermediate V8.

The RX-4 was the only non-European car on test, in a sport sedan segment that had expanded greatly since the early '70s. Difficult auto times of 55mph speed limit, smog motors, and CB radio usage to keep tabs on 'Smokey,' saw enthusiasts pin their hopes on small, nimble sports sedans to expunge auto boredom. Forget about the days of gearing a car to cross the ¼ mile at top speed. As with domestics, the smog years saw all cars place more emphasis on handling and braking. Even the concept of handling had changed, from the times of teeth-rattler HD suspension, to nuanced road manners allied to comfort.

The lower horsepower and smaller size of cars, after the gas crunch, brought on the rear versus front-drive handling debate. Front-drive was increasingly seen as a sign of modernity, and useful for interior packaging on smaller rides. Power windows, AM/FM radios and a/c were commonly specified options in this crowd, which pushed prices even more skyward. Base stickers in *R&T*'s group of eight ranged from $4500 to $8000. The RX-4's price, with $150 AM/FM radio and $450 a/c options fitted, was a very reasonable $5634.

The tested RX-4 sedan weighed 2720lb, and came with a 13B, featuring one Hitachi four-barrel carb, 9.2-to-one comp, 110bhp at 6000rpm, and 120lb/ft at 4000rpm. In keeping with Mazda rotary tradition, the RX-4 was the quietest at idle, registering 50 dBA. It was also the quietest with maximum revs in first gear, reaching 76 dBA. Mazda's inclusion of an overdrive five-speed, from 1976, and lowering the final drive ratio to 3.64-to-one, equalled 2850rpm at 60mph. Measures to improve gas mileage made the RX-4 more capable of dispatching vast distances of gray interstate effortlessly.

R&T remarked that the RX-4 super cruiser was at its best on the freeway, "At 65-70mph the engine is so quiet you can hear yourself breathe ..."[46] In the test, the RX-4 exhibited short, well-controlled panic stops. It achieved the second lowest brake fade with its disk/drum powered combo. Only the all-disk Lancia Beta did better. The RX-4's slalom speed of 55.7mph was faster than the BMW 320i; its 0.72g skidpad figure just a little behind said BMW and Alfa Alfetta. Zero to sixty was 12.4 seconds, with 18.8 seconds at 75mph for the ¼ mile and a 112mph top speed.

The RX-4 was like an American sporty car, in that it was a 'numbers' car. Look at the data panel, and it would seem to be a match for its much more expensive European opponents in several quantifiable areas. However, like a Detroit Dazzler, the RX-4 riding on fat, grippy BF Goodrich BR70-13 radials, did its best work on glass smooth surfaces. Stick to playing with freeway ramps, because potholes and backroads were your enemy. The RX-4's best results were fourth places for engine and ventilation – previously it would have garnered first place for engine, but things had changed.

Three years earlier, the RX-4 blasted to sixty in under ten seconds; in 1977, it cared more about gas mileage. This was true: on test, the thermal reactor-equipped RX-4 compared favorably with the 2-liter thermal reactor-equipped BMW 320i, even though the RX-4 was effectively a 2.6-liter car with larger four-door body. The RX-4's economy range was 14-21.5mpg against the BMW's 17-23.5mpg range. Mazda's post-fuel crisis rotary R&D had bridged the rotary to piston gap.

Judgment at Nürburgring ...

Unfortunately, the RX-4 rated last in the group in 11 areas, including exterior finish. A bizarre result, given the test group included a Fiat 131, amongst three Italian cars on deck. In *R&T*'s opinion, the RX-4 exhibited too many of the traits of pre-downsized American cars. This journal had stated it didn't much care for the RX-4's styling, when it chose it for its '10 Best' list, in 1975. In addition, even the RX-2 copped criticism from *Motor Trend,* for being over decorated. However, now *R&T* likened the RX-4 to a Schuco toy.

The observations were even stronger concerning the interior, where the velour trim was considered "late American boudoir" and "classic Las Vegas." The most intense summary came from one *R&T* scribe, who said the 1977 RX-4 was like an American car that didn't grow up. Oh my, *R&T*'s judgements missed out on three realities. Firstly, domestic cars hadn't improved that much. GM may have spent a fortune on its new '77 full-size line, but they were merely plainer, scaled-down versions, which lacked the oversize charm of their predecessors. Secondly, the most popular cars in 1977 America were the GM F body and Ford Thunderbird. Both were flashier, pricier revisions of pre-gas crunch designs. Thirdly, some people just like Schuco toys and Vegas! The late '70s and early '80s were a time when it was fashionable for US motoring press to criticize US cars. With the Boss 302 and Cuda past icons dead and buried, *R&T* took delight in lambasting Detroit, using Mazda as a proxy.

The RX-4's front console-integrated armrest may have interfered with the five-speed stick's usage, but even a smogged mpg-saving 13B could still perform. The RX-4 was still the fastest car in the eight-car test group by a wide margin. The RX-4 topped out at 112mph, next fastest was the BMW 320i on just 104mph. The 320i and Saab 99 EMS star cars could match RX-4 acceleration, but the 13B's 110bhp seemed more capable than the BMW's identical 110bhp rating. For price, the Saab was getting close to seven grand, and the diminutive

The second gen Luce in Series III form on its October 1975 debut. With the fuel crisis, piston versions like this AP1800 were rising in popularity. Note the Mercedesesque grille, fashionable at the time. (Courtesy Mazda)

Bimmer was moving within striking distance of $8000 list. *R&T* felt Mazda had redone the RX-4 from a driver's car into a family car. However, at only five grand list price, the RX-4 seemed a reasonable compromise.

The styling which *R&T* took exception to was the revised Luce body, introduced in October 1975. The Luce Series III, upon which the export RX-4 was now based, involved a revised, flatter front fascia. The front fascia featured a flat plastic, slat-type grille which lent the Luce the popular 'Mercedes' visage of the day. The rear fascia involved a flat plastic decorative panel with recessed taillights. In between, lay the same upkicked rear fender line styling brought by Luce Mk 2, in '72.

The latest RX-4s now sported the increasingly common lower front spoiler, and, inside, there lay an RX-5 coupe-sourced steering wheel. There were mild suspension revisions to the Series II layout, that brought slight improvements in ride and handling. More noticeable was the RX-4's performance drop off, due to the search for more mpg, and the Series III weight gain. The non-US export 13B motor still sported 130 wild horses, but more emphasis on torque and a 280lb weight increase, compared to the original RX-4, didn't bode well for the ¼ mile.

To improve economy, Mazda made the final drive ratio a taller 3.64:1, versus the previous 3.9 ratio. Thus, the ¼ mile was now low 17s, compared to early 13B cars doing high 15s and low 16s. However, export markets could enjoy the greater availability of the 195/70 13in tire option on new RX-4s. Also, introduced with Luce Series III was a more powerful four-cylinder choice. The 2-liter 'MA' code inline four had a SOHC layout and produced 103bhp with 123lb/ft of torque. The Luce Series III lasted for two years, giving way to a rebodied, puffed out replacement called Luce Legato.

Luce Legato – an upscale Luce

The Luce Legato was introduced at the 1977 Tokyo Auto Salon, and represented the final new model created with US overtones. It had been normal Detroit practice to launch new versions with bigger dimensions, using revised sheetmetal on an existing platform. Luce Legato followed this formula. The Luce Legato was 182in long, 66.5in wide, and sat on a 102.8in wheelbase. Bodystyles involved four-door sedan, four-door pillarless hardtop and, from February 1979, a wagon edition.

Luce Legato was the biggest inhouse-designed car Mazda had yet released, and was intended to replace existing Luce variants, including RX-4, as well as the semi-imported Roadpacer luxury car. As a final hurrah for the 15-year Detroit influence on Japanese car styling, the Luce Legato was extravagance personified. Imposing, as only a squared up shape can be, the visage involved stacked headlamps and a formal grille. The result was similar to the US Ford Granada luxury compact.

Introduced in the fall of 1977, the Luce Legato was the third reworking of the second gen Luce. The Luce Legato was known for its American styling overtones, four-door hardtop and coupe absence. A 1979 MY Luce Legato 2000SE is displayed. (Courtesy Mazda)

By 1979, the Luce Legato range started at ¥996,000, with the latest version of the 1.8-liter I4 that powered the '60s Luce. With the 90bhp edition 2-liter MA four pot, manufacturer quoted top speed was exactly 100mph. An academic outcome given Japan's urban congestion and 62mph national speed limit. However, sumptuous comfort was certainly provided for, with this final manifestation of the 1972 second gen Luce platform. With an eye to the second gas crunch, Mazda revived its diesel past with a 2.2-liter diesel four-cylinder Luce Legato option, introduced in September 1980.

The 2.2-liter I4 diesel was from the era when diesels were definitely diesels. That meant 66bhp and 104lb/ft, along with leisurely performance. Perfectly adequate in a Tokyo traffic jam, with the Luce Legato's excellent a/c running. For excitement, the range did offer the familiar 12A and 13B rotaries, since Kenichi Yamamoto and a dedicated Mazda engineering cohort were determined to keep the rotary motor spinning. However, there was no Luce Legato coupe; that task was fulfilled by the Cosmo AP /RX-5 coupe. As a range, the Luce Legato lasted until late 1981, although the Luce Legato wagon soldiered on in production until March 1988.

The export version of Luce Legato was called 929L, the '929' suggesting the piston motor within, and the 'L' indicating the Legato body incarnation. For the UK market, the 929L wagon was exclusively powered by the aforementioned 1970cc MA inline four. Look at that 1988 model year export wagon, and one can see the ghost of the RX-4 wagon from a decade earlier. All one needed was a 13B motor swap. in Japan the Luce Legato was available with 12A/13B power, but these versions weren't exported. The Luce Legato was from the era when Mazda gave rotary a low profile.

Another RX bites the dust ...

The RX-4 did exist in export markets like America, Australia and Asian countries after the Luce Legato's 1977 fall introduction. These RX-4s available 18 months or so thereafter, were built before the 1977 summer factory holidays. As with many speedy '70s cars, the fuel crisis and recession saw such production remnants linger. Current collectors would jump at the prospect of a zero-mile, unregistered RX-4, but 1978/79 was a different time, when most were more into the Mazda 323/GLC.

So it was that the RX-4 sedan and wagon finished up in America, at the close of 1978 MY. In Australia, the Luce Series II based RX-4 was retailing at $5014 for the sedan and $5195 for coupe by 1976. The revised 'Mercedes grille' Series III version reached Australia in April 1976. Through all this time, the RX-4 was well priced and good value, but sales dwindled due to perceived poor gas mileage. In the wake of the energy crisis, Mazda Motors sold just 436 rotary cars between May 1976 and March 1977.

In theory, by May 1976 Australian new Mazda rotary car sales were limited to the RX-4 and RX-5 coupe. Given economic reality, the RX-4 coupe said goodbye to Australia at the start of 1977, leaving the sedan, at $6382, as the sole RX-4 representative. The RX-4 sedan remained available through June 1979, and, by this hour, all eyes were on the new RX-7 sports car. Things weren't moving in the showroom, or trackside for the RX-4. There was a poor outing at Australia's top Bathurst touring car event, where the big RX-4 was outpaced by the faster 12A-powered RX-3s. However, international rallies did see the RX-4 finish on the podium, so all was not lost.

The Cannonball Run … minus Burt …

The RX-5's presence saw the RX-4 coupe withdrawn from many export markets, but there were still places for RX-4 and Mazda's rotary to shine, like the Cannonball Run. The Cannonball Baker Sea-To-Shining-Sea Memorial Trophy Dash, was a real life coast-to-coast US road race, held four times in the 1970s. Conceived by Brock Yates and fellow *Car and Driver* editor, Steve Smith, in 1971, it sought to show that rapid auto travel could be conducted reasonably safely. The race took on even more significance with the arrival of the 1974 55mph national speed limit.

There were a number of road race Hollywood movies inspired by the real life Cannonball Run. In 1972, Fred DeVan made it from sea to shining sea in 39 hours and 29 minutes using a Mazda RX-2; he finished sixth in the race. An RX-4 did the 1975 Cannonball Run in 39 hours and 22 minutes, coming eighth, showing the single dizzy 13B's reliability. The RX-4's racing drivers were Pierre Honegger, Tom Kozlowski, Jeff Martini and Ray Walle. In 1979, Christine Catalano, Richard Doherty and Tad Richardson used an RX-7 to come sixth in 35 hours and 17 minutes.

That proved Mazda rotary reliability on the road; the Aero Design DG-1 proved it in the sky. David Garber designed the plane using rotary power – just one was built. The Aero Design DG-1 was a US racing aircraft registered N10E, intended to beat the world airspeed record for piston engined aircraft. The single seater used two 330bhp Mazda RX-3-sourced 12As, one driving a tractor propeller with the other driving a pusher propeller. The DG-1 had a very streamlined bullet-shaped fuselage and mid-wing cruciform tail.

The plane's first flight was on July 25 1977. The 20-foot plane had an empty weight of 1700lb and maximum speed of 450mph. The Aero Design DG-1 had a 460-mile range, could reach an altitude of 24,000ft, and could climb at 3000ft per minute. If only Mazda's mid-'70s sales rate could have climbed like that. Interest in rotary was on the decline, and the RX-4 had been selectively withdrawn from some markets after the fuel crisis. In the UK, the RX-4 left as early as the middle of 1976. What could Mazda do to maintain rotary interest? The company tried value added luxury, with a special coupe from the constellations.

The New Cosmo

In the midst of falling interest in the rotary engine, and Mazda financial woes, just when you thought it was safe to go back in the water, Mazda introduced a new rotary shark called Cosmo AP. This was the first time Mazda had dusted off the Cosmo nameplate since its ground breaking two-seater 110S sports car had said adieu in 1972. This new Cosmo was a very different two-door car, and made its international debut at the 1975 Frankfurt auto show. Something of a poke in the eye, given the rocky state of NSU's Ro80, and the fact rotary was a German invention in the first place.

The CD Cosmo coupe made an October 1975 Japanese debut, as part of Mazda's fall lineup for 1976 model year. The latest Cosmo was a boulevardier sports car, inspired by the sports/luxury intermediate personal American cars, so popular in early '70s America. The Chevrolet Monte Carlo and AMC Matador coupe were inspirations. The new Cosmo, unlike the original, was exported widely early on, and went by several names. It was Cosmo AP as a piston and rotary range in Japan, and rotary only in America, where it was simply called Cosmo.

Other export markets got piston and rotary versions of the new Mazda two-door. However, in such places, the piston edition was called 121, and the rotary variant was RX-5. RX-5 was an appropriate name, because the new model was based on the Luce/RX-4 coupe, albeit with many engineering upgrades and styling revisions. It was a larger, more advanced, more refined and luxurious Luce coupe. It also fitted in with US personal car style of longer, lower and sleeker, but with true Japanese engineering substance.

The CD Cosmo had the sophistication of four-wheel disk brakes and four-wheel coils. It didn't have the rumored rear independent suspension, but represented a major RX-4 reworking nonetheless. At the front were MacPherson struts, swaybar, and lower A arms instead of RX-4's lateral arms. At the rear, Cosmo featured a live axle managed by five trailing links, and Panhard rod. The RX-4 had rear drum brakes and leaf springs. The RX-5's suspension promised superior comfort, and so did Cosmo's interior.

Plush would be an understatement: interior upholstery included a choice of standard crushed velvet, or non-breathing vinyl. The latter tended to be popular on domestic and imported cars in '70s America, given that well done vinyl had the look of leather and was easy to clean. Real leather was a rare and expensive option at the time, and involved much more care than the manufacturer-treated leather of the 21st century. In addition, there was wood trim – an accepted and expected accoutrement on sports/luxury cars of the hour. The CD Cosmo's dashboard used a faux wood veneer. However, the manual shifter knob, steering wheel and between-the-seats handbrake lever, were made of the real forest fresh variety.

The CD Cosmo wasn't a cheap car, but, compared to the spartan, plastic-abound interiors of much more expensive German two-door sedans, Mazda delivered the luxury one paid for. It could be said Cosmo had the posh high line interior of traditional banker's hotrods, with the ergonomic benefit of reclining seats. The reborn 1975 Cosmo's interior would have made Huggy Bear feel right at home, and the exterior was certainly pimped out. When *Road Test* tried a CD Cosmo for size, it received many inquiries from fellow motorists asking what the flashy two-door was.

Cosmo was now a styled coupe, which was code for two-door hardtop with a formal grille; something Rolls-Royce started, Ford made affordable with Lincolns and big Thunderbirds, and others followed. The Cosmo's grille wasn't exactly like a mid-'70s Olds Cutlass' grille, but

Making its debut at the 1975 Frankfurt Motor Show, the Mazda Cosmo AP Series I was a more refined and luxurious development of the successful RX-4 Coupe. (Courtesy Mazda)

wasn't a million miles away. Proof of this was *Road Test*'s Cosmo prompting an Olds Cutlass owner at a Los Angeles traffic light to ask what the Cosmo was, and if it was new. It seemed Mazda's styling boys knew Detroit better than ol' Henry, Walter or even Mr Sloan.

The CD Cosmo's opera windows no doubt helped create such visual similarity. To date Audi, BMW and Mercedes haven't done opera windows, Mazda did with CD Cosmo. Even more shocking was the fact Cosmo's fancy C-pillar glass panes were functional. It was enough to induce an infarction in a Detroit bean counter. It has been speculated Ford took CD Cosmo's profile as inspiration for its 1977 downsized Thunderbird. However, the Ford's opera windows weren't functional. Perhaps Mazda had bunnies in mind when designing its personal car?

Cosmic introductions

The CD Cosmo's North American introduction took place in 1976 at Mazda Motors of America's Big Sur Rally. A race running from LA to San Francisco. The Japanese two-door was displayed at the Century Plaza Hotel. Playboy bunnies and a marching band were in attendance. Apparently the interior of the Californian Playboy mansion is darker and mustier than publicity would have one believe. Thus, the bunnies would have appreciated the CD Cosmo's functional opera windows, or maybe they would have preferred to take a bus? Given it was California, and smog was an issue, public transportation made sense. Even here Mazda had a rotary answer.

In the Parkway Rotary 26 of 1974, Mazda had the largest form of rotary transport it had ever made, the Parkway was a bus. Normally Mazda's Parkway bus series had regular piston engines, but this variant had the RX-4 thermal reactor-type 13B Wankel making 135PS. The intention wasn't high-performance, just rotary's pollution fighting properties in an urban smog environment, where public transport would be expected. Having many people aboard a Parkway would also make the most of the gasoline the 13B was burning. Given such buses are normally diesel-powered, this was another cleaner burning feather in the Parkway Rotary 26's environmental cap.

The Parkway Rotary 26 was 243.9in long and weighed 6360lb. The bus had a 75mph top speed, irrelevant in a tight, congested urban environment. More important was that 129.3in wheelbase that allowed lots of people to be good citizens. That 13B was also soon found in the CD Cosmo. It's more sensible to take a bus or train than drive in a Japanese city. The idea of the CD Cosmo sharing its 13B with you, a friend and some luggage, suddenly seems selfish. It explained the 'personal car' tag worn by sports/lux two-doors of such ilk.

In Japan, the CD Cosmo started off with Mazda's familiar 1.8-liter four. The single overhead cam motor made 100PS and 110lb/ft of torque, then it was on to your choice of 12A or 13B rotaries. Piston or rotary, the CD two-door was a pollution fighter, so carried the Cosmo AP nameplate in Japan with pride. The mechanical and luxury upgrades over RX-4, such as 14in wheels and crushed velvet interior, were shared by all CD Cosmos. Thus, it wasn't a cheap car. The range started with the 1800 Custom Special, moved up to the 12A-powered Custom Special and finished with the 13B-motorvated Limited. The Limited's ¥1,795,000 base sticker included all the fruit.

The top introduced Japanese Cosmo AP was the equivalent of over $6000 US. Given cars are one of Japan's few, relatively cheaper, domestic goods to buy, this made Cosmo AP rather special. A big coupe for Japan, the CD Cosmo was 176.2in long, 66.1in wide and sat on the Luce 98.8in wheelbase. The lightest version was 2469lb, with the 13B Limited Cosmo AP tipping the scales at around 2650lb. The American spec Cosmo utilized the RX-4's federalized 110 horse 13B, and weighed 2825lb. With bumper overriders, the CD Cosmo was 179in long – but the US edition was 182in long.

REPU – Mazda's pick me up

The added weight and length were mostly down to the US 5mph bumpers. Once again not as much of an eyesore as the equivalent 5mph units on German imports, but an enthusiast turn off nonetheless. Trucks, commercial vehicles such as vans, attracted lower emissions and bumper restrictions; even easier, CAFE requirements, when they arrived in 1978. This was the motivation behind the iconic Dodge L'il Red Express, and that whole 'Vibrant Vannie' customized van movement of the late '70s. Mazda paved the way for all that, with its 1974 REPU.

The REPU (Rotary Engine Pick-Up) truck was

The legendary North American directed 1974-77, 13B-motorvated REPU mini truck. *Road & Track* clocked a REPU at 0-60mph in 11 seconds. Faster than the 11.2 seconds *Road Test* magazine timed a 1975 Trans Am 400 at! (Courtesy www.mazdas247.com)

the first new rotary model introduced, after the 1973/74 gas crunch. It arrived, in April 1974, at a base price of $3495, and was aimed solely at the North American market. In a nutshell, it was the Mazda B1600 light truck, with apt mods to accept the smogged down 110 horse 13B, the kind found in an RX-4. Small, light trucks had been popular since the dawn of the '70s, and would continue to be fashionable into the '80s. Their popularity spiked at the height of the second gas crunch. Recall the Rabbit-based VW Caddy/ Rabbit pick-up?

The appeal was low purchase price, easy maneuverability and good gas mileage, compared to a normal size V8 truck. Often the light trucks were Japanese models sold as captive imports by the Complacent Three using different nameplates. Such four-cylinder trucks were also dog slow, so Mazda's REPU very quickly made amends. *Road & Track* sampled

A 1975 Mazda REPU in New Zealand. The rotary REPU was targeted at America, this pickup was imported from Bakersfield, California. It is finished in House of Kolor Kandy Apple Red, with Spies Hecker Gold base coat. The undercarriage has 3M chip guard, plus Kandy Apple Red and gold detailing. (Courtesy Haydon Little)

one in 1974, and found it faster than the final US BMW 2002s. The REPU could do 103mph and accelerate from 0-60mph in 11 seconds. Top speed was delivered at 6850rpm, and REPU could hit its 7000rpm redline in the first three gears of its four-speed manual.

This was frisky behavior by 1974 pollution-controlled standards, and the kind of high rpm action not seen since pre-smog times. A 4.62 final drive ratio and four on the floor were the kind of hardware last seen on a '60s pony car, not a mini truck. It was performance with a clean conscience, the REPU had Hydro Carbon, Carbon Monoxide and Nitrogen Oxide readings of 2.3g, 14g and 1.3g per mile respectively. 1970 federal pollution standards had 4.1g and 34g for hydrocarbons and carbon monoxide respectively. This was the standard a Mustang Boss 302 could meet. The proposed 1975 standard for nitrogen oxide was 3.1g per mile.

All the above shows how ahead of the curve Mazda's 13B motor was. The REPU, or Mazda Rotary Pickup to use its formal name, had a chassis that allowed the 13B's lively nature to be enjoyed. The layout was conventional Mazda front independent MacPherson strut, rear live axle leaf-sprung '70s hardware. A front swaybar was included, along with Bridgestone Skyway Deluxe 7.35 14in tires for 5½in wide steel rims.

Front and rear track were 57in and 56in respectively, with front and rear weight distribution on 53/47 per cent. The REPU sat on a 104in wheelbase and weighed 2865lb, which suggested a fun ride. Indeed, *Road & Track* declared the rotary pickup to be nimble, with a better than average ride for a mini truck. The skid pad figure was 0.683g and overall brake rating was judged very good by *R&T*. Brakes were by 10.1in disk/10.2 x 1.75in drum power brakes with vacuum servo, producing a 286 foot stop from 80mph.

The REPU had a 1400lb load rating, 37.7cu ft of bed space and 8in-worth of ground clearance. Carrying on with the practicalities, the rotary rig had average fuel consumption of 16.5mpg, and relied on a 20.4-gallon tank. Riding around at 70mph the interior noise level was 79 dBA. Although REPU was mini truck in nature, not car based, there were size and performance similarities to a compact-based Ford Ranchero 289 V8. The 1966 Ranchero also had 7.35-14in tires, identical weight distribution, the same fuel consumption, a 10.3-second 0-60mph time and lower top speed of 95mph.

The REPU's RX-3/RX-4 usual suspension layout, has been modified by Matt at T.D.S. New Zealand. Brakes are by RX-7 Series IV disks/calipers, with Simmons 18 x 8in aluminum rims. The 13B's induction is by 48 IDA Weber, on a custom stainless steel manifold with nylon risers and 4½in K&N filter. (Courtesy Haydon Little)

No one offered this performance/size combo on a pickup by the mid '70s, except Mazda. By 1974, one had to go to a 460ci V8 Ranchero to get a one second 0-60mph advantage on REPU – by now Ranchero was a much bigger rig, costing nearly six grand. With the modest options one could specify on REPU, AM radio, stripe kit, side mirrors and tonneau cover, price topped out at $3800. Then there was Mazda North America's new warranty: a normal 12 months/12,000 miles on the REPU in general, but 36 months/50,000 miles on the rotary engine. To prove how tough the 12A and 13B were, piston Mazdas had the usual 12/12 warranty for their motors.

This was probably worth more than Mazda's 'Tough' motor ad slogan of the day. Five years on from R100, Mazda's oil change interval had improved from 2000 miles to 4000 miles. Good, but still not the 6000-mile interval one would expect on a normal powerplant. The one thing *R&T* did take issue with was battery location. The REPU's battery was part exposed under the rear right-hand side fender, with access flap and security padlock. The kind of lock one would find on a front gate. The arrangement gave easy access, on what was a commercial vehicle.

The exposed battery was normal practice on Japanese heavy-duty trucks, but *R&T* saw it as vulnerable to theft. In low-crime Japan it was ok; in America it was a liability. The public thought it was a steal – 14,366 REPUs were purchased in North America in 1974. This was about equal to all BMWs sold in North America

A customized peripheral ported 13B, with new RX-7 Series IV sideplates and housings, two RX-8 rotors slotted for 3mm carbon apex seals and RX-7 Series VI eccentric shaft. 20B stat gears, RX-7 Series VI solid corner seals and springs, plus new RX-8 side seals, springs and counterweights. (Courtesy Haydon Little)

that year. Buyers were probably mini-truck owners looking for more performance, as well as former domestic devotees looking for lost performance and value for money, in mid-'70s America.

Sadly, REPU sales dropped off sharply thereafter. Only 113 of the charming little trucks were sold in 1975, and just 632 and 1161 found new homes in 1976 and 1977 respectively. Perhaps Mazda satisfied the REPU's niche early on. Apart from short-lived novelty value, REPU was affected by the same gas price, recessionary factors that slowed sales of domestic and imported enthusiast rides at the same time. Soon after REPU, Mazda launched a large rotary-powered model

A custom red and white vinyl interior. A new weather seal kit has also been fitted. Note the bench seat indentation for intermediate shifter ratio selection. A Japanese market RX-7 Series III 12A turbo five-speed gearbox, has been connected to a standard REPU driveshaft and differential. (Courtesy Haydon Little)

This REPU dashboard has been amended to include a 'Rev Rite' rev counter, and Autometer gauges. Back in 1974 pollution controlled America, the REPU's party trick was being able to hit its seven grand redline in the four-speed's first three gears! (Courtesy Haydon Little)

that might have appealed to US buyers, the 1975 Roadpacer AP.

Almost lost in translation – Roadpacer AP

The REPU's 173in length, 67in width, 61in height and 8in ground clearance were miniscule compared to Roadpacer AP. Simply put, REPU and Roadpacer shared a 13B, but the latter was the biggest, heaviest Mazda production car made to that point. It was also an historically significant car, because, to date, Roadpacer had been the only General Motors-related vehicle to see series production with a rotary powerplant. An ironic ride, considering all the R&D work GM had put into its GMRCE.

The Roadpacer's appearance coincided with the period in Mazda's history when rotary was at a crossroads. The car represented decision inertia, founded in the fact that any business plan is made in advance and may not be appropriate when executed. It might also be said that given REPU and Roadpacer, Mazda were living in denial concerning the fuel crisis. In any case, Roadpacer started when GM and Mazda got talking in the early '70s. Mazda had a reputation for making rotary work; GM were still working on rotary, especially its GMRCE.

GM wanted to slot GMRCE into Monza and Corvette. Possible customers, like AMC with its Pacer, wanted to buy GMRCE for use in their cars. Thus, GM wanted to get the skinny from Mazda on what made rotary tick. Mazda wished to sell a large executive car in Japan, to take on Japanese land yachts proffered

Modified with a 5 x 114mm rim bolt pattern, this REPU's peripheral ported 13B makes 272bhp at the rear wheels! The exhaust system involves 2in steam pipe ceramakromed headers, 2 x 18in Rota resonators into 2 x 12in Rota resonators, ending in a 2½in boiler muffler. To assure high performance, hardware fitted includes a Holley Red pump, new Bosch coils and NGK racing sparkplugs! (Courtesy Haydon Little)

In its 1976 Guide to Sports & GT cars, *Road & Track* jokingly speculated that Japanese buyers might indeed like the US-aimed Cosmo AP Coupe. They did indeed; over 55,000 were sold in Japan in the CD platform's first year! (Courtesy Mazda)

by big boys Nissan and Toyota. Mazda didn't have a car larger than the family Luce, so got assistance from GM. As a quid pro quo for Mazda's rotary advice, GM suggested the Holden Kingswood from its Aussie subsidiary General Motors-Holden as a best fit.

The Kingswood was a rear-drive, live-axled family chariot, sized somewhere between a Toyota Crown and pre-gas crunch US intermediate. This incarnation of Australia's iconic 'own car' was launched in 1971, as the Holden HQ. Its chief distinction, apart from Pontiac styling cues, was four-wheel coil suspension. Power came from Holden's inline sixes of 2.85- to 3.3-liter displacement, or Holden's small block 4.2- and 5-liter V8s. All motors were overhead valve cast iron units. Mazda saw the upmarket Premier variant, with four circular headlamp visage, as most appropriate, but the motors had to go.

There were tax advantages in Japan to installing a small displacement, low pollution, Japanese-sourced motor. That logic meant the 13B would sit between the Kingswood's front suspension towers. So it was, that Holden shipped out engineless Premier four-door sedans to Japan, whereupon Mazda installed the 13B Wankel at Hiroshima. This thermal reactor single dizzy 13B made 136bhp at 6000rpm and 102lb/ft of torque. A single four-barrel Hitachi carb fed the 1308cc rotary, which had a 9.4-to-one compression ratio. That's not all Mazda fitted. In keeping with the Roadpacer AP's limo nature, stick shifts were out, and the three-speed JATCO zombie, operating through a column shift, was in.

Mazda's figures put the Roadpacer at 1575kg, the heaviest Mazda car to take the 13B. To get the car off the line, a 4.444 final drive ratio was specified, and the JATCO had ratios of 2.458 (first), 1.458 (second) and 1.000 (top) for the three-speeder. The substitution of the 13B held promise for Roadpacer. The normal Holden sixes were good on torque, but breathless otherwise. The 13B made more power than Holden's I6 'Red Motor,' and the wickedly short rear end ratio with the torque-amplifying torque converter took care of the low end. The 13B also weighed much less than the Holden's US-style cast iron donks, so this was the best handling Premier that Holden never built.

First and foremost, this was a limo for 'hard working' public servants and VIPs, so the Premier's 5in-wide steel rims and beauty hubcaps remained, and Mazda stacked on additional luxo equipment and gadgets. Once Roadpacer AP hit 10kph, the standard power door locks automatically activated, and a chime system alerted drivers when the limo had reached 90kph. Good warning for chauffeurs, because Japan's speed limit is only 100kph. Mazda's Wankels are Rolls-Royce quiet at speed, which made the Roadpacer's interior a great place to enjoy its deluxe stereo system, operated from the front or rear compartment.

Mazda stats gave Roadpacer AP dimensions

The Cosmo AP Series I interior pictured in October 1975. The effective HVAC system, and mostly real wood trim are visible. Many American critics were not impressed by the overly plush, US personal car type interior. (Courtesy Mazda)

as 4850mm length, 1880mm width and 1460mm height. The limo had a 75-liter gas tank, sat on a 2830mm wheelbase, with 160mm of ground clearance and top speed of 157kph. Conveniently, Japan and Australia are both right-hand drive countries, so the Kingswood/Roadpacer came with the steering column in the correct location. Price for Roadpacer AP was a kingly ¥3.8 million, or around 13 grand, at the car's October 1975 intro. This was twice the price of Mazda's Cosmo AP Super coupe, but Roadpacer was supposed to be the ultimate Japanese luxury ride.

It is commonly thought Toyota Crown and Nissan Cedric were Mazda's Roadpacer competitors. However, true rivals were a size up from these large Japanese sedans. One should consider the contemporary Toyota Century D-Type and Nissan President limos, powered by 3.4- and 4.4-liter V8 motors respectively. Luxury big cars in the old skool American idiom; exclusively automatic in transmission and all features, with no sporting pretensions whatsoever. That said, the Toyota Century which resembled yesteryear's Lincoln, had 170 horses and could do 170kph.

Thus, Roadpacer was a mite down on firepower and speed compared to its V8 rivals. However, its 9mpg thirst in pedal to the metal – or should that be deep cut pile – action- matched the Century and President. It equaled them in luxury, at a cost saving. In 1979, the Roadpacer AP was ¥3,835,000, the Toyota and Nissan were ¥3,876,000 and ¥3,846,000 respectively. Just enough for a government official to show their department was making a difference. A difference in style occurred through the Roadpacer's run. In line with the stylistic and mechanical upgrades done by Holden, the Roadpacer kept pace with the transition from Kingswood HJ to HX. The HX was Australian-introduced in mid-1976.

Holden's quality control wasn't up to Mazda's high standards, requiring the Hiroshima plant to fix up the supplied cars. Mazda's added gizmos increased complexity and introduced electronic gremlins. Nevertheless, over 800 Roadpacer APs were sold by Mazda, between 1975 and 1979, although Mazda got no new supply from Holden post-1977. The Roadpacer AP was more of a success than commonly believed: over 800 embassies and government departments was quite a number. The Roadpacer program was ended, because Holden was discontinuing its Kingswood in favor of the smaller Opel sourced Senator sedan.

The Mazda Roadpacer AP of 1975-79, was an amalgam of the Australian Holden Kingswood Premier body, with the RX-4 automatic's 13B/JATCO power team. Shown on debut in October 1975, the Roadpacer AP was a VIP mobile, targeting the Nissan President and Toyota Century V8 limos. (Courtesy Mazda)

Sumitomo Bank cleans house at Mazda

Mazda had introduced its puffed out Luce-based Legato, and this 12A/13B rotary available model did whatever a Roadpacer AP could do. Thus, Toyo Kogyo bid farewell to the Aussie sedan, and was undergoing a transitional period, when some feared the firm might be saying goodbye to rotary too. Mazda had seemed oblivious to the gas crunch, and kept churning out Wankel machines. So, by the year's end, Mazda had a 140,000-unit rotary car stockpile in Japan, and over 50,000 surplus rotary models for North America.

It seemed that the future the people expected didn't transpire. Many planned technologies for the '70s were based on big scale and cheap oil. That future was thought to include one-million-tonne oil tankers, nuclear-powered submarine tankers and tri-hulled cargo ships. This last vessel type was designed to reduce water resistance, and increase speed. The emphasis was on speed and convenience, not economy. Hence the hope of giant ocean-going hovercraft.

The hovercraft was another vessel which had its advantages, but, like rotary, it was thirsty on gas. Just like rotary, that wasn't a problem when gas was cheap, but OPEC changed the rules. Overnight, thoughts of hypersonic planes and passenger-carrying rockets making the

Atlantic crossing in 25 minutes, seemed like permanent science fiction. The prediction of a nuclear-powered jumbo jet carrying 1000 people, only partly came true 40 years later with the Airbus A380.

There were also the concepts that appeared, but didn't have the right stuff to remain. The idea of high speed cylindrical trains, traveling through underground vacuum tubes at 6000kph, had a precedent. In the 19th century, Brunel had devised an atmospheric railway, using vacuum power to overcome gradients.[47] Tootling along in Tokyo with a Cosmo AP rotary provided the satisfaction of a concept realized. However, business reality was bringing Mazda down to earth. Still heavily focused on rotary, Mazda's sales numbers didn't pick up once the first gas crunch eased. The numbers did improve for other companies.

1975 Mazda sales were 22% lower than 1974's result, and, by the end of 1975 calendar year, Mazda was close to bankrupt. 1975 saw a loss of ¥17.3 billion or around $60 million. Approximately 25% of industrial jobs in Hiroshima were Mazda connected, and this had the Sumitomo bank worried. The bank was Mazda's second largest shareholder and creditor, with over $200 million to be lost if Mazda went under. The bank had to step in and rescue Mazda. So it was that Sumitomo bank put some of its guys on Mazda's board of directors, to rectify the red ink.

A key appointment was Tsutomu Murai as Mazda's executive VP in December 1974. Tsutomu Murai had the power to make key personnel changes, which included making Yoshiki Yamasaki, former Hiroshima plant boss, head of production. It was also the end of the Matsuda family's five-decade autocratic reign of Mazda. Kouhei Matsuda, standing company President, took the heat. Employees were afraid of Matsuda san, and woe betide anyone brave enough to deliver bad news. Thus, the company muddled on for too long, set on a rotary course.

Tsutomu Murai, and some Mazda executives, looked for new strategies to dig Toyo Kogyo out of the corporate hole. The first move was to make its one time hot seller better value. For America, the by-now coupe only RX-3 of March 1977, was 40lb lighter for more mpg and $150 cheaper to flatter the hip pocket. A sub-four grand bait price and five-year/75,000 mile warranty, was a short run move to lure buyers back from the dark side. In Japan, a 'Dispatched Worker Program' was initiated, to replenish lost salesmen that had left Mazda dealers after the first gas crunch.

Company volunteers undertook a two-week sales training course, and were then sent off to parts of the country where dealers were short-handed. At its peak, nearly 3000 volunteers were in the scheme. Realizing the dire financial straits Mazda was in, a compliant company union accepted delayed and smaller bonuses, to protect the workforce from further layoffs and base salary reductions. The collective management also realized it was time for less rotary. So the new 1977 GLC-type Familia and 1978 Capella/626 didn't have a Wankel. Plus, rotary Luce Legatos were mostly for Japanese consumption.

A reordering of business, and making products the international public actually wanted, put Mazda in a much stronger position by the end of 1977. The firm even enjoyed better relations with component suppliers. Symbolizing the new state of play, Kouhei Matsuda handed over Mazda's presidency to Yoshiki Yamasaki. All of this, including the important arrival of the round 323/GLC, was very timely, because Mazda had its house in order before the Iranian Revolution-influenced second World Fuel Crisis of 1979/80. OPEC took pity on the planet and only doubled the price of oil overnight this time.

World Fuel Crisis II

Experiences around the world were similar to the 1973/74 episode, but there was more to it than just OPEC. In America, the gas lines were back, and so were the anecdotes. In mid-1979, at a LA gas station, a pistol-toting young man jumped a line of 50 motorists to fill up. Slightly earlier, a pregnant woman was beaten up by car owners, because they thought she jumped her place in the line. It was a case of love thy neighbor, but only after the gas tank was full. West Coast shortages were also exacerbated by California's environmental myopic vision of a lead free utopia.

Leaded gasoline the state had, but a shortage of refinery capacity for unleaded gas contributed to long gas lines. With more and more cars taking the catalytic converter/unleaded emissions route, motorists needed that unleaded gas. In England, the gas station price rose over one third between mid-1978 and mid-1979, and the fuel crisis hadn't even started yet. This locality was still using leaded gas. Writing for *CAR* in 1979, Edward Francis noted, in the article 'Down on the forecourt,' that there were fewer independently-owned gas stations by the '70s. Moving through the decade, there was a UK trend to fewer, large, big oil company-owned gas stations supplying less gas, to more motorists.(48)

European experiences of the second gas crunch looked like what the Japanese had gone through in 1973/74. In Greece, an odd numbers licensing system banned half the nation's cars on alternate weekends, except for tourists. Greece also adopted a temporary 50mph speed limit, TV broadcasts were restricted, and there was a ban on neon signs. In France, there was a government campaign to reduce motorist gasoline usage, using the mythical 'Gaspi' creature, that represented one liter of wasted gas. Using gas station-provided guidebooks, one would become a Gaspi hunter, doing things like pumping tires 4.5psi over recommendation, to save a liter of gas and slay the dreaded Gaspi.

Diesel car popularity was on the rise in Europe, diesel car economy was better, and diesel attracted a lower government excise. On a global basis, the 20-member International Energy Agency called for oil usage cuts by all, if any one member was caught short by over 7%. The rumor was that Belgium, Sweden and Japan were already past their quota by spring 1979. All the above showed how important the price of oil, and car fuel economy, now was. If the rotary engine was to survive, something special had to be done.

Mazda's Project Phoenix

Mazda's rotary champion, Kenichi Yamamoto, was still around, and still supported the cause of Wankel engines built in Hiroshima. As a Mazda company director, and boss of rotary development, he was able to convince the Sumitomo Bank that Mazda's rotary engine was a viable concern. The dream of putting a 12A in everything from a GLC on up was over, but Sumitomo Bank bought into the idea of Mazda using rotary in a more selective way. The agreement was based on Kenichi Yamamoto's promise of improvements in rotary engine pollution control, and better fuel economy.

Yamamoto san had proof that this was already under way: he was in charge of Project Phoenix, which sought to raise rotary from the gas crunch ashes by getting more precious mpg. The aim was to improve 12A/13B economy by 20% in 1975, and by 40% for 1976. Mazda got rotary working in the first place; now its R&D tried to boost economy and reduce manufacturing costs. Apart from TCP and SIP construction methods, Mazda redesigned the 12A/13B combustion chamber. The MDR chamber shape was followed by LDR, and Mazda tried to limit ancillary power loss too. Torque and pollution control took priority over horsepower, as Mazda looked carefully for better EPA mileage numbers.

Tougher car … tougher engine

Along the way, twin changed to single dizzy, and the Wankel warranty improved yet again. When the 12A/13B were at three years/50,000 miles, Mazda compared its quality to Rolls-Royce; now it had the confidence, in 1977, to offer a standard five years/75,000 miles on the 12A and 13B that might be powering one's North American RX-3, RX-4 or Cosmo coupe. Unlike Mazda's previous three-year warranty, the five-year one was transferable. That is, if the first owner sold their car before the five-year/75,000-mile limit expired, subsequent owners would enjoy the warranty balance.

There was no additional cost for the first or subsequent owners to enjoy the five-year/75,000-mile rotary warranty, but, as before, it only applied to new North American Mazdas sold. It did not work retrospectively. However, at a time when consumers were getting short-changed by inflation-affected, unreliable smog-controlled new cars, that solid warranty was welcome indeed. Mazda also

A 1976 RX-5 racing in Australia. To raise awareness of the Mazda Cosmo/RX-5 in America, one New York Mazda dealer entered a Cosmo Coupe in the 1976 24 Hours of Daytona! (Courtesy www.ausrotary.com)

worked in some Cosmo coupe improvements for 1977 MY. In its first model year of 1976, the Cosmo AP had a rear gray plastic beauty tail trim panel. The next year the gray panel was swapped for a tailwidth wide reflector strip.

Market perceptions of Cosmo AP

As if that wasn't fancy enough, Mazda brought out a more expensive Landau-roofed Cosmo AP, in July 1977, for the Japanese market. If the normal fastback Cosmo AP wasn't Detroit enough for you, then the Cosmo L would seal the deal. A notchback roof with padded vinyl top was in evidence. Indeed, in Detroit parlance, the glass-pillared hardtop might have been called a formal roof. Either way, Cosmo II's extensive standard equipment, posh interior and exterior, would distract one's mind from the 13B's altered state.

The effect of Project Phoenix manifested itself in the performance figures *Road & Track* recorded at Orange County International Raceway. Compared to the RX-4 *R&T* tested in 1974, the Cosmo coupe was decidedly slower in 1976. Using the latest federalized 13B 0-60mph worsened from 9.7 to 11.2 seconds, with the ¼ mile deteriorating from 17.4 seconds at 82mph, to 18.7 seconds at 76mph. Both were manual transmissions cars, but the final drive ratio was now taller, 3.64-to-one versus the previous 3.90-to-one. Plus, with all the design upgrades and plushness over RX-4, the Cosmo coupe was 175lb heftier. However, gas mileage had substantially improved.

Compared to the RX-4's 17.5mpg overall *R&T* figure, the magazine now got 20.5mpg. No doubt the standard five-speed overdrive manual gearbox helped. 1976 was the first year Mazda made a five-speed available in North America. In common with other companies searching for mpg, it was the old four-speed with an overdrive ratio added. *R&T* found the box positive and direct, but especially sticky in the lower gears until the gearbox fluid warmed up. The reworked 13B could still reach redline in the first three gears. However, Mazda was more concerned about economy, and the EPA gas mileage ratings, which had been its nemesis for years.

The Mazda rotary had long been synonymous with high-performance, and this was still true in the depressed mid- to late-'70s, when luxo cars were king. *Road & Track* tested a Caddy Seville 350 V8 and Mercedes 280S sedan in 1975, with 0-60mph times of 13.3 and 16.3 seconds respectively. Next to this, a Cosmo coupe was going like grease lightning, with a plusher interior than both cars put together. However, of greater import in the smog era was driveability: did one's ride start

The interior of an Australian spec RX-5 Coupe, with optional JATCO console automatic shifter. In some export markets the Cosmo AP was called the RX-5, with piston editions denoted 121. (Courtesy www.ausrotary.com)

and run properly? The general consensus was that Cosmo was very good.

R&T judged Cosmo's semi-auto choke a boon. Pull it out on start-up, with the device shutting off automatically, when the engine coolant hit a pre-set temp. *Road Test*'s 1977 Cosmo ran even stronger, doing a 17.8-second ¼ mile. This magazine said the 13B felt stronger than the advertised power, and titled its report 'Powered by a 13B rotary motor, this Japanese muscle car can fly.' This particular Cosmo coupe out-economied a Datsun 810, getting 25.9mpg, which only dropped to 20mpg in performance testing.

Going back to *R&T*'s Cosmo, the magazine said the model didn't display the backfiring or deceleration stumbling that *R&T* experienced on previous rotary Mazdas. However, *R&T*'s 1977 RX-4 sedan, with the same revised 13B, did an 18.8-second ¼ mile at 75mph, with an overall economy of 18mpg. In addition, this 13B had the quirk of a 4- to 5-second lag on acceleration rate, being resumed if one took the foot off the loud pedal, and re-applied thereafter. Cars with the same spec 13B/five-speed power team, but three different results. Put it down to the performance/economy lottery caused by smog controls.

Other cars, domestic and imported, also showed significant variation in testing, between the same, and different, magazine test samples. For the record, the retuned 13B made 110 net horses at six grand, the same as before. However, torque had changed from 117lb/ft at 3500rpm to 120lb/ft at 4000rpm. *Road Test*'s Cosmo was quick enough to match a contemporary base-engine Corvette. As a value assessment, *Road Test* compared the Cosmo with the Chevy Monza Towne coupe V8. The Monza, ironically, was originally intended by GM to debut with a rotary engine.

As things stood, the Chevy was $4876 against the similarly-optioned $5800 Cosmo. Indeed, one could also get a midsize Chevy Monte Carlo for less loot, the class of car that inspired the Cosmo in the first place. Still, one couldn't get four-wheel disk brakes on Monza, nor a five-year engine warranty on the Monte's V8. Then there were Cosmo's standard reclining buckets, a feature GM had an aversion towards. *Road Test* judged Cosmo more economical and slightly faster than Monza V8, not to mention one of the best value for money rides in class.

Fit and finish by Toyo Kogyo was a class above anything GM could deliver, even if the Cosmo's interior and exterior raised concerns. The standard wall-to-wall carpeting, AM/FM radio, tint, fast glass and full instrumentation with 8000rpm tach and 130mph speedo, were welcome. Indeed, Cosmo featured a powered, adjustable driver door-mounted reversing mirror, which was a faddish feature of the hour. However, the nature of said interior didn't go down so well with the reviewers. The most strident criticism came from *Road & Track*, showing its historical pro-import-style bias.

With similar feelings for the RX-4's Las Vegas decor, *R&T* considered the Cosmo's interior more in keeping with a brothel than a sports car. Much of its staff didn't much care for the US personal car lavishness of Cosmo. However, its staff did concede Cosmo was comfy, especially spacious in front, and not bad in the rear for a 2+2. Excellent ergonomics and handy stalk controls for headlamp dimmer and wipers were *R&T*-mentioned, as was the test car's optional a/c system. Very sound air distribution from Mazda's traditional end-of-dash eyeball swivel vents, as well as two center ones. The a/c could be blended with the standard heat and vent system to achieve an optimal result, regardless of encountered clime.

R&T was surprised Mazda's 'shift up or die' tach warning buzzer was absent from Cosmo. The 13B was as smooth and redline willing as ever – was the omission an oversight or intended? The Cosmo coupe was definitely designed with America in mind. It was the car Mazda hoped would revive its fortunes, in this once-important rotary market. Industry folks also thought this was the goal of the pending two-door. Given US market cars had become a veritable pachinko parlor symphony of chimes and buzzers, perhaps Mazda thought they should leave one out? Most '70s domestics and imports had audible warnings for doors left ajar and seatbelt usage; a further tach buzzer might have proved too annoying in a mini luxo personal car.

The exterior left *R&T* staff cold. The Cosmo's styling was considered dull. Once again, any US personal car cue connections were either frowned upon or ignored. *Road Test* was kinder, noting that styling was a subjective matter and stating that the slightly odd rear ¼ window became endearing. Handling and ride produced a four-star consensus. While miffed about independent suspension not being aboard, *R&T* judged Cosmo a fine handling/riding car. The more techy rear suspension was considered a worthwhile improvement over RX-4. *Road Test* felt the same, except that the ride was a bit firm.

Everyone noted Cosmo's reduced handling prowess on imperfect surfaces, as well as Mazda's established precise feel recirculating ball steering, known for minimal play about the center. 1976 saw Mazda offer Cosmo and RX-4 with optional power-assisted steering for the first time. As the ultimate sports/luxo version of the RX-4 genre, *Road & Track* judged Cosmo coupe as a good effort. However, as a 'new' model designed to excite, bring something new, and return flagging Mazda North American sales, Cosmo was considered questionable.

The Cosmo's brakes symbolized its story. Four-wheel disks sounded like an advancement over RX-4, but *R&T* found a surprising amount of fade. *Road Test* found absolutely no brake fade, but the 157½ foot stop from 60mph was only average. The RX-4's disk/drum set up had been considered excellent already, so once again the Cosmo's rate of return seemed negligible over RX-4 coupe. *Road & Track* opined that Mazda had produced a car it thought would go down a storm in the States, then added "Or maybe they [the Japanese] like it?"[49]

Mazda's take on the luxo US intermediate, the Cosmo Landau. With 99kW 13B this flagship could do 180kph (112mph), but all that luxury slowed things down. Mazda's official figure for the 77kW 12A RX-7 said the sports car could touch 190kph. (Courtesy Mazda)

History shows Cosmo coupe, or RX-5, went down like a lead balloon in America. It seemed buyers in this locale wanted 'all new,' not just improved. However, the facts also show the Japanese really did dig Cosmo AP. Over 55,000 were sold in the two-door's first year, and it soon settled down to over 3500 units per month. The Cosmo AP was like a new Savanna for Mazda, and, for a time, was Japan's top selling sports/luxo personal car, and even had imitators. The Nissan Gazelle personal car had a Trans Am-like Gazelle hood graphic, plus Landau and faux opera window treatment.

Road & Track may have thought Cosmo's handbrake lever, steering wheel and shifter knob weren't friends of the forest, but they were real. So too were the Cosmo's opera windows. In Japan at least, Cosmo seemed like the real deal, and quite a deal. With the optional $190 14in factory aluminum rims, the 1977 Cosmo L looked like it was doing 180kph, whilst standing still. Using the top 99Kw 13B it could do this speed, and match Nissan's six-pot Gazelle. However, not even Nissan's Fairlady-derived straight six could match the 13B's smoothness.

Cosmo AP's base sticker 1979 premium over Luce Legato was ¥1,105,000 versus ¥996,000. Using the 66Kw 2-liter I4 Luce Legato could touch exactly 100mph. However, the blockish sedan didn't stir the imagination like Cosmo. It wasn't a global success as the RX-5; the piston 121 fared a shade better. That said, strong home sales saw Cosmo AP continue, in 1979-81 Series II form, as a Japanese market exclusive. Good sales meant, overall, Cosmo AP was a profitable Mazda model. The piston/rotary Cosmo range continued into the '80s, starting with the 1982 edition, based on the new HB Luce platform. Other rotary-powered cars weren't so fortunate.

Whatever happened to the Ro80?

That late '60s technical marvel from Neckarsulm started with a bang, and ended in a puff of smoke, but, in the beginning, success seemed assured. As a 2-liter West German executive car, the Ro80 was tops. Germans historically liked the refinement of small sixes in the 2-liter class, and NSU's two-rotor 995cc Wankel was smoother than any piston powerplant. Quiet too, designed for restful autobahn cruising, the NSU motor had a soft whir, compared to the Mazda 10A's torque-biased, harder edge. The Ro80's 0.355 Cd factor was unusual for the day, as was the nose down, tail up styling. This car was designed to fly through the air.

Four-wheel independent suspension, four-wheel disk brakes and three-speed semi-auto Fichtel und Sachs gearbox, crumple zone safety body and first rate power steering in a compact-sized front-drive package, made the Ro80 the Citroën DS of the late '60s. Compared to this, the BMW 2000 sedan was old strudel, and Daimler-Benz made stale strudel. The Bavarian's 520 successor of 1972 was also uber conventional, even sporting rear drums. Mercedes' 1968 Compact was also very by-the-numbers, with offend-no-one three-box styling. For bahn burning, little NSU had outdone its larger German rivals in every department, except, as it would transpire, motor durability.

The euphoria generated by the Ro80 banished any thoughts of a pending Titanic disaster; the press spoke with one positive voice. Britain's *Motor* magazine titled its February 3 1968, NSU Ro80 road test 'Car of the Year – or Decade?' As European Car of the Year, NSU adcopy merely mirrored the sentiment. "Enjoy The Future Now." Objective fellows became decidedly giddy with delight. One of them was *CAR*'s Ronald Barker, who recalled the heady days, 20 years down the road, when picking up a 14-year-old Ro80 in 1988.

As an English person, Barker admitted the Ro80 overcame a personal bias against buying German. It started with a fat press kit and a flip number electric clock, encased in the then-fashionable brown plastic decorative shell trim. The clock carried a silver inscription plaque which said, "Premiere NSU Ro80 August 1968." Barker said, in 1988, that the clock expired years earlier in a puff of smoke. Much the same happened to the Ro80, but, before it did, there was time for show and please do tell.

Lunch with Sir Alec

So enamored with Ro80 was Barker, he contacted NSU UK PR man Alan Wheatley to invite over top NSU development engineer Dr Walter Froede. Barker then escorted Herr Froede to luncheon with British Leyland's top people, past and present, taking along a Ro80 as a conversation piece. Present at the Longbridge do were BL's chief engineer Charlie Griffin, suspension supremo Alex Moulton and the legendary Alec 'Mr Mini' Issigonis. A nice lunch and discussion were had – not too concerned with cars, according to Barker. The group then went for a drive with the Ro80, whereupon the BL folks said nice things about the car's ride comfort and handling.

Rather rudely, the BL crew were more silent on the rotary subject than the Ro80's own two-rotor motor. The good doktor took it in his stride, but maybe that was because he knew about the elephant in the room better than anyone. In the early '70s, NSU engineering and marketing men held several press conferences in London hotels. Here, claims were advanced on how the latest Ro80 motor had longer seal life and better fuel economy. At one such shindig, *Autocar*'s Stuart Bladon informed Ronald Barker that *Autocar*'s long-term Ro80 test car had been superb. However, the car's rotor apex seals had just expired on the way to the 1972 press conference they were attending.(50)

The Ro80's charm vanished in a cloud of blue smoke. If ever one wanted a car to make it good, it was here and now with the Ro80, but it just wasn't happening. Illustrated dictionaries would have been well advised to carry a picture of the Ro80's apex seal under the Achilles heel entry. Long before that 1972 press conference, the fate of NSU and Ro80 had been sealed.

Ro80, the Macbeth of cars

Very quickly, the NSU rotor apex seal problem surfaced, and NSU started handing out free replacement rotaries under warranty by the truckload. The Ro80 motor was something of a work in progress, and didn't take kindly to stop, start city driving. As a small company, NSU adopted the British practice of R&D on the fly. NSU shareholders didn't much care for 'free' and 'truckload,' and so it was that a stormy shareholder meeting saw the decision to sell 59.5% of NSU shares to VW.(51)

Audi NSU Auto Union AG

In 1969, the boards of VW, AutoUnion and NSU agreed to the Auto Union-NSU merger, creating Audi NSU Auto Union AG. VW held the majority interest, and wanted NSU because of its new front-drive K70 sedan. Anxious to move out of the air-cooled, rear-drive Beetle era, the K70 was seen as the path to the future. The real path came with VW's own Golf. In the meantime, NSU was paired with VW's reborn prestige brand Audi. The Ro80 was sold alongside the new Audi 100, and those rotor seal problems didn't go away with the corporate merger.

In Australia, NSU's concessionaire was John Caskey Holdings (JCH). JCH said NSU had tested its rotary in all conditions imaginable, and that it was indestructible and that JCH would give the Ro80 an 18-month/18,000-mile warranty. Unfortunately, the Ro80 proved as unreliable in Australia as elsewhere. It was common for Ro80 owners driving past each other to hold up fingers, signifying what number replacement engine they were on. JCH closed in 1973, whereupon unsold Australian Ro80 stock was wholesaled at half retail price.

In West Germany, when the replacement engines stopped coming, pragmatic motorists resorted to the German Ford Taunus V4. It was a rough motor, but it was compact and the next best thing, given how far forward the NSU Wankel sat in the Ro80's nose. In 1993, UK Ro80 specialist Simon Kremer of Ro Techniks said he had conversations with former NSU employees, and, at the very least, a Ro80 coupe was planned. Sadly, the problems with the NSU rotary engine, and VW takeover, meant the Ro80 stayed pretty stagnant until the last one rolled out of Neckarsulm in 1977.

Kremer also said that towards the end of Ro80 production, engine reliability was getting solved. However, the gently driven 1977 Ro80 *Thoroughbred & Classic Cars* featured in its retrospective 1993 article, suggested otherwise. Driven 25,000 miles between 1986 and 1992, this Ro80 had just had its NSU rotor tip seals replaced.[(52)] GM shelved its GMRCE because, apart from lousy gas mileage, it couldn't get better than 30,000 miles out of rotary without changing those seals. By the 1990s, specialists claimed they could rebuild a Ro80 motor with reliability included. It seems hard to imagine how small firms could solve the wear problem, when giants like GM and Mercedes had failed.

In the '90s, the Mazda 12A could be rebuilt with new parts for half the price of a rebuilt NSU motor. And the 12A brought larger displacement, more torque, five extra horses, an 80,000-mile life and a greater ability to deal with stop-start urban driving. Thus, when the original Mazda RX-7 got popular in Europe, during the '80s, the Ro80's engine swap of choice became the 12A. With this motor, the Ro80 became the car it should have been from the start.

If only NSU had swallowed its pride and bought in 10As from Mazda. That motor was available from the start of the Ro80's life. As it stood, Graham Robson bestowed a fitting epitaph with "Look, touch, but drive only gently."[(53)] Neckarsulm lived on as a place to make Porsche 924s and 944s. In 1985, the VW Group simplified Audi's name from Audi NSU Auto Union AG to Audi AG. With this, the final vestige of the 37,204 Ro80s was almost laid to rest, but not quite.

In 1987, the Ro80 was reincarnated as the aerodynamic new B3 Audi 80. Heretofore, the Audi 80 had been rather brick-like, now it took on the corporate 1983 aero Audi 100 style, but also many of the Ro80's ideas. There was the surefooted front-drive chassis, forward-mounted motor for excellent directional stability, high-tailed compact aero body. The public and press wowed over this new Audi 80, so very modern and the perfect partner for Audi's Vorsprung durch Technik slogan. Older heads had seen it before with even more striking styling, and less understeer courtesy of a much smoother and lighter rotary powerplant.

Praise by omission

The 1980s Audis were known for excellent gas mileage, linked to tall gearing and that jello mold styling. In contrast, the Ro80 had a second Achilles heel with fuel economy. For top speed, 0-60mph and overall economy, *Autocar* got 110mph/13.8 seconds/22.7mpg, with the Mercedes 230/4; with the Ro80, the figures were 107mph/13.9 seconds/18.2mpg. Poor gas mileage in Europe was the final kiss of death. Ronald Barker envisioned the mood on deck as the good ship NSU sank towards Davy Jones' locker, "There was a time when license fees, coming in from all over the globe, must have helped sustain life at Neckarsulm, while free replacement power units were being distributed in bulk to meet all the guarantee claims."[54]

Nowhere in Barker's article was Mazda's name mentioned, not even once. Indeed, the only comment on Mazda's Wankel, in the whole issue, concerned said motor's smoothness. It seemed Mazda had done such an excellent job making rotary reliable, that 20 years on, the Japanese marque wasn't even associated with the Ro80 debacle in people's minds. Mazda was one of the aforementioned companies handing in license money to NSU. So was GM, via Curtiss-Wright. GM was paying 'ol CW $5 million every six months to keep its '75 Monza rotary dream alive. The mighty one was even showing off its GMRCE at the 1973 Frankfurt Motor Show, in a flashy Vette proto.

Dreamt up in those heady days before the fuel crisis, when GM had loads of money and time on its hands, the XP-897 GT showcar was ordered by GM's Ed Cole. This dream Corvette study was designed around the two-rotor GMRCE, with style courtesy of the GM Experimental Studio. Built on a modified Porsche 914 chassis, XP-897 GT featured a Pininfarina-constructed steel body. The mid-engine sports car had its 180 horse GMRCE sitting transversely, driving through an automatic transaxle planned for the future GM X car.

Displayed around the time of the first gas crunch, and with unreliable apex rotor seal durability, GM knew this car was going to remain a show pony. By 1997, it ended up with UK car collector Tom Falconer in Kent, and was using a Mazda 13B rotary. Well, if two rotors were good, four must be better? Hence GM's four-rotor 1973 Experimental Showcar Corvette. This study was done to match the four-rotor Wankels that Mercedes and Mazda had showed. The XP-882 chassis had been used earlier as a Corvette showcar, but here the transverse 400 cube V8 had been tossed in favor of two joined dual rotor RC2-195 GM Research Engineering units.

The result was the equivalent of 585 cubic inches and over 500 net horses, something people salivated over as smog controls started to bite. This package, with Bill Mitchell-directed gullwing body, did the 1973 show circuit before being quietly mothballed. However, the car did make a show circuit comeback as the 1976 Aerovette, by which time people were more concerned with the cheapest subcompact they could shoehorn themselves into to beat the gas crisis and inflation. The regular C3 Corvette plodded on, getting slower and more expensive with each passing year.

The public never got a gullwing mid-engine Vette, rotary powered or otherwise. However, they did receive a Wankel-powered Citroën, and many wish they hadn't. The new Citroën GS of 1970 was a super clean sheet design European small family car, but the rotary engine Bi-rotor edition was a commercial lemon of the first order. It was as unreliable as the French working week is short. The model was on offer to dedicated Citroën devotees as a commercial trial. By the time the trial was over, owners were told they could keep the cars if they agreed to termination of the Citroën service agreement.

In other words, any more problems and it's your baby. Some audacious souls actually kept the cars, and the few surviving GS Birotors have become valuable collector cars. The Birotor's Comotor engine was a joint venture product, cooked up by Citroën and NSU. The commercial failure of the rotary GS put an end to the motor's future. GM had also announced, by September 1974, that its GMRCE was on ice indefinitely. All this had put enough red ink in Citroën's ledger, that rotary, plus the new CX, pushed the firm into Peugeot's hands in 1974. It was an understatement to say Mazda had succeeded where others had failed, but could even determined Toyo Kogyo make rotary work in the '80s?

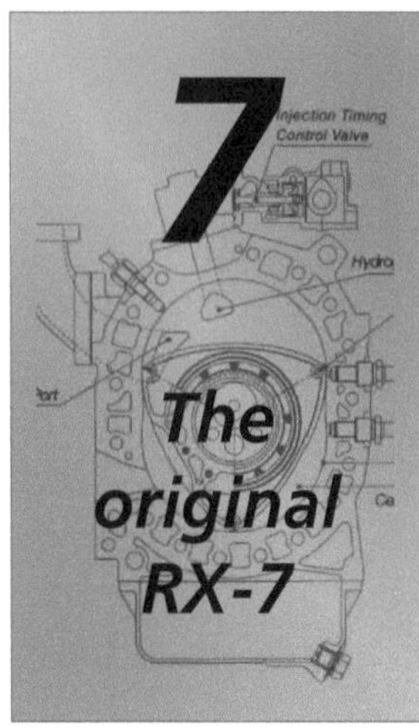

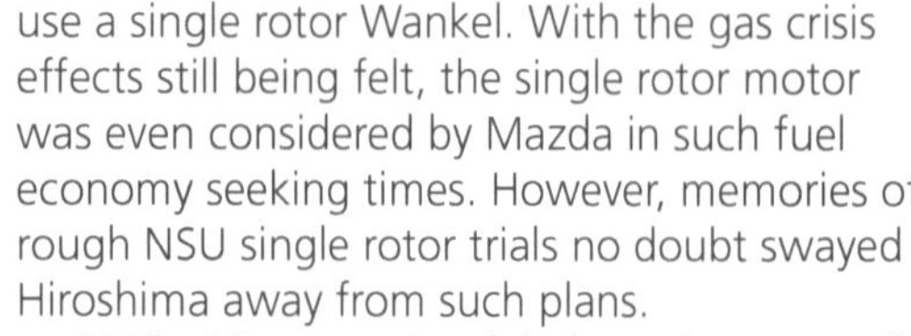

Out of the mouths of babes ... and *Road & Track* ...

The mid to late '70s wasn't a good time to be a sports car. With the upheavals of the gas crunch, recession, insurance premiums etc, corporate parents had little love for their two-door sports car offspring. Witness how GM had ignored the Corvette, BL sent the rubber-bumper MGB to Coventry, and Porsche made punters pay through the nose for badge cachet. As the Datsun 260Z morphed into the 280ZX, one might have thought all was lost, but Toyo Kogyo still had fond recollections of its snappy '60s Cosmo Sport 110S.

Just before fingers became too arthritic to don stringback gloves, Mazda was working on something special, and somehow *Road & Track* knew. In *R&T*'s 1976 Guide to Sports & GT cars issue Cosmo coupe assessment, it said what Mazda really needed to revive fortunes in North America was a sports car. In addition, this would be the correct home for Mazda's still-amazing rotary engine. A sports car to take on the Fiat X1/9 and Porsche 924 wouldn't steal sales from existing sedan-based rotary Mazdas. *R&T* also speculated such a sports car might use a single rotor Wankel. With the gas crisis effects still being felt, the single rotor motor was even considered by Mazda in such fuel economy seeking times. However, memories of rough NSU single rotor trials no doubt swayed Hiroshima away from such plans.

R&T's vision wasn't solely from the Monrovia HQ crystal ball, there had been rumors circulating that Mazda had been working on a sports car since 1974. The rumor got even stronger at the hour of the 1977 US RX-3 SP. Mazda's '70s sales experience guided it towards sports car thinking. Out of all its rotary ranges, the sporty Savanna RX-3 had been its top seller, and most immune to the gas crunch. Over 50% of Savanna/RX-3s sold had been coupes – more encouragement for the sports car route. If anyone is going to tolerate rotary's thirst in a fuel crisis, it will more likely be a sports car buyer.

A Chevy fan's recollection of the US RX-3 suggested a sports car would be a good home for rotary, "I met a guy who had a '73 Mazda wagon; it revved over 12,000 if I remember correctly. Weird sensation, not much sound, but it would go pretty fast." The name of Mazda's new hero? That would be RX-7. In Japan it was Savanna RX-7 – such was the high esteem in which the Japanese regarded the old Savanna (RX-3), that its name lived on. Seven years winning over the Japanese public with the Savanna nameplate would have been wasted marketing, if the Savanna moniker was ditched.

In export markets, the new car would be called plain RX-7, the Savanna name being unknown to all but aficionados outside Japan. Mazda purposely skipped RX-6, feeling it didn't sound nice. Toyo Kogyo was definitely influenced by the pre-existing Triumph TR7, launched in 1975. Indeed, the Triumph was certainly a Mazda marketing target for RX-7 in America for spec and pricing. The older Lotus Super 7, and the lucky nature of the number seven in Western culture, probably also convinced Mazda that RX-7 was the right nametag.

This was the car unveiled to a select group of US auto journalists, in late February 1978. Back then Chuck Nerpel recounted the unveiling in the May 1978 issue of *Motor Trend*. As Nerpel said, the Japanese do a better job of keeping their new cars a secret. Secrecy at Mazda's Miyoshi proving grounds on Hiroshima's outskirts came courtesy of a high barbwire

The Miyoshi proving grounds were completed by Mazda in the mid 1960s. The Cosmo Sport 110S, and all Mazdas thereafter, have received a good workout at the facility. (Courtesy Mazda)

chainlink fence, security guard patrol and veritable forest cover. Completed in the mid '60s, Miyoshi's high-banked track, electronically timed dragstrip, rough paved areas, dirt roads and water baths had all the trial and tribulations any automobile could possibly endure.

Defining the sporting pedigree

Mazda's designers had a relatively easy time with RX-7, codenamed Project X605. The Hiroshima designers and engineers never gave up on the possibility of another sports car post Cosmo Sport, and they were rewarded with creative freedom on Project X605. Chief stylist M Maeda san was clear on RX-7 being a clean sheet design, with no management directions to look like anything else. However, there were some design parameters laid down. Project X605 was to have lots of interior room – a practical consideration for Mazda's once-important North American market. The shape was to have low aerodynamic drag and good see-out visibility, along with an integrated roof rollbar to cope with possible federal roof strength tests. No convertible variants for this little Mazda.

In spite of the abovementioned freedom, the RX-7's pop-up headlamp visage bore some resemblance to the Porsche 924. The middle section's purposely designed modern jet fighter-style greenhouse and rear fascia, were reminiscent of the Mazda Cosmo Sport 110S. The rear fascia's high-mounted indentation home for the rear license plate, was called a 'Baroque Depression' by *Road & Track*'s Werner Buhrer, when that journal carried out styling analysis of the RX-7.

A fundamental philosophy distinction, between the '60s Cosmo Sport and '70s RX-7, was that the latter was going to be an affordable, volume model. RX-7 project chief Moriyuki Watanabe stated that the RX-7 was designed to be less complex and easier to make than the low volume Cosmo Sport. Practical safety concerns meant that apart from the roof rollbar, the RX-7 unibody had extra box framing around the passenger compartment, plus door cavity side impact bars. Increasing importance of aerodynamics for fuel economy saw the original RX-7 shape finished up at the Japan Auto Research Institute (JARI). Here, the wind tunnel facility was used to test full scale models.

Completing the aero work at JARI saw a drag coefficient of 0.36, very sound for the era. This reading rose to 0.381 when the pop-up headlamps were activated for night riding. Pop-up headlamps were popular sports car items for the time. Even though the RX-7 used familiar visual clues, the overall effect was quite unique, and judged attractive by press and public alike. The late '70s weren't known for the beauty of its sporty cars. The Jaguar XJS, Aston Martin Lagonda and Stutz Blackhawk seemed to exemplify some perverse contemporary correlation between expense and ugliness.

The RX-7 wisely avoided an overt interpretation of the fashionable wedge route taken by other '70s luminaries, like the Triumph TR7, Alfa Alfetta GTV coupe and VW Scirocco. Given that the RX-7 was styled entirely inhouse, the car raised the question: why did creations from other parts of the globe have to be so appearance-challenged? The RX-7's interior held no surprises. As per sports car practice of the day, essential instruments, and no more, in a driver facing binnacle, center console with HVAC controls, stereo, traditional 'between-the-seats' handbrake and floor shifter, Mazda's super-effective end-of-dash swivel eyeball vents and no wood trim whatsoever.

A grip of the spoked leather-covered tiller, and casual look around, informed one of comfy space. Interior planning for RX-7 saw the sports car as two-seater for North America, and 2+2 for Japan and most other export markets. With the small folding rear seats of the 2+2 export spec, Britain's *Autocar* discerned front/rear legroom of 40/25½in, with the stock front

The FB Savanna RX-7's introductory 100-horse 12A/four-speed power team on the car's March 1978 release. In May 1978 *Motor Trend* commented on the 12A's reliability, and Mazda's ten years of rotary development and production. (Courtesy Mazda)

reclining buckets moved all the way back on their runners. Lift the large unframed glass hatch, and trunk accommodation transpired to be 4cu/ft, rising to nine units with the rear seats folded.

RX-7 nuts and bolts

The RX-7 had full width bumpers that the Fiat X1/9 didn't have, and multi-colored taillight combo in place of the Trans Am's 'go dim and guess' red taillamps. Underneath what looked like a sports car, Toyo Kogyo engineered a true sports car. In the best traditions of the MG T series and Porsche's 356, sedan components were refined for adventurous driving. In the RX-7's case that meant the basic layout from the RX-3 coupe, but with a great amount of development work. Yes, the RX-3's recirculating ball steering made it over, but on RX-7 a broader steering shaft reduced distortion and added feel plus precision.

Given non-power steering was at hand, recirculating ball steering may have had a reputation for being a bit dead about the center, but transmitted less road shock and was lighter in parking lots than rack and pinion. The RX-7's steering box was also a heavier duty unit than on RX-3s. Once again, MacPherson strut front suspension, coils and anti-swaybar were present. However, there was a tensioning rod for front and rear location of the lower strut. The lower part of the coil spring was now tapered, so it could be closer to the kingpin axis. Such revised geometry meant narrower steering offset, less roadshock through the steering column, and more stable braking.

The original RX-7, shown with its earliest dashboard, continued Mazda's excellent HVAC system reputation. Since R100 days, those dash-end eyeball swivel vents have been legendary for superb through flow. (Courtesy Mazda)

The RX-7 and Porsche 924 both had MacPherson strut front ends, but RX-7 utilized a rear live axle, not the 924's independent rear end. A retrogressive move at first glance, but Mazda had things under control. In the '60s, Fiat and Alfa did excellent handling live-axle cars, that had said live axles properly located. The RX-7 was just such a car. Mazda played around with a sophisticatedly located live axle on the CD Cosmo coupe. This was a moderate success, but, with RX-7, Mazda switched from Panhard rod to race-proven Watts linkage for live-axle lateral location.

Factory-backed racing RX-3s had used Watts linkage. The CD Cosmo's Panhard rod would have produced a less than satisfactory roll center, and have made RX-7 75mm longer. RX-7 rear suspension also featured coils, but not the RX-3's leaf springs, four longitudinal arms, gas-filled Kayaba shocks and on the upspec RX-7 GS, an 18mm anti-swaybar. The rear shocks were widely spaced and nearly vertical, valved for equal bound and rebound. RX-7 damper setting was selected for softness on low speed bumps for good ride, firming up at speed for greater control.

When the Porsche 924 came out, it was initially known for its magic carpet ride at speed, which deteriorated badly at lower velocity on poor surfaces. This was especially true on US roads, and Mazda wanted to avoid this embarrassment with RX-7. Braking was courtesy of conventional power assisted 9in front disks and 8in rear drums, like a 924 too. Connecting all this good stuff to the road were four-bolt 13in rims and tires. Mazda's standard spec RX-7 four-speed manual, which the company hoped to sell in America for under $7 grand, yen/$ strength permitting, had 13 x 5in perforated steel rims wearing 165 HR steel radials.

Then came the optional version, GS in Mazda parlance and 500 bucks pricier, with 185/70 HR 13in steel radials; all one would want given power steering was unavailable. Pushing the parking lot workout limit were optional 13 x 5.5in aluminum rims. Continuing Japanese tradition of comprehensive standard spec, the base RX-7 came with rev counter, voltmeter, quartz clock, reclining buckets, tint glass, AM/FM stereo radio and front anti-swaybar. Options included tilt-up removable sunroof, air-conditioning, automatic transmission and those aforementioned alloys.

However, one standard feature that defined

RX-7 was that 12A rotary engine. At one time, your Mazda wouldn't leave home without one, but, even by 1978, it made Mazda's sports car special – and determined the car's layout. Mazda engineers had considered a rear-drive mid-engine layout early on, as per Fiat X1/9, but being rotary made Mazda's 'front midship' set up the right sports car ticket. By placing the small, bucket-sized 12A just behind the front axle line, Mazda avoided the practical, and handling, problems of mid-engined sports cars –that is, poor space efficiency, excessive vehicle width, a difficult sill to climb over, poor rearward vision, poor trunk, and a propensity to spin out of control once the high grip limit has been passed.

The Cosmo Sport 110S and RX-7 had one important thing in common: they were the only Mazda rotary cars not to have a piston-bodied equivalent. That showed Mazda's rotary faith in RX-7, and closed the door to RX-7 clone creation.

Mazda's 12A atmo motor, the only choice for early RX-7s, used a four-barrel carb and made 100bhp SAE at 6000rpm and 105lb/ft at 4000rpm on 91 octane unleaded. In Japan, the engine was called 35-cid plus 2, a reference to the 12A's two rotors that took displacement to 70ci. Not a whole bundle of power, and RX-7's 54/46% weight distribution wasn't the 50/50% expected. Mazda launched RX-7 with a thermal reactor 12A, saying it might well go catalytic converter/unleaded, as with other cars, if federal emissions regs got much stricter.

However, all the above seemed small beer next to the important question of reliability. Up to RX-7, Mazda had made 930,000 rotary-powered cars and light trucks; this spoke volumes to consumers. Mazda had introduced their SIP process in mid 1973 to get the chrome layer onto the inside of the combustion chamber easier, in order to hold that crucial protective lubrication film. However, the engineers, with their constantly working test cells, made other improvements to increase durability and efficiency – the inside of a Wankel combustion chamber is a tough place to be.

To further protect the apex seals, now made of iron-based material, the contact area was a 'chilled layer,' crystallized by an electron beam. The side of the combustion chamber was beefed up by gas-nitrizing treatment. This produced a very thin, but corrosion and wear resistant, area. The whole point was to reduce wear, protect the seals, achieve a good seal, and thus maintain the compression ratio. The corner button seal was now flexible. Flexible seals stopped wasted gas going to the exhaust, and helped keep in heat. The last point was key, given the intrinsic poor thermal efficiency of rotary.

To deal with the cool running nature of rotary, the size and shape of the combustion chamber, plus leading sparkplug position, had been altered. There were now three areas of intense burn, evenly spaced around the center ignition electrode, where previously there had been just two. To overcome a well-known Mazda rotary hot start problem, the 12A/13B application electric starter motor now opened the throttle slightly, when coolant temp was over 140F. Hot start problems on all kinds of pollution-controlled cars was a hot button topic in the '70s. Compared to final US RX-3 days, the 12A had gained five horses. Apart from returning to a 4bbl carb, the size of the secondary intake port was now larger and reshaped for better breathing.

Improved 12A breathing also raised economy, as did a smaller and redesigned carb float. The latter item had the side benefit of reducing fuel starvation in hard cornering, another universal problem on performance carb cars. Put all the improvements under one hood, and this was the best 12A Hiroshima had yet made. It was used to power a car with manufacturer dimensions of 4285mm length, 1650mm width and, 260mm height, with starting weight of 1065kg. In imperial measurements, 168in length, 65in width and 49in height for a 2300lb two-seater.

Turning circle was only 31.5ft, showing the benefits of rear-drive on the 95in wheelbase car. However, the most important stat was the 56in/55in front/rear track. Narrow tracks had been the bugbear of early rotary Mazdas. Now the RX-7 still looked cute, but wide track implied handling would be well up to snuff. On the optional 185/70 13in radials, Mazda spoke of a test facility skidpad figure of 0.84g and associated 60mph slalom cone speed.

Factory figures for a five-speed RX-7 GS with standard 3.9:1 final drive showed 0-60mph in 9.2 seconds with ¼-mile sprint in 16.7 seconds. For automatic RX-7s these times worsened to 10.6 and 18 seconds respectively. Maximum torque being set at 4000rpm saw the in gear

The Savanna nameplate was held in such high regard in Japan during 1971-78 that Mazda christened its new sports car Savanna RX-7. It took on MGB, Triumph TR7, Datsun 280ZX and Porsche 924 in its early years. (Courtesy Mazda)

50-70mph acceleration run done in six seconds using fourth gear. Utilizing a 14.5 US-gallon gas tank the RX-7 aimed to go far with projected EPA numbers of 19mpg city and 29mpg highway. The combined overall figure was hoped to be 23mpg.

All the above stats were efficient by late '70s standards. Given the performance and smoothness Wankel delivered in a sports car format, no one could label RX-7 a gas guzzler, not even the EPA. Make no mistake, the RX-7 was a sports car, not a coupe sedan or grand tourer. In fact, it kind of upstaged the sophisticated-seeming RX-5 stablemate with 13B motor. The RX-7 out-accelerated, handled and braked the four-wheel disked RX-5, on mere 12A motorvation. With an EPA 14mpg 1980 Turbo Trans Am looming, RX-7 was looking dynamite. Plus, even the plastic mastodon was worried.

Slipping to a 17-second ¼-mile state for the average 350 V8/automatic combo, the C3 Vette was looking a mite oversize and wasteful next to RX-7. It was fitting that America should indirectly name the original RX-7. The first series RX-7 got the nickname SA22C, from the 1978-80 Series I VIN start. However, come the 1981-83 Series II, the start code in North America changed to FB. This was due to the US Department of Transportation forcing a 17-digit VIN changeover. Some world markets held on to the old SA22C prefix, but many others, including the UK, switched to the FB start from 1981.

The FB tag stuck in subsequent informal naming parlance, and with ensuing RX-7s being known as FC and FD chassis, it's a convenient tag. Whatever the handle, the original RX-7 made its Japanese market debut in March 1978. Letting the RX-4 and Cosmo vacate the area, the RX-7 was a 1979 MY debutante in North America, reached the UK in September 1979. It also reached Australia in 1979 calendar year, at $14,850. International rollouts took longer back in the day, and always commenced with the home market.

Mazda: no longer just rotary

Mazda had become a two-tier company, famous for some reliable, if a tad dull, economy cars, as well as the rotary ranges. The 808 with straight four, and GLC/323, put the rice on the Hiroshima table. The Mazda marketing machine wanted Joe Q Public to know that it wasn't just the rotary company anymore. The US ad for the 1978 GLC Sport (Familia/323) said, "Great Little piston engine." Ordinarily, car ads don't mention the fact that the car has a piston engine as a sales point. It would be like boasting one's model had four wheels, hardly unique. However, Mazda was trying to deprogram the US mindset that it had lovingly created earlier.

By saying 'piston' and the GLC Sport having an ad signpost clearly showing 35mpg city/46mpg highway, Mazda was saying its Japanese import economy credentials were as good as any other brand in the late '70s. The GLC starter sticker of $3248 also spelt low-cost motoring. The Sport edition's combination of floorshift, perforated steel rims with trim rings/radials, sports two-spoke steering wheel, and contemporary fashion statement hood and body profile decals, announced one's CAFE racer intentions.

The paint and tape spelt glitz; the ex 808 'Mizer' 1272cc SOHC I4 equaled economy. In Japan, there was a 985cc Familia version to save even more yen. That said, nothing saved Mazda like the all-new, front-drive BD Familia of 1980-84. Very close in style and layout to the original VW Golf, this cheese wedge Mazda marked a strong comeback for the company in Japan. On a number of occasions, the BD's sales unseated the mighty Corolla as the king of vanilla flavor small family cars – a real poke in the eye to giant Toyota, and its ultra-conservative rear-drive Corolla.

To survive after the fuel crisis, Mazda went sensible, and the public approved. To get out of the red and into the black meant putting exciting models on the back burner. It's a strategy *CAR*'s Paul Horrell identified in the

September 1994 article, 'The Madness that is Mazda.' Horrell also described the sad exodus from rotary, "Then came the oil shock, and California went back to drugs and Honda Civics."[55] They did buy an awful lot of Civics, Mizers and GLCs. Even in Japan, Kenichi Yamamoto's agreement with the Sumitomo Bank saw rotary remain a sideshow.

RX-7 versus 924 et al ...

Rotary Luce Legatos and Cosmo APs might not be well known outside Japan, but the FB RX-7 was. In international minds, the RX-7 was the last rotary vestige. It came out a year after the Ro80 met its Waterloo. Fortunately, by 1978/79, people were in the mood to take another look at rotary, in the shapely and affordable form of Savanna RX-7. It was especially good value next to quasi rival, the Porsche 924. Porsche may be a two-syllable word, but it was also a five-figure coupe. The 924 was hard to ignore; it was the new 'entry level' Porsche.

Porsche signs were plastered on billboards around the Mont Fuji circuit during the final Formula One race of 1976 held in Japan. Even before this, it seems Mazda got hold of a 924 as a benchmark study for half the RX-7's gestation period. Chuck Nerpel of *Motor Trend* noticed the 924's presence at the press unveiling of RX-7, in late February 1978, at the Miyoshi test facility. According to Mazda, the solitary 924 was there with the RX-7 trio, in case journos wished to make a comparison.

Motor magazine UK tested the 12A RX-7 five-speed: it did 119mph and 0-60mph in nine seconds. The same magazine also sampled the 2-liter 924, which got to 121.3mph and sprinted to 60 in 9.3 seconds. The Mazda was 169in long and 66in wide, according to *Motor*; for Porsche the figures were 166in and 67in respectively. One would expect the Porsche to cost more, and it did. In 1985, the 924 Lux was £12,123, the better-equipped FB RX-7 was £10,500. Being a Porsche, the 924 got into Group 8 insurance; the RX-7, the thriftier Group 7.

Overlooking the badge cachet premium, in looks, size and performance, the cars seemed very similar, but were they really? The Porsche used the VW/Audi 2-liter I4 with fuel-injection. A sturdy device, but rather agricultural in manner. The 924 could do 120mph plus, but its audio soundtrack made disco sound like Mozart. In contrast, the RX-7 revved so easily and smoothly a 6800rpm change up a cog warning buzzer was included, lest drivers take revs to eight grand or even worse. Roger Bell mentioned in *Autocar* that the RX-7's 12A ran as sweetly as a bumble-bee on cruise.

The FB RX-7 delivered Mazda its first Le Mans success. In 1979, an American privateer entered a FB RX-7, completed the 24-hour test and finished 21st overall. It was the first rotary-powered vehicle to complete the French endurance race. (Courtesy Mazda)

The source of such praise came from *Autocar*'s 1999 observation of the 100 Greatest Sports Cars Of All Time. The original FB RX-7 was there, so were the BMW M1, C2 Corvette and King of the Hill Vette. However, the Porsche 924 was not, and neither was the 944. The Porsche 968 was included, and this '90s sports car could trace its lineage to ye olde 924. However, the FD RX-7 was there too, as a '90s 968 contemporary ride. Unlike Porsche, Mazda's progressive FD RX-7 had only two things in common with the FB RX-7: there was the RX-7 name; and a derivative of the 13B Wankel that was seen in the FB's final hours.

The 968 was the Zuffenhausen filling in the Hiroshima sushi roll. It seemed the rival had become the master. Roger Bell extended the usual praise concerning Mazda's rotary steadfastness, "The Japanese company was the only one to make a success of it ..."[56] To make the *Autocar* Top 100 with an engine that no one else had made a production success was like reinventing the wheel. *Autocar* also thought highly of RX-7 in 1981, when it was included in a classy, high price and performance Euro field. The RX-7 was amongst comparison cars in the *Autocar* April 25 1981 report on Porsche's 924 Turbo.

At just £8549, the 12A atmo RX-7 was much, much cheaper and slower than luminaries like the Maserati Merak, Lotus Eclat, BMW M535i etc, but *Autocar* said, "... we have included the Mazda RX-7 which has considerable novelty appeal with its Wankel

The FB RX-7 was codenamed Project X605. Work on the rotary sports car started in 1974, with Moriyuki Watanabe as Project Head. The FB was largely a clean sheet design with few compromises. (Courtesy Mazda)

engine ..." Interestingly, the RX-7 was the only non-British/European car in the comparison. The Datsun Z car had moved on to the 280ZX by this stage, and was no longer considered 'enthusiast comparable.' *Autocar*'s Autotest of RX-7 occurred soon after the car hit the UK market. The November 24 1979 test divulged a 113mph terminal velocity, 0-60mph in 10.1 seconds and 18.2mpg overall.

It was a sign of the RX-7's dedicated sports car nature, that many people were prepared to buy a vehicle with fuel economy in the teens, during the second fuel crisis of 1979/80. It was also a sign of the RX-7's worth that *Autocar* should subsequently compare it with rivals capable of comprehensively outgunning it in acceleration and top speed, with only marginally worse gas mileage. Both the rotary concept and RX-7 had appeal beyond the mere 'Numbers Car.' In 1981, Mazda didn't yet make a turbo to take on the blown 924, but *Autocar* felt atmo RX-7 was a worthy low-priced exotic.

An *Autocar* RX-7 grievance concerned wheel hop. On uneven surfaced corners, an unrefined patter would result. In the May 1978 *Motor Trend* RX-7 intro, Chuck Nerpel remarked on the Detroit-style judder/wheel hop on maximum acceleration take offs. Nerpel mentioned that firmer bushings in the four-link longitudinal arms of the rear suspension would cure this, but ride comfort would be adversely affected. Such was the compromise nature of a live axle in a sports car application, well located or otherwise. It would make US pony car devotees feel right at home, but would be alien in the independently sprung 924.

In all other spheres of operation, the RX-7 proved a most excellent handler. Nerpel mentioned how one could take hands off the steering wheel at 120mph in the top lane of the Miyoshi test track's three parabolic turns with no drama. Steering was generally precise, and lighter than a rack-and-pinioned car. Ride was comfier overall than Porsche 924, and slight understeer was the first safe reaction when a corner was taken a tad too fast in RX-7. One avoided the 924's torque tube, transaxle complication, and having to dull a mid-engine car's steering reflexes to make it safe for public consumption. It would seem the good Front Midship was the optimum vessel to set sail on.

To match the 924's 2+2 format, early US-sold RX-7s employed a dealer-fitted rear jump seat option. In spite of the meagre '+2' part of the RX-7 equation, the formula equalled good North American value. Although not quite up to the factory skidpad figure, *Road & Track*'s $8295 RX-7 GS five-speed came surprisingly close in other areas. The 0-60mph time was an identical 9.2 seconds, the 59.3mph slalom speed almost at the factory's 60mph. *R&T*'s 0.779g reading was still better than it achieved with the RX-7's rivals, the Porsche 924 and Datsun 280ZX automatic.

The re-emissioned 1980 924 five-speed did 0-60mph in 10.6 seconds, recorded 0.766g and a 58.9mph slalom speed with 23mpg overall, against RX-7's 22mpg. The Datsun achieved 10.2 seconds, 0.76g and 56.5mph respectively, with lower fuel economy than either and a 2.8-liter I6 unable to match the 12A's smooth eagerness. The 924 cost $16,770 and the Datsun listed for $9899. The stats showed Mazda's great strides in fuel economy, to nearly

A Japanese spec RX-7 pictured in March 1979. In a November 24 1979 Autotest, the UK's *Autocar* magazine found its five-speed RX-7 capable of 0-60mph in 10.1 seconds, a 113mph top speed and 18.2mpg overall. Thirsty for the speed, but the RX-7 was UK-admired for its sports car nature. (Courtesy Mazda)

The 1979 Luce Legato four-door pillared sedan, called 929L in export markets as a piston version. With 66kW four-cylinder motor Mazda claimed a 160kph (100mph) top speed, for this rear-driver. With a 13B, North Americans would recognize the 929L as the departed RX-4. (Courtesy Mazda)

match the thrift of a slower four-cylinder car. They also showed that even with a three-way cat and unleaded gas, 924 couldn't match the emissions efficiency of RX-7.

In Europe, a 924 did 0-60mph in around nine seconds, and got close to 30mpg. In America, the Porsche succumbed to the performance dilution other imports suffered, when being pollution controlled. On the other hand, in Mazda rotary tradition, the RX-7 showed a redline eagerness alien to the times. Apart from the expensive, sports sedan-like 924, there were oversized GM F body coupes, and the Datsun Z car was catering more for luxury than sport. In the search for comfort, the Triumph TR7 also seemed like a soft GT machine, especially in V8 form. Thus, the RX-7 was fast becoming the affordable, sports car default choice. The demise of the MGB merely underlined this development.

RX-7 LS & Series II

For 1980 model year, with changes introduced in October 1979, RX-7s boasted higher grade interior trim. The North American 1980 RX-7 GS had a starting list price of under eight grand, with optional aluminum rims costing $273. Copying the European spelling use of 'litre,' which Pontiac had embraced to convey new wave late '70s 'road car' performance, in its 1980 RX-7 ad, Mazda was pushing the post-muscle car spirit of overall speed. Fast progress in the corners, not just the ¼ mile. Even though long defunct, it's possible Mazda kept stating "Mazda's rotary engine licensed by NSU/WANKEL," in ads to exploit the newly fashionable European-theme performance concept.

Whatever the motivation, the method was working and RX-7 was getting popular in America. In stepped the value-added special edition to set one apart from the madding crowd; it was called RX-7 LS. Introduced in North America for 1980 model year, the LS stood for a 'Leather Sport' full deluxe brown leather interior. At a time when real leather interiors, and sport for that matter, were rare, the RX-7 LS had desirable value beyond the mere common paint and tape specials of the era.

2500 RX-7 LS cars were theoretically built for North America, and could be thought of as an upscale RX-7 GS. The exterior featured B-pillar LS badging and unequal width dual gold pinstripes. After the muscle car era subsided, pinstriping was the new power tuning and an art in itself. The cars came with FB RX-7's optional 5.5in wide alloys, with LS specific gold centers. All the decoration bathed against main exterior colors of Aurora White, Brilliant Black, Solar Gold and Sonic Bronze. It's believed the numbers for the respective exterior colors were 1000/1000/500 and 250. This exceeds the intended 2500 total, and Mazda never gave a color choice number breakdown, just an advertised total, which RX-7 LS popularity exceeded. AM/FM stereo radio and sunroof were standard on RX-7 LS; not so on BMW 320i.

Paint and tape special editions were often created by dealers, using parts which could be catalogue ordered. Wishing to steer showroom traffic in their direction, saw a few more special GS cars created than originally planned. Japanese car makers got a reputation for quickly releasing either new models, or much-revised versions and the upgraded RX-7 Series II made a 1981

In 1979 still limited to 12A power, but the rotary RX-7 sports car was now the only Mazda Wankel car exported internationally. Its lithe, purist nature contrasted with the contemporary Vegasesque Datsun 280ZX. (Courtesy Mazda)

model year debut. The most obvious change was a smoother front and rear fascia restyle. Front spoilers were in vogue, so Mazda combined the front bumper/air dam in an integrated fashion to lower the drag coefficient.

Automakers were just starting to use aero tricks to boost fuel economy in the wake of the second gas crunch, and RX-7's restyle lowered the Cd from 0.36 to 0.34 – very nice for 1981. The tail end saw the demise of the Baroque Depression, in favor of the wider, flush lens covers in the style of a late '70s Trans Am. The new taillights were neater, and so was RX-7's handling. The propensity to oversteer was reduced, courtesy of a thinner rear swaybar and tire change. Previous Bridgestone RD 116 tires gave way to RD 204 equivalents from the same manufacturer, which provided more grip.

The RX-7 Series II also saw Mazda dump its long-favored thermal reactor emissions control apparatus. The combustion of leftover hydrocarbons and carbon monoxide in the thermal reactor, with an air pump to enrich the burn, had been common Mazda practice. Sometimes the air pump added air directly into the thermal reactor; at other times additional air was directed to the exhaust ports. However, federal pollution law was getting too strict, and US government moves to ban leaded gas by the end of 1984 would nullify the cost savings of the thirsty thermal reactor method. So it was that 12A joined the catalytic converter/unleaded crowd, with RX-7 gas mileage benefits.

Normally, one could option an RX-7 GS, or LS with automatic and or a/c. However, given the RX-3 lineage, all this stuff went on a car

A Mazda 323/GLC of 1979 vintage. The round-shaped, rear-drive GLC hatch was a serious Mazda money maker. However, the all-new 1981 front-drive 323/GLC would be even more commercially successful. This new hatch would have the US Ford Escort as a kissing cousin. (Courtesy Mazda)

West Germany welcomes Mazda! The FB RX-7 pictured, together with Cosmo AP and Luce Legato, were the three passenger rotary cars Mazda was making in 1980. (Courtesy Mazda)

with rear drum brakes. When the RX-7 was sneak peaked to chosen press early in 1978, a non-drivable racing RX-7 was shown with four-wheel disk brakes and a handbrake mechanism. This was taken as a sign of how the production RX-7 would evolve. In fact, the Porsche 924 also started disk/drum and went to four-wheel disks itself. Thus, four-wheel disk brakes became a production reality on RX-7 Series II, with the GSL variant.

RX-7 at the track

Cosmetically RX-7 Series II had moved from exposed steel bumpers to integrated plastic covered units, wide black rubber protective side body moldings and wraparound taillights. However, the RX-7 GSL's four-wheel disks and clutch type limited-slip differential wouldn't be noticed by the casual observer. Racing improved the breed – the production RX-3 12A homologated the 12A for racing, and the RX-7's upgrades spoke of a trackside connection too. This was the era when the car that teams raced had a strong engineering and layout relationship to the cars that people could buy. All over the world, winning on Sunday helped sell RX-7s on Monday.

Britain had been a lukewarm recipient of rotary Mazdas. Thirsty performance didn't help sales, and one was more likely to see a Ford Capri or Vauxhall Firenza winning a touring car race. The UK market received the RX-7 Series II upgrades in June 1981. The UK RX-7 had always been five-speed manual in nature, whereas in North America and Japan one could get an automatic RX-7. With the Series II changes, the UK RX-7 received four-wheel disk brakes as standard, and the 12A 105 to 115PS power hike.

Re-tested with the more potent 12A, *What Car?* magazine found the UK RX-7 good for 0-60mph in 8.8 seconds, with a 121mph top speed and 21mpg overall fuel economy. However, before all this, the RX-7 was the first rotary Mazda to make it big in Britain. It was admired from the start, and quickly made inroads into UK tin top racing. The car's success was with the TWR (Tom Walkinshaw Racing) team.

Headed by Tom Walkinshaw, TWR used to race BMW 3.0 CSLs and Ford Capris, but achieved notoriety when Mazda contracted it to handle the Mazda works team in the BTCC (British Touring Car Championship). In this era, the BTCC focus was the 1980 Tricentrol RAC British Saloon Car Championship. TWR driver Win Percy won the driver's title back to back, in 1980 and 1981. Percy dominated Class B, covering 1601cc to 2300cc cars, achieving ten consecutive wins in 1980, and eight consecutive victories in 1981. Other classes were D (up to 1300cc), C (1301cc to 1600cc) and A (2301cc to 3500cc).

Class B was where the main protagonists lay. Successful combatants like the Ford Capris of Gordon Spice and Andy Rouse, Triumph Dolomite Sprint and Alfa Alfetta GTAm were all class B cars. Class A had arisen in 1981, under pressure from British Leyland. BL wanted to get its Rover 3500 SD1 3.5-liter V8 sedan in amongst the action. Using the ex-Buick/Olds/Pontiac V8 this sedan was fast in 1981, but had teething troubles in the pre-Vitesse era. The RX-7 was the only non UK/Euro front runner, and certainly served it up to once-dominant cars like the Capri and Dolomite.

There was some controversy concerning the TWR RX-7 triumph, in the sense that it was a saloon (sedan) championship, and the RX-7 was definitely a sports car. However, whilst the Dolomite and Firenza coupes of yore were sedan and sedan/coupe, the Ford Capri was certainly not a sedan either, and no one ever said boo about the Capri taking part. TWR took its success on to the 1981 Spa 24 Hours, where its RX-7 achieved outright victory. At Spa-Francorchamps, the RX-7 had more than a two-lap winning margin over the second place BMW 530i. In doing so, Mazda avenged BMW's triumph over the R100, in the 1970 edition of the same race.

Inspired by its 1981 international achievement, TWR took the RX-7 to Le Mans in 1982. Using a suitably aero-enhanced FB RX-7, with Nikon sponsorship, the TWR RX-7 was raced by the Tom Walkinshaw, Chuck Nicholson and Peter Lovett trio. Sadly, the TWR RX-7 retired before the 24 hours were up, due to engine failure. After its Mazda association, which included making some enhanced RX-7 turbo road cars with bodykit/decals for sale through some UK Mazda dealers, TWR moved to the Jaguar camp. Racing the Jag XJ-S, and offering tuner-improved XJ-S and XJ sedans, TWR had entered a new and successful racing chapter.

Mazda tried Le Mans on for size itself, using modified examples of the FB RX-7. The company's first attempt at the 24-hour endurance race came in 1979. Mazda Motorsport Division came up with the FB RX-7-based Mazda 252i. Unfortunately, the 252i wasn't quick enough to qualify for the 24 Hours of Le Mans. However, the same year there was inaugural rotary success at Le Mans – using an RX-7. Entered by an American privateer, the RX-7 completed the race and came 21st overall. Mazda was hard at work on the evolutionary RX-7-based 253, but this also failed to qualify for Le Mans in 1981.

Typical Mazda perseverance saw it try again and succeed, in 1982. Mazda sent over two of its latest RX-7-based 254 racers; one expired, and the other managed 14th overall. Not an earth-moving experience, but the original RX-7 did allow Mazda to go the distance at Le Mans for the first time. Even Carroll Shelby found the Cobra had Le Mans limitations. This led to the GT40, and Mazda too turned to something sports car specialized, to achieve victory at the 24 Hours of Le Mans. However, there were still plenty of races the FB RX-7 could do well in; it was perfect for road course touring car events.

In 1981, the RX-7 got titles in SCCA (Sports Car Club of America), Pro-Rally series and the BTCS (Belgian Touring Car Series). Most importantly, the FB RX-7 became a veritable tour de force in US IMSA racing. The car type that would scoop many victories was shown to journalists at Mazda's Miyoshi test facility, in February 1978.

The proto, non-drivable racer had hardware that could be ordered from US Mazda dealers, from early 1979. Recall the zenith of the pony car SCCA racing from ten years earlier, where go fast parts were on offer to privateer racers and general public alike; in this instance, lightweight body panels, and bodykit consisting of flared fenders, front air dam, rear spoiler – and even racing decal stripes – were in evidence. Mazda thoroughness dictated the RX-7 perform well and look right on the track, so it took care of the pinstriping. Price of this bolide was undisclosed at the viewing, but included a full race peripheral-port atmo rotary with modified combustion chamber, two-barrel 45 DCLE Weber carb and no pollution controls. This 220 plus net horse engine was a rotary puzzle. Under the US license agreement that Curtiss-Wright had with Mazda concerning using a rotary in America, the rotary engine could be sold as part of a car, or parts could be imported to fix the motor in said car.

Mazda's loaves and fishes …

Under the license CW had with the by-now-defunct NSU, a US sub licensee couldn't import a complete motor, unrelated to the car it was going to be fitted to. The specialized engine-building process to create that racing peripheral port fire breather required more than replacement parts; it needed Mazda factory expertise. The NSU/CW license agreement had created an unusual engine practice in North America. Like VW with the Stateside Bug, Mazda set up a thorough dealer plan concerning maintenance and repair, to protect the solid reputation of its rotary engine.

The 1980 Savanna RX-7 GT with tartan upholstery, like Triumph TR7s and Porsche 924s of the day. As per its Savanna/RX-3 predecessor, the new RX-7 had a sportier GT variant. In 1981, the RX-7 made its ATCC debut in Australia's Sandown 400. (Courtesy Mazda)

Periodically, a 10A or 12A would be disassembled, and wear-related parts replaced. This entailed fitting new gaskets, using Mazda-specific disassembly tools and procedures to avoid incorrect or infrequent servicing, and prevent engine failure. To maintain quality and introduce greater practice uniformity, Mazda replaced the orderly disassembly plan with a core exchange program. Under the program, donated engine cores would be rebuilt with replacement parts, and reintroduced through the dealer supply chain.

To keep things legit, a dealer would have to have a customer's car VIN and the donated core, for Mazda records, before a replacement recon motor could be given to the customer. To speed up the process, dealers hunted for 'Easter eggs' by getting rotary Mazda VINs to go with found cores. Thus, recon motors could be made in advance, 'here's one I made earlier'-style, ready for customer sale. It became a competitive dealer business, to have a ready supply of remanufactured rotary 10As and 12As ready to go off the shelf, for an attractive price. To achieve this end, dealer employees even investigated junkyards for car VINs and associated cores.

The core exchange program was carried out with such energy that, by the early '80s, dealer shelves were overstocked with reborn 10As and

A 1980 US RX-7 advert drawing upon the FB's sporting exploits at Bonneville, and in the IMSA GTU category, to push sales of the road-going RX-7. Even with optional aluminum rims specified, the FB RX-7 was affordable, and good value for money. (Courtesy Mazda)

The Mazda RX-7. It's no secret the car is a phenomenal success. As is. And it's no secret why.

The front mid-engine RX-7 is a truly remarkable combination of beautiful aerodynamic design, uncanny quickness and exceptional balance and handling.

But hardly one to rest on its laurels, the '79 RX-7 set a world speed record of 183.904 mph at the Bonneville Salt Flats. This specially-prepared** RX-7 shattered the old record of 167.208 mph for Class E Grand Touring Cars, held by a Corvette.

And now, road racing will never be quite the same, with lean, mean rotary-engine RX-7s to reckon with in IMSA's GTU under-2.5 litre class.

The Mazda RX-7. It's one great sports car. And one great sports car value.

*Manufacturer's suggested retail price under $8000 for GS model shown (slightly higher in California). Actual prices established by dealers. Taxes, license, freight, optional equipment and any other dealer charges are extra. (Wide alloy wheels shown above $275 extra, slightly higher in some states.) All prices effective 12/15/78 and subject to change without notice.

**Standard engine replaced by larger engine modified to 323 hp. Car was lowered to reduce wind resistance and special aluminum discs used as wheel covers to reduce drag.

Mazda's rotary engine licensed by NSU-WANKEL

mazda

The more you look, the more you like.

12As. Sitting quietly boxed in clear plastic wrap, the glut of units were sold off cheap. Improved Mazda rotary reliability, and fewer Mazda models needing rotary, just RX-7 in America by 1979, rendered the biblical feeding of the five thousand unnecessary. It was necessary to find a licensing loophole, so the RX-7 could race with factory peripheral ported rotaries. This was achieved, and soon the FB RX-7 was dominating IMSA's GTU class of sub 2.5-liter machines.

RX-7 loving IMSA GTU

The warning shot was fired in Mazda's 1980 US RX-7 advert titled, "Over 183mph. Under 2.5 litres. Around $8000." The intention to enter IMSA's sub 2.5-liter GTU class was stated, and, by the end of 1980, the objective was achieved. In 1980, Walt Bohren drove the Racing Beat-prepared RX-7 to GTU title triumph, the outcome of an RX-7 winning car was never in doubt. The manufacturer's title was secured with the RX-7's fourth straight 1980 win, and there were still three races to go. It was wrapped up at the 245-lap Mosport Enduro in Canada, on August 15 1980. The winning car was the #17 Akai/AMsoil-sponsored Racing Beat RX-7 of driver trio Jeff Kline, Walt Bohren and John Morton. Bohren and Kline were lying first and third in the driver's championship at the time. Brad Frisselle was second in the championship, and became second in the race with Jim Downing in an RX-7. Third place was taken by the Z&W Enterprises RX-7 of Pierre Honegger and Ernesto Soto. It was the fourth time in 1980's GTU series that Mazda achieved a 1-2-3 result.

While the RX-7 was GTU king, drivers like Jim Downing and Roger Mandeville were showing the way in RS Racing Stocks, using the older RX-3. Roger Mandeville set a new lap record at the August 15 1980 Mosport Enduro, doing a 1:31.41 at an average speed of 96.843mph on lap 193. Not only that, the race took place under very hot conditions. The drivers showed signs of wear, the Mazda rotary never did. Whereas the NSU Wankel had trouble coping with normal driving, Mazda's Wankel handled race trials with aplomb. It was the start of an unbroken FB RX-7 string of success.

At the 1979 International Motor Sports Association (IMSA) season opener, the February 1979 Daytona 24-Hour Race, RX-7 won the GTU class and came fifth overall. RX-7 emphatically outclassed GTU class, for a 1-2 finish in that category. FB RX-7 took out all the IMSA GTU titles between 1980 and 1987, and, unlike NASCAR, this mini racer was closely related to the RX-7 one could actually buy. The end of 1980 race season sale price

Tom Walkinshaw Racing (TWR) could count the UK's 1980 and 1981 BTCC, plus the 1981 Spa-Francorchamps 24-Hour Race, amongst its FB successes. Its turbo-fettled RX-7 was one of the aftermarket blown FBs available through UK Mazda dealers in the early to mid '80s. (Courtesy Mazda)

The 1983 MY all-new front-drive Capella (626) four-door at its September 1982 debut. It was 1983 *Motor Trend* Import Car of The Year. There was a fuel-injected turbo variant, but no rotary. (Courtesy Mazda)

for the winning Racing Beat fettled RX-7 was $65,000, a lot more than the eight grand for a showroom RX-7 GS, but one received benefits.

The IMSA GTU RX-7's 12A 70ci motor had Lucas mechanical fuel-injection, and a peripheral ported 260 horses at 9500rpm, with 160lb/ft at eight grand. Using a 5.67:1 rear end and 0.88 top five-speed, the 2250lb RX-7 could do 137mph and 165mph with Daytona gearing. Zero to 60mph was 5.6 seconds with a 14.1-second ¼ mile at 106mph. It drank like a musclecar too, doing 6mpg in race trim. Goodyear Bluestreak Sports Car tires on 16 x 11.5in spun aluminum, cast aluminum center three-piece modular BBS rims, helped deliver a 1.04g skidpad figure …

Amazing stats, but the underlying RX-7 elements were still present. That meant independent MacPherson strut suspension, with coil springs and swaybar. At the rear, one would still find a live axle, four trailing links, compound Watts linkage, coils and swaybar. The FB's recirculating ball non power steering was there, the race car sported 2.4 turns lock-to-lock. The 12in front/11.8in rear disk brakes were much bigger than stock, and weren't power assisted. The 12A's rotors were series controlled to keep a lid on the mods. With the fundamental FB retained, racing RX-7s generated a positive race-to-road car connection that could only help sales. Even the 9.4:1 compression ratio of the 1150cc 12A (rotor radius x width x eccentricity = 210mm x 70mm x 30mm), seemed streetable if good hi test was to hand.

In 1981, Lee Mueller won GTU class in the Kent Racing RX-7. 1982 saw the GTU class format change, with most teams participating in the whole racing season. Jim Downing took the 1982 title, pushing Roger Mandeville into second place. Joe Varde was quick in 1982, but less consistent in his Casey Montex RX-7. 1983 saw Roger Mandeville win the GTU title in an RX-7, beating ex-team-mate Jim Downing, also in an RX-7. Former AMC stalwart Amos Johnson came third in his Team Highball RX-7.

The Team Highball RX-7 mimicked the success of the Team Highball Gremlin at Daytona. Once again using Johnson's racing No 7, the No 7 Team Highball RX-7 won the Daytona 24-Hour Race GTU class a record four consecutive times. Out of 82 races, it managed a consistent 64 top ten finishes. Fourth place in the 1983 GTU driver's title race went to John Maffucci. Moving into 1984, Jack Baldwin drove his CCR RX-7 to GTU driver's title victory, with Jack Dunham and Jeff Kline second and third respectively in Mazda RX-7s. There was some irony in the exotic Porsche 924 GTR of John Schneider coming fourth in the championship. The racetrack doesn't notice badge cachet.

In 1985, the GTU displacement ceiling was increased from 2.5 to 3 liters, but the RX-7 on 70ci (1.1 liters) still won out. However, this time Jack Baldwin earned his second straight GTU driver's title, after a hard struggle against Chris Cord in the AAR Toyota Celica. The FB RX-7 also provided a stepping stone for rising star Tommy Kendall. Driving the ex-Jim Downing CCR Mazda RX-7 to his first title in 1986. Kendall just beat Roger Mandeville's RX-7 in 1986, then won again using the CCR RX-7 to claim the 1987 driver's GTU title.

The 1982 model year Mazda Luce replaced Luce Legato. The US-inspired Luce look of 1972-81 was gone, but Legato's rear-drive format and four-door hardtop availability were kept. (Courtesy Mazda)

Amos Johnson was second in the 1987 GTU driver's title race, using the No 7 Team Highball RX-7. Third was Terry Visger in the fast Huffaker Pontiac Fiero, but Visger didn't enter enough races to be a title contender. Tommy Kendall went on to win four SCCA Trans Am titles between 1990 and 1997. He also broke Mark Donohue's long standing Sunoco Camaro consecutive win record in 1997. Kendall became much associated with success in the Roush Mustang Cobra, but the winning started with the relatively humble FB RX-7. There also always seems to be some strange historical connection between Mazda and Ford.

The 1982 fourth gen HB platform Luce RE (Rotary Engine) four-door. The ability to specify Mazda's 12A and 13B rotaries in the sober-suited Luce four-door created the ultimate Japanese street sleeper. With NSU's Ro80 discontinued, Mazda entered the '80s as the sole rotary purveyor. (Courtesy Mazda)

RX-7 & Australian Touring Car Championship

If Tommy Kendall provided an example of going from Mazda to Ford, Allan Moffat showed sometimes one moves from Ford to Mazda. Canadian racer Moffat became legendary in 1970s Australian touring car racing, culminating in the famous 1977 1-2 formation Ford Falcon finish at Bathurst with Colin Bond. However, the Mad Max Road Warrior Falcon V8 coupe was soon to go out of production. Moffat had lost official Ford backing, so continuing to campaign the Falcon V8 coupe was going to be financially tough. Fortunately, Mazda Australia approached Allan Moffat early in 1979, with the idea of running the new FB RX-7 in Australian touring car racing.

As an exploratory move, Moffat traveled to America to test Jerry Wright's JLC Racing IMSA RX-7. Moffat was impressed the JLC racing mechanics didn't have to lift the hood once during extensive racetrack testing. Allan Moffat brought the JLC Racing RX-7 to Australia, where the car was raced at the Sandown round of the 1980 Sports Sedan Championship. The car finished sixth in two heats. Even before this, Moffat got into discussions with Australian authority CAMS on the legality of using a peripheral port racing engine. He knew a mere bridge port 12A wouldn't cut it against the local Ford Falcon and Holden Commodore V8s, in going for outright race victory. Peripheral porting was initially approved, then rejected, and Moffat had to just get on with building a race RX-7 for the ATCC.

The racing RX-7 was not that distant from the model found in Aussie showrooms. There was a bridge port 12A, Mazda five-speed manual with 3.5 to 5.5:1 final drive ratios, depending on which circuit was at hand. A Mazda racing differential was employed, along with heavy-duty suspension using firmer shocks, coils and bushings. There were also 10in wide rims, with grippy tires to fill the flared arches of the ATCC Group C era bodykit. By the time Moffat got the Downunder RX-7 program moving, RX-7 racing in Japan and America was established, so hardware was bountiful.

Engines came race-ready from Mazda Japan, and brakes, differential, gearbox, bodykit and other homologated parts were also Japanese or North American sourced. Whatever else was required fell to custom manufacture by Ron Harrop and Team Moffat. The race car had a dogleg five-speed box, where second to fifth are in the 'H' and first is a pitlane crawl ratio. The driver was catered for by a tight-fitting fiberglass seat. Apart from a racing harness, there were also large pads on the transmission tunnel and driver's door, plus a sturdy footwell footrest, to help keep the driver in place. Otherwise, normal FB footwell pedal placement prevailed.

Most FB RX-7s had a large central tach. However, this time it read to 10,000rpm and there was no redline. A secondary needle was carried up by the main tach needle, to serve as the rev limbo pole. To the left of the tach were three temperature gauges for coolant, engine oil and gearbox oil. To the right side were gauges for fuel pressure, oil pressure and differential oil temperature. The center dashboard had a row of switches for electric fuel pumps, differential oil cooler pump, gearbox oil cooler pump, with the ignition switch closest to the driver. The master battery switch was on the left-hand side of the transmission tunnel.

The RX-7 racer's fuel lines could be seen through the rear hatch glass, and were shielded from the interior by a plexiglass panel. Those lines supplied fuel to the bridge port 12A's Weber 48 IDA carb. The slick shod RX-7 received Rothmans tobacco sponsorship. Specifically, the Peter Stuyvesant cigarette brand. The car made its ATCC debut at the 1981 Sandown 400, where Allan Moffat qualified tenth and finished sixth. At the major Bathurst touring car race, in October 1981, the RX-7 qualified fifth. While lying fourth, Moffat handed the keys to Le Mans legend Derek Bell, and the car finished third overall.

At Surfers Paradise in November 1981, Moffat got his first RX-7 victory. The flat, flowing Surfers Paradise circuit suited the RX-7 very well. Indeed, the experiences of the RX-7 in the ATCC during 1981-84, showed the driving characteristics of the rotary powered RX-7. V8 Aussie touring cars had a lot of low end torque, heavy clutches and could reach very high top speeds on long straights. The RX-7 managed to be an outright victory contender, and yet was the complete antithesis of the V8 cars. The RX-7 felt like an enhanced version of the regular road car – That is, a nice-handling, well-balanced machine with light controls.

The clutch wasn't V8 brutal, since the 12A rotary didn't make a truckload of torque. As compensation one got that never ending rise of rotary power, more revs equalled more go. It was seamless, but the driver had to be mentally on form all the time. Without a lot of torque, it was necessary to maintain speed through the corners, keep the revs up, but not too high. It was easy to go way off the normal 9500-10,000rpm shift points and trash the Wankel, tough as the motor was. However, too few revs and the Weber carb would supply too much fuel to the 12A. This over supply would make the motor stammer, which was hard on the transmission.

The 12A's power came in around 6000rpm, so one had a narrow range of power, speed and balance equal to the hardest Sudoku challenge. At 7/10th pace, the RX-7's light steering seemed more user friendly than V8 rivals, but Allan Moffat said that at 10/10th in a race environment, getting the most from the FB RX-7 was hard work. Power was a hurdle for Moffat to overcome. After the 1981 Surfers Paradise success, Moffat used the RX-7 for a class win in the Guia 200 Macau touring car race. He then went to Japan, to work with Mazda engineers to make the car faster. The work paid off; Moffat's RX-7 was 1.8 seconds quicker at the 1982 Sandown ATCC race, but still trailed the V8s of Dick Johnson and Peter Brock.

Allan Moffat finished a distant fourth at Sandown, and damaged the 12A on the long straights of Symmons Plains whilst trying to match the V8s. Moffat took pole and won round five's race at Lakeside. He also won round eight at Surfers Paradise, despite a collision with Johnson's Ford Falcon. The September Sandown 400 saw Moffat debut in a new car. His old car went to Gregg Hansford and Lucio Cesario. Moffat won in spite of allegations that he had speeded in pitlane. 1982's Bathurst wasn't too hot. Moffat had Mazda factory racer Yoshimi Katayama as co-driver. Unfortunately, their car only managed sixth overall. Holden's Commodores were especially dominant after being granted rulebook freedoms.

Moffat achieved a come-from-behind victory to win the 1982 Surfers Paradise 300, passing Dick Johnson's Falcon V8 in the process. He also passed Peter Brock and Allan Grice to win the Adelaide 300, claiming the 1982 ATCC Endurance Championship title in doing so. The sparks were flying in 1983 for RX-7 too. Moffat won round one at Calder, and round four at Wanneroo, using a light fuel load strategy. He got pole position at Adelaide's round five, but came second to Brock by a mere bumper bar. It was the closest finish in the ATCC's history. Then came moves to make the RX-7 more competitive.

Moffat managed to get CAMS to permit the 13B's usage, despite opposition teams protesting. The 12A-motorvated RX-7 beat the fast Nissan Bluebird Turbo to win round seven at Oran Park. RX-7 was able to utilize the bigger 13B engine at round eight. However, the Ford and Holden camps convinced CAMS that it would only be a level playing field, if their respective Falcons and Commodores could use bigger rims and spoilers. In the face of this development, Moffat was able to move CAMS to allow fuel-injection for his RX-7.

Still a Small Giant

What did the established Ford and Holden camps have to fear from a small sports car that just moved from a 70ci engine to an 80ci edition? Ford and Holden teams had been campaigning their V8 cars for over a decade in the ATCC. It was a testimony to the effectiveness of the FB RX-7 and rotary engine, that Mazda's newcomer package should be seen as such a threat by the pushrod establishment. The concessions CAMS granted to Ford and Holden seemed excessive. Allan Moffat told *Modern Motor* magazine's Barry Lake, in 1984, that the carb 12A RX-7 and fuel-injected 13B RX-7 racers would have to be driven back-to-back several times, for the power difference to be discerned.

In any case, 1983 saw Moffat win his fourth ATCC title, and further show the reliability of the RX-7. At the September 1983 Sandown 400, Grice blew a motor, Brock broke a hub and Allan Moffat managed to come from behind to victory in RX-7. So it was on to the October 1983 Bathurst 1000, and what would be the RX-7's best result at the great race. Moffat qualified outside the top ten, but Bathurst is an all-day enduro and the RX-7's great race fuel economy put him in the lead. However, in the end, Peter Brock used team-mate John Harvey's Commodore to win the race, once his own Holden had expired. Allan Moffat came second.

1984's racing season witnessed some gremlins. The crew had tried to warm the 13B up faster by restricting the front fascia air intake. Unfortunately, a faulty warning system failed to show the engine was overheating, and a number of 13B's were lost. Moffat managed to win round three at Wanneroo, but missed much of the championship because of an accident at round four's Surfers Paradise. Moffat's RX-7 was rear-ended by a Ford Falcon, causing him to suffer broken knuckles.

Allan Moffat returned to win the Oran Park 250 endurance race with Gregg Hansford. Showing, again, the shortcomings of RX-7 and rotary, Moffat had trouble with 1984's Sandown 500 in September. He used to do well here, but the track layout was altered to include new slow corners. Suiting the torquier V8s, Brock's Commodore came first, Moffat's RX-7 was second. At October 1984's Bathurst 1000, Moffat partnered Gregg Hansford to come third in the team's second car. An early race collision damaged the team's first car, which couldn't continue very long after repairs.

The Commodore V8s were too strong at Bathurst in 1984, but there was still Mazda cheer to be had. At the final race of the year, Moffat's RX-7 team cars came second and third. This allowed Mazda to clinch the ATCC's Manufacturer's title, but it would be the end of factory-backed RX-7s in the ATCC. The Australian series was changing from Group C to international Group A rules. This would let in European stars like the BMW 635 CSi, Jaguar XJ-S and Volvo 240 Turbo. Unfortunately, Mazda was unwilling to fund a Group A FB RX-7. The FB was coming to the end of its production life.

Thus, 1984 would be the final year Moffat would campaign the RX-7 in the ATCC, despite his own faith in the car – he owned a red RX-7 himself, at the time. As a final fling, Allan Moffat took the FB RX-7 to America in early 1985, for the legendary Daytona 24-Hour race. The car was entered in GTO class where it would be facing faster, more specialized machinery, like sports prototypes. Moffat's team made modifications to its ATCC RX-7. This involved small changes to the rear spoiler and front suspension, plus removal of part of the interior to save weight.

The RX-7 qualified 40th in a field of 76 entrants. However, after six hours Moffat's car was lying 12th, and after 16 hours was ninth. Unfortunately, the car's 13B was hit by a stone, forcing the car to stop for repairs. It ended up coming 24th overall. Going back to the topic of the ATCC, the RX-7's inroads were impressive, given the extent authorities went to to protect the competitiveness of the local V8 cars. To move the series back to a local affair between Ford Australia and Holden, all-wheel drive, turbo cars were subsequently banned. This was to end the dominance of the Nissan Skyline. The remaining BMW M3 was neither all-wheel drive, nor turboed. Therefore, authorities stacked a weight penalty on the little car, as well as a 7500rpm rev limiter on its four-cylinder engine. It was the end of Group A, and now you know why the powers that be feared peripheral ported FB RX-7s.

Everything … but NASCAR!

The success at the 24 Hours of Daytona wasn't the only 1985 triumph for RX-7. The FB RX-7 came third outright in the 1985 Acropolis Rally held in Greece. This represented round six of the FIA World Rally Championship, which transpired from May 25 to May 31. Ingvar Carlsson and Benny Melander's RX-7 completed the rally in 11 hours eight minutes and 25 seconds. First place went to Timo Salonen and Seppo Harjanne's Peugeot 205 T16, and second was claimed by Stig Blomqvist and Bjorn Cederberg's Audi Quattro Sport.

The Acropolis Rally represented the RX-7's best FIA rally result to that point, in the Group B supercar era. It was a time dominated by high tech, specialized all-wheel drive, turbo cars where 600bhp wasn't uncommon. The Peugeot 205 T16 was a mid-engine rally weapon, far removed from the front-drive production 205. The Quattro Sport as made in a 220 unit homologation run of 304bhp road cars, costing $90 grand between 1983-87. Thus, it was only when the entry list was poor that more mundane machinery, relatively, like RX-7 and Porsche 911 SC RS could get up the field. As a Japanese car at the Acropolis Rally, the RX-7 achieved the primary objective of finishing ahead of the Nissan 240 RS driven by Shekhar and Yvonne Mehta.(57)

The FB RX-7 was the nimble little rear-drive sports car that could have achieved more in world rallying in an earlier era. In America, speed was judged more in a straight line, than darting through forest stages on loose surfaces. The mecca for straight-line speed was Bonneville's salt flats, and even here the FB made its mark, with help from Racing Beat. US rotary specialist Racing Beat specially prepared a 1979 FB RX-7 to take on the Bonneville Salt Flats. The FB in question used a larger, souped up 323 horse Wankel, aluminum disc wheel covers and lowered suspension.

Setting records on salt flats is harder than it looks. Cars can be a handful at speed as tires squirm for grip on a powdery, glass smooth surface. Drivers try various techniques and aero tricks to reach their speed objectives. The FB RX-7 by Racing Beat came away with a new Class E Grand Touring Cars record of 183.904mph set on the Bonneville Salt Flats. The old record of 167.208mph was held by a Corvette. Once again rotary had lived up to its V8 alternative performance billing, and forget about the valve float. In Japan, another record breaker was also rotary powered.

Mazda HB Cosmo & Elford 626 Turbo

1981 was the final model year for the CD Cosmo in Japan. For 1982 MY, it was replaced by the new post-Luce Legato, HB Luce platform-related Cosmo. The Luce was still rear-drive, which meant taking lots of rotary power wouldn't be a problem: lie tondemo gozaimasen, or no worries. At first, the HB Cosmo was launched in piston form only, but new 1982 six-port 12As and the latest 13Bs were soon available.

The HB Luce/Cosmo range of 1982 to 1986 represents the only time in automotive history a car has offered piston gasoline, rotary and diesel powerplants. The 2.2-liter I4 diesel was still a Luce option. As before, Cosmo action started with the piston 1.8-liter VC SOHC I4, accompanied by the 2-liter MA and 2-liter FE design SOHC I4s. Concerning rotary choices, one had the 12A-SPI, 12A Turbo, and automatic transmission power team-only 13B-RESI. One could option the HB sedan body with a rotary, but all eyes were on the pop-up-headlamped Cosmo coupe Rotary Turbo of 1982.

The 1982, Cosmo coupe Rotary Turbo 12A was officially Japan's fastest production car, until the FJ20ET-powered R30 Nissan Skyline came along. However, for muscle, Mazda now had a piston alternative, in the form of the turbo version of its FE SOHC inline four pot. This 'FET' 1998cc fuel-injected turbo made 120bhp and 150lb/ft. It was an engine option in Japan, as well as some Eastern Europe and Middle East markets. This motor could be chosen in the Luce/929 coupe, also with pop-ups, as a way to get the Cosmo coupe Turbo's performance with much better gas mileage. In any case, the Cosmo wasn't around in the aforementioned export markets.

The Cosmo coupe had a 1984 Series II makeover that brought blackout pillars. Apart from being Mazda's flagship, the 1982 Cosmo coupe RE Turbo also happened to be the world's first turbocharged rotary production car. It was an important precedent, because turbo rotaries would be Mazda's lead performance angle until 2002. Before that, turbo motors were headline news. Coming out of the fuel crisis, everyone wanted to know how to make a small economical engine behave like a big powerful engine on demand; the answer was forced induction.

If it doesn't go, then blow! – Turbo Mazdas

Instead of power-sapping, belt-driven superchargers of yore, automakers channeled wasted exhaust gases to spin a turbine, and turbocharge their gasoline and diesel engines of the 1970s, and 1980s. It was something even used on bikes. The 1980s Honda CX500 Turbo bike had reverse writing 'Turbo' script on its front fairing above the headlamp. The aforementioned Mazda FET motor was a Japanese spec catalytic converter engine requiring unleaded gas.

To get such benefits in the leaded gas 1980s UK market, some turned to Mazda dealer/tuner Elford. Located in Bournemouth, Dorset, Elford Turbo Ltd had a respected turbo conversion for the popular front-drive Mazda 626, that didn't affect the factory new car warranty. With the bolt on installation, a Garrett T3 turbo was mounted on a custom cast iron exhaust manifold. The turbo blew through a special Weber DMTT carb.

Boost was mild, with a max of 4psi, and was combined with retarded ignition to ward off detonation, and colder sparkplugs. A custom stainless steel front section exhaust pipe was included with the £1190 kit, which could be fitted by Elford for £125. The £8039, 1985 Mazda 626 2-liter GLX coupe was a natural candidate. With the turbo kit, fourth gear 50-70mph acceleration was cut from 9.7 to 6.1 seconds. Elford advertisements claimed its 626 Turbo outperformed the standard FB RX-7, still current at the time.

The 626 Turbo could be picked up from Elford, or ordered through any UK Mazda dealer. An exciting mover, and perhaps the only thing better in UK Mazda land was the Elford RX-7 Turbo. Various companies like Elford and TWR had turbo conversions for the popular FB RX-7 in the UK. A great chassis, now it had the power a classic rear-driver could easily harness. Enjoy torque sans torquesteer. Elford's 626 Turbo could be had from £8999 driveaway at late 1985 pricing. The Elford RX-7 Turbo was £13,999 driveaway from Elford direct.

Japanese automakers were a little slow adopting the turbo route to performance. European machinery like the BMW 2002 Turbo and Saab 99 Turbo were the first modern cars to bring turbo mainstream, along with the 1978 Buick Turbo Regal and 1979 Ford Mustang. Then came the 280ZX Turbo, automatic-only at first and with a factory 0-60mph claim of 7.1 seconds. This turbo Datsun was introduced in mid 1981 and matched the Corvette's price, whilst bettering its performance. The Elford RX-7 Turbo had similar performance, recorded in *CAR* magazine.

As of September 1985, the standard RX-7 was listed at £11,499 with 0-60mph in nine seconds and 115mph top end. Urban 56mph and 75mph steady state UK economy figures were given as 17.9/35.8/28.8mpg respectively.

UK Mazda dealer Elford provided right-hand drive converted turbo FB RX-7s, and 626s that ran on leaded gasoline. At the time, factory turbo versions of these cars were unleaded Japanese market only. (Courtesy Mazda)

The Japanese market 1984 FB RX-7 Turbo, pictured on its September 1983 debut. Note the trim rings, plus front bumper and sail panel 'RX-7 Turbo' callouts. Wishing to protect its rotary's hard-won North American reliability reputation, Mazda kept this blown 12A variant at home. (Courtesy Mazda)

The Elford RX-7 Turbo cost £12,938 (list price), with 0-60mph in 7.5 seconds and a 130mph terminal velocity. Fuel economy recorded by *CAR* was in the 17mpg to 25mpg (UK mpg) range.[58] Thus, the turbo version was rather sharp value. The Elford Turbo was almost on a performance par with the Euro spec Porsche 944 Lux, a car costing £17,551. Great performance and minimal gas mileage penalty from Dorset's largest Mazda dealer. However, what about Hiroshima's turbocharged FB? Step forward the 1984 RX-7 Turbo Series III.

Introduced in the fall of 1983, the Japanese market RX-7 Turbo had a factory claimed top speed of 135mph. It has often been said the FB RX-7 was planned to take on the mighty Nissan Z car, and the RX-7 Turbo was a natural nemesis for the 280ZX Turbo, but it wasn't exported to America. Management in Japan decided it wouldn't risk the rotary's hard fought reliability reputation by sending the RX-7 Turbo Stateside. They were no doubt mindful of the turbo warranty claims of hard driven Fox Mustangs and 1980-81 Turbo Trans Ams. Owners can be unsympathetic maintenance wise. Turbocharger problems might have unfairly tainted the Mazda rotary.

An Australian RX-7 Series III wearing a personalized 'SA22CT' license plate. The 'SA22C' part represents the 1978-85 FB RX-7 early chassis prefix; the 'T' part indicates this car has been modified with a turbo. (Courtesy www.ausrotary.com)

The Japanese RX-7 Turbo used a non-intercooled 12A Wankel, as in the 1982 HB Cosmo coupe RE Turbo. It had subtle red script front side bumper and sail panel 'RX-7 Turbo' callouts. Otherwise, the steel rims and trim rings suggested it was just another GT, quite the street sleeper. North America didn't miss out, that market alone received the latest Series III FB with a new version of the bigger atmo 13B. Like the Japanese turbo, the upscale sports/luxo North American RX-7 GSL-SE was an unleaded, catalytic converter spec car with much higher power and torque.

The GSL-SE's 13B had a 'Dynamic Effect' intake system, six-port induction and EGI denoted electronic fuel-injection, instead of the 12A's carb. It was enough to kick outputs to 135bhp at six grand and 133lb/ft at 2750rpm. For Japan and America, the six-port design was a headline counter to Honda's three-valve per cylinder high output I4 seen in the new 1984 Honda CRX coupe. When the RX-7 was at the rumor stage, it was thought it might rival the Corvette, and with 13B it looked like it had. The magazine testing consensus suggested a sub eight second 0-60mph time. This equated with a late '70s Corvette with L82 350 and four-speed.

In keeping with the times, the five-speed 80ci GSL-SE, and RX-7 Series III in general, represented a fashionable sports luxury combo. The GSL's clutch type limited-slip differential and four-wheel disk brakes came along for the ride. The brakes were larger, and Mazda used 14in rims on the RX-7 Series III, along with lugnuts instead of bolts as previously, with a new spacing pattern of 4 x 114.3mm (4 x 4.5in). North American RX-7 Series IIIs had a unique instrument display that didn't have a centrally placed tach. The central tach had been normal RX-7 fare.

The North American RX-7 Series III also had a unique code designation, called P132. Internationally, this 1984-85 RX-7 was simply named Series III. Other Series III upgrades included the return of the RX-7's external oil cooler. The 1983 'beehive' water-oil heat exchanger had proved troublesome. From the start, the RX-7 had a firewall mounted mini electric winch to pull in the choke on carb cars, if the driver forgot. However, the Series III/P132 brought even more convenience features.

The FB RX-7 Series III had the option of an overdrive four-speed automatic in some markets, and optional power steering. The latter was standard on the super luxo Australian spec FB RX-7 Limited. 14in alloys, two-tone exterior paint, deluxe interior trim, power windows and air-conditioning made this RX-7 anything, but limited. Even so, the new RX-7 Limited cost $23,120, which undercut the final 280ZXs and new 28 grand Nissan 300ZX, in the Aussie market. At the helm lay a three-spoke sports wheel and the revised Series III instrument panel seen outside North America.

Work at the five-speed manual controls and the 12A-powered RX-7 Limited did the standing 400-meter sprint in 17 seconds, about what the original 1978 model could do, as luxo features undid 12A power gains in the interim. This made Limited slower than new kids on the block like Mitsubishi's Starion Turbo or Alfa GTV6, but it matched the new 300ZX, and that was enough for Mazda. The Limited represented a nearly ten-grand increase in the Australian price of an RX-7 since its late '70s intro. The FB had changed, it was no longer the pure sports car it once was. However, memories of Triumph TR6s and MGBs were fading fast.

The Australian spec FB RX-7 Series III never got the 13B motor, nor a turbo. However, this car has been modified to feature both. The FB chassis was always a good handler looking for more power. (Courtesy www.ausrotary.com)

The Australian RX-7 Series III of 1984-85 brought an upscale 'Limited' variant with two-tone paint, luxo trim, a/c etc. It competed with the Datsun 280ZX and Nissan 300ZX luxury cruisers, fashionable at the time. (Courtesy www.ausrotary.com)

FB RX-7, sports car of its time ...

The international public were quite taken by the plush extravagance of the new 300ZX, so the RX-7 Limited indulged the masses with the sports/luxury they wanted. The new Z car, Starion Turbo and Honda CRX were Japanese headlines the six-year-old FB RX-7 had to contend with. Highly opinionated *CAR* moved the FB down to Adequate in its 'The Good, The Bad & The Ugly' section, by the FB's late life. Positive points were performance, smoothness and keen pricing. Negative aspects were seat comfort/support, a downscale interior and hard ride comfort. Summing up, *CAR* said, "Fast, desirable, best days over." Well, Mazda were just months away from introducing an all new RX-7, and the FB was seven years old.

In the August 1984 issue of *CAR,* LJK Setright looked back on two Japanese cars he liked, the FB RX-7 and new generation 1983 Honda Prelude. The conclusion was champagne taste on a beer budget. They were described as comfy touring cars that could cover ground quickly, without encouraging drivers to explore the chassis limit in the manner of an Alfa. Setright said they were modest in power, luxurious in appointment, very practical, but superlative in no particular area. Thus, if you liked to waft along in a Jag XJS or Mercedes 280CE, but didn't like the asking prices, the Japanese duo would suffice, or was this the car the FB RX-7 had become?

Known as P132 series in North America, this third iteration of the original RX-7, saw the successful little sports car through its final couple of model years, 1984-85. Mods here involve MSD module, FC oil cooler, Racing Beat suspension and exhaust, plus 15in Ronals. (Courtesy Jim Chung)

LJK Setright described his first RX-7 experience, in the late '70s, as involving a car with a rougher-than-Prelude ride, and light, smooth steering that was a bit dead about center. He judged the sports car as well made. Mazda was noted as tops for quality amongst Japanese companies, offering an excellent standard of fit and finish, matched by few anywhere in the world. Fast forward to the 1984 RX-7 Series III, and Mazda claimed it had improved the RX-7's recirculating ball steering. LJK Setright said it just felt stiffer and harder work, not better.

CAR's Ian Fraser chipped in with the comment that the FB RX-7 was showing its age, but that the front midship layout was an intrinsically sound sports car format. He also gave the view that Mazda's engineers had made changes to the RX-7 with the Series III, targeting the wrong customers at the behest of marketing.[59] These comments concerned the plush, luxury angle that Mazda had taken with the Series III to match the 280ZX and 300ZX coupes; at the time people were indeed showing a greater preference for grand tourers than sports cars, so RX-7 adapted.

Even in its own lifetime, the FB RX-7 was acknowledged in Japan and internationally as a modern classic. In the 1984 Tamiya Catalogue, the Japanese plastic kit maker gave the story so far. The 1:24 scale glue kit was called

Mazda Savanna RX-7 (model id no2416). It was a yellow-colored model of the FB RX-7, measuring 182mm long, that carried the reverse decal script Savanna RX-7 between the pop-up headlamps. The kit version, with Mazda factory sunroof, was Toyo Kogyo-released in November 1980, according to Tamiya. The company described FB RX-7 thus, "Unveiled to the public in 1978, the Savanna RX-7 received wild acclaim from all who saw it."[(60)]

Tamiya's Savanna RX-7 description also noted the front midship layout, and mentioned Mazda's 100 touring car race victories by 1976. This latter fact actually referred to the older RX-3, but showed that, in Japanese consciousness, the RX-7 represented a continuation of the Savanna legacy that began in 1971. The plain success of the RX-7 as a roadcar – its racing credentials are beyond question – just requires observation of contemporary sporting car rivals from inside and outside Japan: the Isuzu Piazza showed how not to impress enthusiasts.

Created with an eye to the VW Scirocco's US success, and a pressing need to replace its ageing 117 coupe, Isuzu produced the 1980s Piazza coupe. The Ital Design Giugiaro looks promised much, but the humble mechanicals reminded one of that saying concerning the farmhouse animal starting with 'P' that decides to don lipstick before going out for an evening. With ties to GM, the substance was no surprise. The Piazza drew from the Isuzu and GM T car parts shelf. Apart from the snazzy styling, the interior featured instrument binnacle switchgear pods and electronic dash readouts designed to amuse rather than inform during traffic jams and 55mph cruises.

Motor's Richard Bremner looked at a Piazza in 1984 in a report titled, 'Piazza – full of eastern promise?' The Japanese spec cat-equipped unleaded 2-liter DOHC I4 was unwilling, and the conclusion was, "For European drivers, it is best admired from afar."[(61)] Credit Mazda for designing a smog motor with some fire – that was the Wankel appeal. Not only that, the FB RX-7 chassis had the dynamics to take the fight right to the Porsche 924 – judged Porsche's best handler of the day. It was a similar story in America, with another distant GM cousin called Fiero.

The plan was good: utilize existing GM corporate hardware with a new spaceframed, plastic paneled mid-engine, rear-drive two-seater sports car. On the early Pontiac

The North American RX-7 Series III had a unique instrument cluster, it was the only original RX-7 without a centrally placed tachometer. With front buckets fully back, RX-7 2+2s had front/rear legroom dimensions of 40/25½in. This FB has dual pulleys with underdriven water pump, and oil pan baffle plate. (Courtesy Jim Chung)

To meet stricter pollution laws Mazda changed its emissions control strategy from thermal reactor/leaded, to catalytic converter/unleaded gas on RX-7 Series II. This RX-7 Series III came with the base 12A carb motor, which is now fitted with Racing Beat accessories and Cartech turbo kit. (Courtesy Jim Chung)

With its front midship layout, 2400lb weight, size and mostly two-seater nature, the FB RX-7 was like a forerunner of the Miata (MX-5). The successful original RX-7 was never a factory ragtop. However, its enthusiast nature helped explain the commercial achievements of the later Miata. Toxico Illuminas, Racing Beat flywheel and oil pressure regulator aid performance on this FB. (Courtesy Jim Chung)

In spite of the front midship layout, placing the rotary engine just behind the front axle line meant that the original RX-7 was still nose-heavy. That said, its 54:46% weight distribution didn't prevent it from being one of the best handlers of its era. CP racing strut tower brace, OEM rear spoiler and LSD help this sports car stick to the road. (Courtesy Jim Chung)

A North American 1984 RX-7 GSL. In its second from last model year the FB RX-7 was an unqualified success. Dominant in IMSA GTU racing, excellent Kelley Blue Book resale value, and solid reputation with the public. (Courtesy Wayne Justice)

Another view of the Series III FB RX-7's unique P132 North American dashboard. GSL upgrades over older FBs involved clutch-type LSD and four-wheel disk brakes. (Courtesy Wayne Justice)

British Leyland North America priced its Triumph TR7 sports car relatively low compared to other markets, to remain competitive with the FB RX-7. (Courtesy Wayne Justice)

Apart from the Datsun Z car, the FB RX-7 had the Porsche 924, Fiat X1/9, Pontiac Fiero, and even C3 Corvette as competitors! It made out alright, thanks to rotary power. (Courtesy Wayne Justice)

Fieros, GM parts let the concept down. Rear suspension was from the GM X car, the front suspension from the T car. Motorvation was courtesy of GM's mileage savior the Iron Duke I4. The car had all independent suspension and four-wheel disks, but such ingredients alone do not a sports car maketh. It was a valiant attempt, but the clunky components created something heavier than ideal, and more sedan than sports car in feel.

The Iron Duke I4 motor didn't want to play ball; the Fiero needed more firepower. That would be the Citation V6, but this cast iron lovely made things even heavier. *Road & Track* value/performance compared Fiero against its only possible North American market rivals, the RX-7 and Fiat/Bertone X1/9. The Mazda was the only car that could do 0-60mph in under ten seconds. It was also the only one with a chance of a 2+2 layout. The price range in September 1983 was a projected $9000 for Fiero, with the Mazda and X1/9 established around the 11 and 16 grand levels respectively.

The conclusion was that Fiero was a nice starting point, but RX-7 was much more powerful and closer to a real sports car. The Fiat was seen as underpowered, but a superb nimble handler. However, even its 27mpg economy couldn't overcome that steep purchase price. Then there was the Fiat's fragility, 'built to last an Italian summer' and 'Fix It Again Tony' were popular descriptions – or epitaphs. The RX-7 consumed 21mpg, but was infinitely better made, and only marginally pricier than Fiero. Once depreciation was factored in, the Hiroshima Hero was probably cheaper.

Ford may have had Total Performance, but Mazda gave total value with the FB RX-7. By 1984, Mazda could show some decent EPA economy figures, 19 city and 29 highway mpg for a 12A-powered RX-7 GSL. Switching to a cat converter and unleaded had helped Mazda sidestep the rich fuel mix thermal reactor approach of yore. Mazda's quality and its rotary's reliability equaled a January/February 1984 *Kelley Blue Book* resale value for a 1981 RX-7 GSL of 93.4% of the original sticker price. In representing a reliable, value for money, attractive model conforming to sports car ideals, the RX-7 was unique in its era.

The FB's popularity from intro time saw long US waiting lists, and some unscrupulous dealers charging three grand over list price. Quite something on a sub 10K car. By the end of its run, 474,565 RX-7s had rolled off the Hiroshima assembly line, 377,878 of which were US sold. The car finished in Australia with the aptly named 1985 RX-7 Finale. This limited edition had special decals, and a blacked out section between the window and rear hatch. The Finale was loaded with all power options, and came with a brass plaque inscribed with the car's sequence number and the epitaph, 'Last of a Legend.'

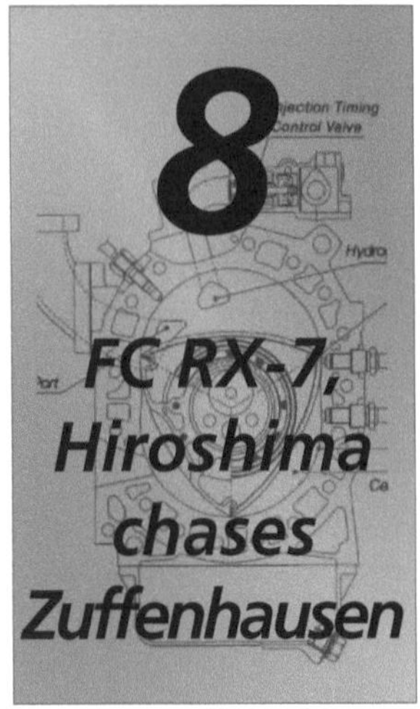

Benchmarking Porsche 944

An openly stated goal of the new 1986 model year FC chassis RX-7 was to match or better Porsche's 944 for less money. An ambitious goal, but as noted in *Fast Lane*'s December 1985 Porsche 944 Lux versus Mitsubishi Starion encounter, the Japanese automakers were less scared of taking on Porsche than European brands. Mazda was very confident at the FC RX-7's introduction, with a plan of innovation and image building to take the company into the early '90s. The aim was to create as much cache with the public for the Mazda brand as was enjoyed by Audi, BMW and Saab. A Mazda spokesman said, "We know their products are no better than ours."[62]

The 944 target was as much about necessity as anything else. Basically a steel-flared fendered version of the 924, with half a 928 V8, the Porsche 944 had captured the international sports coupe imagination. Not exactly beautiful, but its broad shoulder-padded image, coincided with '80s Yuppiedom. This new sub species of human evolution needed something to drive, somewhere to place their aluminum briefcases, and Porsche 944s or VW Golf GTis sufficed. The irony was that 944 was mostly made at the old NSU Neckarsulm factory that made the unfortunate Ro80.

Benchmarking is often an inescapable part of auto design life. The Mazda 121 subcompact used Fiat's Uno, and the Subaru Legacy utilized the Mercedes 190 and BMW 325i for dynamics. Toyota bought a new Porsche Cayman each year, during the 2012 Toyota 86's four-year development. The market dominance of Porsche 944 saw it systematically incorporated into the Mazda FC RX-7 development program. Looking back, many have felt the close shadowing of the 944 by FC RX-7 cost the new rotary the uniqueness possessed by the FB original.

UK's *CAR* magazine was in on the FC with its usual 'The Good, The Bad And The Ugly' comments. In the late '80s, it placed RX-7 in the 'Interesting' section, along with Porsche's 944, but delivered its expected two cents. Positive points for the £15,555 RX-7 atmo were smooth rotary engine, value; with negative attributes being bone-jarring ride, not-so-nimble handling, and the coupe's intent on being '944-like.' Conclusion was "Shameless aping doesn't pay." Then again, perhaps it did? The 944 cost £24,771 with an identical 135mph top speed.[63]

The Porsche beat RX-7 on acceleration and economy with 0-60mph in 7.5 rather than 8.5 seconds, and 30.6mpg, not 22.9mpg in *CAR*'s UK testing. *CAR*'s 944 comments revolved around Porsche's dreamland prices, and a wish that the 944 was more accessible. Such was Zuffenhausen's badge lure. The 944 similarity factor was most aired by the UK press, perhaps a bit miffed that, by this stage of the '80s, its car industry was largely out of the affordable sports car business. For example, can you say Reliant Scimitar?

In any case, it even made positive words on the FC RX-7 sound like backhanded praise. Observing the new 1986 cars in 'Tester's Year,' *Motor*'s Daniel Ward noted, "The Mazda RX-7 is a handsome machine, better-looking than the 944 the Japanese copied …."[64] Writing in the *Daily Express Guide To 1987 World Cars*, Gordon Wilkins took a more diplomatic line, saying the new Savanna RX-7 had "strong European echoes." Adding to this, it was stated that the new chassis had been carefully developed for good stability and handling.[65]

Judging a book by its cover – FC styling

At this time, good handling, small exterior dimensions and subtle styling were still seen as exclusively European properties. Perhaps the respective handling and style excesses of the Mitsubishi Starion and 1984 300 ZX didn't help? In any event, the FC RX-7 was labeled as the IBM clone PC of car, even though, stylistically, there were just two 944 elements Mazda were looking at for FC. One was a more steeply raked windshield than the FB RX-7. The second was the 944's iconic big rim 'fill

On debut in October 1985, a FC chassis Japanese spec RX-7 GT Limited. The new 1986 FC maintained Mazda tradition by retaining the Savanna name, centrally-placed tach, rear-drive and rotary engine. All FC RX-7s used variations on the 13B theme. (Courtesy Mazda)

A modified 1986 FC RX-7 in Moscow, Russia. This street-ported car has a 13B with Garrett GT3582R turbo. It also has Rage rims, sized 17 x 8in front and 17 x 9in rearwards. Originally in rough shape, the owner's first action was to restore the steel unibody. (Courtesy Alexander Savchuk)

The rolling road tells no lies. The result was 396 horses at 6700rpm at the rear wheels, dyno proven. Solid motor and tranny mounts feature, along with Walbro 255 LPH fuel pump, Perma-Cool 1070 oil thermostat and CX-Racing FD RX-7 radiator. (Courtesy Alexander Savchuk)

the arches,' minimal overhang, wheel at each extreme corner.

Beyond such elements, 944 and FC RX-7 diverged. The 944 had crisper edges, the FC RX-7 more rounded and organic. The story was reversed on the inside. For '86 MY the 944 sported a revised, rounded, organic dash, whereas RX-7 took a LEGO block approach – completely in keeping with clean, functional '80s dash practice, but lacking in charm compared to Mazda's '70s interiors. Most FC attention concerned the exterior, where the front was regarded as very close to the 944. Indeed, the mid-front fascia crease line made the Mitsubishi Starion and 944 peas from the same pod, whereas the RX-7 had a much more rounded front.

At first sight, *Road & Track* declared 944

A star in Russian tuner magazines, this modded FC RX-7 Turbo has M-1 Sport, Duraflex bodykit. M-1 Sport 20mm and 30mm Duraflex front and rear fender extenders feature respectively. D-1 Carbon Duraflex hood, Ganador reversing mirrors and JDM taillights complete the visual treat. (Courtesy Alexander Savchuk)

The interior features Sparco EVO buckets, roll cage and Racing Safety ignition switch panel. Haltech electronics are used for the IQ3 dash gauges, ECU (PS 1000), boost controller and 02 sensor. The Mazda 13B manual box is worked by a TCS short shifter, and through an ACT heavy duty clutch with 6 puck sprung disc. An ACT Streetlight flywheel is also employed, along with welded differential. (Courtesy Alexander Savchuk)

This modified 13B Turbo Wankel has an Atkins Solid Corner seal, FD RX-7 corner seal springs and FD RX-7 oil pressure regulator, along with NGK BR8EIX sparkplugs. Block off plates are used to eliminate smog gear, like EGR. The cold start injector from the throttle body was deep-sixed. Primary injectors are RC 750CC (x2), with secondary units being RC 1600 CC (x2). A dual-sheaf Racing Beat alternator pulley is utilized. (Courtesy Alexander Savchuk)

front, Dodge Daytona middle and third gen Camaro rear. Its conclusion was: derivative styling. Then again, how different can one make a pop-up headlamped coupe look, without resorting to wedge styling? Internationally, the FC RX-7 look was judged anywhere from sexy to conformingly pleasant, but *Autocar*'s Mark Gillies gave some further 1986 insights. Gillies said that, in Britain, very few liked the FC RX-7's styling. However, Gillies said he personally appreciated the FC's appearance, feeling it was more dramatically styled and better looking than the Porsche 924S on test. He also thought the RX-7's front was like a baby Corvette, which Gillies considered a positive feature.

This 1986 FC RX-7 Turbo's handling is aided by an HKS Hyper Max D kit, along with Super Steering angle and Toe Elimitor kits by Racing Beat. Bushings, swaybars and camber rod are sourced from Delrin, Godspeed and TCS respectively. Brake disks and pads are from Brake Labs, with brake lines from Apex. (Courtesy Alexander Savchuk)

FC Engineering – RX-7 goes high tech

As per the interior, the new RX-7 exterior moved away from the stylistic showmanship and badgework of the '70s. The FC had even less exterior decoration than the FB RX-7. Look up on the FC's 5mph integrated nosecone/bumper, and the neat 'Mazda' corporate front decal script was apparent. It was all very eighties, as was the new RX-7's mechanical spec. The FB had been constrained by budget. This meant retaining RX-3 hardware, and giving up the 924-style one-piece tailgate. Mazda designers settled on an all-glass hatch to cut cost. However, compromise was a dirty word concerning FC RX-7.

The FC RX-7 had all independent suspension, and four-wheel disk brakes from the start. The layout was like Porsche 924/944, minus the transaxle. Thus, a see-through diagram would show front MacPherson struts, lower A arms, coils, tube shocks and swaybar. Rear suspension involved semi-trailing arms, camber control arms on the drop links, tri-axial floating hubs, coils, tube shocks and swaybar. The rear suspension terms were code for passive rear wheel steer. Four-wheel steering was in vogue at the time, with Toyo Kogyo at the tech forefront.

At the 1984 Tokyo Auto Salon, Mazda exhibited an active four-wheel steering layout, indirectly controlled by computer. In 1987, one could buy a Mazda 626 with four-wheel steering; the GD Capella platform had a 626 2.0i GT 4WS five-door variant. The 4WS Honda Prelude was another luminary of the era. However, engineers increasingly sought easier ways to get handling benefits. Subaru's chief engineer Masaru Katsurada said a speed-sensing, computer-controlled 4WS 626-style system was tried on the original Legacy at proto stage in 1986, but was abandoned.

The FC RX-7 also avoided the complexity, and, some would say gimmick nature, of active 4WS. However, its suspension system sought the same outcome of controlling camber. The engineers achieved this mechanically by utilising links, bushings, levers and bearings, plus a design precedent embodied by the 1985-89 BF chassis Mazda Familia/323. This hatchback introduced TTL (Twin Trapezoidal Link). TTL helped the rear suspension prevent the rear wheels going toe-out during hard cornering, which would cause instability. The FC refined TTL with DTSS (Dynamic Tracking Suspension System) .

A 1986 Japanese spec Savanna RX-7 GT-X. With the FC RX-7 starting at a minimum of 2656lb, it was heavier than the smaller FB RX-7. This necessitated the 148 DIN PS 13B atmo rotary, as the new export base motor. The old FB got by with the smaller 12A. (Courtesy Mazda)

To retain low speed agility and a nimble nature, DTSS allowed the rear wheels to toe-out. Then, around the 0.4g to 0.5g lateral load point, the rear wheels would switch to toe-in for stability under hard acceleration, cornering and braking scenarios. Thus, the FC RX-7 avoided the wild oversteer exhibited by some high-performance cars, because their rear suspension permitted too much camber change. Mazda also tried to bake its own cake and eat it with the front suspension. Here, the FC followed the asymmetrical front suspension linkages of the GC Capella.

The FC RX-7 front suspension possessed a wide based lower A-arm, with lots of forged aluminum to reduce unsprung weight, which benefits handling. Normally, anti-dive front suspension geometry causes a harsh ride under braking, and on bumpy surfaces. Mazda's solution was to fit the A-arm fronts with soft longitudinal bushings, and fit firm bushings in the transverse direction. In trying to make suspension less of a compromise, Mazda had active suspension concerning shock absorbers for high line FC RX-7s. Another '80s high tech phenomenon, active suspension tried to combine ride comfort and handling in the one package.

By now, conventional adjustable springs and dampers were seen as old hat, at least in racing. At the highest level, active suspension implied replacing conventional hardware with aircraft tech hydraulics. Lotus was at the forefront of such tech, and incorporated an 'Active Ride' system into its 1983 grand prix car. Lotus had development contracts with four car makers, including GM and Volvo, to productionize Active Ride. A Volvo 760 Turbo proto showed the system in action. A micro computer administered changes in fluid pressure of the hydraulic cylinders would produce the optimal ride/handling balance for any situation.

In the future, post 1990, Active Ride was foreseen as a common option in the price range of a/c or ABS. In the real life 1986, Mazda delivered upscale RX-7s with AAS or Auto Adjusting Suspension. AAS involved using a computer to adjust shock absorber firmness to the ideal level. The computer would observe data on vehicle speed, acceleration, braking and steering wheel angle to work out lateral acceleration. A micro computer would work out what to do, with a signal sent to the shock absorber actuators to respond. The adjustment would occur in micro seconds.

With three levels of firmness, the shocks would vary between normal, firm and hard. Amble along under 50mph and the FC would cruise on the softest setting, changing to front shock level two the moment 50mph was attained. If the sensors said serious action was happening – heavy acceleration, cornering or braking – the computer would tell the actuators to go level three hard on all four wheels at once. The car's computer would make all these calls by itself. However, the driver had some input, via two console buttons marked Normal (Level one) and Sport (Level two). Naturally, if one floored the loud pedal under 30mph, the system would automatically go level three to minimize tail squat.

On the Mazda Miyoshi proving grounds, AAS was effective in delivering the right ride for any occasion. The same was tried with the FC's steering. Answering criticism concerning the FB's 'dead about center' recirc ball system, Hiroshima went rack and pinion on FC RX-7, with a high tech assistance device for upscale RX-7s. If one's FC had the optional power steering, a computer would work out the optimal power assist, judged on vehicle speed, cornering force and tire grip. The adjustment was done via valves and servos.

The FC RX-7's body had some special properties, beyond the 944 comparo. Aerodynamics were very key in the '80s, as a sales point, and to improve gas mileage. At 0.31, the stock FC had a very good drag coefficient. With the optional aero package, consisting of rear spoiler, small air dam and front fender well extensions, the drag coefficient was just 0.29. This bettered the trailblazing 1983 aero Audi 100. The FC's rear hatch wiper parked vertically to reduce drag, and a triple rubber seal around the door perimeter made for a quality door closing action. There was even a 'Flash-To-Pass' port, a small flush-mounted glass window placed ahead of the retracted pop-up quartz headlight. Flash-To-Pass allowed the FC's driver to flash their lights to pass, without having to raise the pop-ups.

Inside, Mazda continued its tradition of fine ergonomics, albeit with less panache than in old RX-4 days. The legendary eyeball swivel dash vents were gone, and a modern, blockish, gray plastic dash molding contained full sports car instrumentation. A very large central tach was surrounded by a sizable speedo and more analogue gauges, of ¼ sweep nature. The ¼ sweepers covered oil pressure, water temp, fuel and battery charge. Above the center console was a vehicle status panel, which included a quartz digital clock.

The instrument binnacle had all relevant control switches. On the left were the lights, turn signal, flashers, and on the right were cruise control, windshield wipers and environmental items. The sports steering wheel was mounted 0.2in eccentrically to afford a clearer view of the tach. As with other Japanese cars fore/aft, lumbar and back angle seat adjustment came standard, for the FC's velour or optional leather front buckets. The sporting icing on the cake was forged aluminum brake and clutch pedals.

Even though the materials weren't up to German quality, the FC easily out-ergonomicked the Porsche 924/944, and those controls harnessed a more powerful 13B. As per the US, FB RX-7 GSL-SE and EGI (Electronic Gas Injection) 79.8ci 13B was on hand, but the 9.4:1 comp motor had refinements. The six-port injected 13B now made 146bhp at 6500rpm and 138lb/ft at 3500 pm. These were SAE net figures, and, as with Porsche and its 944, Mazda was going with a one-world spec, unleaded gas-ready motor. In Japan, the same engine was rated at 148 DIN horses.

The 13B improvements involved a change to pulse chamber dimensions of the tuned intake system. This permitted improved intake charge filling. The latest 13B had reduced internal friction, thanks to smaller apex and side seals. Rotor weight was reduced 14% and exhaust diameter tubing was increased. Finally, different port timing allowed the redline to be 500rpm higher than in FB days. Whatever reliability qualms people had over 12A RX-7s were now gone. The 13B of 1986 MY was declared indestructible, and was the standard FC powerplant. The new RX-7 needed a bigger, more powerful engine, since the FC was larger and heavier than the outgoing FB.

FC stats for the export atmo 13B 1986 RX-7, commenced with a 2656lb coupe. With 169in length, 66.5in width and 50in height, plus manufacturer claimed top of 130mph. *Autocar*'s April 2 1986 figures were 134mph, with 0-60mph in 8.5 seconds, so the claimed figures seemed legit. US testers always seem to get better 0-60mph times out of cars, probably due to Stateside ¼-mile familiarity; the FC RX-7 was no exception. According to *Motor Trend*'s Ron Grable in January 1986, one of the six test fleet FCs at the US Seattle press show-and-tell managed 0-60mph in 7.7 seconds.

This figure equaled the outgoing FB GSL-SE's best. It also matched the time *Road & Track* got with the less smog/CAFE-controlled pre-1980 four-speed L82 Corvette. However, the FC was a bigger beast than the FB, and came with 17/24mpg city/highway EPA numbers. That the FC achieved this efficiency was due to Mazda's engineers fearing the US gas guzzler tax enough to keep weight to a minimum. Mazda approached the FC's creation in a systematic fashion. Chief project engineer on FC RX-7 was Akio Uchiyama. Most FB RX-7s were sold in North America, so Uchiyama and his team spent some time in America checking market tastes.

Owner profiles were studied for the FB RX-7 and popular rival sports cars, which included the wildly admired Porsche 944. The 944 was an original benchmark FC goal, so the Porsche's popularity showed Mazda was on the right track. Catering to market tastes also meant FC RX-7 wouldn't be as pure a sports car as FB RX-7. Owner surveys, and prevailing early '80s economic conditions, dictated that gas mileage mattered. Indeed, FC RX-7 development took a one-month break towards the end of the FC's design phase, around May 1983, because Mazda was concerned about the US gas guzzler tax.

The tax added a surcharge to purchase price, to encourage car buyers to choose thriftier vehicles. To make sure FC RX-7 wouldn't get unfairly slugged, Mazda pared down the pounds as best it could. As a result, the FC featured more alloy parts than any new Mazda since the R360 microcar. Aluminum was used for the front suspension arms, engine mount brackets, front brake callipers and optional hood choice. An aluminum jack even saved 1.3kg. The FC's new hatch arrangement had a steel sash around the perimeter, mating to the body with a rubber seal. This method relied on the sash to provide strength, allowing the hatch glass to be thinner. The upshot was a ten-pound weight saving.

The US RX-7 FC turbo arrived in the North American market, for 1986½ model year, with 182 SAE net horses. Turbo versions can be visually distinguished by the hoodscoop feeding air to the engine-top-mounted intercooler. The turbo arrived in time for a horsepower battle, in a revived North American sporty car market. (Courtesy Alex Tong)

No hoodscoop meant a normally aspirated, world export market 13B was present. The upscale US RX-7 FC GXL with 15in rims carried a base price of $16,645. This handily undercut the early 1986 $22,950 base of the revised Porsche 944 that the FC was shadowing. (Courtesy Alex Tong)

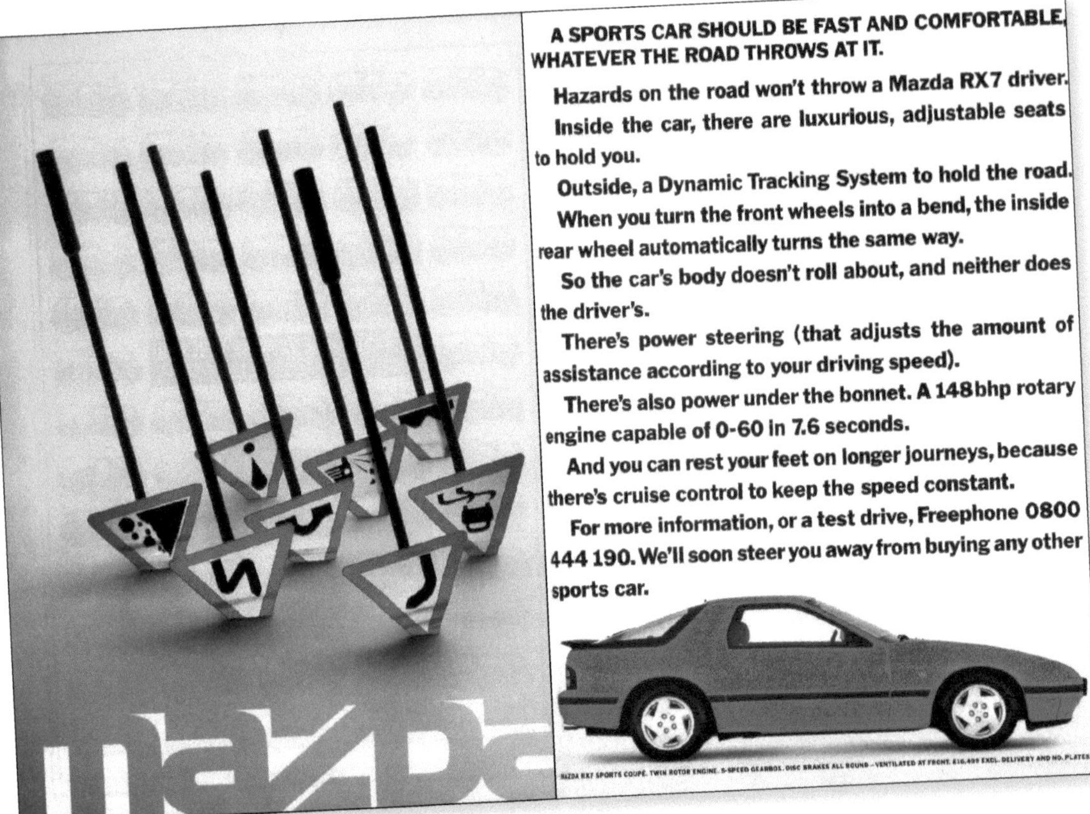

A 1988 RX-7 with 148 bhp 13B motor. (Courtesy Mazda)

The 200 bhp 1989 RX-7 Turbo II convertible. (Courtesy Mazda)

Those inevitable comparisons

To maintain quality feel in a world of weight saving, Mazda put a triple seal around the door perimeter. Perhaps weight saving motivated so many companies to switch from badges to decals in the '80s?! In spite of the seal tricks, the FC, and other new lighter designs, lacked the quality heft of older models. The comment was made that a Porsche 924/944 door thunked closed with greater reassurance. In addition, despite Mazda's great strides in rotary gas mileage and weight savings, the new FC RX-7 came off second best in economy/performance balance comparos.

Autocar tested the FC RX-7 in 1986, the Lotus Esprit S3 atmo in late 1984, and the Corvette TPI in late 1985. For top speed, 0-60mph and overall UK mpg, the three manual cars produced respective results of 134mph/8.5 seconds/18.7mpg, 130mph/7.3 seconds/23.2mpg and 151mph/6 seconds/17.6mpg. Okay, the Mazda had a debut UK price of £13,995, with the Lotus on £17,980, but the rotary sports car still didn't deliver the go its mpg suggested.

The new wave of light, affordable sporty front-drivers were interesting. The Celica GT 2-liter I4 had 150bhp and a 130mph top end. Mazda's RX-7 even had some internal competition from its BF Familia/323 Turbo all-wheel drive performance hatch. With a DOHC, 16-valve, intercooled turbo 1.6-liter I4, this 'hot hatch' matched the atmo 13B rotary's 148 DIN bhp rating, and did 0-60mph in 7.9 seconds. The four-cylinder didn't provide the 13B's smooth power trip, but did give 23.4mpg economy, even though top speed was a mere 125mph according to *Autocar*. *Autocar & Motor* made the following critical RX-7 atmo comment, "Powerful argument for piston engines."(66)

The advances in engine technology and the rise of high-performance hatchbacks were giving RX-7 a hard time. There was even a junior 'pocket rocket' hatch class surfing the technical wave. An early example was the diminutive Suzuki Swift GTi, with the world's first 16-valve DOHC 1.3 EPI motor in a production car. The 1.3-liter made 101 DIN bhp, and matched RX-7's mid eight-second 0-60mph sprint. Top speed was only 112mph, but the Swift GTi and other hot hatches had served notice to the sports car world. The hatches were front-drive, and lacked traditional swoopy coupe styling, but in the case of the Swift GTi, cost a mite under half the RX-7's price.

FC RX-7 reception

The value of rear-drive and sexy looks was getting pricey. However, FC RX-7 was looked forward to greatly, after the successful FB RX-7. This was certainly so in Japan. When doing the FC, Mazda chose the P747 development code, because it gave no idea of the configuration of the new RX-7. People wanted to know. *Motor* magazine's correspondent in Japan, Kevin Radley, divulged some accurate spy/rumor info in January 1985. He said the new car would have a wraparound lifting hatch, independent rear suspension, an uprated atmo 13B and supercharged 200-horse 13B.

The preview info was incorrect about other elements: the forced induction method, and the adoption of the RX-8 name, at least as far as the 20th century went. The *Motor* spy drawing was quite accurate, except the nose was rather Starion origami-like, and blister Can Am fenders very noticeable versus the final, smoother FC.(67)

In Japan, the new FC stuck to tradition, retaining the FB's Savanna RX-7 tag verbatim. In America, the feeling was that FC was so 'all new,' it should be called RX-8. The North American importer was Mazda Motors of America, located in Rancho Dominguez, California. It was hoped the top RX-7 GXL

Autocar's stats for the 1986 FC RX-7 atmo had 134mph top speed, 0-60mph in 8.5 seconds and 18.7mpg overall. For a 1986 Corvette the figures were 151mph, 0-60mph in 6 seconds and 17.6mpg overall. The RX-7 was increasingly seen as thirsty for the performance. (Courtesy Cameron Bentley)

The FC RX-7 interior, pictured in April 1989; note the rear jump seats. As with other 1980s cars, the FC RX-7 had blander interior and exterior designs compared to '70s predecessors. Well put together, but the plastics lacked the quality touch of the Porsche 944 that the FC was benchmarked against. (Courtesy Mazda)

On debut in October 1988, the turbocharged 200 horse 13B was felt to give the FC RX-7 the performance its looks promised. The intercooler sat atop the 13B, and its script said it all! Note the Denso a/c compressor to the left of the 13B's radiator fan. (Courtesy Mazda)

would come in under 17 grand, with the basic edition under $12,000.

Unlike in FB days, one didn't receive more power in a pack with extra luxury. All North American FCs initially used the atmo 13B. True to the promise, the FC RX-7 GXL arrived at $16,645, with a lot more fruit than the starter $22,950 Porsche 944. The basic RX-7 was very plain in spec and came with 185/70 14in radials. The RX-7 GXL had front- and rear-vented disk brakes, with four-piston front calipers, plus 15in alloys with 205/60 Bridgestone Potenzas.

Apart from AAS, DTSS and smart power steering, GXL options ran to a/c, power sunroof, burglar alarm, leather seating, Pioneer CD player and even an aluminum hood. Magazine testers and enthusiasts alike were miffed that one couldn't get the base car with GXL's better rim/tire package. Testing the RX-7 GXL caused this opinion, as many felt the car's '80s high-tech handling gizmos got between driver and car. The DTSS camber controller wasn't so apparent, but the computer-controlled steering and shocks were another matter.

However, objectively the FC handling had to be judged an improvement on FB RX-7. Weight distribution was improved to 51:49% from 54:46%, and sudden oversteer was more under control. Lap times on a given track were also better. At the Seattle press launch, FB and FC RX-7s, with five-speed manual and EGI 13Bs, were run at Kent Raceway. The new FC was 2.5 seconds quicker than its FB predecessor, and just 0.5 second slower than the Porsche 944 on hand. *Road & Track* tested the 1986 RX-7 GXL and Porsche 944 at Willow Springs International Raceway, once again 944 won out.

At Willow Springs, the RX-7 GXL was 1.5 seconds slower than the 944. – At first, it had been 2.6 seconds slower. Feeling the car wasn't right, Mazda flew in Takaaki Ito, the manager of chassis design department number three. Ito san and a couple of Mazda assistants replaced some suspension bushings that weren't up to spec, and the GXL was much improved. Then *R&T* tried an RX-7 with optional Sport Package, a lighter car with larger brake rotors and no AAS. The RX-7 Sport was less than 0.5 second slower per lap than the 944. However, somehow, all FCs seemed to exhibit erratic rear brake locking.

In the *Autocar* April 2 1986, 'Two Of A Kind' Porsche 924S/FC RX-7 comparo test, Mark

Gillies said one had to drive the new FC Alain Prost smooth, not Keke Rosberg rough. UK cars were basically five-speed manual only GXLs on FC debut, and the standard computer control AAS smart shocks reacted sharply to driver inputs. No sudden movements brought the best results. The UK FC RX-7 arrival with 205/60 VR 15in tires, radio cassette player and sunroof as standard, but power steering was unavailable.

Looking back on the April 2 1986 test, *Autocar* said the FC was let down by softer suspension settings aimed at the North American market. The non-power rack and pinion steering was judged lacking in feel. Plus, in spite of the 4.10 final drive, Gillies said one was always a cog lower in the FC versus the Porsche 924S. Tested on the UK's West Country roads, Gillies felt the RX-7 wasn't quite as competent as the 924S, but was more exciting and definitely a serious sports car.

The FC RX-7 made its UK TV debut on the BBC's *Top Gear* motoring show in 1986, where, predictably, it was tested against the newly re-engined Porsche 924S. Audiences experienced the trademark rotary warning buzzer, telling the driver to change up close to 7000rpm. It's interesting to note that every UK FC road test, after *Autocar*'s initial report, complained about the FC RX-7's suspension being too harsh. It was also noteworthy that on UK debut in 1986, the FC was exactly £1500 cheaper than the first rung on the Zuffenhausen ladder.

With 10.9in front and 10.7in rear-vented disk brakes, and 15 x 6in alloys wrapped in Bridgestone Potenza RE71 tires, plus AAS and DTSS, upscale FC RX-7s had the spec on paper, and nearly in practice. Chalk up the difference in RX-7 versus 924/944 ability to the price difference, and the fact Porsche had been dealing solely with sports cars since 1948. Getting something that started close to Hitler's Bug, to handle, would make a company wise about traversing bumps and going around corners. The RX-7's Japanese-style lighter controls, and chassis behavior would suit the far greater number of customers that could afford an RX-7, compared to a Porsche.

Market greetings! Hello, FC RX-7 …

In Japan, the latest RX-7 quickly took on the position of one of the country's hero cars, and the competition was as intense as ever. The situation was shown in the 1988 edition of the Fujimi kit model car catalogue. Versions of the 'New Savanna RX-7' were available in 'Inch Up Mini' 1:48 scale (kit #00006-IM6 New Savanna RX-7) and 'Inch Up Disk' 1:24 scale (kit #03034 ID-34 New Savanna RX-7). There were also versions of Japan's other newish performance cars: Nissan MID4, Nissan Skyline Seventh Generation, new front-drive Toyota Celica 2000 GT, Toyota Soarer 3.0 GT, Toyota MR2, revised Nissan 300 ZX, Honda Prelude XX and that rear-drive legend, Toyota Sprinter Trueno.[68]

Kenichi Yamamoto, pictured while Mazda president from 1984-87. Yamamoto san and his 47 Samurai engineers got the rotary humming in the 1960s. In the wake of the fuel crisis, Yamamoto also convinced Sumitomo Bank that rotary was still a wise investment. (Courtesy Mazda)

So many cars, and the RX-7 was the only rotary, a feature that was still Mazda's calling card. That quality was also still a North American draw card, a continent that seemed to like the company's '80s designs. The front-drive GLC took up where the original left off. *Motor Trend* bestowed its Import Car Of The Year title on the new front-drive Capella/626 in 1983, and the same accolade went to the FC RX-7 in 1986. The sports scene was getting intense in North America, too, at FC intro.

With world gas prices on the way down, and CAFE frozen for the next 30 years, automakers renounced their vow of abstinence and started making the good stuff again. There were 5.7-liter GM F bodies, turbo I4 Mopars and 24-valve I6 Toyota Celica Supras, plus countless affordable 16-valve front-drivers. Then there was the 1987 Ford Mustang GT 5.0, costing only $11,324. Mazda responded with a mid-1986 MY FC RX-7 Turbo packing 182bhp (SAE), and a 1988 ragtop. Power was back, and so too were open top cars, now that roll-over safety law fears had subsided.

The RX-7 Turbo could match the acceleration of a 5-liter Mustang or 5.7-liter GM F body, but at a far higher price. However, with that price came much greater chassis sophistication,

Note the steel rims of this FC RX-7 GT. Mazda's Takaharu 'Koby' Kobayakawa, FD RX-7 program manager, was adamant that the price leader FC approach to keeping RX-7 sales volume high was bad news. (Courtesy Mazda)

build quality, and appeal to a different, upscale buyer. The Turbo was a good PR halo car, and the regular RX-7 in Japan. Publicity can also be achieved through media exposure. The great US popularity of the original RX-7, meant the FB got around without Mazda really trying. Sally Field's journalist character in the 1981 movie *Absence of Malice* drove an RX-7.

Three FB RX-7s featured in a final season episode of *The Fall Guy*, starring Lee Majors. Here the cars were supposed to be water-damaged stock, and got used in some exciting stuntwork, where the FB's nimble nature was a boon. In the late '80s, Mazda took a more formal PR approach, with actor and car/racing enthusiast James Garner doing US Mazda TV ads. The advertising included the FC RX-7 convertible, which was technically interesting as well as attractive. It was claimed to be the first ragtop with an integral windblocker. The rigid panel folded up from behind the rear passenger seats. It blocked drafts, but also reduced the FC ragtop to pure two-seater status.

Mazda also claimed its car was the first production convertible where the entire convertible assembly dropped as a complete unit into the rear body cavity. To drop the top, unlatch two header catches, power lower the top halfway, then manually fold down the rigid section, power lowering to complete. It was by no means completely automated, but with some patience, the roof's rigid center section could be removed to fashion a targa top – yet another Porsche connection. Popular in the '80s, the FC convertible had optional audio speaker containing headrests. There was also

One of the greatest high performance engines of the '90s, the iconic Mazda 20B-REW. Powering the 1990 JC Cosmo, this huge 2-liter rotary has been the only triple rotor Wankel to date in production. (Courtesy Chris Stredwick)

a leather snap-fasten tonneau cover to keep things neat.

Help from Henry – the Ford connection

Not so neat was the atmo-only nature of the snazzy FC RX-7 convertible, in the North American and Australian markets. To get show-with-go and the turbo ragtop, one had to reside in Japan or the UK. Mazda as a corporation had been doing some hands-across-the-water cooperation with America, in the form of the Ford Motor Company. After decades of historical coincidences, and a buy-in attempt where Ford tried to nab rotary and Mazda refused, Dearborn and Hiroshima had a meeting of the minds. In the early '70s, Henry Ford II declared Mazda worthless beyond Wankel, but now ...

In the brave new post-Iacocca world, it seemed Ford and Mazda needed each other. Ford had been sawing Mavericks in two to create affordable subcompacts, but now needed a small car tech partner, to help create a Pinto-replacing front-drive hatch for the '80s. There were also several projects where even a giant like Ford lacked expertise; Hiroshima could help. Mazda was successfully restructuring away from rotary dependence during the late '70s. However, rotary had been a financial drain. Mazda needed to fund a range of modern '80s front-drivers and remain a largely independent automaker.

The upshot was Ford Motor Co taking a 7% stake in Mazda during 1979, quickly increasing to 20% by the early '80s. And so started a number of joint design, production and distribution ventures. The first noticeable one was the new Mazda Familia BD of 1980. It was a front-drive hatch, done with Ford aid, and was the platform basis for the new US 1981 MY Ford Escort. Ford Australia made clone versions of the Familia BD, as the Ford Laser, around this time. The Australian Ford Telstar was derived from Mazda's new front-drive Capella/626. Both replaced the rear-drive European Ford Escort and Cortina that Ford Australia had been making for years.

The program even saw Ford Australia make the Ghia-designed Ford/Mercury Capri. This was a 2+2 front-drive roadster utilizing Mazda 323 mechanicals. The car was aimed at and exported to America. In spite of product placement in a car show scene on an episode of US sitcom *Cheers*, this particular Capri was a limited success. People were flocking to Mazda showrooms to grab a Miata. Mazda had a plan to actually make cars in America. To short circuit the yen/dollar exchange rate, and overcome import quotas, Mazda wanted to emulate Nissan and Honda. At first, it was going solo.

In 1984, Japan's third biggest automaker was considering a vacant Detroit Ford plant, but didn't wish to be involved with Ford. A Mazda spokesman said, "We want to do it our way."[69] As things turned out, Mazda's first US plant had Ford involvement. Ford was working on a modern front-drive Mustang replacement for the Fox platform in the '80s, but the project was outside Ford's expertise. Mazda were doing a cool coupe based on the next gen front-drive GD Capella/626. Ford thought, let the next Mustang be a cousin of the upcoming Mazda MX-6. However, before this could transpire a national 'Save the Foxstang' campaign brewed up, showing Mustang devotees against the idea of a non-V8, front-drive Stang.

In spite of the tenuous connection between the graceful '60s Shelby Mustang, and plastic clad '80s GT 5.0, many felt the status quo was worth preserving. The upshot was Ford prising off 'Mustang IV' badges from the prototypes, and applying the '80s cyber-like 'Probe' nameplate instead. Mazda built this Ford Probe, alongside its 626 and MX-6, thereby achieving commercial viability concerning its first US factory. That plant was the $550 million Flat Rock, Michigan facility. As part of completing Probe, Ford engineers and designers made a trip to Hiroshima. In Japan, they played with the exterior, interior and driving dynamics to get

Unlike other companies, Mazda had the decency to include a turbo boost gauge on its FC RX-7 Turbo. At least one could keep tabs on the activity of the twin-scroll Hitachi-made turbo. Air conditioning and Pioneer CD player represented typically excellent Japanese standard equipment for the price. (Courtesy Mazda)

The HC platform Luce saw the nameplate jump from midsize to fullsize in September 1986. The piston version was still called 929 in export markets. This HC generation was the first time North America met the piston 929 (1988 MY). (Courtesy Mazda)

Probe right for North America. Don Sherman said the Probe was probably the nicest car Ford never built.[70]

Ford interest extended to Mazda's small pickups, hence the B series/Ford Courier connection. To overcome cost problems of making US subcompacts, there was the Ford Festiva, a Kia Korean-made version of the Mazda 121. However, concerning this Kia Pride, Mazda stated it merely provided tech assistance to the Korean firm. In any case, FC RX-7 sales sauntered on; around 86,000 FC RX-7s were sold Stateside in the car's first '86 MY. Sales peaked in North America in 1988 model year. However, as a sports car, how sporty was the FC RX-7?

The original NA chassis Miata, pictured in 1989, and sold as the Eunos Roadster in Japan. The Miata used the front midship layout first seen on the FB RX-7, and pioneered the Powerplant Frame (PPF), which would be used on the FD RX-7. (Courtesy Mazda)

FC RX-7, how good the sports car?

The answer was: very. The FC RX-7 carried on FB tradition by winning the 1989 and 1990 IMSA GTU titles. It was a FC RX-7 that took out the RX-7's 100th victory in IMSA GTU life. This happened in September 1990, in San Antonio, Texas. Then there was the big success of New Zealand racer Peter Farrell, in the 1993 IMSA Firehawk series, using an Agfa-sponsored FC RX-7. To commemorate the RX-7's long GTU success, the North American market saw a formalised version of the 1986-87 RX-7 Sport, which was basically a light atmo car with the good rim/tire/brake pack; and as a special 1988 US version, say hello to the RX-7 GTU.

The 13B atmo-powered GTU used the 15in five-bolt GXL rims with 205/60 tires, four-piston front callipers with associated bigger-than-base rotors, front and rear spoilers, firmed up suspension, clutch pack LSD, and shorter 4.3:1 final drive ratio. The usual ratio was 4.11:1. Logically, to achieve Colin Chapman's speed by adding lightness, the GTU did without power steering, radio, a/c or sunroof. However, to earn a little value-added greenbacks, some dealers sold cars with dealer-installed sunroofs.

Featuring a cloth interior, the GTU wasn't exactly showroom eye candy, but *Road & Track* liked it. In a choice between the loaded commemorative 10th Anniversary 16in rimmed, turbocharged, all white RX-7 and the stripper GTU, *R&T* felt the GTU was the real enthusiast's ticket. After all, who doesn't enjoy a stripper on their birthday? In 1989 model year, the FC RX-7 adopted the international improvements of the Series V, and the new North American base became the RX-7 GTU. Upscale of this was the performance-directed GTU-S. 1989 was the first time US FC RX-7s adopted a viscous-type LSD.

As an enhanced atmo lightweight, the GTU-S featured the convertible's aluminum hood, quicker FC RX-7 steering ratio and the ten-horse Series IV to V upgrade, but not the planned 20B rotor tip, due to engineering issues. Unfortunately, the GTU-S didn't sell well, only 2000 units in 1989 and a mere 400 copies in 1990, the variant's last year. Mazda North America never marketed the GTU versions properly, and buyers were confused as to which FC was the hot one. The GTU tag was dropped, and, for 1990, the base RX-7, though technically the same, was simply called RX-7.

On a cosmetic level, 1986-87 RX-7 Series IVs had squarer taillights, and black bumper and door rubstrips. The 1989-92 cars had round 'RX-3 tribute'-style taillights, and color-coded rubstrips. Fuel-injection engine management was upgraded, and, using Japanese DIN ratings, the atmo 13B moved from 148bhp/138lb/ft to 161bhp/140lb/ft. The turbo 13B rose from 185bhp/183lb/ft to 200bhp /195lb/ft. The latter was another Mazda milestone, and *Performance Car*'s Kevin Blick described the achievement in the 1990 March issue, 'Southern Comforts' Porsche 944 S2 versus RX-7 Turbo II convertible encounter compare, as follows, "painstakingly improved over the years by Mazda to its present turbocharged, intercooled and electronically managed 200bhp zenith."

Note well, the intercooler sitting atop the venerable 13B, receiving cool dense air via the forward facing hoodscoop. Lift the hood and '13B Intercooled Turbo II' was emblazoned in red on the silver intercooler housing. Being the second turbo RX-7 post-FB days, Turbo II was a logical nomenclature. Unlike the lag-prone Mitsubishi Starion, Mazda's blower answered the call of the wild from just 2000rpm, even in top. Hiroshima's trick was an Hitachi 'Twin Scroll' turbo, that spooled virtually from the get go. Mazda accurately claimed 150mph and 0-60mph in just over six seconds. Enough to match a Chevy Chevelle SS 454, but the Turbo II came with a cat converter and used unleaded gas in all markets.

With an environmentally-clear conscience, Mazda added a 'Turbo II' front fender callout decal behind the wheel well, and, in terms of driving experience, one was always in front. A 1990 MY RX-7 Turbo II convertible ad said, 'You'll Never Forget The First Time You Open It Up." With that 'wind-Jammer,' it also claimed "So the only thing that really gets blown is your mind." The Turbo II coupe and convertible made their UK market debut in the fall of 1989, at £21,999 and £23,999 respectively. Like Japan, but unlike America and Australia, the UK market had its ragtop with a Turbo 13B. Like all FC ragtops, it also had the refinement of a real, heated, glass rear window. Something the front-engined Porsche ragtop didn't have.

The UK Turbo II ragtop came with leather interior and power top standard. However, the convertible couldn't be ordered with ABS. A curious omission in the high tech '80s, and even more strange, given the UK Turbo II coupe could have ABS. Maybe some of Henry Ford's 'safety doesn't sell' was rubbing off on Mazda?! On FC release, ABS was a Japanese market option. That said, as far as North America went, chief chassis and handling engineer Takiguchi san said they would try ABS out in Japan first. With the bad vibes from Audi 5000s experiencing beserk cruise control, the option caution was understandable.

In any case, the Turbo II's 13B greatly closed the door on street car porting, the former engine mod of choice. Mild, extend, bridge, J/Monster and peripheral, the idea was to increase the size of the intake port, so more fuel and air could be ingested to make more power. Trouble was, the bigger the hole, the lower the low end torque and driveability. Noise, poor fuel economy and reduced Wankel life accompanied wild porting. From bridge porting onwards, an 'eyebrow' opening is added alongside the normal port. The bridge becomes smaller with more advanced porting, eventually risking the rotor's corner seals falling out.

Monster porting sees the aperture hole extend past the rotor face, into the housing water seal/O-ring area. This requires the seal to be cut back and filled with a metal-type sealant like Devcon. Depending on the extent

1990 Savanna RX-7 GT-X. In designing the FC RX-7, Mazda sought to copy the big-wheel, flared-fender, minimal-overhang look popularized by the 1980s Porsche 944. (Courtesy Mazda)

The HC Luce was available with a bewildering variety of power teams in Japan. Internationally, this bodystyle was known for its excellent 3-liter V6, but in Japan it could be had with the turbo 13B. The low volume HC Luce Rotary Turbo's place was taken by the spectacular 1990 Cosmo. (Courtesy Mazda)

of porting, the water gallery may have to be blocked off and even more sealant filling done. In spite of the blocking and filling, coolant still leaks through the seals.

Peripheral porting is the wildest mod, with the side ports filled in and new circular intake ports done through the rotor housing. A tubular intake manifold is an easy peripheral port identifier. Peripheral porting creates a Wankel motor with a 2000rpm idle speed, and 6- to 12-month engine life, or under 7500 miles. Thus, to avoid such performance pitfalls, a 200-horse 13B Turbo II unit is the RX-3 street car drop in choice par excellence.

Very special RX-7 Turbos

For the peak in factory-provided refined performance, one sought out the Japanese market RX-7 Savanna Infini Series. The ultimate Turbo FCs were made in a low volume run, 600 units per annum, with annual changes from 1987 to 1991. Identified by an Infini logo on the tail – the sight most drivers would see – there was also an Infini logo steering wheel, 15in BBS alloys, aero bodykits, bronze tinted window glass and special exterior colors for each year of availability.

The aluminum hood and scoop were on the functional side, as were upgraded sports suspension, modified ECU and weight saving measures. The floor bar on the passenger side was a nod to the 'boy racer' '80s era. Infini Series I came out for 1987 MY, with the Series II as a 1988 debutante. Both were FC RX-7 Series IV spec cars, and were limited to white or black exteriors. The Infini Series III arrived in 1990, with the Series IV coming out in 1991. These were FC RX-7 Series V-based, the Infini Series III was painted in Forest Green alone, with the Infini Series IV available in Forest Green or Noble Green.

Pictured in March 1991, the Series IV Infini was based on the FC Savanna RX-7 Series V. Between 1987 and 1991, Mazda made a low volume run of ultimate FC RX-7s. These turbocharged Japanese spec Infini cars were considered the finest RX-7s of the pre FD era. (Courtesy Mazda)

Mazda also offered go-faster, inhouse tuner accessories for the Japanese spec RX-7 Savanna via its Mazdaspeed catalogue. The 1998 edition carried a bodykit with front spoiler, rear spoiler base and intercooler scoop. Handling could be improved with a Ride-Height Adjustable Suspension Unit set, utilising Eibach springs. Reinforced Stabilizer bars and aluminum shock tower strut bar, along with Sports Rubber Bushings, could also be fitted to sharpen handling. A mechanical system limited-slip differential helped maximize traction.

To help get the blown 13B's power to the LSD, Mazdaspeed did a Twin plate Clutch, special Clutch Cover and Lightweight Flywheel made of chrome molybdenum steel with a nitrided surface. To facilitate shifting, Mazdaspeed's Sports Shifter had an anti-vibration rubber on the shift lever. It was designed to make positive feel shifts, with throws shortened by around 25%, creating 'snap-of-the-wrist' shifting. High-performance brake pads and Teflon Brake Lines, covered with stainless steel mesh, all improved the FC's active safety.

All the above showed Mazdaspeed was as obsessive as any tuner inside, or outside, Japan. However, for flash you can't touch a limited edition. The 1500-unit run of 10th Anniversary RX-7s of 1988 were an instant collector car goldmine. A Crystal White monochromatic exterior, with matching white bodyside moldings, taillight housings, side mirrors and 16in seven-spoke alloy rims. Gold rotor shaped 10th Anniversary Edition fender badges let bystanders know this Turbo II-motorvated coupe had met the bling quota. Inside, one found an all black leather interior, leather wrapped steering wheel with 10th Anniversary Edition center piece, plus Italian Momo shifter and boot surround.

The 10th Ann's exterior had Infini-style bronze tinted glass. Moving from Series IV to Series V the FC increased one inch in length, from 168.9in to 169.9in. The sales numbers for FC totaled 272,027 units, another increase, but not as numerous as its FB predecessor. As a final hurrah, Mazda did a limited run of 500-loaded Turbo II ragtops for the Japanese market 1992 model year. Poor America never got the blown convertible. North America took around 5000 FC ragtops in 1988, less over the 1989-91 timeframe. Indeed, although FCs were on a continual rise globally, thanks to Japanese sales, they were on a US decline since the '88 MY peak.

Although that limited edition 1992 Turbo II convertible had glamor, it was an original 1986 FC RX-7 that would become the fastest FC. The car in question was the Racing Beat-prepared RX-7 that visited Bonneville salt flats for 1986's Speed Week. The project was managed by Racing Beat's chief engineer Jim Mederer, and concerned the Grand Touring Sports class. Here the engine and chassis could be modified greatly, but the bodyshape was off limits; tachiiri kinshi. Only some FC parts were used on the front suspension, none at the rear and the driveline was a FC parts free zone too.

To keep a small frontal area, special rims of 21 x 5.5in dimensions, with tall tires, were employed. Goodyear Funny Car tires lived out back, with a custom Racing Beat five tubular link rear suspension utilising Porsche 911 stub-axle carriers. There weren't any rear brakes. The original plan was to import four Mazda competition dept Japanese GTP endurance turbo 13Bs, but these were discovered to be not durable enough. Racing Beat instead created a custom-modified 13B turbo. This bridge-ported unit had a 7.5:1 comp ratio, dry sump lubrication and Bosch/Kugelfischer mechanical fuel-injection hardware.

The Hitachi twin turbos used exotic metals that had to be imported. This pertained to the turbine housings and exhaust pipes made from special alloy steel, heat resistant to 2100F. An air-to-water intercooler was utilized, with a capacity of three gallons of chilled water. A rear reservoir had a mix of ice and water, with ice cubes added prior to each record pass. The intercooler dropped the intake temp from 280 degrees to just 45, allowing the 13B to make 530bhp at 8500rpm using 14.7psi of boost. Power went through a $6000 five-speed Weismann Transmissions crashbox, and driveline with Summers Brothers spool drive in Porsche instrument grade bearings.

Spinning its Enkei rims, the Racing Beat FC RX-7 set a blown GT record of 238.442mph. The record still stands to this day.[71] As a commercial record breaker, FC RX-7 was certainly good enough for Mazda to continue with the RX-7 concept. With the late '80s recession, Porsche 944 was on the skids. It prompted Porsche to cut 944 '88 MY production by 50%. Most unsold Porsches were US 944s, so no reason to shadow Zuffenhausen anymore. With the next RX-7, Hiroshima would reveal a truly unique and uncompromising sports car.

The finale for the FC RX-7 chassis, the Japanese spec Savanna Winning Limited turbo 13B powered sports car, pictured in September 1991. Impressive, but the new wave of Japanese supercars were quickly upstaging the single turbo FC RX-7. (Courtesy Mazda)

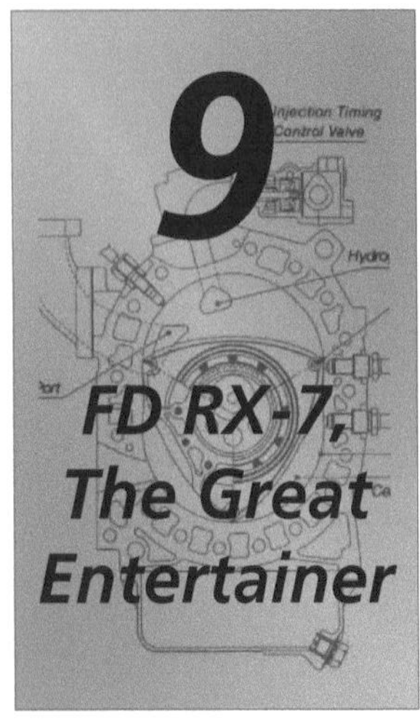

Exciting design ideas

By the late '80s Mazda didn't have a very exciting fleet of cars. Models like the 1987 DA chassis 121 subcompact, aging 929L wagon and even the FC RX-7, were worthy, but rather bland, fare. In 1988, Mazda engaged in the Kansei program, an empirical approach to creating enthusiast cars. First signs of Mazda's new wave cars came with the 1989 Mazda MX-5, called Miata in North America. Unveiled at the Chicago Auto Show, on February 10 1989, Mazda's Experiment No 5 reinvented ye olde British style two-seater roadster, and was an instant hit worldwide. Popular with public and critics alike, the MX-5's genesis involved a 1976 discussion between *Motor Trend*'s Bob Hall, rotary savior Kenichi Yamamoto and Mazda R&D boss Gai Arai, on what kind of car Mazda should make in the future.

The answer was a modern version of the '60s Lotus Elan, and the idea was followed up by Mazda's new 1982 Southern California design studio. Its Duo 101 proposal involved rear-drive; and the MX-5 had the chassis-stiffening Powerplant Frame (PPF). The NA MX-5 followed the FB RX-7's front midship layout, and having the PPF's rigid engine to diff connection also helped with the superlative handling. In Japan, the MX-5 was sold as the upscale Eunos Roadster, and this classy Lexus, Infiniti rival brand also issued forth the ultra sports, luxury fourth gen JC chassis Eunos Cosmo, of 1990.

Loosely based on Mazda's '85 MX-03 concept car, the '90s Cosmo was an elegant coupe, powered by a twin turbo 13B, and spectacular triple rotor, twin turbo 20B-REW. Displacing 1962cc, the 20B-REW was the largest Wankel unit Mazda put into volume production, and the only triple rotor car it has productionized. Producing the Japanese limit of 280PS and 297lb/ft at a mere 1800rpm, the Eunos Cosmo 20B-REW could do 0-60mph in six seconds. If the customary 180kph limiter was removed, the Cosmo could touch 158mph – a lot of speed for the luxury fittings aboard.

For those who thought rotary engines didn't make enough torque, Mazda produced its JC Cosmo Coupe with optional three-rotor 20B REW. Making the Japanese manufacturer-agreed 280PS ceiling, but also with 297lb/ft of torque! (Courtesy Mazda)

The 1990 Eunos JC Cosmo featured 'offend no one' styling, and much techno-gadget wizardry. If one couldn't quite stretch to the three-rotor 20B REW option, the standard 13B turbo motorvated the two-door just fine. (Courtesy Mazda)

The Eunos Cosmo majored in luxury as much as power, and was expensive to buy and feed. It was the first Cosmo, since the '60s original, to be solely rotary powered. Made from February 1990 to September 1995, the 8875 production run was split 60:40% between the 13B and 20B twin turbo editions. (Courtesy Mazda)

The JC platform Cosmo Coupe's interior, with driver-side TV screen closed. This 1990s dream mobile featured state of the art driver and entertainment electronic aids. However, like other Japanese supercars conceived during the high flying '80s, the early '90s recession hurt its commercial prospects. (Courtesy Mazda)

In the September 1994 issue of *CAR*, on page 79, Paul Horrell declared that the Cosmo 20B sounded like a jet fighter taking off, with acceleration that made one feel like they were entering orbit! However, he commented that the car's styling wouldn't frighten grandma. The Eunos Cosmo was the ultimate street sleeper. (Courtesy Mazda)

Apart from the sumptuous leather interior, the Eunos Cosmo was the first car in the world with optional GPS. It was Japan's first car with the 'Palmnet' serial data communications system for ECU to ECAT operation. The Cosmo's Car Control System CRT color touch screen interface could work the climate control, mobile phone, GPS, NTSC TV and tuner/CD player. Official exports to Europe and America, via Mazda's planned Amati dealer network didn't come to pass. Apart from gray market importing, the Eunos Cosmo remained a largely Japanese only model.

FD RX-7: Koby san's vision

One was an international hit, the other a Japanese rarity. However, the Miata and JC Cosmo would influence the new 1991 FD RX-7 in terms of chassis and firepower respectively. RX-7 program manager and car guy Takaharu Kobayakawa, known as Koby, set out the new FD's goal: "Fastest volume – production sports car with unrivaled acceleration feeling." No secret was made of Mazda wishing to match the Honda NSX's numbers at half the price. The NSX had an aluminum monocoque, 282mm brake rotors, a high output 3-liter V6, and was handbuilt at the special Tochigii factory. It quickly built up a reputation as a user-friendly exotic car.

The RX-7 came with 294mm brake rotors, and had comparable stats. In *Motor Trend*'s July 1993, 'The Fastest From The Far East' compare test, the FD RX-7 was a bit quicker in 0-60mph,

A technical drawing of the Mazda HRX (Hydrogen Rotary Engine) from October 1991. The rotary engine has proven more adept at using hydrogen than piston engines. Mazda has been continually developing the rotary's hydrogen capability. (Courtesy Mazda

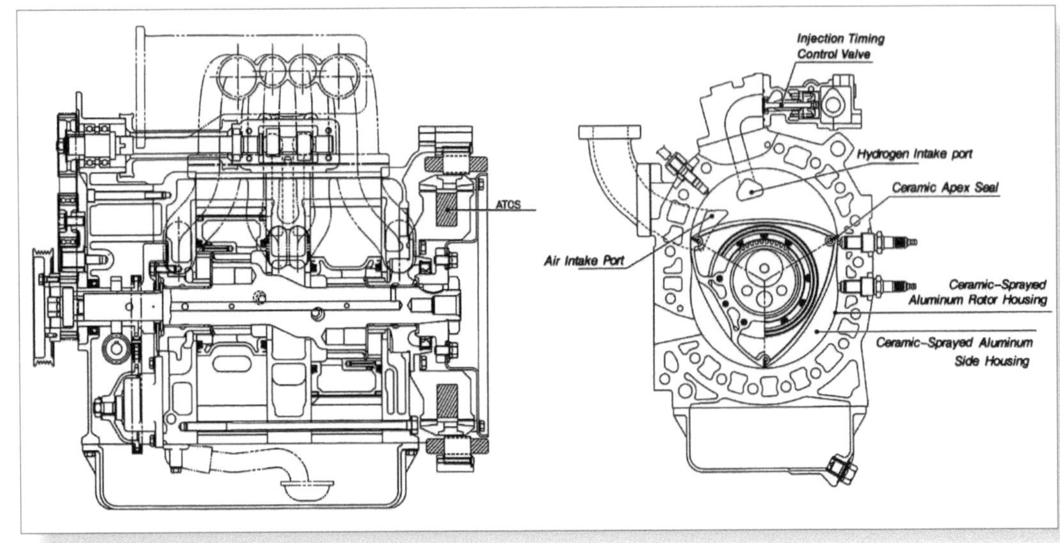

registering 5.3 seconds and matched the NSX's 13.9 second ¼-mile time. After 1320ft, the NSX and RX-7 were doing 100.9mph and 99.7mph respectively. The 2800lb RX-7 R1 came with one airbag, a 17cu ft cargo capacity and a twin turbo 13B, making 255bhp at 6500rpm and 217lb/ft at 5000rpm. Cost was $32,500. The 3020lb NSX had dual airbags, 5cu ft luggage area and a V6, making 270bhp at 7100rpm and 210lb/ft at 5300rpm. Unfortunately the NSX cost $68,600.

The above numbers did mean something, because the RX-7 proved in many independent tests that it could outlap the iconic NSX. In *Road & Track*'s March 1992, 'The Best-Handling Sports Cars in America' track test, the RX-7 slayed all on the Southern Californian Streets of Willow Springs. The FD RX-7 in R1 spec set a 1:05.64 lap time, better than the NSX's 1:07.14 and even the extra-outrageously-expensive Porsche 911 Turbo's 1:05.73. To achieve this kind of overall performance, with an unconventional engine and a low price, Mazda employed some unusual engineering tricks. To some, a madcap weight-reduction program from FC to FD RX-7.

The HRX could represent the rotary's past and future. Speaking to *The Telegraph Motoring* at the 2012 Moscow Motor Show, Mazda CEO Takashi Yamanouchi said rotary had a role in a low emissions future. (Courtesy Mazda)

Compared to FC RX-7, Mazda dropped 150lb, and using a mid luxo UK FD example 1992 RX-7. the driver up kerb weight was just 2965lb. This included driver airbag, a/c, ABS, side intrusion bars and cruise control. Mazda engaged in three rounds of weight saving to achieve this, with aluminum for the jack, suspension wishbones, thin wired dipstick, squeeze cast 16in aluminum rims and reduced greenhouse glass (20lb). Three pounds saved via a smaller radiator. The FD had some of the lightest seats in the auto industry, using fiberglass reinforced polypropylene for a base they weighed 33lb each.

The aluminum hood weighed just 18lb, but that was the only non-steel panel. To keep costs down versus NSX, FD RX-7 went conventional. 20lb were saved through a single tube exhaust, single muffler and thinwall casting of the final drive housing. The Miata-style laminated stamped steel PPF (Power Plant Frame) improved chassis rigidity and saved more weight. Rigidly connecting engine to diff, and bolting the whole drivetrain to the chassis at two points, over seven feet apart, had been done on the C4 Corvette. However, on the FD RX-7 it actually worked. Less final drive wind up and more traction delivered.

FD suspension was all independent, double wishbone front and rear, with four coils. A break from the FC's Porsche 924/944 set up, but the FD did follow the FC's rear camber control properties of DTSS. An electronic torque sensing Torsen differential worked with the PPF to get the power down, and was one of the first of its kind on a production car. On the handling-biased FD R1, an engine bay strut tower brace and Z-rated 225/50 Bridgestone Expedia S-01s, were fitted to the FD's 16 x 8in alloys. The tubular swaybars were sized 30mm at the front and 17.3mm rearwards. As with the top FCs, the front sported four-piston brake callipers, but only single pot rear units, as was '90s fashion.

Each front brake had a front air dam cooling inlet and exhaust, to take hot air from the nose mounted oil cooler. The airflow ducted over the wheel well and away from the brakes and shocks to keep them cool. Combined with Mazda's longstanding front midship layout, the FD RX-7 R1 turned in a 0.95g skidpad figure, accompanying a 66.4mph slalom stat when tested by *Road & Track*. It was posted, in the magazine's April 1992 issue, that the FD RX-7 registered the highest mass produced car skidpad figure in the journal's test history.

The FD's chassis was sophisticated in a conventional, rather than an electronic, manner. Liquid-filled sliding and rigid rubber bushings were pressed into the attachment points of the aluminum suspension. To make the FD fly, Mazda cooked up a new 255PS twin turbo version of the 13B, seen in the earlier 1990 JC Cosmo. It was the kind of twin sequential turbo set up seen on a Porsche 959. The primary turbo got exhaust gases from both rotor chambers, it took care of low end torque. Turbo two received a little gas on a closed loop; it spun to 140,000rpm on standby. The second Turbo came in around 4800rpm, with a view to deliver over 10psi boost at peak power. Max power came at 6500rpm, with 217lb/ft at 5000rpm.

The turbos were two Hitachi HT12 units, and the traditional warning buzzer chimed in at the 7000rpm redline. The intercooler now lived in the front fascia's nose, for improved cool air access. The 'W' in the six-port 13B REW title, stood for the twin turbo system. 'RE,' as before, implied a rotary engine. A 4.10:1 final drive and tight gear ratios worked with the rotary's power linearity. The five-speed's ratios were 3.48 (first), 2.01 (second), 1.39 (third), 1.00 (fourth) and overdrive 0.70 (fifth). With 2.9 turns lock-to-lock, the FD had the spec of a serious sports car; it also had the look. That look was '90s 'Gothic Curve,' and came courtesy of the Californian design studio. Andrew English noted in *Fast Lane*'s August 1992 Porsche 968/ Nissan 300ZX/RX-7 comparo, that, designwise, the FD RX-7 and Dodge Viper both hailed from California, adding that the designers probably curtly nodded their Ray Bans at each other at the local sushi bar. *CAR* magazine put the FD in the 'Interesting' part of its 'The Good the Bad and the Ugly.' Positive points in its May 1993 issue were "Gerry Anderson shape, Thunderbirds go," negative points were simply put as "Dipsomania." Conclusion was "Light,

The third generation FD RX-7 followed the 1984 Corvette and 1989 Miata by having a PPF (Powerplant Frame). The PPF achieved a solid engine to differential connection, to improve chassis rigidity and handling. (Courtesy Mazda)

Shown in December 1991, the FD RX-7 was Infini branded in Japan. The 1991 debutant was a twin sequential turbo, no compromise 255PS fireball. It benchmarked the much more expensive Honda NSX's performance stats. However, whereas the mid-engined NSX was rather restrained, the FD was extremely raucous. (Courtesy Mazda)

The FD was criticized in export markets for its tight cabin. Durability of dashboard surfaces and fittings was also questionable. Mazda improved matters in 1994 MY. In Japan, the FD RX-7 was available in 2+2 configuration, and with a four-speed automatic. (Courtesy Mazda)

The FD RX-7 twin sequential turbo 13B-REW. With 9:1 comp ratio it made 255PS at 6500rpm, enough to allow the FD to do 0-100mph in 13 seconds! Note the Nippon Denso A/C compressor and serpentine belt system. The latter was normal '90s fare for handling accessories. (Courtesy Mazda)

fantastic." At a debut UK price of £32,536 and with stats of 156mph, 0-60mph in 5.1 seconds and 25.5mpg, the British considered the 1993 RX-7 good enough value to put a Porsche 968 in the shade.

The allusion to the '60s UK *Thunderbirds* puppet animation series was appropriate: the FD RX-7 had that dream car look. Plus, the world hadn't seen curves like this since Raquel Welch starred in *One Million Years BC*! It was certainly back to the '60s, in a good way. Mazda even incorporated greenhouse and rear fascia elements of the original Cosmo Sport – another '60s model that was rather easy on the eye. The wedge look of the '70s, and blockish '80s were out. The organic, curved theme continued into the FD's cockpit. Reminiscent of an early '70s Vette, said many.

FD RX-7 1993 MY USA

Drilled alloy pedals, large chrome-bezelled analogue gauges, in an arcing dash, with traditionally centrally placed RX-7 tach – everything looked old school, but was screwed together tight. However, as per most Mazdas since the '70s, plastics and general materials were a bit cheap. Fortunately, the FD RX-7 was inexpensive in America. Measuring 168.5in for length, 68.9in for width and 48.4in high on a 95.5in wheelbase, the diminutive FD was good value for money. It made a 1993 MY North American debut in base, Touring and R1 guises. Base was the $31,300 stripper from hell, a rare friend of no one. Touring was the sensible $34,300, 2862lb choice, and came with leather seating surfaces, tilt/slide sunroof, halogen foglights, rear wiper/washer, extra sound insulation and trunk mounted subwoofer system.

A concession to the West Coast custom car scene, the Touring had a banging Bose Acoustic Wave audio system. At $32,300 and 2800lb, came the sporty R1, a no compromise racer. The R1 weighed a bit more than the base car's 2789lb, since its furnishings encompassed Z-rated tires, two engine oil coolers, front brake fascia ducts, stiffer suspension, front shock tower brace, special R1 cloth upholstery and a rear spoiler resembling an import tuner scene rite of passage. Mazda wouldn't even let journalists photograph the last item at the press intro. The R1 couldn't have cruise control, and $800 leather interior was the only option.

Problems surfaced quickly. People didn't

like the distinct nature of the three option packages. The R1 was a bit sporty, unless your last name was Andretti. The interior trim also dissolved faster than stirred Tang. Yes, everyone loved the FD, it was a hoot of a sports car, and many agreed more of a thoroughbred than a contemporary V8 mid-engine car wearing a prancing horse badge. However, it needed some refinement. That said, the FD was *Motor Trend*'s 1993 Import Car of the Year.

Playboy magazine put the new FD against the also new Dodge Viper in 1993, judging the FD the better overall machine. The FD RX-7 also scored *Playboy*'s Car of the Year 1993 title; smart bunnies indeed. The FD RX-7 was included in *Car and Driver*'s annual 'Ten Best' list, throughout its 1993-95 North American availability. With the 1992 *Autocar & Motor* Awards, the FD RX-7 got a 'Highly commended' and description of "Lean and lithe with uniquely pure curves."[72] Even so, to answer buyer complaints, Mazda made the ride of 1994 base and Touring FDs softer. The company applied more durable underside paint to resist stonechips. Interior surfaces were also more durable for '94 MY, original matte black paint peeled too easily.

The sports US 'R' version also got changes, to rear swaybar, revalved dampers, softer bushings, more steering caster and power steering pump adjustment for stability. It was renamed R2, was softer in nature with easier on the eye rear spoiler and Pirelli P-Zero tires. The R version now commanded a $2000 premium, but had a more dent-resistant front air dam; and dual airbags were standard US FD fare. '94 MY US FDs had 'one-touch' driver power window and map pockets to meet the oddments space shortfall. There was also an optional steel sunroof, it was glass in '93 MY.

Japan's FD RX-7 and other hotshots

PEG (Popular Equipment Group) put popular option combos in one pack, ie sunroof, cargo cover, leather seating surfaces, but no front fogs or Bose stereo. Where specified one still had to part-disassemble the Bose stereo's trunk ducting to access the FD's space saver spare. In Japan, the FD's little eccentricities were more easily overlooked, as it was sold under the upscale Efini brand. Versions of this 1992-95 Series VI RX-7 encompassed Type R, Type RB, A-spec, and the top dog Type RZ. There was also a slightly de-tuned Touring X edition which had a four-speed automatic, unavailable in the UK.

The wild FD RX-7 existed against a background of new Japanese supercars. In addition to the latest Nissan Skyline, there was the new twin turbo 300ZX (*Motor Trend* 1990 Import Car of the Year), Mitsubishi 3000 GT VR-4 (*Motor Trend* 1991 Import Car of the Year), Subaru's SVX, and 1994 Toyota Supra Turbo. So apart from Honda NSX, Japan was coming up with mind-blowing fast, high tech speed machines. In terms of figures, the Supra was the new top canine, in a fast moving pack of auto one-upmanship.

The Mitsubishi, Subaru and Skyline GT-R were all-wheel drive machines. The Mitsubishi and Skyline had four-wheel steer and forced induction six cylinders of power. The 300ZX had 'Super HICAS' rear-wheel steer, and shamed the Corvette towards adopting the LT1 V8. The Supra had power and luxury, due to a Lexus sibling. However, the FD RX-7 was alone

Making its debut at the 1991 Geneva Motor Show, the Eunos Presso or Mazda MX-3 was a bold, front-drive 1.8-liter V6 coupe. Another of Mazda's exciting early '90s niche players. (Courtesy Mazda)

Making a 1992 debut, the Eunos 500 was a Mazda 626-based upscale sports/luxury sedan BMW 3 series alternative. The early '90s recession limited the extent and success of the Eunos brand. (Courtesy Mazda)

The 1992 Autozam brand AZ-1: a mid engine, gullwing, rear-drive Kei class sports car! Made in cooperation with Suzuki, the Suzuki Cara was the sister model, the 657cc turbo/intercooled three-cylinder 12-valve AZ-1 was another victim of early '90s recession. (Courtesy Mazda)

in this crowd, by not being a heavyweight GT machine. It didn't place technology as the driving force behind its appeal. In addition, it was by far the best looking car of its era.

The Supra had a strange pinched haunch, narrow track. Capable of an unlimited 181mph, and faster accelerating than the Ferrari 348 and Porsche 911 Turbo, according to a UK July 1993 *What Car?* test. However, the car's rear wing brought forth a cartoon suggesting the Supra's stylist gained experience designing shopping carts.[73] Mazda put out a number of interesting cars in the 1990-94 period. The 1991 121 'Bubble Car' was the first retro small car. The MX-3 1.8-liter V6 front-drive coupe represented bold thinking, as did the glorious handling, mid-engine AZ-1.

Hailing from 1992-94, the Autozam youth brand AZ-1 was done in conjunction with Kei car partner Suzuki, whose sister car was the Cara. Steel monocoque, fiberglass reinforced panels, Miura-style headlights and gullwing doors. With a 657cc turbo and intercooled three cylinder, the AZ-1 must be one of the most exotic and fun microcars in history. The exciting new Mazdas of 1990-94 were overseen by company design general manager Shigenori Fukuda, a closet Jaguar fan. Indeed, Mazda had a number of interesting models and projects going at this time.

Big Dreams – M2, Amati & Jaguar

M2 Inc, aka 'Mazda Too,' was started in November 1991, to create niche rides from mainstream Mazda models. Run by boss Mr Masakatsu Kato, the Japanese father of the NA MX-5, and assisted by Hirotaka Tachibana, who did the FC RX-7's suspension dynamics, M2 went beyond mere cosmetics. The company did a series of much upgraded Cafe Roadsters based on the NA MX-5. There was an M2 building with HQ in Tokyo, and the showroom in the affiliated Setagaya-ku Matsudarotari Building. Grander still, Mazda planned a full scale luxury brand.

The influence of Lexus and Infiniti were inescapable. Subaru was even working on an all-wheel drive, twin turbo, luxury Estremo prototype in 1987. Toyota's Hiroyuki Watanabe saw the planned Aristo as a BMW 735i rival. Work started in 1986 on this Majesta derivative with Ital design looks, twin turbo V6 and one foot tall in-car audio subwoofers. There was a lot of blue sky thinking coming out of the boom time 1980s. For Mazda, it was a luxury car line called Amati.

Amati was a ¥50 billion project with V8 and V12 sedans at the top of the tree. The V12 would have trumped the Lexus LS400. Mazda planned a US HQ, and had 70 special dealers in North America picked out, for the spring of 1994. Sadly, the grand plan didn't come to fruition. The cars were made at a state of the art new Hofu plant, which would set a new standard in quality control. Pressure to stop came from Ford, and was mainly due to the 1990 world recession. The recession was global, was particularly felt in Asia and Japan, and would drag on through to the mid '90s.

Mazda already made a number of niche products like the MX-3, and an entire Amati line was going to be a bridge too far. Japan's Nikkei issued a pre tax profit/loss forecast for Japan's nine main automakers for the 1992-93 financial year. Losses for Nissan, Isuzu and Daihatsu were predicted, with reduced profits forseen at Toyota, Honda, Mitsubishi and Mazda. Even small car king Suzuki was going to make less profit, and Nissan was going to close their highly regarded Zama factory in 1995. In 1992, Mitsubishi tried a refurbished used luxury car scheme. The first batch of 200 'new/old' Cimas sold out in a week.

To push cars, cosmetic giant Shiseido trialled spraying fragrances in showroom stock at five Tokyo car dealers. Over 80% of the 116 people surveyed said it had a positive sales effect. It contrasted with Toyota's AMLUX (Automobile & Luxe) showroom showcase in Tokyo's Ikebukuro district. Done in the style of a 1930s' view of buildings of the future, the modern multi-storey complex told a six chapter story of cars and people, in unusual fashion. There were Perspex tables composed of boxes showing Toyotas in various diorama settings, such as a desert, a seaside, and even an active volcano.(74)

Ask for any Toyota luxury car brochure you like at AMLUX, and a beautiful AMLUX lady would give you a large format brochure, with 90gsm art paper, leatherette cover, nicely presented in an envelope. There were no salesmen at AMLUX; its job was to entice visitors, whereupon they would go to a regular Toyota dealer and buy a car. Sadly, by the mid '90s, this wasn't happening as often as it used to. There was rising interest in small vehicles, especially Kei class rides of a utilitarian nature. By the late '80s, Kei cars were reviving, so Mazda brought back its Carol nameplate, under the Autozam youth brand, in 1989.

The reborn Carol was made for Mazda by Suzuki on an Alto platform. In 1995, the 660cc Suzuki Wagon R overtook the Toyota Corolla as Japan's number one selling car. Mazda's usual sales stalwart, the Mazda Familia, wasn't doing well in Japan. However, there was a waiting list for Mazda's new small, tall MPV, the Bongo Friendee. So popular indeed, that Mazdaspeed even made go faster accessories for this unlikely hero. One could add Eibach springs, high-performance brake pads and TYPE-II Sports Sound Muffler made of baffled stainless steel to a Bongo Friendee. This format of vehicle was such a hot seller, Mazda gave the greenlight to the BU-X wagon in 1996. This mini MPV had been seen at the Tokyo Auto Salon.

Mazda's 1996-2002 Demio DW was done as a tall, mini MPV. However, it wasn't all utility. That Mazdaspeed TYPE-II muffler could also be bought for the Eunos 500. The grand Amati plan may have been axed, but some models from the luxury scheme did see production at Hofu. The Eunos 500, aka Xedos 6, was a close relative of the Capella/626; flawless build quality with a smooth V6 option. As a 1990 sports/luxury alternative to the BMW 3 series, it was more luxury than sports, but did achieve some conquest sales. There was also the larger Eunos 800/Xedos 9/Mazda Millenia.

The Eunos 800 was even more luxo-directed than its little brother. It was well specified, well built, but didn't have the driving dynamics of a BMW 5 series. However, it did have a Miller Cycle V6 motor. In typical Mazda style, here

Mazda's flagship Eunos Cosmo Coupe was made in Series II form during 1994-95. In video games, the car appeared in Sega GT, the first two Gran Turismo games, and the arcade series Wangan Midnight: Maximum Tune 1, 2 and 3. (Courtesy Mazda)

was another unconventional engine format productionized. Using the 1940s idea patented by American engineer Ralph Miller, the Miller Cycle Motor reduced the usual energy lost by a four-stroke engine on compression stroke. On the Mazda motor, the Miller idea introduced a fifth cycle, where the intake valve was left open longer. A supercharger was then employed to do compression, over the range where it's better at said task than a piston.

Ol' Henry – Ford business

The efficiency gain allowed Mazda to advance ignition timing, for even better performance and economy. Ford was behind plans to achieve luxury economies of scale by harmonizing Mazda with Jaguar, especially involving Amati. Jaguar's engineering team visited Japan in the fall of 1992, to discuss use of components from the Amati program. Indeed, Ford execs liked the idea of the baby Jag X-Type being built at the Hofu plant. However, Jaguar chairman Nick Scheele said the Mazda parts were inappropriate for a Jag, and that there was no point producing the car halfway across the globe, when Browns Lane had spare capacity.(75)

Jaguar eventually based its S-Type on the Lincoln LS. The X-Type Jag ended up based on the Ford Mondeo, built at a UK Ford factory. In modern times, under Indian TATA corporate ownership, Jaguar is very interested in moving execs and production to China. The traditional Browns Lane factory closed years earlier.
To overcome the strong yen and get more European market share, Mazda long planned to make cars in Europe. In the hope of following in

Toyota's and Nissan's footsteps, Ford's Saarlouis site was mentioned, in February 1990, as a possible top choice for joint Ford and Mazda European production. Unfortunately, the early '90s recession curtailed such plans.

In February 1993, Japan's largest newspaper *Asahi Shimbun* claimed that the Ford/Mazda plan, discussed since the late '80s, was at an end. Mazda denied the claim. However, Mazda did establish a small German design studio. This Frankfurt studio came up with the attractive 1995 Familia five-door hatchback, and the 2009 MX-5 Superlight concept car that celebrated the MX-5's 20th birthday. On a more mundane level, the 1990 launch of the Ford Escort GT represented a joint venture with Mazda, where Escorts and 323s would come off the same line. Earlier, Mazda even tried to sell some Fords in Japan, through its Autorama dealer group in the '80s.

The recession adversely affected the lovable Autozam AZ-1, and caused the 1995 demise of M2 Inc.; although the latter's work was continued by Mazdaspeed, which was absorbed into Mazda formally in the late 1990s, as subsidiary company Mazda Auto Tokyo. FD RX-7 project chief Takaharu Kobayakawa stated in the fall of 1994, as new company design general manager, that there would be no FD RX-7 convertible, nor hi po turbo edition of the new 1995 Familia. Mazda were in the red by the mid '90s and parent Ford wanted Hiroshima to go sensible.

FD RX-7 aftermarket afterburners

By late 1994, Ford had long owned 25% of Mazda, and Ford's Henry Wallace had become Mazda's Vice President. The new 1995 Mazda Familia would be a cornerstone of Ford's global small car program. However, Ford had no control over go fast tuners, who cooked up some very spicy, modified FD RX-7s – such as the PFS (Peter Farrell Supercars) Ltd Edn; The Manassas, Virginia outfit charged $13,800, in 1994, on top of a stock RX-7, to create performance better than 911 Turbo at over twice the price. That performance was 0-60mph in 4.4 seconds in a 2780lb car, using an uprated 13B-REW with 360bhp at 7000rpm and 300lb/ft at 4800rpm.[76]

PFS included a custom, larger, handmade aluminum intercooler and air intake. The intake was an aluminum piece with 'Peter Farrell PF Supercars' script. PFS got Doug Wallace to rework a programmable Crane ECU, normally seen on late model Mustangs and Camaros. Indeed, one could have an electronic valve controller with three push buttons allowing up to 14psi of boost. Space was made for the bigger intercooler by replacing the stock airbox with twin foam filtered air intakes. A 3in cat back exhaust and 4.3:1 rear ratio were included, with the option of a Centerforce clutch.

PFS specified O-Z Mito rims sized 17 x 8.5in front and 17 x 10in rear. Tires were by BF Goodrich whose Comp T/As were 235/45 ZRs on the front, and 275/40 ZRs out back. Custom

The FD RX-7 has seen wilder mods than previous RX-7s, reflecting its flamboyant twin turbo nature. This 1993 example was purchased by its current owner in March 1998, and was Malta Car Domain People's Choice Award champ in 2010. It features a Turbonetics turbo, Blitz blow-off valve, and GReddy intercooler. (Courtesy www.cardomain.com/ride/3883705/1993-mazda-RX-7)

progressive wound coils lowered the FD 0.75in, swaybars were larger and combined with gas dampers which had an eight-position valve adjustment on the side. Overall the suspension was 60% stiffer, and some aero add ons also aided to glue PFS Ltd Edn to terra firma.

Naturally Japan had its tuners too. Originally just a car dealer in Ota-ku (Tokyo), Kitamagome Knight Sports' tuning operation was started by Makoto Kamazuka, a successful racer, in 1971. Racing a R100 in touring car events was done on the side. In August 1973, the work of Knight Sports Co Ltd was formally established, with selling race and rally rotary hop up parts as the core business. In 1974, Knight Sports even started exporting parts to America. Competitionwise, a modified R100 was entered in Japan's Touring Car Endurance Series.

At the 1976 Rolex 24-Hour Daytona race, Makoto Kamazuka successfully challenged high powered BMWs, before his RX-3 retired after 17 hours. He won the Indonesian Grand Prix of 1980, in a modified Mazda RX-3 GSII; the Macau Grand Prix; and a touring car race at Japan's Tsukuba circuit, in 1991, using a single turbo FC RX-7. Kamazuka san then quit racing to concentrate on the tuning business. By the end of the '70s, Knight Sports was exporting throughout South East Asia. The business moved from Kitamagome to its current site, South Magome Ward, in 1981. 1990 saw the first formal use of the Knight Sports Co Ltd name. In 2004, Knight Sport's vehicles gained the right to keep Mazda's normal new car warranty.

Present Knight Sports business covers Demio DE, Axela BL, Roadster NC, FC and FD RX-7, plus SE3P RX-8. So visit the Minamigome part of Tokyo on Route 1. Displayed at the 1998 Tokyo Auto Salon, its Type RS RX-7 had one big turbo and 480bhp at 6500rpm and 40lb/ft at 6000rpm. Upgrades included a Tilton double-disk clutch, HKS stainless steel exhaust manifold, HKS ECU, Pomec racing dry-type battery. There was a toggle switch behind the steering wheel to increase boost by 40%, but no traction control. 12.4in brake rotors, racing carbon metallic brake pads and a conventional mechanical LSD came too. To avoid blocking the radiator, a custom V type configuration oversize aluminum intercooler was mounted almost horizontally behind the air dam, with the rear part tilted up 45 degrees. Kayada twin tube dampers were part of a suspension utilizing mostly squeeze cast or forged aluminum parts. Knight Sports added its own two-way adjustable rear wing, which raised the drag factor to 0.30. Apart from Knight Sports decals and sponsor signage, the TAS showcar had special bodykit.

The Knight Sports FD RX-7 had a tuner figure for the standing 400 meters of 11.75 seconds. A Mazda 'Time Trap' electronic stopwatch was

To achieve a 12-second ¼ mile and 0-60mph in 3.7 seconds, Apexi engine electronics, Apexi ignition and Monster brand cable wiring are employed. Inside this FD, Kicker subwoofers keep the audio sweet-sounding. (Courtesy www.cardomain.com/ride/3883705/1993-mazda-RX-7)

Included hardware mods on this 1993 FD RX-7 run to D1 spec radiator cap and Kakimoto exhaust. Blitz gauges keep the driver informed on the rotary's progress. (Courtesy www.cardomain.com/ride/3883705/1993-mazda-RX-7)

Matching the extra horses, this FD RX-7 features a D2 Racing Big-Brake Kit, Air Ride springs, Ruff Racing rims and Nankang tires. An RE-Amemiya bodykit helps the visuals, with Bride bucket seats holding the driver in place. (Courtesy www.cardomain.com/ride/3883705/1993-mazda-RX-7)

on the steering column to time ETs, and racing 'Bride' bucket seats gripped the driver. The car gripped the road with 18in Enkei rims wrapped in 235/40 ZR Yokohama Advans. Knight Sports' surcharge was $31,000, and it had an Australian agent.[77] Its tuned car looked like the ultimate FD RX-7, until one visited VeilSide. This Japanese tuner is based near Tsukuba Circuit, and the company's name represents a reverse amalgam of the founder Yokomaku Hiranao's first name. Yoko means 'side' and maku means 'veil'.

It was back in July 1995 that the tuner received the Japanese Ministry of Transportation's approval to sell its fancy aero bodykit parts. VeilSide's 'Fortune' bodykit replaces all exterior panels, bar the roof, on FD RX-7. At $11,000, the Fortune kit is aptly named, and the most expensive Japanese car kit VeilSide offers. The firm also does engine tuning, and its work can be seen in *The Fast and the Furious* movie franchise.

In its October 1993 'Four Seasons Test,' *Automobile* magazine said the FD RX-7's quick steering, stiff suspension and big tires made it a top autocrosser, but an average daily driver. Car design does involve compromise. (Courtesy Mazda)

Sounds awesome, but people always want more. To this end, try the triple rotor 20B conversion for FD RX-7, engineered by Pettit Racing. Called the Pettit Racing TKT Banzai Edition, this crazy device had a 550-horse 20B with parallel turbos. The TKT Banzai Edn's primary turbo was larger than stock, and featured flat turbine blades for torque. The second turbo's curved blades were for top end power. A computer-designed custom subframe accepted the 20B. A much larger intercooler was placed in the front air dam. A larger aluminum radiator, custom ECU and a special wiring harness tidied the messy stock arrangement – all done by Pettit Racing.

Changes were made to the 20B itself. The company street-ported and blueprinted the motor, and had the rotors CNC machined to accept heavy-duty tungsten coated apex seals. The 550bhp was facilitated by larger fuel injectors, high flow fuel pump and a new fuel pressure regulator. A Centerforce Dual Friction clutch and billet flywheel handled the 20B's

Originally a US 1993 RX-7 Touring, modifications for serious track action involve changing to a single TDX61 turbo twin scroll Turblown unit and Vmount Intercooler/radiator. Turbo Source Inconel heat shields are employed on the turbo, downpipe, turbo manifold and wastegate dump tubes. Two Tial MV-R water-cooled 38mm wastegates are also part of the performance equation. (Courtesy Shawn Christenson)

colossal poke. The 20B added 90lb versus the 13B-REW, but a stainless steel cat back exhaust and 8.5lb flywheel saved 80lb. A light 1000amp dry cell battery was placed behind the driver.

It wasn't all about power, GAB 8 way adjustable shocks, Eibach Trak Pro springs, along with two Trak Pro swaybars provided handling aid. Lightweight 18in Forgeline rims with Bridgestone S-02 tires were tough for the times. At 2740lb the TKT Banzai Edn weighed slightly less than a normal RX-7. However, there was nothing normal about 11.5 second ¼ mile, or $35,000 in parts and labor for just the 20B conversion.

Fortunately, Mazdaspeed had some more affordable upgrade items for the FD RX-7 in the late '90s. There was the wind tunnel-tested AERO TYPE-1 bodykit set, Mazdaspeed's most elaborate. It consisted of sculpted AERO Bonnet, Front Nose, jumbo Rear Wing, side skirts and fender extenders. The TYPE-II had a front nose with indicator lights and lenses like a '60s Toyota 2000 GT. Mazdaspeed's range of alloy rims carried the tuner's experience of transferring racing car rim tech to street use.

Mazdaspeed's Ride-Height Adjustable Suspension Unit used Eibach springs, and lowered the FD's suspension 20-30mm. The Reinforced Stabilizer bars and aluminum shock tower strut bar, sports rubber bushings and mechanical type LSD were all beneficial to handling. Stepping up the 13B-REW's power made Mazdaspeed's Twinplate Clutch essential.

Painted in Plasti Dipped Matte Red, this FD RX-7 uses Shine Auto Spec bodykit. Parts involve Spec B 25mm front-extended fenders, Spec B 25mm molded in rear flares, Spec S front bumper, Spec S rear diffuser and GT sideskirts. Enkei RPF1 rims have a 15mm offset and are sized 18 x 9.5in front and 18 x 10.5in rear. Dampers are Koni Yellows, with Eibach 720 Pro-Kit front and 530 Pro-Kit rear. (Courtesy Shawn Christenson)

To reach 481 horses and 395lb/ft, 22lb of turbo boost is used with a custom Adaptronic 440 series ECU. Custom wiring harness and four AEM coils provide this 13B's spark. A custom cold air intake for the turbo, with its own heatshield, is included. The intercooler even has its own 800 CFM fan. Fuel is metered from a 20-gallon fuel cell by an electric pump capable of coping with a 1500 horsepower motor. Two ID1000 primary injectors are used, along with two ID2000 secondary injectors. Fuel returns through a 19-row fuel cooler with 360 CFM fan. (Courtesy Shawn Christenson)

There was a Clutch Cover for the smooth engaging competition asbestos free clutch disk, and heavier duty 'metal disk.' To reduce inertia, start spinning Mazdaspeed's Lightweight Flywheel made of chrome molybdenum steel, with a nitride surface.

High-performance brake pads, teflon brakelines and special silicone lead plug wires, were all available for FD RX-7, as were TYPE-I and TYPE-II sports mufflers. Made for FD RX-7, plus NA/NB MX-5 and Familia, were Sports Driving Meter dash gauges. These featured white dial faces, red numerals and orange needles. Numbers were placed outside the scale and illumination was red. Mazdaspeed even had a Carbon Look Dash Panel for FD RX-7 and NA MX-5. Using a special printing technology, the dash surface received a print of the carbon material.

Air pump, a/c compressor, heater core and power steering have all been eliminated. There are no HVAC dash controls, radio and speakers have gone, too. Functional items like Speedwire six-control switch panel, Speed Hut custom gauges (with RX-7 script!), six-point rollcage and Proxy R888 tires sized 275/35/18in front and 315/30/18in rear are present. Note how the C5 Vette in the background has stolen FD styling cues! (Courtesy Shawn Christenson)

With a near 160mph top speed and 0-60mph in under five seconds, the FD RX-7 twin turbo was initially welcomed in America. However, its specialized sports nature and fragility limited sales. Mazda worked in durability fixes for its second US MY of 1994. (Courtesy Alex Tong)

FD RX-7 racing exploits

Mazdaspeed specially developed a 15W-40 fully synthetic engine oil, called 'Rotary 1,' just for Wankel motors. For those adding serious power, and or contemplating intensive track use, Mazdaspeed made a Reinforced Power Plant Frame for FD RX-7. This item was created using special hand rolled steel, boosting PPF strength 18% with no weight increase. In truth, the largely stock FD acquitted itself admirably well in Australian production car racing. At the 1992 12-hour production race held at Bathurst, the FD RX-7 beat everything easily. The field included a BMW M5, Honda NSX driven by Jack Brabham, and the new Porsche 968.

This was the FD's first competitive outing anywhere, and the winning driver trio involved Charlie O'Brien, Gary Waldon and Mark Gibbs. A further two victories in the same 12-hour race occurred at Bathurst Mount Panorama, in 1993 and 1994. Once again, Porsche 968 was trounced. 1995 was the last year Mazda officially entered the FD in the 12-hour production car race. This time, the venue was Eastern Creek raceway, but the result was the same. The RX-7 won again, and a few months later this very same winning FD was on the podium at the Targa Tasmania tarmac rally. As an Australian model homologation special, the 1995 RX-7 SP helped the factory-backed production racers legally compete. An initial 25 were made, but popularity saw that number rise to 35. The SP version had 274bhp and 263lb/ft, weight saving materials, larger front and rear spoilers and 17in rims. Mazda Australia gave 0-62mph as 5.3 seconds and 13.6 seconds for the ¼ mile. The RX-7 SP retailed for $101,610 Australian dollars.

To commemorate this Australian racing success, Mazda released the RX-7 Series VIII-based 2001 Bathurst R. This was a Japanese only market model. In America, the FD RX-7 continued the RX-7's SCCA success, with triumphs for Don Kearney in NE Division and John Finger in SE Division. Pettit Racing won the 1998 GT2 Road Racing Championship, using a street 1993 RX-7, with mere bolt on accessories. Dominating the series, the Pettit RX-7 amassed a 140-point total, 63 points clear of second place in the championship.

More specialized was the RX-7 PFS Supercar campaigned by New Zealand racer Peter Farrell's outfit in the early '90s IMSA series. Mazda Japan contracted Farrell's operation to do a FD racer for the series, via journalist/racer amigo Steve Potter, the manager of Mazda's East Coast publicity office. Mazda liked the idea that the new IMSA Supercar Series involved few mods. IMSA then recognized low volume production cars like the Lotus X180R, but the PFS Supercar RX-7 still did fine. Unfortunately, the early '90s recession proved the car's

A 1994 RX-7 Series VI, wearing the final Japanese-style Series VIII (1999-2002) bodykit. This FD RX-7 has also been modified with HKS adjustable suspension, working with 18in Volk Racing SE37A bronze rims. (Courtesy Binny Onqa)

Listening to buyer demands, the 1994 North American FD RX-7 had an optional PEG (Performance Equipment Group) pack. PEG brought together popular items (leather seating and sunroof) under the one option umbrella. It didn't include front fog lights or the complex FD Bose stereo. (Courtesy Binny Onqa)

In the September 1992 issue of Sports Car International, on page 35, David Colman's opinion on autocrossing and the FD RX-7 was: 'The sport of the 1990s has met the car of the decade.' (Courtesy Binny Onqa)

worst enemy. Mazda closed its motorsports department at the end of 1992. Farrell ran his RX-7 Supercar in only three races during 1993.

The PFS Supercar retailed for $70 grand, and Farrell's company sold three to Mazda's Italian distributor. These exports dominated their class in the 1993 Italian Supercar Series, and Supercars they truly were. 420bhp at eight grand, 320lb/ft at 4800rpm, front and rear track were 58.2in and final drive ratio 4.11:1. A 15-gallon fuel cell was employed, along with Penske remote reservoir shocks. Rims were 17 x 8.5in on the front and rear, front brake ventilated rotors measured 13 x 1.75in, with rear rotors being stock FD 11.6in issue. How fast was a Supercar? Try 0-60mph in 3.8 seconds, ¼ mile in 11.9 seconds at 122mph, with a terminal velocity of 185mph. It could also stop from 60mph in a scant 100 feet.

The Le Mans challenge

As good as any RX-7 based racer was, Mazdaspeed soon worked out one needed a dedicated sports car to challenge Le Mans. Thus, its first big success in France came in 1983, with the 717C, powered by its trusty 13B rotary. 1983 saw new regs at Le Mans, with a new Group C Junior class renamed Group C2, in 1984. In 1984, Mazda motorsport formally became Mazdaspeed Co Ltd. The 1983 Prototype Group C Junior class 717C's body and chassis were built by Mooncraft with Mazda's help. Mazda's team of two 717Cs were the only Group C Junior cars finishing Le Mans in 1983. They came 12th and 18th overall.

In 1984, two evolved 727Cs visited Le Mans, plus two 13B-powered Lola T616s, sponsored by BF Goodrich. The Lolas came first and third in class, tenth and 12th overall. The Mazda factory cars managed fourth and sixth in class, equating to 15th and 20th overall. This result showed Mazda Wankels didn't always power Mazdas at Le Mans. In 1970, a Belgium team put a 10A in its Chevron B16, but it retired after four hours due to coolant pipe failure. In 1973, the Japanese Sigma Automotive Team put together its Sigma MC73 with a 12A, which unfortunately expired in the 11th hour. In 1974, the updated Sigma MC74 did finish the 24-hour duration, but was classified DNF because it completed insufficient laps.

Mazda's 1985 Le Mans campaign revolved around the 737C, with its two-car team coming third and sixth in class, representing 19th and 24th overall. The 737C had been expected to win its class. 1986 was special for the use of Mazda's new triple rotor 13G, in its team of two 757s. Sadly, both retired early with driveshaft troubles. The 13G is better known by the title 20B, which Mazda has called the motor from November 1987. Mazda tried the triple rotor 757s again at Le Mans in 1987. This time, one retired early, but the other 757 came seventh overall. This represented the best result by a Japanese automaker at Le Mans to that point in time.

At 1988's Le Mans, Mazda's new quad rotor 13J-M, where 'M' stood for modified, powered two Mazda 767 racers. One 20B-powered 757 machine also competed. The 767 was the best placed Japanese car from the fourth to 16th hours. Unfortunately, both then suffered exhaust manifold problems, causing the 767s to slow down and finish 17th and 19th overall. The 757 endured a brake rotor crack, but still came 15th overall. Not the kind of progress Mazdaspeed wanted. 1989 saw the aggressive

After trying continuously since 1979 to win the prestigious 24 Hours of Le Mans, Mazda's Motorsport Division triumphed in 1991 with its 787B racer. The 787B has been the only rotary-powered car, and first Japanese car to date to win at Le Mans. (Courtesy Mazda)

campaign called 'Operation Rollback.' Mazda sent three 767Bs with Type 13J-Ms to France; two cars crashed in qualifying.

Fortunately, all three 767Bs completed the 24 hours, with enough laps under their belts. One came seventh overall, and, by covering 4980km, it recorded the longest distance run by a Japanese car at Sarthe. The other two 767Bs managed ninth and 12th overall. 1990 was a real let down. Mazda brought its new 787, with also-new quad rotor R26B motor. One car had fuel problems, the other electrical; both gave up the ghost prior to race end. With authorities about to introduce new regs that would outlaw rotary engines, 1991's Le Mans would be a do or die exercise. Fortunately, Mazda chose the 'do' option, but needed its latest 787B sports car for the 59th running of Le Mans.

The 787B involved revised suspension geometry, which allowed bigger rims, in turn permitting larger brake rotors which were now carbon ceramic. The R26B featured three sparkplugs per rotor chamber, and, for '91, a continuously variable intake system. The variable length telescopic intake pipes, were ECU puppet-stringed via electric motors and a cable/pulley set up.

Compared to 787, the latest 787B had a 25mm longer wheelbase, 15mm narrower front track and small suspension changes. For 1991, Mazda would field two 787Bs and one 787 for Le Mans. The 787 series was designed by Nigel Stroud, specifically to use the Mazda four-rotor motor and a Porsche synchro gearbox like a Porsche 962. The rotary engine helped 787B to be a shorter, more compact car than Le Mans rivals. Stroud strove for low weight and small frontal area, rather than ground effects. Mazdaspeed in Japan did the carbon composite body.

The 787B utilized carbon fiber composites with honeycomb structure for the entire chassis. The carbon fiber monocoque was made by a specialist English company, and the cars were completed by Mazdaspeed. The part of the chassis aft of the cockpit was a tubular structure, that carried the rear suspension and engine. The engine wasn't structurally stressed. Front and rear suspension were by double transverse wishbones. They were acted on directly by Bilstein shocks and springs, transversely mounted at the rear. Manual rack and pinion steering was present.

The quad rotor R26B 787B motor that powered Mazda's winner at the 1991 Le Mans 24-Hour race. Making 700PS at 9000rpm, the R26B maintained flexibility via variable length telescopic intake manifold piping. Pipe length was controlled via ECU, electric motors, and a cable/pulley system. (Courtesy Mazda)

With the 787B racer Mazda set a fast pace combined with low fuel consumption (seven liters of fuel per lap), that the opposition couldn't match. For the Le Mans 24 Hours, the 787B was limited to 674 gallons of gas. In racing, Mazda has shown the rotary engine to be very frugal. (Courtesy Mazda)

A Miyoshi Proving Ground tribute to the 1991 Le Mans-triumphant Mazda 787B racer, erected on the January 12 2007. 20th anniversary celebrations were held at Le Mans in 2011, marking the 787B's victory. TV actor and Mazda spokesperson Patrick Dempsey was on hand for the festivities. (Courtesy Mazda)

Technical specs involved 654cc x four rotors with 700PS at 9000rpm and 600Nm at 6500rpm. Mazda electronic fuel-injection managed the R26B, with its power going through a five-speed manual box and Borg & Beck triple plate clutch. Carbon Industries outboard ventilated carbon rotors and pads slowed the 787B down. Mazda's metric exterior dimensions were 4782mm for length, 1994mm for width, height of 1003mm, all on a 2662mm wheelbase. Front track was 1534mm, with rear track at 1504mm. Weight had to be at least 830kg, and fuel came from a 100-liter ATL fuel cell.

Takaharu Kobayakawa, aka Koby, was in charge of Mazdaspeed's motorsport activities. Mazdaspeed got Le Mans legend Jacky Ickx as an advisor. Ickx put Mazdaspeed onto the Oreca racing team of Hugues de Chaunacs. Thus, the Oreca team prepared the three Mazda race cars, and reserve car, in France. The 1991 Le Mans event was run to a fuel consumption formula, since fuel per car was restricted to 2550 liters. A handwritten sticker above the dash instruments reminded the driver of the seven liters per lap target. Engine revs and fuel consumption were permanently shown in the instrument display.

Driver teams involved the #18 787B's David Kennedy, Stefan Johansson and Maurizio Sandro-Sala. The #55 787B had Volker Weidler, Johnny Herbert and Bertrand Gachot. The #56 787 was driven by Takashi Yorino, Yojiro Terada and Pierre Dieudonne.

Rolling on Rays brand rims of 18 x 12in front with Dunlop brand 300/640/R18 tires, and 18 x 14.75in rear with 355/710/R18 tires, the 787B lapped over five seconds faster than the 787. For qualifying, the rev limit was 9000rpm, with 8500rpm for the actual race. The 787B's carbon ceramic brakes were a first for any car maker, and certainly helped Mazda. The #55, #18 and #56 cars qualified 12th, 17th and 24th respectively. However, they were demoted to 19th, 23rd and 30th respectively, because authorities gave favorable positions to the C1 class cars that they were trying to promote.

The opposition from Jaguar, Peugeot and Mercedes couldn't match Mazda's pace for the set fuel limit, highlighting the race winning Wankel format. Mazda's bright orange and green 'Renown' livery #55 car took the Le Mans checkered flag. Mazda's car #18 came sixth, and car #56 was eighth. The winning car was taken to Japan and disassembled in front of the media. The car could have done another 24 hours of Le Mans. The third 787B was built to replace the Le Mans winner for the remaining rounds of the sports car championship. However, there were no more good season results, since the remaining sprint type races didn't suit the 787B.

It was the second 787B, chassis #002, that was the glorymobile. The 787B made its debut at the May 1991 Fuji 1000km race, where #002 came first in GTP class and sixth overall. The car's next race was at Le Mans, where its young driver trio achieved victory. The #002 car was then promptly retired, and mostly kept in Mazda's museum. It had several outings in the late '90s, when the rear end got slightly damaged. However, it was restored by Mazdaspeed in time for the 20th Anniversary of its Le Mans win. Former Mazda works drivers tested it and car #002 was then flown to Le Mans.

As part of the 20th Anniversary celebrations, Mazda spokesperson and actor Patrick Dempsey tried out #002. It was then driven on Saturday morning by Johnny Herbert. The unusual rotary sound has made the Renown racer a crowd favorite. Kit maker Tamiya has even paid tribute to car #002 with an early '90s 1:10 scale radio-controlled electric model (#58102). Looking just like the Renown racer and ready to be sold in its 1992 catalogue, but only 450mm long and weighing just 1.280kg.[78] The kit is somewhat of a collector item too.

Unfortunately, Mazda's piston move for 1992's Le Mans wasn't successful. The V10-

powered TWR machine couldn't touch the Peugeot 905s. Mazda officially withdrew from sports car racinq at the end of 1992. Even worse, the company never capitalized on the Le Mans triumph in advertising its roadcars. As a company more concerned with stemming red ink, and keeping a rotary car in production, the 787B's legacy would remain in the history books alone.

FD RX-7 – defining the legacy

The new second gen NB MX-5 of 1999 MY took styling cues from the FD RX-7 – if only RX-7 could have followed its little brother's sales example. Unfortunately, the FD RX-7 arrived in recessionary times, and a generational shift away from ultra fast cars. In March 1993, *CAR*'s US correspondent Jamie Kitman mentioned how piloting the latest Jag XJ-S 6-liter, 40th Anniversary LT1 Vette, ZR-1 Vette and FD RX-7 raised nary a glance from young people, more interested in their Game Boys and 16-bit electronic hardware. In 1993, *Automobile* magazine was yet another journal to award the FD RX-7.

Automobile's January issue proclaimed FD its 'Design Of The Year.' However, the same journal listed FD caveats in its October 1993 issue. Its 'Four Seasons Test' showed that enthusiasts should be careful about what they wish for: they might actually get it. The FD was a real race car for the road, and that meant, on a daily driver basis, the car was often more committed to driving than the driver. The GT siding 300ZX Turbo accumulated twice as many North American sales in the FD RX-7's first 18 months on market. Mazda's obsessive weight-lightening program also added to the FD's reliability woes. Plus, there were some recalls to consider.

First was a fire-related recall, requiring more heat resistant fuel lines under the intake manifold. A fan control unit was now set to run the radiator's electric fans if the coolant got too hot, even if the motor was off. Stronger and more heat resistant cooling system parts were introduced. The changes covered water pump bearing housing, coolant level sensor, radiator upper hose, thermostat gasket and all water hoses above the engine. Third round of changes concerned the braking vacuum check valve and hose leading to the brake booster. The original sometimes stuck, meaning no brake power assist.

A second generation Mazda MX-5 in France. The piston-engined MX-5 has always been an easier sell in gas-expensive Europe than any rotary Mazda. Mazda had sold around 430,000 MX-5s worldwide by the start of the second gen model in 1998. (Courtesy Paul Baylis)

During the reign of this NB MX-5, the 2000 Guiness Book of World Records pronounced the MX-5 the best selling two-seat sports car in history! Unfortunately, the specialized nature of the FD RX-7 meant Mazda's rotary sports car was only sold in Japan from 1999 onwards. (Courtesy Paul Baylis)

The NB MX-5 took styling cues from the FD RX-7. However, the latter was absent from European price lists for most of its life. In diesel-loving Europe, Mazda's 1991 Le Mans victory was sometimes mentioned in adverts. The fact that the triumph was achieved by rotary power was often omitted. (Courtesy Paul Baylis)

The FD RX-7 Series VIII's base 16in alloy rim, pictured in January 1999. Here, the rim carries Mazda's contemporary corporate 'M' logo. Back in 1991, Japanese market FD RX-7 Series VI cars had earlier-design squeeze cast alloys, with the Infini logo, that the FD was originally sold under in Japan. (Courtesy Mazda)

Cracking of the factory squeeze cast alloys, warped brake rotors and suspension clunks also appeared for some owners. The sequential twin turbo system proved complex, with the bi-turbo actuation mechanism sometimes proving troublesome. Thus, one didn't always get the full promised boost. The FD RX-7 required a caring owner and regular servicing for best results. The FD's first year Stateside was its best, with 9976 sold. By 1995 MY, only the base and R2 versions remained. Owners had to be careful of detonation causing the 13B-REW's apex seals to expire.

For 1995, PEG was renamed PEP (Popular Equipment Package). PEP included a sunroof, cargo cover, leather seating surfaces and foglights. However, a reliable gas gauge wasn't included. For this, many turned to the aftermarket. Mazda said North America wouldn't receive any 1996 RX-7s until the market took up the slow selling '95s. In the end, 1995 turned out to be the RX-7's final North American model year.

A third gen FD chassis RX-7 racer, taking part in America's SCCA GT-3 class of sports car racing. (Courtesy Lynn E Hanover)

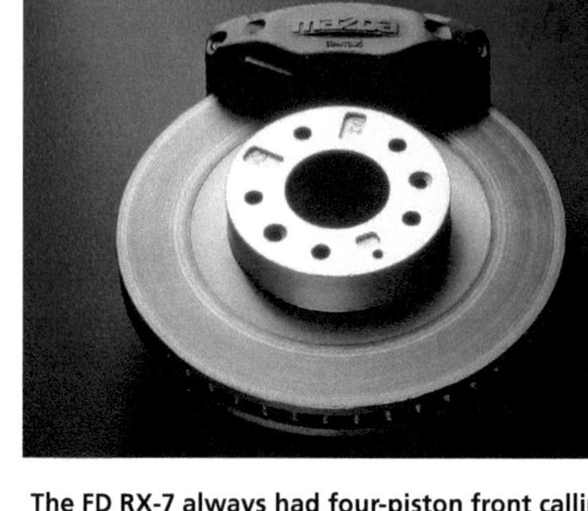

The FD RX-7 always had four-piston front callipers. However, the 1999-2002 RX-7 Series VIII saw the availability of 17in rims and 314mm brake rotors, shown here. On the Japanese tuner scene, foreign brand names, like Brembo, carry more cachet than stock Sumitomo callipers. (Courtesy Mazda)

A sports car to remember ...

In the UK, the FD RX-7 was much liked by the critics. From the cleverly concealed C door pillar flap, to the PPF, here was a car with style and substance; more exciting to drive, and way better value, than the normal Porsche 968. However, the FD had a propensity to oversteer, which became pronounced after a few hot laps, when the rear tires became overly warm. The UK press judged the FD's steering as precise, but rather light, which gave little warning of that pending oversteer. This was one Japanese car that was tricky to drift.

The FD RX-7 had foibles not seen since a '60s Citroën, but *Autocar* noted in retrospect, "Only a hard ride spoiled the most beautiful of Mazda's rotary-engined coupes."[79] *Autocar* put the FB and FD RX-7s in its list of 100 Greatest Sports Cars Of All Time, back in 1999, and said the FD had the sexiest shape this side of a Ferrari. The FD's ride was jittery on Britain's imperfect roads, and *CAR* judged the firm Porsche 968CS as offering better ride comfort. However, recession and declining interest in sports cars were the FD's real problems in Britain, and elsewhere.

The depressed sports car market saw many companies cut their prices to move stock. The single spec two-seater, manual transmission-only UK FD RX-7 Series VI wasn't overpriced to start with. It came with driver side airbag, ABS, a/c and cruise control. (The UK 300 ZX Bi-Turbo and Porsche 968 couldn't even be optioned with airbag at the time.) Nevertheless, to improve slow sales, the price of a FD was cut from over £32,000 to under £26,000 during 1993. Owners of earlier sold UK FDs were refunded the difference. UK testers felt the RX-7 R1 would be more fun, but it wasn't available, and sometimes a car can be too exclusive.

Porsche never had many UK dealers, but only 29 UK Mazda dealers were capable of servicing a FD RX-7. For the Renault Alpine A610, it was just six. Nothing exotic about Mazda's warranty though. A610 had one year, Porsche 968 two years, but FD RX-7 carried a three-year factory warranty. Even in the '90s, the 13B was still one tough rotary. However, none of the above helped sales, and the official Mazda-supplied UK FD ended in 1996. Then, in the late '90s, the FD RX-7 returned to the British Isles in upgraded 1996-98 Series VII trim. It was part of the UK's gray market Japanese high-performance import wave.

A FD RX-7 Series VIII, with rear wing and tint, in 1999. The FD's rear spoiler had long been a sore point with critics, and was the only item detracting from the FD's timeless beauty. However, these were the days of the Japanese import tuner craze. (Courtesy Mazda)

The European scene was a trifle dull at the time, and the idea of previously unavailable, fast Japanese cars limited to 280bhp, seemed most enticing. *CAR*'s Gavin Green set the scene when describing a small import specialist from Bolton, Warrender, "It specializes in Japanese machinery because, increasingly, the Japanese build the best high-performance cars. And because the official Japanese distributors in the UK seem pathologically incapable of selling the cars that enthusiasts actually want ..."[80] It was a big change from 1973, when *CAR* pronounced the RX-3 as having a great engine

The FD RX-7 Series VIII, pictured with rear strut bar. Series VIII Japanese market cars could have 280PS 314Nm (231lb/ft) versions of the twin turbo 13B-REW rotary. Thus, the 314mm brake disks of such cars with 17in rims, and the strut bar, were important chassis upgrades. (Courtesy Mazda)

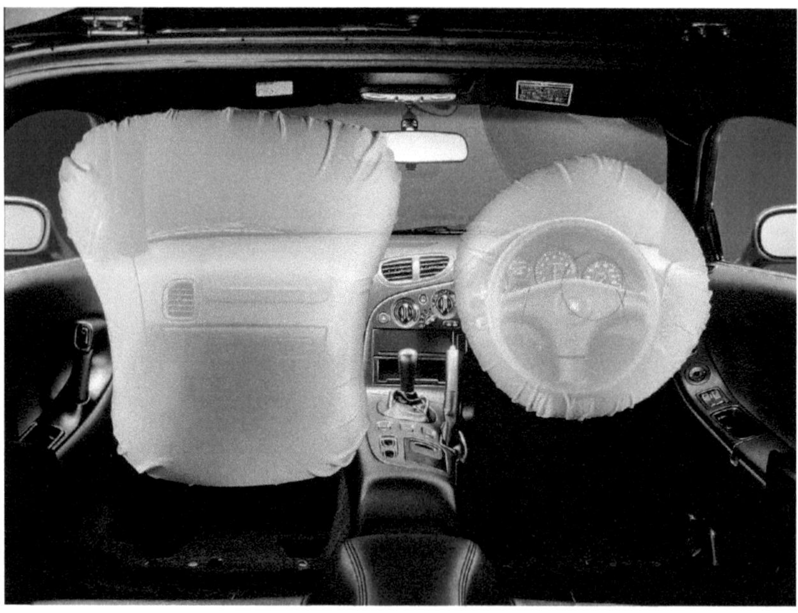

A Japanese spec RX-7 Series VIII Type RS, showing the refinement of dual airbags, in January 1999. The Type RS was the top normal FD at the time. FD was the third RX-7 to face off against Porsche's front-engined sports car series. Against the Porsche 968, Hiroshima still trumped Zuffenhausen for including more standard toys. (Courtesy Mazda)

The imaginative interior of FD RX-7 was a radical '90s move away from the coldly functional FC RX-7's work station of the '80s. Although lacking 21st century gee gaws, such as keyless go, and sat nav, the modernity of this 2001 FD RX-7 Type RS's cockpit still glows. (Courtesy Mazda)

In the depleted early '90s sports car market, the Porsche 968 and Renault Alpine A610 were amongst the FD RX-7's few rivals. All these cars had price cuts in the UK to bolster sales – the FD dropping from £32k plus to under £26k in 1993! A 2001 MY FD RX-7 Type RS2 is shown here. (Courtesy Mazda)

in search of a decent chassis. So it was that the Series VII FD made its way to UK shores. Many more special import FDs came to Britain than ever arrived by official Mazda UK decree.

The Series VII also made its way to New Zealand, and was an unofficial Australian import. By this time, the strong yen made a 1997 RX-7 $89,505 Australian dollars, and very prohibitive. So Aussie RX-7 sales only lingered into 1999 for the final Series VIIs. The FD RX-7 Series VIII, of January 1999 to August 2002, was a Japanese market only car, and represented the ultimate factory RX-7. The Series VII had seen a return to the RX-7, being sold under the Mazda brand name. This version also brought minor changes to simplify vacuum tube routing about the intake manifold, and a 16-bit ECU that went with an increase in turbo boost taking power to 265PS. By now, Mazda only made right-hand drive RX-7s.

The 265PS was the base manual gearbox power level for the Series VIII, which had versions with 280PS and generally upgraded features. The improvements seemed warranted: by April 1996, the sale of cars in Japan had risen 20 months in a row. It seemed Japan was finally exiting the 1990 recession. By May 1998, the FD RX-7 was selling steadily at 200 to 300 units per month in Japan. The Series VII had brought more efficient high flow turbos. This took the output of some versions onto 280PS and 313.8Nm or 231lb/ft, the Japanese legal limit. The front fascia was revised to permit better airflow to the intercooler and radiator. Front and rear headlights were restyled, as was the rear spoiler, which now became adjustable.

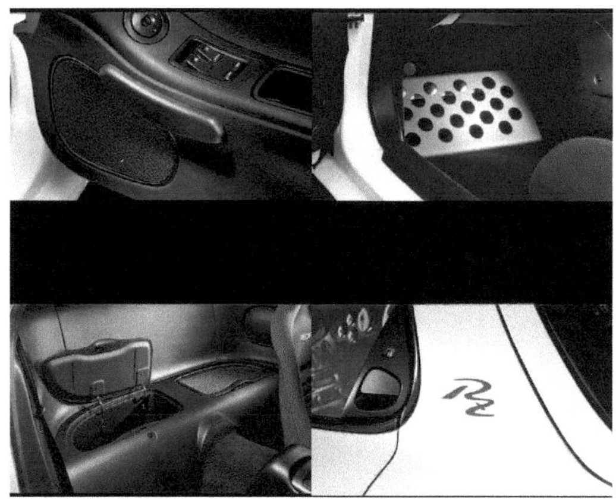

A 2001 MY Mazda RX-7 Series VIII Type RZ; a more specialized version of the top line Type RS. Special features visible are 'RZ' sail panel script and drilled aluminum dead pedal. The Type RZ was 10kg under the already lighter weight 1280kg Type RS. (Courtesy Mazda)

Keeping it in the FD family, the Type RZ's yellow Bilsteins came from the Type RS. The very low volume Type RZ had custom gunmetal-colored BBS rims, new 16-bit ECU, and ABS that braked each wheel independently. The RZ bestowed its lightweight red Recaros upon the two-seat Type-A 'end of FD' Spirit R. (Courtesy Mazda)

Top regular Series VIII was the Type RS, which came with Bilstein dampers, increased brake rotor diameter and brake pad surface area, a shorter final drive ratio and weight reduction measures taking things down to 1280kg. With a nod to practicality, the manual gearbox's fifth speed was made taller. Then there was the very low volume, limited edition Type RZ, with all the Type RS toys, but with weight reduction to 1270kg, plus custom gun metal-colored BBS rims and a custom red racing theme interior.

The Series VIII range brought an ABS system that braked each wheel independently;. Type RB-S, Type R, Type R Bathurst and Type RS were all 2+2 variants. The Type RZ was just a two-seater. 265PS versions came with 217lb/ft. The Type R, Type R Bathurst, Type RS and Type RZ all had 280PS with commensurate upgrades, like 17in rims and 314mm brake rotors. The rims were 17 x 8in with 235/45R 17in tires on the front, and 17 x 8.5in with 255/40R 17in tires rearwards.

The 2001 Japanese market released FD RX-7 Type R Bathurst R1, to commemorate the fourth straight 12-hour production car endurance race victory that the FD achieved in Australia between 1992 and 1995. This picture shows the special parts, such as white face dials and carbon fiber interior trim, that made up the Bathurst R1. (Courtesy Mazda)

Miata Detroit V6 & FD Spirit R

UK and US journals kept reminding readers that the RX-7 was still alive and kicking in Japan. Just as well, because, in Detroit, the Ford boys drew upon FD hardware to create a V6-powered Mazda proto in 2001. Henry's henchmen shoehorned the 3-liter, aluminum block Duratec V6 under a custom hood with forward facing hoodscoop. To cope with the red colored Miata V6's power, the engineers tossed the stock Miata six-speed in favor of the RX-7's five-speed. They also employed the FD's driveshaft, rear differential, axle halfshafts and brakes. Not as nimble as a four-pot Miata, but capable of 0-60mph in 5.8 seconds. Unfortunately, it didn't see production.

The FD RX-7 Spirit R did see production, as a Japanese market Series VIII variant. This 1500-unit limited edition FD, was Mazda's farewell to the RX-7 in 2002. It had all the previous

This 2002 FD RX-7 Type R Bathurst R2 was a belated tribute to a car and homologation special that achieved production car racing success in Australia at the famous Bathurst track in the 1990s. That car was the limited edition 204kW lightweight 1995-97 RX-7 SP Series VI and VII. (Courtesy Mazda)

At 18lb, the normal RX-7 aluminum hood was the only non-steel panel Mazda used. The stock FD RX-7 utilized conventional thin steel panels and weight-saving practices. However, this is the aluminum-paneled Mazdaspeed 'AL' Concept Car, pictured here in January 2003. (Courtesy Mazda)

low volume, limited edition toys, and some new exclusives. The Mazda Press Release hid nothing under a bushell. "The Type-A Spirit R model is the ultimate RX-7, boasting the most outstanding driving performance in its history." The Type-A was a two-seater, five-speed manual version, with lightweight red trim Recaro buckets, as seen in the earlier Type RZ. Over 1000 Spirit Rs were the Type-A version. Titanium Gray was an exclusive Spirit R paint color, chosen on over 700 Spirit Rs.

One could choose a Type-B Spirit R, which was also a manual transmission 280PS car, but of 2+2 configuration. The Type-C was also a 2+2, but with the 255PS 13B-REW and four-speed automatic power team. The Type-A and B retailed for ¥3,998,000 as new cars. The Type-C was ¥3,398,000 at the same time. All Spirit Rs have since become highly collectible in Japan. The FD RX-7 as a general model was also hardly common, compared to the high volume FB and FC. 68,589 FD RX-7s rolled off the Hiroshima assembly line between 1993 and 2002 model years. It was enough to move Mazda to continue rotary into the 21st century.

Part of the all-aluminum front and rear independent double wishbone suspension found on all FD RX-7s. However, on the 2002 FD RX-7 Type R Bathurst R2, such items were uprated and firmer. As per all 280PS FDs, and the earlier Australian market FD RX-7 SP, 17in alloys were standard. (Courtesy Mazda)

Outside Japan, the only access buyers had to the 2001-2002 FD RX-7 Type R Bathurst R1/R2 Series VIII was via gray market imports. The gray market had involved high performance European rides in the early '80s. By the late '90s, it was dominated by the special versions of the Japanese scene. The FD RX-7 was on wish lists, along with Mitsubishi EVOs, Subaru WRXs and Nissan Skylines. (Courtesy Mazda)

Mazda had problems to address with the FD RX-7. The public had cooled off sports cars, and Mazda already had the MX-5 for that job. The FD's limited interior space and high fuel consumption were also commonly aired concerns. Plus, on value, the final US 1995 MY RX-7 R2s were considered pricey, equal to a BMW M3. Rumors about the next Mazda rotary were circulating. By the middle of 1998, the belief was that it would be a non-turbo coupe like the original FB RX-7, and due out in 1999. Mazda's new chief at the time was James Miller. He said rotary was the heart and soul of Mazda, a showroom drawcard and company morale raiser.

Showcar clues – true red ink

It all started in the mid 1990s. At a time when the RX-7 was commercially faltering in export markets, Mazda was in the red, and Ford was putting the squeeze on Hiroshima to make sensible cars. Even so, Mazda unveiled its RX-01 concept car at the 1995 Tokyo Auto Salon. It was a sporty combo of Miata base and new 218PS 13B-MSP (Multi Side Port). Due to economic conditions, the concept went to bed, but a small dedicated team at Mazda kept the project alive. The whole deal eventually sparked management interest, and was allowed to progress to the 1999 RX-EVOLV (RXE) concept car.

If RX-01 was a first draft, then RXE was a much classier, refined indication of what Mazda would put in production in 2003. This time, it was on to the 1999 Tokyo Auto Salon, with critics acknowledging RXE to be much better-finished and integrated than RX-01. The goal was a sports car for four people, and factions inside Mazda wanted to call it RX-8. RXE had some dimensions similar to FD RX-7. RXE length was 168.7in and width 69.3in. However, it was almost 5in taller, and, with a 107.1in wheelbase, the nearly 12in extra answered the FD's tight cabin criticism.

RXE had what Mazda called 'Freestyle' doors, a new take on the old 'Suicide' doors of yore. Thus, there was no center unibody B pillar, and the back doors opened rearwards. This was to allow easier rear cabin access in a compact car. During the RXE's development,

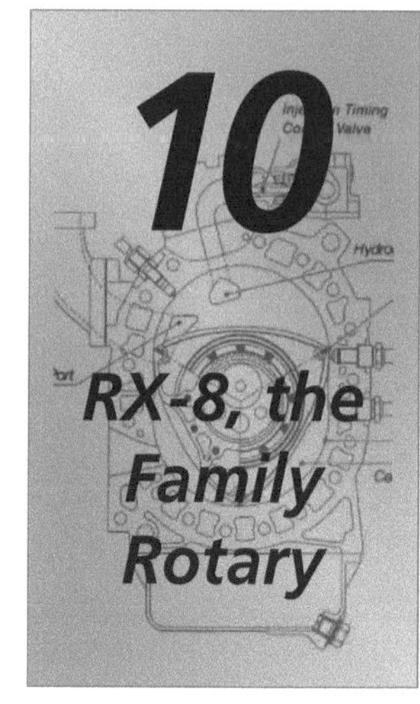

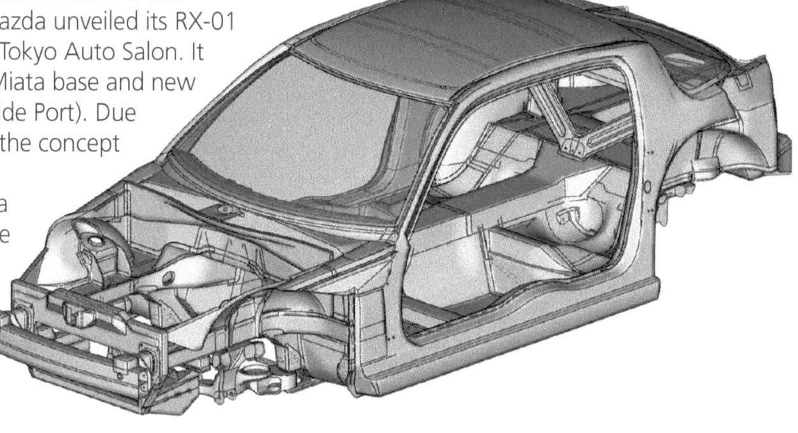

The 2001 Design/Engineering Model for what would become the Mazda RX-8's unibody. Strength of the pillarless structure was maintained by 'hydraforming,' which involves making the unibody under hydraulic pressure; plus, a high mount backbone chassis design. (Courtesy Mazda)

A trio of Mazda rotary technical tour de force! The Le Mans-conquering 787B racer, with RX-8 Design Model, and a FD RX-7 in the background. Unfortunately, Mazda didn't make full use of said Le Mans win to boost road car sales. The 787B was an under-utilized halo car. (Courtesy Mazda)

The Renesis RX-8 rotary motor, shown in January 2001. It had the same 1308cc as per past 13Bs, but side-mounted intake and exhaust ports, higher comp ratio and ultra fine fuel injectors, boosted gas mileage and lowered emissions. In high output six-port form, the Renesis atmo rotary made 250PS. (Courtesy Mazda)

Martin Leach was Mazda's R&D chief. Acknowledging that safety laws might thwart the Freestyle doors, Leach said, "But we will try to keep that part of the design, if we possibly can." The RXE monocoque was made via hydraforming – that is, forming the steel structure under hydraulic pressure. Exterior styling was overseen by Yoichi Sato, the boss of Mazda's Hiroshima Advance Design Studio.

Styling hallmarks were minimal overhangs, a 'cab rearward' look and cues honoring past Mazdas. Thick C pillars and sloping roof recalled the FB RX-7; the double bubble roof, the FD RX-7. At first glance, it looked as though the RXE had no headlamps; in fact a narrow horizontal air intake concealed a pair of very narrow, high intensity discharge lights. A forward-tipping double clamshell hood gave

Mazda created this Cosmo 21 showcar, as a 21st century celebration of the company's first rotary-powered car, the 1967 Cosmo Sport 110S. (Courtesy Mazda)

Shown at the 2002 Tokyo Auto Salon, the Cosmo 21 was built on a Mazda Miata chassis. Power came courtesy of a 250PS RX-8 rotary motor. (Courtesy Mazda)

access to the latest front midship-located 13B. This motor was dubbed Renesis (rotary engine's genesis). Still at 1308cc and matching the current 280PS FD RX-7 Series VIII 13B-REW's output, but without any forced induction …

Mr Leach proudly proclaimed Renesis' achievement, "This is the highest power density ever achieved by a normally-aspirated engine for a roadgoing automobile." It was a continuation of 1995 13B-MSP RE thinking – with refinements. There were redesigned and larger intake and exhaust ports, and a three-stage induction system to optimize chamber filling. Thinner, lightweight rotors permitted a 10,000rpm redline. A higher compression ratio brought better gas mileage, but the usual 13B 654cc chamber size was kept.

For optimal handling, double wishbone suspension existed front and back, with aluminum arms and knuckles. Heavy items, like the gas tank, were within the wheelbase and a 50:50 weight distribution was apparent. It was a design with a low polar moment of inertia. Special 20 in five-spoke alloy rims wearing 225/40 ZR tires front and 245/35 ZR tires rear provided grip and a macho look. The RXE interior was pure style, done by Wu-Huang Chin of Mazda's West Coast US design studio. RXE had brown and silver lightweight sports seats, with transparent wire mesh centers.

Both front and rear seating slid on runners, and the passenger side rear seat had a built-in, fold down child's seat. Instrumentation featured a 280kph speedo and 11 grand tach. There was a red starter button, and a green one marked 'KILL.' A further red button, of one-touch nature, operated the handbrake. On the center console lay a small, silver joystick for the six-speed clutchless transmission. This was backed up by Formula One-style steering wheel mounted paddles, which Mazda called 'Wing Shifts.' Right to change up, left for a downshift.

The driver could avoid any understeer or oversteer via an ACB (Active Cornering Brake) system. This encompassed two steering wheel levers, to work the left and right side rear brakes. The RXE's large four-wheel disk brakes had six piston callipers at the front, and four-piston callipers at the rear. An ID Access smart electronic card opened and locked doors, started the engine and armed the car's security system. The card even stored the driver's skill level, and would reduce power from 280PS to 240PS and 152lb/ft for novice drivers. The design goal for RXE was 0-60mph in under five seconds, and for this aim target weight was a mere 2626lb.

Martin Leach set up a weight-saving 'gram force' to help RXE meet its goals. Mazda also wanted to keep the price down, with Leach saying they were working on what figure the car could be considered affordable in North America. The proposed figure was under ¥3.5 million, or approx $33,000. The RX-01 brought forth the idea of a rotary Miata. Sam Mitani broached the subject of a Renesis Miata, with Mazda, for *Road & Track*. To this, one Mazda engineer responded, "Anything is possible."[81] Mazda came up with just such a vehicle as a showcar for the 2002 Tokyo Auto Salon.

This vehicle was a 35th birthday tribute to the 1967 Cosmo Sport 110S, and Mazda's Wankel production cars. Called Cosmo 21, this showcar used a Miata base, FD RX-7 five-speed and the hi po 250PS Renesis motor. The concept ride had a back-to-the-'60s interior

The interior of the Cosmo 21 showcar. Apart from retro touches, it doesn't look much like the Cosmo Sport original. The Miata basis limited interior design freedom. (Courtesy Mazda)

A December 11 2000 sketch of the RX-8 prototype. Mazda titled it 'four-door sports car' and the company was right. The RX-8 sought to satisfy Miata lovers with a family to take care of. (Courtesy Mazda)

Technically from an earlier time, in practice, the RX-8 was the first vehicle to embody Mazda's Kodo Design Language (KDL). KDL attempts to capture the moment just before stored energy is released in nature, to stir emotion in the car public's heart. Hence RX-8's 'about to pounce on prey' look. (Courtesy Mazda)

and exterior theme, even if the Miata's stouter dimensions meant it didn't look as svelte as the Cosmo Sport 110S.

In modern times, Mazda creations represent an internal competition between its Japanese, US and German design studios. Eventually, management was sold on productionizing RX-EVOLV, chose the RX-8 moniker, and displayed a Design and Engineering model of same, at the 2001 North American International Auto Show. A 'Reference Exhibit' RX-8 was shown at the 2001 Tokyo Auto Salon, pending the final management production decision. The 2001 show exhibits were very close to the factory RX-8, which started rolling off Hiroshima's production line, in February 2003. The extremely positive public reaction to the showcars no doubt swayed Mazda into thinking that it was onto a good thing.

RX-8 … zoom zoom

Initial RX-8 sales exceeded expectations, with production at the Renesis engine plant at full stretch. 60,100 RX-8s were built in 2003.

Celebrating the start of RX-8 production at Hiroshima on February 17 2003. The RX-8 was also assembled in South Africa. Honoring Ford links, this was done at the Ford Motor Co plant in Pretoria. (Courtesy Mazda)

There was even talk of the Renesis motor being fitted to Mazda models outside the RX-8, and a return to an all-new pure sports car RX-7 in 2005. The Freestyle Doors were a bigger publicity generator for RX-8 than even the Renesis motor. Apart from Hydraforming the unibody, the RX-8 also used a high-mount backbone frame. This ran from the front bulkhead, through the upper part of the transmission tunnel, to the rear bulkhead.

Such strength permitted Mazda to reduce body panel thickness. There were also further strategically chosen chassis reinforcement points. Although lacking a B pillar, a virtual pillar existed via the RX-8's reinforced door frame structure. To stop folks accidentally falling out of the four-door coupe on the move, the inner and outer door trim handles were combined. Thus, one couldn't open a rear door, unless the corresponding front door was open. The RX-8 chassis had front long-arm double-wishbone suspension, and a rear-mounted multilink beam. Mazda's PPF locked the powertrain into a single, rigid unit. The front midship layout shortened the gearbox to differential distance, so that in spite of a 2700mm wheelbase, a one-piece carbon fiber propeller shaft could be used on six-speed manual cars, to save weight.

The RX-7 finished with 17in alloy rims; the RX-8 started with 18in items wearing 225/45 ZR-rated footwear. Advancements in suspension tech meant the new car rode better, even with bigger rims and low profile rubber. Motorvating the show, in top spec, was the six-port Renesis making 250PS or 184Kw at 8500rpm and 216Nm of torque at 7500rpm. There was zero overlap between the side-mounted intake and exhaust ports. This promoted improved thermal efficiency, and facilitated a leaner idle mix, versus the 13B-REW. Emissions from the final RX-7s had been a worry. The Renesis' zero overlap meant that when exhaust gas was kept and carried over to the next intake cycle for an extra thorough burn, there was no instability.

Rotaries have long been good on nitrogen oxide, not on hydrocarbons, hence the need to carry over and burn. The cool-natured, great surface area rotary design means more work for the cat converter filter. It has to deal with the pollutants that the Wankel format isn't so good on. The Renesis side-exhaust-port layout kept unburned hydrocarbons for the next combustion cycle. Plus, a newly designed cat worked with a double-skin exhaust manifold. This set-up maintained high exhaust gas temperature to improve cat activation on motor start-up, even in colder climates.

A higher compression ratio, and newly developed ultra fine fuel injectors, sought to improve gas mileage over those final RX-7s too. North America's CAFE standards, and the Smog Nazis of California, were hard rotary task masters. However, Renesis seemed to have the answers. The 250PS Renesis powering the 2004 MY RX-8 six-speed manual passed California's Golden State preserving LEV2-A dictates, and early EPA estimates were 18mpg city/23mpg highway. So Renesis was better than 13B-REW on pollution, economy and durability. No turbos equalled fewer recalls.

Mazda North American Operations provided a warranty extension program for 2004-2008 MY RX-8s of eight years, or 100,000 miles. This covered the rotor housing, internal parts, seals and gaskets. True, the Renesis wasn't exactly a Prius on gasoline, and the Wankel still had a greater-than-piston thirst for oil, but Mazda was making 250PS atmo, versus the FD's 255PS twin turbo, on the same 1308cc. That said, the blowers did supply torque and, back to back, the RX-8 was slower. *Autocar* magazine tested the FD RX-7 and RX-8 in 1992 (8/7/92) and 2003 (16/9/03) respectively.

The stats for the FD RX-7 were 0-60mph in six seconds, 0-100mph in 15.8 seconds, 156mph top speed and 16mpg overall. For RX-8 the respective figures were 7.1 seconds, 18.1 seconds, 142mph and 19.5mpg. The RX-8, at 1300kg, was lighter than the FD's 1310kg. The RX-8 carrying chassis prefix SE3P, utilized weight-saving measures. Mazda used many aluminum and plastic body panels on the RX-8 unibody, plus plastic bumpers. Need it also be said that RX-8 could carry four homosapiens in adequate comfort, with reasonable luggage space. However, in the words of Scott Evans, in the June 9 2010 issue of *Motor Trend*, "This is not a numbers car ..." The RX-8's sublime chassis made its DSC (Dynamic Stability Control) superfluous. Leave it on, and the computer could jerk the rear end back into line. Turn it off, and the driver could fine tune the rear wheel grip level, aided by delicate, electric assist power steering of excellent feel. Mazda showed restraint on rim/tire size, and there was the refinement of six point rubber mounts on the rear subframe.

The RX-8 Mazdaspeed Concept car shown in January 2003. Utilizing its inhouse tuner hardware, Mazda produced 300 Mazdaspeed Version cars in 2003. 300 follow up Mazdaspeed Version IIs were done for 2004, but in Strato Blue only. (Courtesy Mazda)

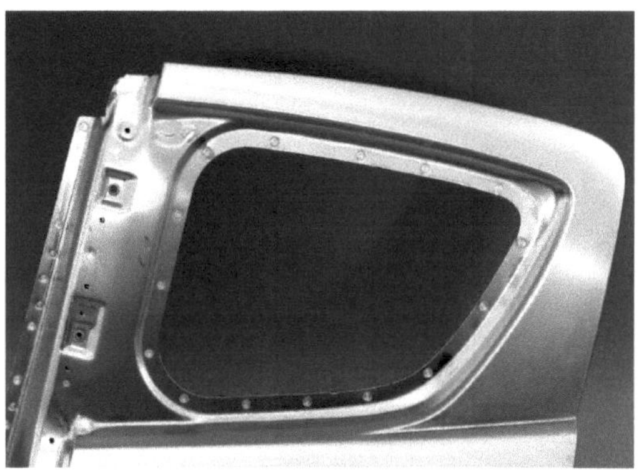

Mazda showing its friction heat method for joining aluminum surfaces, concerning the RX-8's rear door in February 2003. A virtual pillar on RX-8 existed via the reinforced door frame structure. Here, top and bottom latches locked the rear door to the body. (Courtesy Mazda)

The 106.4in wheelbase and 174.2in length were modest, but the 2003 RX-8 could seat two adults and two kids in reasonable comfort. The Freestyle doors were an access boon on this family sports car. The FD RX-7's limited interior space had inhibited that model's sales. (Courtesy Mazda)

A US spec RX-8; *Motor Trend* proffered 2004 MY performance figures of 14.8 seconds at 94.3mph for the ¼ mile. 0-60mph was done in 6.4 seconds, with 60mph to zero in 111ft. The acceleration matched an Acura CL Type-S. However, Mazda's creativity was on a whole new level. (Courtesy Scott Redmond)

Base US RX-8 debut price was $25,180, but that didn't include the Comp Turbo upgraded T618Z and GReddy hardware fitted to this ride. Many North American RX-8 owners have added aftermarket turbo kits. (Courtesy Scott Redmond)

RX-8 handled on road and track

It was commonly agreed that the RX-8 had a solid feeling structure, with compliant suspension. It was handling for adults, rather than boy racers, although the Renesis engine note was reminiscent of yesteryear's Formula One car. In April 1992, *Road & Track* stated that an RX-7 R1 had a slalom speed of 66.4mph and skidpad figure of 0.95g. *Motor Trend*'s May 2003 issue supplied 67.1mph and 0.88g as respective figures for RX-8. The magazine ¼-mile times of 14 and 14.8 seconds for FD RX-7 and RX-8, leant credence to the notion that RX-8 was indeed a sports car with two bonus rear seats.

Experts praised RX-8 handling. Two-time Daytona 24-Hour race winner Randy Pobst put RX-8 ahead of Nissan GT-R, Porsche 911 Turbo and Dodge Viper ACR at Laguna Seca, in *Motor Trend*'s 2008 Best Handling Car compare. More kudos still in *Car and Driver*'s 2010, 'The Best Handling Car in America for Less Than $100,000' challenge. Here an RX-8 R3 came third out of a field of seven cars. Indeed, the RX-8 did some high achieving in motorsport. Earliest was the Japanese one make 'Party Race' 2004 series, sanctioned by the Japanese Automobile Federation (JAF).

For the NR-A/Party Race program, Mazda provided a NR-A kit sold through Mazda

In June 2010, *Motor Trend*'s Scott Evans observed it was necessary to come to the RX-8 wanting a car with its particular qualities. Two-time Daytona 24-Hour race winner Randy Pobst admired RX-8's handling. Conclusion? RX-8 was for dedicated auto enthusiasts. (Courtesy Scott Redmond)

This RX-8's custom interior has a Cobb mount by Proclip, dual-vent pod with fuel pressure and oil pressure, Lotek center pod with oil temp, PLX multi-gauge and boost, full interior LED kit and SARX embroidered floor mats. The factory Bose audio has iPod integration, plus 10in bazooka bass tube, and a Voo Doo shift knob stirs the gearbox. (Courtesy Scott Redmond)

dealers. The kit, designed only for the 250PS RX-8, made the production car track ready. It consisted of rollbar, sports radiator, oil cooler kit, tow hooks and racing brake pads, plus special high temp brake fluid. Also in 2004 was the Mazda sponsored Formula Women series, consisting of an all-lady field, using slightly modified RX-8s. In 2005/6, the RX-8 was in the UK Britcar series endurance races. Mazda Belgium sponsored an RX-8 silhouette racer in that country's GT series.

In North America, the RX-8 participated in the 2006 Grand-Am Cup, and the Street Tuner class of the Koni Challenge Series .Ryan Eversley won both touring car class races in the 2010 SCCA World Challenge Mid-Ohio Grand Prix, using an RX-8. Honoring the RX-8 design integrity, the aforementioned racing examples have involved production-related racers. However, privateer success at the 2008 and 2010 24 Hours of Daytona involved an RX-8 using a 20B Wankel and custom tube frame chassis. The Speed Source Race Engineering team achieved GT-class victories at this event. It represented the 23rd endurance race win at Daytona by a Mazda rotary racing car.

With roadgoing RX-8s, the top 250PS Renesis edition had a 9000rpm redline, but there was also a lower-output version rated at 192PS, with 7500rpm redline. The latter was available with a five-speed manual gearbox or four-speed automatic. At first, an automatic couldn't be found that could cope with a nine grand redline, so it was the 192PS edition that powered shiftless RX-8s. In America, the 192PS version was only seen in automatic form. To avoid misleading advertising Stateside for hi po 250PS Renesis, quite early on its output was declared as 232 SAE net ponies.

Kodo Design Language … RX-8 style

Mazda subsequently did a lower output 215PS (212bhp SAE net) edition of the six-port Renesis. This added excitement for North American automatic RX-8 owners from 2007 MY onwards. However, in a world less concerned with automotive tech details, it was the RX-8's styling that grabbed the most attention. Positively received by press and public alike, the RX-8 may have been the earliest model to express Mazda's 21st century Kodo Design Language. Kodo represents the fusion of 'motion' with movement found in nature. Mazda designers wished to capture the moment energy is released, giving examples such as when a cheetah pounces on prey, or the moment a Kendo sword strikes.

Celebrating the export release of the RX-8 Series II, on January 7 2008. Seeing off the first shipment, extreme left, Mazda's Representative Director Hisakazu Imaki, and to his right Mazda President and CEO Hiroshi Yamamoto. (Courtesy Mazda)

Thus, the RX-8 featured a minimal overhang, muscular, Can Am-fendered look, derived from 1999's Mazda RX-EVOLV, and suggestive of the model's rear-drive nature. The cubic front styling and cab rearward profile modernity, blended with the strong C pillars and sloping rear window angle. It all harked back to the Cosmo Sport 110S and FB RX-7. Like Japan itself, the RX-8 was a seamless blend of ancient and modern. The short, low front was aided by the compact rotary. There was a power bulge hood center with rotary motif. The rear combination lamps had chrome accents, and cute rotor-shaped rear foglamp.

The special edition RX-8s

Low in the rear, fascia dual exhausts were placed on left and right. The RX-8's interior couldn't feature the wild colors and exotic hardware of the RX-EVOLV, but took the showcar's overall theme. It continued the interesting dashboard/console look of FD RX-7, after the blandness of the 1980s. And what could spice up a car range more than the selective release of limited edition models? Things kicked off in Japan, with a special 2003 Mazdaspeed RX-8 edition, predictably called 'Mazdaspeed Version.' This limited edition RX-8 involved a run of just 300 cars. They carried inhouse tuner, and Mazda motorsport good guy, Mazdaspeed's sports accessories such as special cat back exhaust and sportified ECU chip.

Mazdaspeed version came in True Red, Strato Blue Mica or Sunlight Silver exterior colors. There was a 2004 'Mazdaspeed Version II' with uprated equipment. Once again, the production run was 300 cars, but only the Strato Blue Mica color was at hand. There were no Protege, Mazda 3/6 or MX-5 versions done by Mazdaspeed. With inhouse-designed bodykit, suspension tuning, interior improvements, cold air intake etc … the Mazdaspeed RX-8s have become Japanese collector cars.

Mazda was in a quandary, at the start of the 2000s, over whether to use the MPS (Mazda Performance Series) or Mazdaspeed tags for its performance cars. MPS got the nod on a worldwide basis, with MPS applied to the 2006 Mazda 3 MPS 2.3-liter turbo I4 hot hatch. For Japan only, there was the 2004 RX-8 True Red Style. Only available with the True Red exterior color, and black leather interior, this limited edition featured slight trim changes. 2005 saw a special edition RX-8, called 'Sports Prestige Limited' (SPL) in North America, and Shinka in Japan. The latter name meant evolution, appropriately evocative of Japanese art and cultural development. This luxurious GT had a Black Cherry or Galaxy Gray exterior, Parchment leather interior and subtle chromed 18in rims.

The SPL/Shinka followed the Mazdaspeed suspension upgrade formula of revalved Bilstein dampers and a urethane foam injected front suspension crossmember. The latter feature improved chassis rigidity, ride quality and would appear on many special RX-8s. 2150 SPL/Shinkas were planned, but only 1357 were made. 2005 saw the first UK limited edition RX-8 called Evolve. Named after Mazda's 1999 showcar, this RX-8 was based on the 250PS six-speeder. The 500-unit production run involved 400 Copper Red Mica cars and 100 colored Phantom Blue Mica.

The RX-8 Evolve rolled on dark silver 18 x 8in alloys. Special trim pieces encompassed a polished aluminum rotary crest on the front air dam, dark silver bezeled headlamps, sports door mirrors, polished aluminum side air outlet fins, rotary insignia B-pillar decoration and chrome exhaust surrounds. Interior trim included stone leather and Alcantara seat trim, black leather wrapped steering wheel, shifter knob and handbrake lever. Priced at the same level as a leather-optioned UK RX-8, the Evolve was certainly value for money.

May 2006 saw the UK release of the RX-8 PZ. Priced at £25,995, 800 PZs were made. There were 320 Galaxy Gray PZs and 480 Brilliant Black cars. The PZ was a joint project between Mazda UK and the rallying specialist motorsports company Prodrive. Based on the six-speed 250PS version, the PZ had special ten-spoke alloys, sourced from Italian Formula One firm OZ Racing. The theme was dark silver rims, with low drag mirrors, front and rear black mesh grilles and rear spoiler. The rims and carbon fiber rear wing spoiler carried the 'Prodrive' script.

The PZ followed Mazdaspeed's handling recipe of revalved Bilsteins, and Eibach coils that were 60% stiffer than stock, with ride height 15mm under a standard RX-8. The rear fascia greeted onlookers with a custom dual exhaust system, where tailpipes carried Prodrive insignia.

Third UK RX-8 special edition was the Nemesis, based on the RX-8 five-speed with 192PS motor. Thus, it carried 192PS UK standard equipment, such as front fogs, heated front seats, powered driver's seat, climate control, nine-speaker BOSE premium audio with six-disc CD autochanger, black leather-adorned steering wheel, shifter knob and handbrake lever. Then came the Nemesis bounty of Copper Red Mica or Stormy Blue Mica exterior color choices, combined with Stone leather interior. As per previous limiteds, the Nemesis had a polished aluminum rotary crest on the front air dam, polished aluminum side air-outlet trims behind the front wheel arches, special B-pillar trims with rotary crest, and additional Nemesis badging. Nemesis-branded luxury floormats came with Mazda RX-8 logos on the rocker panel dress plates, for a deal representing a £330 saving on a like-specified RX-8. Unfortunately, the order rate proved slow. Although launched in 2006, some Nemesis cars were registered in 2007. Fuel economy in Europe was once again a Mazda rotary bugbear. The numerous special edition RX-8s were part explained by Mazda UK's need to spice up interest in slow moving stock. 200 Copper Red and 150 Stormy Blue Nemesis cars were sold, with each owner entitled to a free Prodrive track day.

Finally, there was the UK RX-8 Kuro. With a run of 500 units, the Kuro was faithful to the Japanese meaning of its name, with a Sparkling Black Mica exterior. The interior had light gray leather, and rocker panel decorative trims stated the car's 500-unit sequence number. Mechanicals were untouched, but there were cosmetic changes to headlights, taillights and interior.

To commemorate the first Mazda rotary, 1967's Cosmo Sport 110S, Mazda released the RX-8 40th Anniversary edition for Japan and North America. The '60s Cosmo Sport was initially white only for exterior color, so, in Japan, the RX-8 40th Anniversary paid tribute with a Marble White exterior. In America, where the Cosmo Sport 110S was little known, the RX-8 40th Ann was painted Metropolitan Gray Mica.

RX-8 in later life

Both Japanese and US RX-8 40th Anns featured a special Cosmo Red leather interior, and new design alloy rims to be seen in the RX-8 Series II of 2009. The 40th Ann cars had sportier suspension with Bilstein dampers, and urethane foam injected into the front suspension crossmember. The US RX-8 40th Ann made a 2008 model year showing in North America only. It paved the way for the worldwide RX-8 Series II's 2009 MY debut. Now the RX-8 came with a trapezoidal strut tower, and more rigid carbon fiber driveshaft. Rear suspension geometry was revised, and, along with a 90lb weight reduction, overall handling was improved.

Manual transmission RX-8s had their final drive ratio shortened from 4.444 to 4.777, to get the cars off the line with greater alacrity. Front and rear bumpers were restyled for more aggression, complimented by a revised front fascia. Redesigned front and rear headlamps were of sportier nature, and larger 90mm exhaust pipe outlets were added. The Series IIs also featured the new style five-spoke 'Rotary Engine' theme aluminum rims, on a normal RX-8 in asymmetric form. Width, height and wheelbase remained at 69.7in, 52.8in and 106.4in respectively. However, length increased from 174.2in to 176in; and there was a new R3 variant.

The next generation '16X' Renesis, pictured on October 24 2007. At the 2012 Moscow Motor Show, Mazda CEO Takashi Yamanouchi said the rotary engine would still figure in Mazda's future concerning low emissions/ hybrid applications. (Courtesy Mazda)

RX-8 R3 ...

The RX-8 R3 was a 2009 MY entrant, carrying on the sporty tradition of the FD RX-7 R1s and R2s, but in a more refined form, with fewer pitfalls. Cosmetically, there was a rear deck wing, slightly more aggressive front splitter and lower fascia. Rocker panel side skirts, Xenon HID headlamps and 19in BBS forged alloys with 225/40 R19 tires were all functional. Suspension was reworked with the familiar Bilsteins and urethane foam-injected front suspension crossmember. On the inside the front occupants had to fit the Recaros with non-adjustable side bolsters – if one did fit, they were comfy.

R3s also came with a 300W Bose audio system, Bluetooth and a keyless entry/start system. As a sign of how rapidly such car tech was advancing, North American RX-8s had sat nav – available only from midrange models upwards. Plus, the auxiliary input for the Bose stereo was awkwardly placed at the back of the front console cubby, below the armrest center. Later car designs factored in the popular iPod's usage. RX-8 was also sharing features with the MX-5. The roadster had long taken tips from its rotary big brother. Here, the 2006 NC MX-5, whose lead stylist was Moray Callum, featured a muscular fender look. It also followed RX-8's front double wishbone, multi-link rear suspension.

If only RX-8 could offer Miata MX-5's fuel economy. The 2009 RX-8 six-speed North American EPA numbers were 16 city/22 highway mpg, or slightly worse than the 5-liter V8 Mustang of the hour. A 1.3-liter 232-horse Wankel out-drinking Henry's 412bhp V8 pony, was making RX-8 an increasingly hard model to sell Stateside. So were emissions. In the UK, grams of CO_2 per kilometer had become a popular pollution measuring stick, by the late 2000s. The 228bhp RX-8 put out 284 units; a 388bhp Mercedes E500 Sport wagon was on 280 units, with just 258 units for sedan. It seemed that the small displacement rotary paid a heavy gas mileage and pollution price, compared to the big, high output V8s.

Ford says ii tabi-o!/bon voyage!

Ford had been close to Mazda since 1979. Mazda was the US giant's small-car-technology partner, supplied light truck designs, and was involved in many joint production and sales distribution projects. The alliance continued to the new lightweight Mazda 2 supermini small car, which was a close cousin of the yet-to-

The Mazda 3 Sky Activ CNG Concept reference exhibit at the 43rd Tokyo Auto Salon. As if tying drivetrain to ECU via Mazda's Sky Activ system wasn't enough, economy with low pollution is maximized by throwing in compressed natural gas, too. (Courtesy Mazda)

arrive 2008 European Ford Fiesta. However, the global financial crisis of 2007/8 saw Ford streamline its operations. It jettisoned Volvo, Jaguar, Aston Martin, and distanced itself from Mazda. As Hiroko Nakata wrote in *The Japan Times,* on May 24 2012, Ford's stake in Mazda had declined from one third to just 2.1 per cent.

Strong competition, the global financial crisis, and appreciating yen hadn't been kind to Mazda. The company had been in the red since 2008, registering its fourth annual, consecutive group net loss to the end of the business year March 2012. Plus, unlike other Japanese automakers, it still largely made cars only in Japan. Seeking new partnerships, Mazda signed a 2012 deal with Fiat. The next MX-5 and a new Alfa sports car would be related, Alfa being in need of a rear-drive platform. Both would be built, alongside each other, at Hiroshima from 2015.

Mazda's hot sellers of today: from left to right, the compact SUV CX5, Mazda 6, and Mazda 3. In Japan, the Mazda 6 and Mazda 3 are called Atenza and Axela respectively. Unfortunately, rotary and Miata no longer make up major Mazda sales action. Mazda still makes red cars, but the company doesn't wish to be *in* the red. (Courtesy Mazda)

Towards the RX-8 Spirit R

It promised to be the best-made Alfa in history. There was also speculation that Mazda would supply its fuel-efficient gasoline engines to Fiat, leaving the Italians to concentrate more on diesels; thereby saving corporate costs. Europe was one cause that hastened the RX-8's demise.

The final limited edition, Japanese only, RX-8 Spirit R, pictured just before market launch on October 7 2011. As if an atmo 250PS rotary motor wasn't enough, Mazda upped the showroom wow factor by reviving suicide rear doors! The RX-8 was one of the few true enthusiast cars of the modern era. It required owner understanding. (Courtesy Mazda)

A final publicity shot for the RX-8, taken on April 26 2012 concerning the very last of the line RX-8 Spirit R. So popular was the RX-8 Spirit R in Japan, that Mazda built 1000 more copies. The very last RX-8 Spirit R came off the Hiroshima line in June 2012. (Courtesy Mazda)

Stricter Euro V emissions standards posed a Renesis problem. As a result, Mazda announced in April 2010, that 2010 MY would be the end for RX-8 on that continent. In May 2010 Mazda stated 2011 MY would be the last, for RX-8 in North America. Emissions and CAFE were cited as reasons.

As much as Mazda is proud of rotary, the company acknowledged RX-8 wasn't selling well in later years. As a small company, it had to put its resources towards conventional models, and the Mazda 3 and 6 were critical and commercial success stories worldwide. In recent times, even the once-mighty MX-5 has become a niche model. Mazda had considered axing rotary, even before 2011 MY. It turns out, Mazda North America had urged Mazda Japan to keep rotary going, because of its commercial halo factor Stateside. As happened with FD RX-7, Mazda launched a Japanese market Spirit R RX-8 special edition, as a fond farewell to the sporty four-door.

The RX-8 Spirit R was a 1000-unit run, announced in October 2011. Manual transmission versions were based on the Japanese RX-8 Type RS, with automatic Spirit Rs patterned off the six-speed electronic auto paddle shifted Type E. The Spirit R's features were disclosed on October 7 2011, with the iteration going on sale, November 24 2011. Orders were almost equally divided between the choice of three exterior colors: Aluminum Metallic, Sparkling Black Mica and Crystal White Pearl Mica. The RX-8 Spirit R was bought by a wide demographic – varied in age, some were rotary fans and some just liked sports cars.

Common to both manual and auto Spirit Rs were Spirit R ornament, front fogs, headlamps and rear combination lights with black bezels, red front and rear brake callipers with larger than standard RX-8 brake rotors, piano black transmission tunnel trim, curtain, and front side SRS airbags. There were also Dynamic Stability Control and traction control driver aids, plus black leather-wrapped steering wheel with red stitching, black leather-wrapped parking brake lever with red stitching, center console box with front seat armrest, and rear lidded console box. Both boxes were covered with synthetic leather and employed red stitching.

Unique to the manual transmission Spirit R were 19in bronze-painted forged aluminum rims. The manuals came with harder Bilstein dampered sports suspension and 225/40R 19 89W tires. There were snug red and black Recaros featuring a mix of leather and cloth; the six-speed's shifter wrapped in black leather with decorative red stitching. The manual RX-8 Spirit Rs were purposely sportier, coming with aero bodykit parts and aluminum pedal set. Automatic Spirit Rs had toned down sports suspension to go with gun metallic-painted 18in aluminum rims, wrapped in less aggressive 225/45R 18 91W tires. Inside were normal black leather, heated front buckets with red stitching and eight-way electric adjustment, plus memory function. The auto console shifter was also trimmed in black leather.

Underlying the enthusiast nature of those prepared to buy rotary in 2011/12, 66% of RX-8 Spirit R buyers chose the manual version. Indeed, this hardcore minority agitated so much, Mazda announced in April 2012 that they would extend the Spirit R's availability for another 1000 units. Now the last RX-8 Spirit R would roll off the Hiroshima line in June 2012.

Outside Japan, the RX-8 was assembled in South Africa at the Ford Motor Co Pretoria Assembly Plant. This was to overcome South Africa's high import duty, and showed Mazda's one-time Ford link. By the end of March 2012, 192,094 RX-8s had been made. Add on the extra 1000 extended Spirit Rs, and Mazda's plan to popularize rotary after the niche FD RX-7 had been a moderate success.

However, critically the RX-8 and Renesis was an unqualified success: as well as 2003 Japanese Car of the Year, the RX-8 was also *Australian Wheels* magazine's 2003 Car of the Year. It was in *Car and Driver*'s Ten Best list in 2004, 2005 and 2006. The Renesis rotary was named 2003 International Engine of the Year. The jury praised Mazda for "its sheer bravery in pursuing the Wankel format and making it work." Renesis also picked up category wins for 'Best New Engine' and 'Best 2.5-liter to 3.0-liter.'[82]

X-Men RX-8

To many enthusiasts, the RX-8 was their hero; but Mazda created a superhero with the 2004 RX-8 X-Men model. Based on a 2004 RX-8, the RX-8 X-Men Car was related to the Hollywood *X-Men* movie franchise. *X-Men 2* director Brian Singer worked closely with Mazda on the project. The director revised the movie script to accommodate the special RX-8's silver screen appearance. As an RX-8 iteration, the X-Men car was painted Mutant Blue, had an 'X'-shaped grille, angry rear spoiler and enlarged 'X' on the body's nameplate. Interior featured a silver and black theme for door trims, seats and steering wheel. There was a communication device placed on the upper center console.

The movie franchise-related 2004 RX-8 X-Men. Painted in Mutant Blue, *X-Men 2* movie director Brian Singer worked with Mazda on the special edition project. He even changed the script to work the car into the film. (Courtesy Mazda)

A rotary future?

UK car market expert James Ruppert had this to say about a three-year-old RX-8 190 with 36,000 miles on the clock, in 2007, "...the RX-8 is still one of few compact coupes that can deliver good looks, space for four people and fine driving dynamics."[83] Little surprise, given RX-8 adhered to the credo of Mazda's Toshihiko Hirai concerning the original NA MX-5: 'jinba ittai,' or 'rider and horse as one body.' All well and good, but, on a practical level, where does rotary go from here? Mazda's own R&D offers a clue.

Mazda CEO Takashi Yamanouchi spoke to the UK's *Telegraph Motoring,* at the 2012 Moscow Motor Show. He said Mazda was committed to rotary, and its role in future low emissions hybrid tech. Mazda has long worked on making rotary compatible with hydrogen; the two seem well suited. At the 2004 North American International Auto Show, the RX-8 HRE (Hydrogen Rotary Engine) was unveiled. This represented the fifth Mazda rotary hydrogen-capable vehicle, and was dual fuel in nature. RX-8 HRE had a 61-liter gasoline tank, and a 110-liter hydrogen tank that stored 2.4kg of hydrogen at 350 bar.

In November 2008 Mazda announced delivery of 30 RX-8 Hydrogen RE cars to the Norwegian hydrogen project HyNor. The RX-8 HRE was the fifth Mazda to have a hydrogen-compliant Wankel motor. (Courtesy Mazda)

November 15 2008, the RX-8 HRE handover ceremony in Oslo. Mazda hydrogen program manager Akihiro Kashiwagi presents the bi-fuel RX-8 HRE to HyNor Chairman Johan Thoresen. (Courtesy Mazda)

In 2005, Mazda got Japanese street approval for RX-8 HRE, and announced, in February 2006, that it would start leasing the HRE to commercial Japanese customers. The first cars leased went to Idemitsu and Iwatani. This was the first time in history that a production hydrogen/gasoline car had been fleet delivered. More ambitious still was Mazda's November 2007 announcement to deliver 30 RX-8 HREs to the Norwegian hydrogen project HyNor.

Running on just hydrogen, the Renesis made 109PS and 140Nm at five grand. Top speed for a five-speed HRE was 170kph, with 0-62mph in ten seconds. Operating range was 100km. On just gasoline, the HRE made 210PS, 222Nm at 5000rpm, with a 550km range.

In 2007, Mazda released info on its Renesis successor, called 16X. This was the codename for a two-rotor Wankel of narrower bore/ longer stroke nature. Like Renesis, it was atmo in nature, but with narrower rotor housing, greater eccentricity and epitrochoidal radius. The aim was to lower rotary's traditional cool-natured, greater surface area character, bringing better thermal efficiency. Displacement changed from the usual 1308cc to 1598cc. Factor in aluminum side housings and direct fuel-injection. Mazda claims fuel economy similar to its 2-liter gasoline I4.

Unfortunately, the global financial crisis, and technical problems meeting the emissions/ economy goals of 16X, have seen the project put on the back burner for now. The rumoured 290-horse 16X, in a suspected new sports car to rival Toyota's 86 coupe, sounds enticing. Mazda's general manager of powertrain development Mitsuo Hitomi has assured rotary fans that 16X won't be abandoned.

Of more immediate concern to Mazda is promoting its Sky Activ tech. This system ties in the drivetrain with the ECU of Mazda's conventional gasoline and diesel cars to maximize efficiency and economy. It takes less R&D cash, and is an easier sell than hybrid. Mazda is certainly looking to the conventional for its bottomline – especially to its CX-5 and CX-9 SUVs. However, one can always dream, and Mazda CEO Takashi Yamanouchi said, "Although RX-8 production is ending, the rotary engine will always represent the spirit of Mazda, and Mazda remains committed to its ongoing development."

The Mazda RX-8 HRE was a five-speed variant, with an extra 110-liter tank storing 2.4kg of hydrogen. Apart from slightly slower acceleration, there were no special concerns about hydrogen operation or performance. The RX-8 could still exceed 100mph. (Courtesy Mazda)

The RX-8 HRE's motor made 210PS on gasoline, and 109PS on hydrogen. Using hydrogen alone this RX-8 HRE could accelerate from 0-62mph in 10 seconds. With a combined range of 650km, the RX-8 HRE was a practical low emissions vehicle. (Courtesy Mazda)

Epilogue

Never say never; that's one thing James Bond and Mazda CEO Masamichi Kogai have in common. In the Mazda RX-Vision sports car concept, unveiled at the 2015 Tokyo Motor Show, Mazda included front engine/rear-drive, KODO styling and … a rotary engine.

At the unveiling of the CX3 baby SUV, Mazda fended off questions, saying sports car and rotary were off the table. It seems, it was keeping something up its sleeve.

Although vague on specifics, Mazda has confided that its 'Reference Exhibit' has a next gen 'SKYACTIV-R' rotary motor. This borrows Mazda's contemporary efficiency tag for harmonizing electronics and hardware. The Hiroshima concern stressed that it never stopped rotary R&D; plus that the rotary symbolizes the company's 'never-stop-challenging' spirit, and that it wants to put something like RX-Vision into mass production at some point. The original 1967 Cosmo Sport was mentioned at the press release.

Then, as now, rotary sets Mazda apart from other automakers!

The Mazda RX-Vision Concept was a surprise participant at the 2015 Tokyo Motor Show. It re-affirmed Mazda's commitment to gasoline rotary powerplants. (Courtesy Mazda)

Technical details on the hoped-for sports car were few, outside of RX-Vision being rear-drive, front-engined and rotary-powered. So tantalizing was the promotion, in fact, that Mazda didn't even show the motor! (Courtesy Mazda)

Harking back to rotary and rear-drive sports cars, but RX-Vision embodies current Mazda KODO styling and SKYACTIV efficiency tech. Named 'Most Beautiful Concept Car of the Year' at the January 2016 Festival Automobile International in Paris. (Courtesy Mazda)

In spite of the GFC and buyers baying for economical SUVs, you can't keep a good rotary down! Now dubbed SKYACTIV-R, the rotary powerplant still makes Mazda a unique company. (Courtesy Mazda)

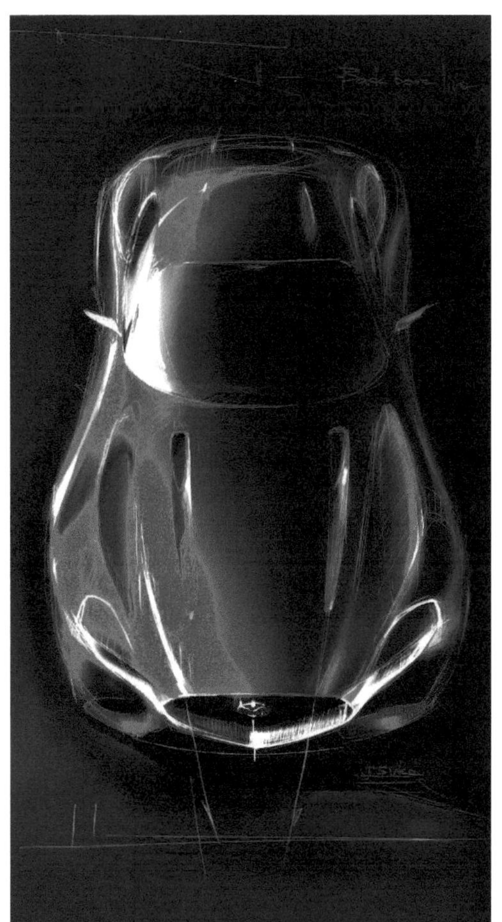

The Mazda RX-Vision shown at the Geneva 2016 show. (Courtesy Mazda)

Appendix

Mazda specification tables

1971 Mazda R100

US 1971 Model Year price	$2495.
Dimensions	150.8in length, 58in width, 53in height, 89in wheelbase.
Structure & Weight	Steel unibody, 2010lb (with full tank of gas).
Engine	10A two rotor rotary (491cc x 2); Carb: Hitachi KCB-306 4bbl two-stage, 110bhp @ 7000rpm, 100lb/ft @ 4000rpm (1970 Canadian advertised SAE gross ratings).
Gearbox	Full synchro four-speed manual floorshift (3.7 final drive).
Front Suspension	MacPherson struts, coils, swaybar.
Rear Suspension	Live axle & semi-elliptical leafs.
Brakes	9.6in solid front disk, 7.9in rear drum.
Wheels/Tires	Steel 14 x 4in rims/145/70SR14 Dunlop radials (export spec).
Performance/Economy	110mph (estimate), 0-60mph 10.8 seconds, 16-24 US mpg (Figures: *Car and Driver*, November 1970, page 38).

The R100, or Familia Presto Rotary Coupe, was Mazda's first mainstream rotary car. Based on the second generation Mazda Familia small rear-drive family car, the R100 was available from 1968 to 1973. Success on the racetracks earned it the nickname 'Small Giant.'

1977 Mazda RX-4 Sedan

US 1977 Model Year price	$5034 (base list).
Options fitted	factory a/c ($450), AM/FM radio (S150).
Dimensions	179in length, 65in width, 56in height, 99in wheelbase.
Structure & Weight	Steel unibody, 2720lb.
Engine	13B two rotor rotary (654cc x 2); Carb: Hitachi 4bbl two-stage, 110bhp @ 6000rpm, 120lb/ft @ 4000rpm (SAE net).
Gearbox	Full synchro five-speed overdrive manual floorshift (3.64 final drive).
Front Suspension	MacPherson struts, coils, swaybar.
Rear Suspension	Live axle & semi-elliptical leafs.
Brakes	9.1in power front disk, 9in rear drum.
Wheels/Tires	Perforated steel 13 x 5.5in rims/BR70-13 BF Goodrich radials.
Performance/Economy	112mph, 0-60mph 12.4 seconds, 0.72g skidpad, 14-21.5 US mpg (Vehicle price/test data: *Road & Track*, March 1977).

Introduced in October 1972, the rear-drive Luce was Mazda's big car. The rotary engined version was known as the RX-4 internationally. The RX-4 introduced the large 13B rotary motor, and new standards in acceleration and top speed for a Wankel Mazda. However, *Road & Track*'s 9.7 second 0-60mph time of April 1974, diminished as Mazda retuned the 13B for better economy. Still, with the widest stock rims/tires, the RX-4 was Mazda's skidpad and slalom numero uno!

1980 Racing Beat RX-7 GTU IMSA Racer

US racing season end sale price	$65,000 (ono).
Dimensions	170.1in length, 75in width, 46in height, 95.3in wheelbase.
Structure & Weight	Steel unibody, 2250lb.
Engine	12A two rotor rotary (575cc x 2), Lucas mechanical fuel injection, 260bhp @ 9500rpm, 160lb/ft @ 8000rpm (SAE net), rotor controlled peripheral ported race motor.
Gearbox	Full synchro five-speed overdrive (0.88 top) manual floorshift (5.67 final drive).
Front Suspension	MacPherson struts, coils, swaybar.
Rear Suspension	Live axle, four trailing links, compound Watts Linkage, coils, swaybar.

Brakes	12 x 1.1in front ventilated disk, 11.8 x 0.8in rear ventilated disk (no power assistance).
Wheels/Tires	Front – 16in rim/22 x 10.5in tire (20psi). Rear – 16in rim/25.5 x 12.5in tire (22psi). BBS three-piece spun aluminum modular rim with cast aluminum center, Goodyear Bluestreak Sports Car tire.
Performance/Economy	165mph (Daytona gearing), 0-60mph 5.6 seconds, 1.04g skidpad, 6mpg (Spec/data: Information Bureau, 5900 Wilshire Blvd, LA California).

The original FB chassis RX-7, known as Savanna RX-7 in Japan, so as to honor its illustrious RX-3 predecessor, entered a depressed late '70s sports car world. Objectively, the RX-7 was a purer sports car than its popular 924 and Triumph TR7 rivals, being closer to a Fiat X1/9 in single mindedness. The FB RX-7 underlined its sports car ability, by winning every IMSA GTU manufacturer title between 1980 and 1987, using the kind of racing car described above.

1992 Mazda RX-7 (FD)

UK list price	£27,778.71.
Dimensions	168.5in length, 68.9in width, 48.4in height, 95.5in wheelbase.
Structure & Weight	Steel unibody, 2965lb.
Engine	13B-REW two rotor rotary (654cc x 2), Bosch electronic fuel injection & ignition, 2 x Hitachi HT12 turbos, 237bhp @ 6500rpm, 218lb/ft @ 5000rpm (SAE net).
Gearbox	Full synchro five-speed overdrive (0.70) manual floorshift (4.10 final drive).
Front Suspension	Double wishbones (aluminum), coils, swaybar (30mm tubular).
Rear Suspension	Double wishbones (aluminum), coils, swaybar (17.3mm tubular).
Brakes	294mm ventilated disk x 4 + ABS.
Wheels/Tires	Aluminum 16 x 8in rims (squeeze cast)/225/50ZR16 Bridgestone Expedia.
Performance/Economy	159mph, 0-60mph five seconds, 0.97g skidpad, US EPA city/highway composite 21mpg (Figures: *Fast Lane*, August 1992).

First seen at the 1991 Tokyo Auto Salon, the sexily styled FD RX-7 soon drew praise from journals ranging from *Car and Driver* to *Playboy*! The no compromise two-seater had a twin turbo 13B, to surf the new wave of Japan's early '90s high tech supercars.

2012 Mazda RX-8 GT

Australian Manufacturer recommended retail price, June 2012	$57,692.
Dimensions	176in length, 69.7in width, 52.8in height, 106.4in wheelbase.
Structure & Weight	Steel unibody, 3034lb.
Engine	13B Renesis six-port two-rotor rotary (654cc x 2), Denso electronic fuel injection and ignition, 184kW (250PS) @ 8500rpm, 216Nm @ 7500rpm (Japanese market advertised DIN net ratings).
Gearbox	Full synchro six-speed overdrive (0.787) manual floorshift (4.777 final drive).
Front Suspension	Double wishbones (aluminum), urethane foam-filled front crossmember, Bilstein dampers, coils, swaybar.
Rear Suspension	Multilink, Bilstein dampers, coils, swaybar.
Brakes	12.7in power ventilated front disk, 11.9in ventilated rear disk, ABS, Traction Control.
Wheels/Tires	Forged alloys 19 x 8in rims/225/40R 19 89W radials.
Performance/Economy	0-100kph 7.3 seconds, 0-400 meters 15.2 seconds, 12.9 liters per 100km (95 RON gasoline). (Data: *Wheels magazine*, Australia, November 2008).

With 'Freestyle' doors and seating for four, Mazda's RX-8 tried to address concerns about the FD RX-7's impracticalities. The strategy worked, and RX-8 remained available in most world markets during its 2003-2012 run. RX-8 packed the atmo Renesis rotary, displacing 1308cc but yielding 250PS in high output six-port form. The RX-8 was an early modern era exponent of the 'Coupe four-door.' This auto extrovert was eventually laid low by stricter pollution laws and gas mileage dictates, in North America and Europe. It was an acquired taste that hooked some loyal devotees!

Mazda-related websites

Mazdas 247 – the 24/7 Mazda community

www.mazdas247.com
An online Mazda enthusiast website, established in 2001. Not just limited to rotary models, although the 'Hiroshima Screamers' are well represented!

RX-7 Club

www.rx7club.com
Dedicated to the preservation, modification and enjoyment of Mazda's RX-7 (Savanna RX-7) sports car. The site also has forums for earlier rotary models, and the later RX-8.

NoPistons – Mazda RX-7 & RX-8 rotary forum

www.nopistons.com
The site's name shows its rotary focus! All generations of RX-7, and the RX-8, are catered for. There is also a section for the vintage era Mazda rotary rides!

AusRotary.com

www.ausrotary.com
A large Australian-based site covering rotary Mazdas of all ages, with members all over the world. Great collection of early rotaries on show from sunny climes!

Mazdatrix

www.mazdatrix.com
A Californian rotary specialist. The company has raced FB and FC RX-7s in SCCA E production, as well as the RX-8 in NASA/Grand Am Cup. They also did the 12A motor in Jay Leno's classic Cosmo Sport 110S!

Racing Beat

www.racingbeat.com
Shot to prominence preparing the hot 12A in Car and Driver's RX-2, that competed in the 1973 IMSA Racing Stocks class. The performance specialist has transitioned more into Miata, and other piston models, as Mazda's product emphasis has changed.

Knight Sports

www.knightsports.co.jp
Knight Sports' performance tuning operation, was started out of a Mazda dealer outlet by racer and founder Makoto Kamazuka. The company commenced as a rotary specialist, but as per other Mazda tuners expanded into the piston models. Today it covers Demio, Axela, Miata and rotaries back to FC RX-7. Knight Sports exports throughout South East Asia, and has an agent in Australia: www.nengun.com/knight-sports/

RX8Club.com

www.rx8club.com
An online community for fans of the four door family rotary sports car.

Bibliography

Autocar, "Autocar Performance Data," August 31 1974.
Autocar, June 5 1985.
Autocar, September 19 2007.
Autocar & Motor, February 21 1990.
Autocar & Motor, November 11 1992.
Barker, Ronald, "Dogwatch Frontline," *CAR*, April 1988.
Bell, Roger, "100 Greatest Sports Cars Of All Time," *Autocar*, June 2 1999.
Bremner, Richard, "Piazza-full of eastern promise?" *Motor*, May 19 1984.
CAR, August 1984.
CAR, September 1985.
CAR, April 1988.
CAR, April 1993.
Classic & Sports Car, November 2000.
Consumer Reports, "What's Happening To Auto Pollution Controls," April 1974.
Davis, Pedr and Davis, Tony, *The Best of Circles Audi in Australia*, Blakehurst: Marque Publishing Company, 1992.
Davis, Pedr and Davis, Tony. *Volvo DownUnder A Swedish Success Story*, Blakehurst: Marque Publishing Company, 1990.
Dunne, Jim & Davis, Jim, "PS Puts 10,000 Miles on the New Mazda: Wankel-Powered Car Proves Silent, Powerful, and Trouble-free," *Popular Science*, January 1972.
Ed. Jefferis, David, *Daily Express Guide to World Cars 1994*, Harpenden: Pedigree Books, 1993.
Ed. Tamiya News Editing Room, *1984 Tamiya Catalogue*, Shizuoka: Tamiya Plastic Model Co, 1984.
Ed. Tamiya News Editing Room, *Tamiya Radio Control Guide Book*, Shizuoka: Tamiya Plastic Model Co, 1992.
Fujimi 1988 Catalogue Synthetic, Shizuoka: Fujimi Corporation, 1988.
Glasson, Mick, "Rotary Rated Top Engine," *The West Australian Motoring*, Saturday June 7 2003.
Green, Gavin, "Raw like sushi," CAR, May 1998.
Hales, Mark, "Rotary Club," *Motor*, November 1 1986.
Hardiman, Paul, "NSX Marks The Spot," *Classic & Sports Car*, November 2000.
Harnell, Boyd, "White Knight," *Sports Car International*, October/November 1998.
Horrell, Paul, "The Madness that is Mazda," *CAR*, September 1994.
Lamm, John, "The converter route to a cleaner and healthier environment," *Autocar*, October 10 1984.
Lamm, Michael, "Canada Joins The Rotary Club," *Popular Mechanics*, December 1969.
Lamm, Michael, "PM Owners Report: Mazda RX-2 and RX-3: Enthralled by performance, appalled by mileage," *Popular Mechanics*, July 1974.
Maher, Steve, "Unlikely Choice," *The BMC Experience*, October-December 2012.
McDowell, Bart, "Those Successful Japanese," *National Geographic*, March 1974.
Mitani, Sam, "Mazda's Secret Miatas Revealed," *Road & Track*, September 2001.
Motor, "Thanks A Quarter Million ..." August 14 1985.
Oliver, Ben (editor). *The Best Of CAR: The '70s and '80s*, London: Portico Books, 2008.
Palmer, Brian, "Revolutionary Rotary," *Thoroughbred & Classic Cars*, January 1993.
Pickett, Trevor, "Hooked!" *Perth Street Car*, Vol 15, No 2.

Road & Track: On BMW Cars 1966-1974, Surrey: Brooklands Books, 1985.
Road & Track: On BMW Cars 1975-1978, Surrey: Brooklands Books, 1985.
Road &Track, "R&T Summary," February 1975.
Road &Track, "Ten Best Cars for a Changing World," June 1975.
Road & Track 1976 Guide to Sports & GT cars, "Mazda Cosmo – Ample performance and improved fuel economy but the styling is a disappointment," 1976.
Robinson, Peter, "The supercar Mercedes should have built," *Autocar & Motor*, February 12 1992.
Robson, Graham, *Classic and Sports Car A-Z Of Cars of the 1970s*, Devon: Bay View Books, 1993.
Ruppert, James,"Going UP …" CAR, March 1993.
Rutherford, Michael. "Hot Metal," *Motor*, Jan 3 1987.
Sedgwick, Michael, *Classic Cars of the 1950's and 1960's*, Twickenham: Tiger Books International, 1997.
Sherman, Don, "US Probe to fight off alien imports," *CAR*, April 1988.
Sherman, Don,"At 8550rpm in fifth gear, the only sound you hear is the record breaking," *Car and Driver*, December 1986.
Taylor, Rich, "3-Way Battle RX-7x3," *Sports Car International*, January 1994.
The Children's Treasury Of Knowledge-Transport, Singapore: Time-Life Libraries (Asia), 1975.
Wakefield, Ron, "Mazda weighs US production site," *Motor*, May 19, 1984.
Wakefield, Ron, "Turbo Datsun 280ZX launched on US market," *Motor*, week ending June 20 1981.
Walker, Howard, "New For '85 Coming Soon To A Showroom Near You …" *Motor*, January 5 1985.
Ward, Daniel, "Tester's Year," *Motor*, Jan 3 1987.
Wilkins, Gordon, *Daily Express Guide To 1987 World Cars*, London: Express Newspapers, 1986.
Wood, Jonathan, *Great Marques Of Germany*, London: Viscount Books, 1989.

Footnotes

(1) Brian Palmer, "Revolutionary Rotary," *Thoroughbred & Classic Cars*, January 1993: p60.
(2) *Ibid*, p60.
(3) Pedr Davis and Tony Davis, *The Best of Circles Audi in Australia,* Blakehurst: Marque Publishing Company, 1992: p36.
(4) Michael Sedgwick, *Classic Cars of the 1950's and 1960's*, (Twickenham: Tiger Books International, 1997: p59.
(5) Jonathan Wood, Great Marques Of Germany (London: Viscount Books, 1989: p29.
(6) Pedr Davis and Tony Davis, The Best of Circles Audi in Australia (Blakehurst: Marque Publishing Company, 1992: p72
(7) *Ibid*, p11
(8) *Ibid*, Chapter 7, 1957 & 1959 entries.
(9) Michael Sedgwick, *op cit*, p59.
(10) Ronald Barker, "Dogwatch Frontline," *CAR*, April 1988: p48.
(11) Brian Palmer, *op cit*, p61.
(12) Ronald Barker, *op cit*, p48.
(13) Michael Lamm, "Canada Joins The Rotary Club," *Popular Mechanics*, December 1969: p210.
(14) Paul Hardiman, "NSX Marks The Spot," *Classic & Sports Car*, November 2000: p99.
(15) Michael Sedgwick, op cit, p168.
(16) *Classic & Sports Car*, November 2000, p9.
(17) Ron Wakefield, "Turbo Datsun 280ZX launched on US market," *Motor*, week ending June 20 1981: p40.
(18) Peter Robinson, "The supercar Mercedes should have built," Autocar & Motor, February 12 1992: p56.
(19) Michael Sedgwick, *op cit*, p213.
(20) *Ibid*, p233.
(21) *Ibid*, p232.
(22) *The Children's Treasury Of Knowledge-Transport*, Singapore: Time-Life Libraries Asia, 1975: p10.
(23) Michael Lamm, *op cit*, p212.
(24) *Ibid*, p212.
(25) *Ibid*, p210.
(26) *Ibid*, p212.
(27) Jim Dunne & Jim Davis, "PS Puts 10,000 Miles on the New Mazda: Wankel-Powered Car Proves Silent, Powerful, and Trouble-free," *Popular Science*, January 1972: p83.
(28) *The Children's Treasury Of Knowledge-Transport, op cit*, p27.
(29) *Ibid*, p103.
(30) Michael Lamm, *op cit*, p212.
(31) Michael Lamm, "PM Owners Report: Mazda RX-2 and RX-3: Enthralled by performance, appalled by mileage," *Popular Mechanics*, July 1974: p97.
(32) Bart McDowell, "Those Successful Japanese," *National Geographic*, March 1974: p340.
(33) *Autocar*, "Autocar Performance Data," August 31 1974: p15.
(34) *Road & Track, On BMW Cars 1966-1974*, Surrey: Brooklands Books, 1985: p58.
(35) Pedr Davis and Tony Davis, *Volvo DownUnder A Swedish Success Story*, Blakehurst: Marque Publishing Company, 1990: p64.
(36) John Lamm, "The converter route to a cleaner and healthier environment," *Autocar*, October 10 1984: p21.
(37) Steve Maher, "Unlikely Choice," *The BMC Experience*, October-December 2012: p44.
(38) Trevor Pickett, "Hooked!" *Perth Street Car*, Vol 15 No 2: p114.
(39) Mark Hales, "Rotary Club," *Motor*, November 1 1986: p54.
(40) Ed. Ben Oliver. *The Best Of CAR: The '70s and '80s*, London: Portico Books, 2008: p10.
(41) *Autocar*, August 31 1974: p3.
(42) *Motor*, "Thanks A Quarter Million …" August 14 1985: p70.
(43) Consumer Reports, "What's Happening To Auto Pollution Controls,"April 1974: p348.
(44) *Road &Track*, "R&T Summary,"February 1975: p107.
(45) *Road &Track*, "Ten Best Cars for a Changing World," June 1975: p35.
(46) *Road & Track: On BMW Cars 1975-1978*, Surrey: Brooklands Books, 1985: p37.
(47) *The Children's Treasury Of Knowledge-Transport, op cit*, p110.
(48) Ed. Ben Oliver, *The Best Of CAR: The '70s and '80s*, London: Portico Books, 2008: p50.
(49) *Road & Track 1976 Guide to Sports & GT cars*, "Mazda Cosmo – Ample performance and improved fuel economy but the styling is a disappointment," 1976: p158.
(50) Ronald Barker, *op cit*, p48.
(51) Pedr Davis and Tony Davis, *The Best of Circles Audi in Australia*, Blakehurst: Marque Publishing Company, 1992: 1968 entry.
(52) Brian Palmer, *op cit*, p65.
(53) Graham Robson, *Classic and Sports Car A-Z Of Cars of the 1970s*, Devon: Bay View Books, 1993: p118.
(54) Ronald Barker, *op cit*, p48.

Above and below: 1993 RX7 Touring.

(55) Paul Horrell, "The Madness that is Mazda," *CAR*, September 1994: p79.
(56) Roger Bell, "100 Greatest Sports Cars Of All Time," *Autocar*, June 2 1999: p107.
(57) *Autocar*, June 5 1985: p17.
(58) *CAR*, September 1985: p173.
(59) *CAR*, August 1984: p25.
(60) Ed. Tamiya News Editing Room, *1984 Tamiya Catalogue*, Shizuoka: Tamiya Plastic Model Co, 1984: p15.
(61) Richard Bremner, "Piazza-full of eastern promise?" *Motor*, May 19 1984: p49.
(62) Michael Rutherford, "Hot Metal," *Motor*, Jan 3 1987: p5.
(63) *CAR*, April 1988: p163.
(64) Daniel Ward, "Tester's Year," *Motor*, Jan 3 1987: p28.
(65) Gordon Wilkins, *Daily Express Guide To 1987 World Cars*, London: Express Newspapers, 1986: p39.
(66) *Autocar & Motor*, February 21 1990: p81.
(67) Howard Walker, "New For '85 Coming Soon To A Showroom Near You ..." *Motor*, January 5 1985: p16.
(68) *Fujimi 1988 Catalogue Synthetic*, Shizuoka: Fujimi Corporation, 1988: p12.
(69) Ron Wakefield, "Mazda weighs US production site," *Motor*, May 19 1984: p24.
(70) Don Sherman, "US Probe to fight off alien imports," *CAR*, April 1988: p26.
(71) Don Sherman, "At 8550rpm in fifth gear, the only sound you hear is the record breaking," *Car and Driver*, December 1986: p88.
(72) *Autocar & Motor*, November 11 1992: p79.
(73) Ed. David Jefferis, *Daily Express Guide to World Cars 1994*, Harpenden: Pedigree Books, 1993: p10.
(74) James Ruppert, "Going UP ..." *CAR*, March 1993: p100.
(75) *CAR*, April 1993: p8.
(76) Rich Taylor, "3-Way Battle RX-7x3," *Sports Car International*, January 1994: p36.
(77) Boyd Harnell, "White Knight," *Sports Car International*, October/November 1998: p71.
(78) Ed. Tamiya News Editing Room, *Tamiya Radio Control Guide Book.*, Shizuoka: Tamiya Plastic Model Co, 1992: p37.
(79) *Autocar*, September 19 2007: p83.
(80) Gavin Green, "Raw like sushi," *CAR*, May 1998: p86.
(81) Sam Mitani, "Mazda's Secret Miatas Revealed," *Road & Track*, September 2001: p67.
(82) Mick Glasson, "Rotary Rated Top Engine," *The West Australian Motoring*, Saturday June 7 2003: p5.
(83) *Autocar*, September 19 2007: p71.

Left, below left and below:
1989 RX7 Turbo II (Courtesy Pietro)

Mazda's rotary coupes, the RX-2, RX-4 and FB RX-7. (Courtesy Wheels & Richard Knight Cars)

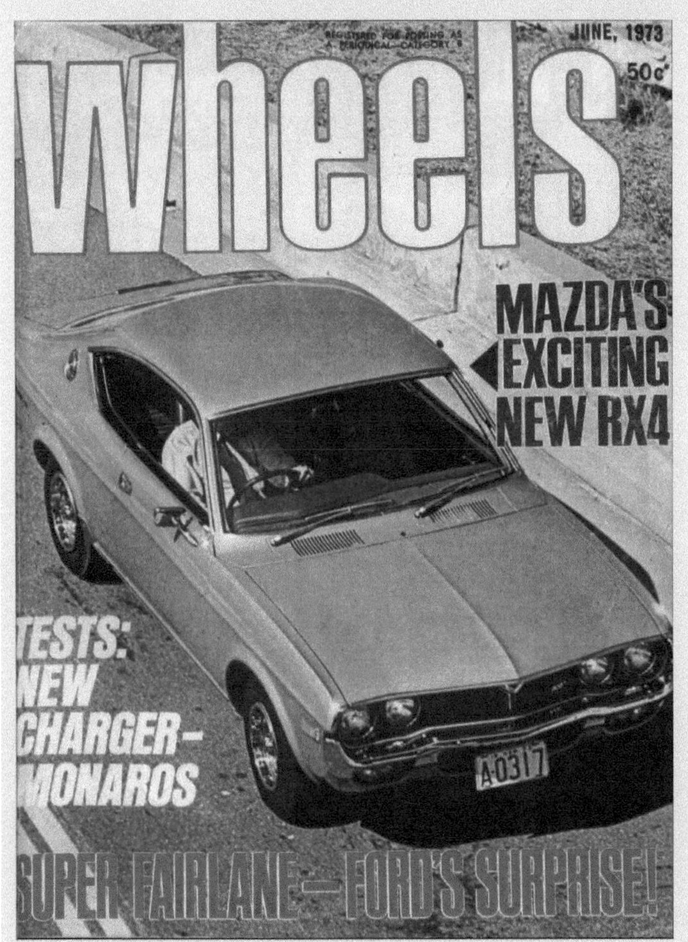

THERE'S THE MAZDA RX7

AND THERE'S A
RICHARD KNIGHT MAZDA RX7

As Britain's largest Mazda RX7 dealer, we always have a wide selection of new and used RX7's to choose from.

Plus, our exclusive range of body kits and accessories can give your RX7 even more style and performance.

So, whichever RX7 you want, at Richard Knight Cars we give you a better choice.

RICHARD KNIGHT CARS Ltd

35a-37 Fairfax Road,
Swiss Cottage,
London, NW6 4EL
(01) 625 5176

45 The Mall,
Ealing,
London, W5
(01) 840 3682

mazda

PERFORMING ART

CHARGED WITH EMOTION. POWERED *WITH* FINESSE.

MAZDA RX-7

Spirited, seductive, arousing. The sensationally sculpted new Mazda RX-7. A graceful low-slung coupé with classic sports car proportions. All lines and curves blending smoothly into an integrated muscular yet elegantly streamlined form. ◇ Powered with finesse, its 0-100km in around 6 seconds will capture the soul of true sports car drivers. At the heart beats an electronically fuel-injected sequential twin turbo, rotary engine, boosting power to 176kW @ 6500rpm, and torque to 294Nm @ 5000rpm. Scorching performance achieved with breath-taking ease. Experience the classic. Mazda RX-7. For the location of your nearest Mazda RX-7 specialist, contact Mazda call free (008) 035 522.

The 1992 FD RX-7, basking in Mazda's Le Mans winning limelight! (Courtesy Mazda)

102 MAZDA 787B
レナウン・チャージマツダ787B

In 1991, the Mazda Motor Company became the first Japanese automobile manufacturer to win the prestigious Le Mans 24 hours endurance race. The Mazda 787B racer is powered by a unique 4-rotor, rotary engine capable of producing 700 horsepower. Tamiya's 1/10th scale R/C model of the Mazda 787B racer provides both racing excitement and realistic scale looks. A rigid bathtub type main chassis is further reinforced with X-member space frames. An FRP T-bar is used for the rear gearbox/suspension plate. The preferred 3-point suspension system uses independent coil springs at the front, while a single, oil damper unit is installed at the rear. A precision ball type differential is used, providing superb cornering performance. Vacuum formed, polycarbonate body shell accurately depicts the sleek styling of its full-sized winner.

(Model Specifications) ● Scale: 1/10th. ● Overall length: 450mm ● Overall width: 212mm ● Overall height: 112mm ● Wheelbase: 270mm ● Tread: Front 170mm, rear 157mm ● Weight fully equipped Approx. 1,280g ● Tire width/diameter: Front 28/64mm, rear 45/68mm ● Body: Vacuum formed of polycarbonate (Lexan) ● Frame: Impact resistant resin, bathtub/space frame with a rear FRP T-shaped plate ● Suspension: Front independent coil spring damped unit, rear single coil over oil filled damper unit ● Ball type differential gearing ● Motor: 540 type ● Gear ratio: 1:5.0 ● Power source: Tamiya Ni-Cd 7.2V Racing Pack ● Radio control unit: Requires Tamiya R/C System or other 2 chan. R/C equipment (Battery and radio unit available separately)

Ford tried to buy Mazda to get the rotary engine. The two companies then became partners, and both have won Le Mans. Above right: Hidemi Aoki is with the Fresh Cherries Fords. (Courtesy Tamiya & www.nepoeht.com)

Also by Marc Cranswick –

Volkswagen's first mid-size car, was also its final new design in a 30-year air cooled odyssey. The Type 4 411 and 412 held to VW tradition, while introducing new engineering directions and refinements. VW's biggest ever car faced off against mainstream competition. Would Dr Porsche's ideals still hold out, for VW's transitional car?

ISBN: 978-1-787115-22-4
Hardback • 25x20.7cm • 184 pages • 223 colour pictures

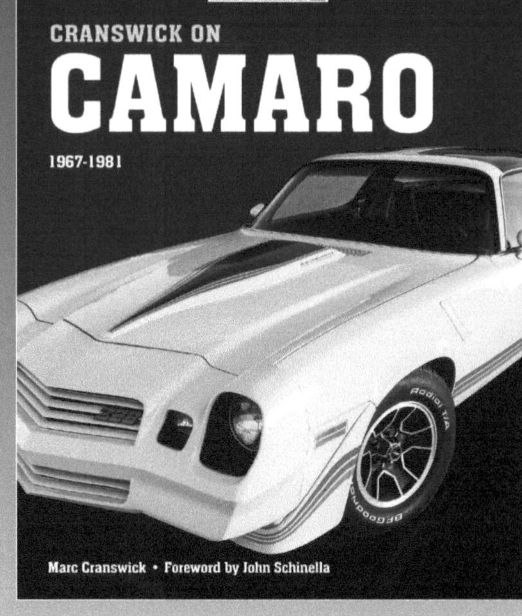

Covering Chevrolet's specialized sport coupe, during the classic 1967-81 era. Relive those outlandish hi po Camaros, from legendary speed shops Baldwin-Motion, Dana, Nickey and Yenko. Fuel crisis, insurance and the EPA? Don't worry, the Bowtie boys had your back in the showroom, and on the track.

ISBN: 978-1-787116-68-9
Hardback • 25x20.7cm • 184 pages • 223 pictures

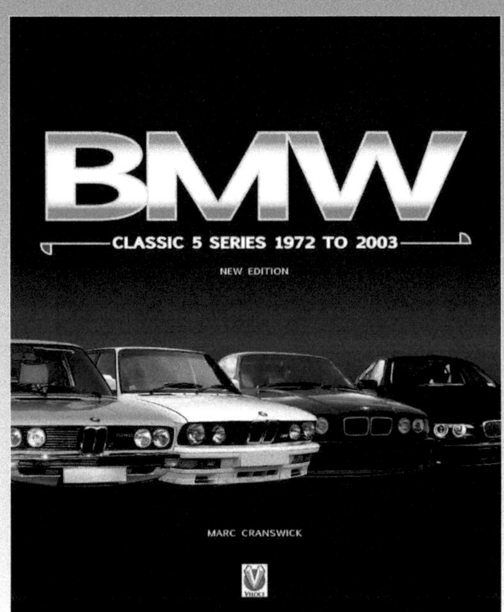

A look at BMW's 5 series in the classic era. Observes model changes and development from 1972, to the end of e39 5 series production. Complete descriptions and pictures of BMW Motorsport cars, plus the exotic tuner specials from Germany. BMW's rise in business internationally is also examined.

ISBN: 978-1-787117-75-4
Paperback • 25x20.7cm • 232 pages • 250 pictures

For more information and price details, visit our website at www.veloce.co.uk • email: info@veloce.co.uk
• Tel: +44(0)1305 260068

Also from Veloce –

Updated fourth edition of this definitive history of the successful & long-lived RX-7. Mazda's boldness in using Felix Wankel's engine design imbued the RX-7 with huge driver appeal; close to half a million cars had already been sold by 1986.

ISBN: 978-1-787111-33-2
Paperback • 20.7 x 25cm • 216 pages • over 240 pictures

For more info on Veloce titles,
visit our website at www.veloce.co.uk
email: info@veloce.co.uk
Tel: +44(0)1305 260068

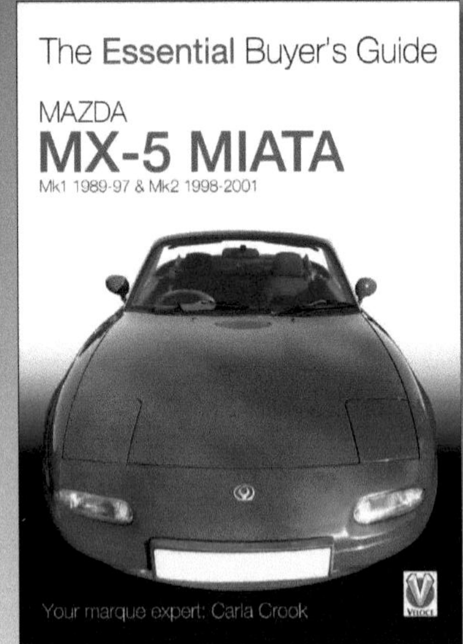

ISBN: 978-1-845842-31-4
Paperback
• 19.5 x 13.9cm
• 64 pages
• 107 colour pictures

ISBN: 978-1-845848-67-5
Paperback • 19.5 x 13.9cm
• 64 pages
• 100 pictures

Having these books in your pocket is just like having a marque expert by your side. Benefit from the authors' years of real ownership experience, learn how to spot a bad car quickly, and how to assess a promising one like a true professional. Get the right car at the right price!

For more info on Veloce titles, visit our website at www.veloce.co.uk
• email: info@veloce.co.uk • Tel: +44(0)1305 260068

Index